Teaching in the Secondary School

SIXTH EDITION

Tom V. Savage
Santa Clara University

Marsha K. Savage
Santa Clara University

David G. Armstrong
Late of the University of North Carolina at Greensboro

PEARSON
Merrill
Prentice Hall

Upper Saddle River, New Jersey
Columbus, Ohio

Library of Congress Cataloging in Publication Data

Savage, Tom V.
Teaching in the secondary school / Tom V. Savage, Marsha K. Savage, David G. Armstrong.—6th ed.
p. cm.
Armstrong's name appears first on the earlier edition.
Includes bibliographical references and index.
ISBN 0-13-119441-0 (alk. paper)
1. High school teaching—United States. 2. Education, Secondary—United States. I. Savage, Marsha Kent, 1952- II. Armstrong, David G. III. Title.
LB1737.U6A75 2006
373.1102—dc22

2005003469

Vice President and Executive Publisher: Jeffery W. Johnston
Executive Editor: Debra A. Stollenwerk
Senior Editorial Assistant: Mary Morrill
Production Editor: Kris Roach
Production Coordination: GGS Book Services, Atlantic Highlands
Design Coordinator: Diane C. Lorenzo
Cover Designer: Jeff Vanik
Cover Image: FotoSearch
Photo Coordinator: Monica Merkel
Production Manager: Pamela D. Bennett
Director of Marketing: Ann Castel Davis
Marketing Manager: Darcy Betts Prybella
Marketing Coordinator: Brian Mounts

This book was set in Jansen Text by GGS Book Services, Atlantic Highlands. It was printed and bound by Hamilton Printing. The cover was printed by Coral Graphic Services, Inc.

Photo Credits: Scott Cunningham/Merrill, pp. 15, 70, 123, 145, 193, 203, 231, 271, 301; Anna Elias-Sevilla/Prentice Hall School Division, p. 236; Tony Freeman/PhotoEdit, p. 33; Larry Hamill/Merrill, p. 88; Will Hart/PhotoEdit, p. 104; Ken Karp/Prentice Hall School Division, p. 289; Kathy Kirtland/Merrill, p. 117; KS Studios/Merrill, p. 343; David Mager/Pearson Learning Photo Studio, p. 257; Anthony Magnacca/Merrill, pp. 40, 214, 364, 370, 413; Jeff Maloney/Getty Images, Inc.–Photodisc, p. 5; Karen Mancinelli/Pearson Learning Photo Studio, p. 2; Pearson Learning Photo Studio, p. 399; Barbara Schwartz/Merrill, pp. 175, 390; Peter Stone/Black Star, p. 373; U.S. National Education Association, p. 418; Anne Vega/Merrill, pp. 10, 59, 91, 317; Tom Watson/Merrill, p. 228.

Pearson Education Ltd.
Pearson Education Singapore Pte. Ltd.
Pearson Education Canada, Ltd.
Pearson Education—Japan
Pearson Education Australia Pty. Limited
Pearson Education North Asia Ltd.
Pearson Educación de Mexico, S.A. de C.V.
Pearson Education Malaysia Pte. Ltd.

PEARSON
Merrill
Prentice Hall

10 9 8 7 6 5 4 3 2
ISBN: 0-13-119441-0

Preface

Being a teacher can be tremendously rewarding when students learn and get excited about school. However, it can be very discouraging and frustrating when they do not. Attaining the rewards of teaching does not happen by chance; it requires considerable knowledge and skill.

This text provides information for those who are interested in becoming secondary school teachers. It addresses the wide range of knowledge, skills, and attitudes that a person must possess: an understanding of students, recognition of educational issues that impact students and teachers, ability to plan lessons, awareness of legal obligations and responsibilities, and willingness to engage in professional growth, to name a few.

The authors of this text do not intend to provide all the answers for persons planning careers in education. Since education is constantly changing, there can be no prescription or set of answers for all of the difficult challenges that teachers face. Rather, we intend to provide the readers with basic principles and concepts that can be used and applied in a variety of teaching circumstances.

Organization of This Text

Earlier editions of *Teaching in the Secondary School* have been used successfully in courses covering secondary education methods, introduction to teaching, issues in education, and secondary curriculum. We have designed the text to be flexible so that users can organize the chapter sequence in ways that best fit their needs.

The organization that we have chosen addresses *the societal context of secondary education* in part 1. In this section, we intend to provide some historical, philosophical, and social background for secondary education and to illuminate the impact of changes on students and society. A second purpose is to help readers understand the significant changes that are taking place in education and allow them to place these changes within a societal and historical context.

In part 2, we focus on *preparation for teaching*. Research indicates that one of the key elements in becoming an effective teacher is productive planning. Therefore, in this section we have included chapters that focus on becoming a reflective teacher, selecting and organizing content for instruction, differentiating instruction in order to accommodate the diverse needs found in typical classrooms, planning units and lessons, and managing the classroom.

Part 3 focuses on *the act of teaching*. We have provided diverse models of teaching, including direct instruction, various approaches useful in attaining higher-level learning outcomes, and productive uses of small-group and cooperative learning. Successful instruction also requires that students are able to process and comprehend the material that they encounter. Therefore, we have included a chapter on reading across the curriculum. In addition, we consider assessment as an integral part of instruction. For this reason, a chapter on the assessment of student learning rounds out this section.

Part 4 includes two chapters on the professional context. Chapter 14 discusses issues relating to legal rights and responsibilities. Chapter 15 explains that teachers must be lifelong learners and that professional growth will continue throughout their teaching careers.

In addition to providing information that will be useful for readers contemplating a career in education, the material in the text will serve as a valuable resource for teachers in the classroom.

Special Features of This Text

Several features in this text will help readers maximize their comprehension and learning. Those features include the following:

- **Graphic Organizers.** At the beginning of each chapter, we have provided a graphic organizer that visually displays the relationships among the various elements of the chapter. This can provide a useful scaffold for the readers throughout the chapter.
- **Chapter Introduction.** The introduction aims to help set the stage for the content that is presented in the chapter.
- **More from the Web.** In each chapter, we have listed websites that promote understanding of the chapter contents.
- **Bulleted Objectives.** At the onset of each chapter, the objectives identify important material that readers should learn.
- **For Your Portfolio.** We have linked the content of most of the chapters to the INTASC standards for beginning teachers. In these chapters, the reader is challenged to select material that demonstrates their understanding of the INTASC standards for inclusion in a portfolio.
- **Critical Incidents.** In most chapters, we present a critical incident to help readers engage in reflective thinking about situations that today's teachers face.
- **What Do You Think?** This feature provides opportunities for readers to examine personal beliefs and convictions related to key issues and concerns.
- **Figures.** Reinforcing textual content illustrations graphically present important relationships.
- **Key Ideas in Summary.** This feature completes the instructional cycle that begins with the graphic organizer. The graphic organizer provides a preview and a scaffold for chapter content, the content unfolds, and the key ideas conclude the chapter reinforcing what readers have learned.
- **Reflections.** These sections at the end of each chapter engage readers in critical thinking about some of the issues that have been discussed in the chapter.
- **Learning Extensions.** These extensions challenge readers to apply and extend what they have learned in the chapter.
- **References.** The references direct readers to source material that the authors have used.

New to This Edition

Each chapter in this edition has been reviewed and updated. New content has been included, and, where appropriate, outdated content has been deleted. New features that are especially noteworthy in this edition include the following:

- **An entire chapter devoted to "Reading Across the Curriculum."** Most educators recognize that reading instruction should not end in the elementary school. Helping students read and process print information is the responsibility of *all* teachers. This chapter includes powerful approaches that secondary teachers can use in all content areas to help their students read and comprehend print material.
- **A chapter on "Differentiated Instruction."** The great diversity of students and a growing awareness that not all students learn the same way have led secondary teachers to realize that they must learn how to alter their instruction in order to meet the needs of all students in the classroom. This chapter provides a rationale for differentiating instruction and discusses alternative means of implementation.
- **A totally revised chapter on "Assessing Student Learning."** Recent emphasis on accountability and high-stakes testing requires that every teacher must understand assessment issues and how to identify what students have learned. This chapter has been totally revised to better assist readers in understanding and responding to assessment issues.
- **A revised chapter on planning units and objectives.** Feedback from users of the fifth edition suggested the need for more specific and concrete information on planning. We have attempted to add that detail.
- **More content on foundations.** In order to provide a context for understanding the contemporary status of secondary schools and suggestions for change, context on the historical, philosophical, and social foundations has been added to chapters 1 and 2.
- **Improved chapter order.** In the fifth edition, the chapter on diversity was chapter 6 and was included in the planning section. We believe that student diversity needs to be discussed earlier and is really more a part of the social context, so we moved it to chapter 3. We also felt that the discussion of legal issues in chapter 4 as a part of the social context broke the flow of the chapters from understanding the context to planning and then to instruction. Therefore, we moved it to chapter 14 as a part of the section on the professional context. Feedback from users indicated a desire to have the chapter on planning addressed earlier in the text. Therefore, we moved it up to chapter 6 in this edition.

We hope that these changes will improve the flow of information to and the professional growth of users of the text.

Acknowledgments

Any book requires the participation of a variety of individuals. We are pleased to acknowledge the contributions of the following individuals who reviewed preliminary versions of the chapters and provided useful feedback: Theodore E. Andrews, Southern

Illinois University; Paul D. Bland, Emporia State University; John-Michael Bodi, Bridgewater State College; Jacquelyn Culpepper, Mercer University; Ellen C. Stewart Fleishman; J. M. Hilton, Metro State College; Mary C. Markowitz, Ohio University.

In addition, we particularly thank Debbie Stollenwerk, our editor, and the helpful staff at Merrill/Prentice Hall. They have provided recommendations and suggestions for the cover and the photographs as well as well as the substance of the final version of the manuscript.

Finally, we especially acknowledge David Armstrong. His untimely passing just as we began the sixth edition was a great loss. David made great contributions to secondary education and social studies education in his more than 30 years in higher education. He was not only a valued colleague but also a good friend. It is fitting that his ideas and contributions live on through this text.

TVS
MKS

Educator Learning Center: An Invaluable Online Resource

Merrill Education and the Association for Supervision and Curriculum Development (ASCD) invite you to take advantage of a new online resource, one that provides access to the top research and proven strategies associated with ASCD and Merrill—the Educator Learning Center. At **www.educatorlearningcenter.com**, you will find resources that will enhance your students' understanding of course topics and of current educational issues, in addition to being invaluable for further research.

How the Educator Learning Center Will Help Your Students Become Better Teachers

With the combined resources of Merrill Education and ASCD, you and your students will find a wealth of tools and materials to better prepare them for the classroom.

Research

- More than 600 articles from the ASCD journal *Educational Leadership* discuss everyday issues faced by practicing teachers.
- A direct link on the site to Research Navigator™ gives students access to many of the leading education journals, as well as extensive content detailing the research process.
- Excerpts from Merrill Education texts give your students insights on important topics of instructional methods, diverse populations, assessment, classroom management, technology, and refining classroom practice.

Classroom Practice

- Hundreds of lesson plans and teaching strategies are categorized by content area and age range.
- Case studies and classroom video footage provide virtual field experience for student reflection.
- Computer simulations and other electronic tools keep your students abreast of today's classrooms and current technologies.

Look into the Value of Educator Learning Center Yourself

A four-month subscription to Educator Learning Center is $25 but is **FREE** when packaged with any Merrill Education text. In order for your students to have access to this site, you must use this special value-pack ISBN number **WHEN** placing your textbook order with the bookstore: 0-13-169280-1. Your students will then receive a copy of the text packaged with a free ASCD pincode. To preview the value of this website to you and your students, please go to **www.educatorlearningcenter.com** and click on "Demo."

Brief Contents

Contents

NOTE: Every effort has been made to provide accurate and current Internet information in this book. However, the Internet and information posted on it are constantly changing, so it is inevitable that some of the Internet addresses listed in this textbook will change.

Teaching in the Secondary School

SIXTH EDITION

PART 1 *The Setting Today*

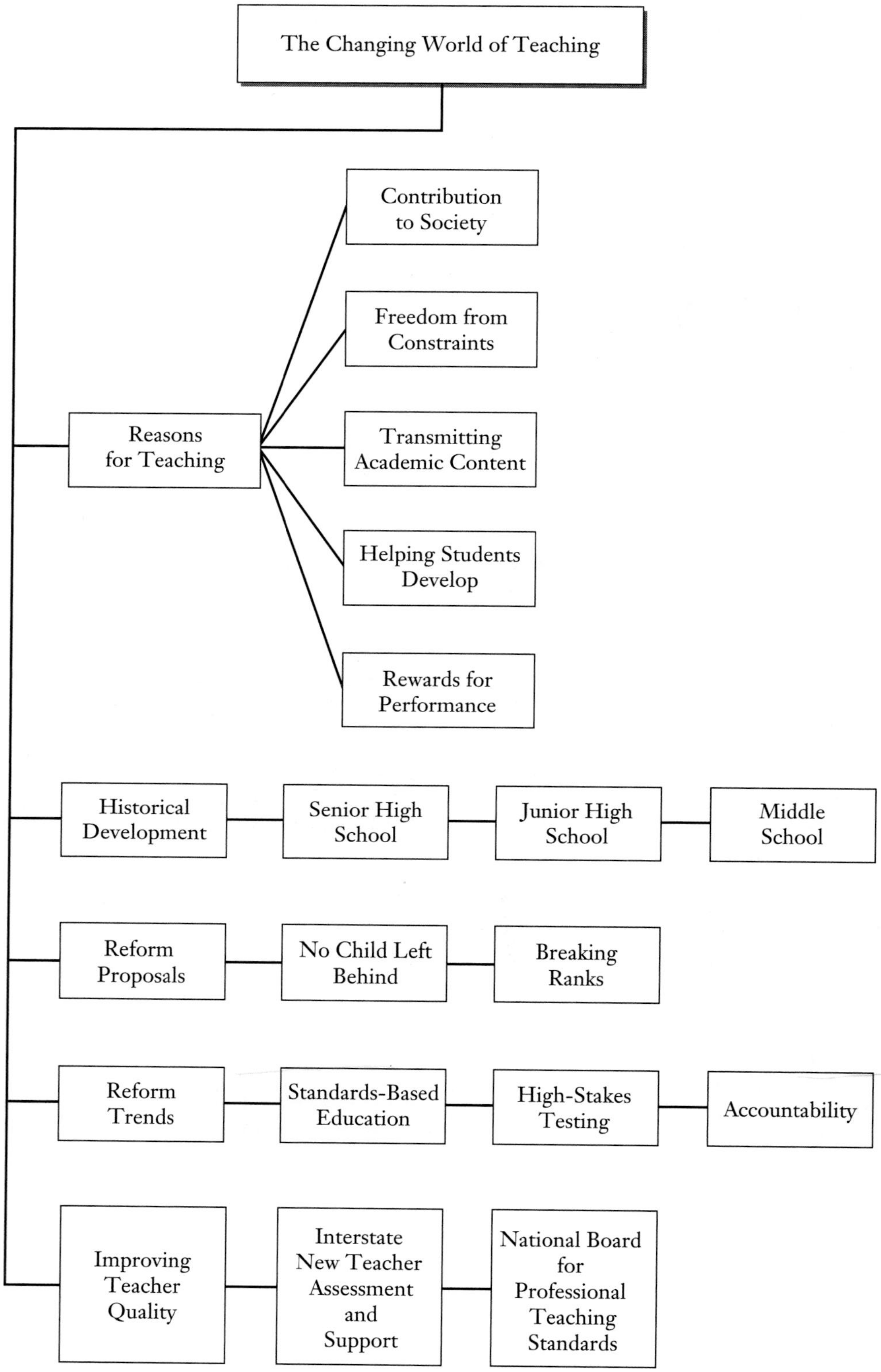

Figure 1.1
Graphic Organizer

CHAPTER **1**

The Changing World of Teaching

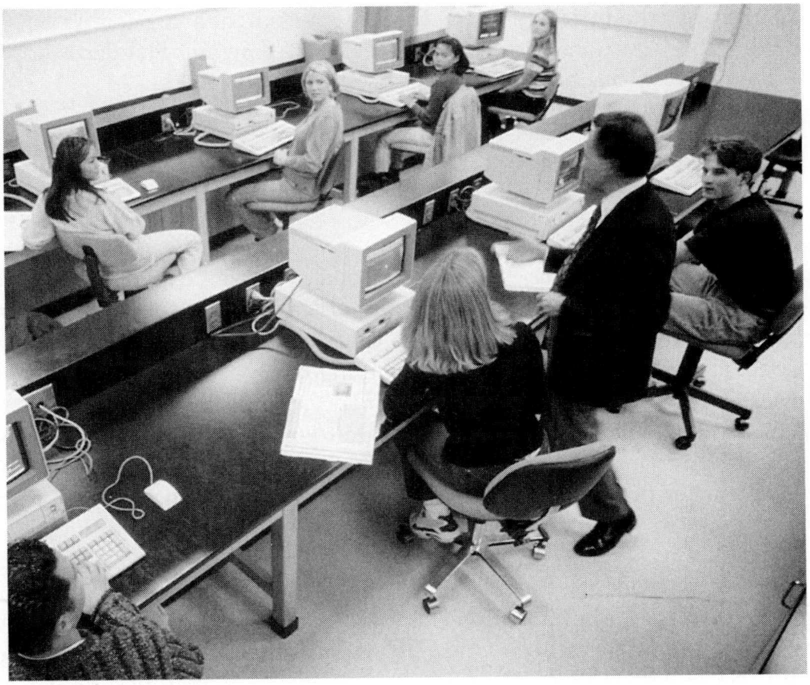

OBJECTIVES

This chapter will help you

- understand that change is a constant of life for secondary school teachers;
- clarify reasons for becoming a secondary school teacher;
- trace the development of secondary education;
- define the difference in philosophy between the middle school and the junior high school;
- state the basic elements of *No Child Left Behind*;
- compare the report *Breaking Ranks* with *No Child Left Behind*;
- explain the rationale for standards-based education;
- state the arguments for and against high-stakes testing;
- define accountability; and
- describe some ways the Interstate New Teacher Assessment and Support Consortium and the National Board for Professional Teaching Standards hope to improve the quality of teachers in the nation's classrooms.

Introduction

Nearly everyone has vivid memories of their secondary school experience. Some of the memories are good, some are not. This is because secondary education occurs at a critical time in the lives of individuals. It is a time of seeking independence, developing self-concept and identity, and basically coming of age. It is a time of life when the decisions that are made have lifelong consequences.

Some of us developed interests through special programs such as athletics, debate, drama, and music that continue to influence and enrich our lives. Many of us encountered a special teacher or coach who influenced our lives in dramatic ways. In fact, many people choose to be secondary school teachers because of the influence of a special teacher.

However, for many students, the secondary school experience was impersonal and irrelevant. The National Commission on the High School Senior Year (2001) found that students who did not demonstrate their prowess in academics, athletics, or music went through school with no counselor, teacher, or adult knowing him or her well. For them, their high school experience was impersonal and irrelevant to their lives. They became disengaged and alienated from school.

The secondary school years are important years where the lives of individuals are influenced in powerful ways. Yet there are many who worry that secondary education is not keeping up with contemporary demands. The National Commission on the High School Senior Year (2001) notes that schools and education are related to economic growth in ways that coal, mineral deposits, and manufacturing processes were to earlier generations. They conclude that contemporary demands require all students to take at least two years of formal education beyond the senior year.

The graphic organizer at the beginning of the chapter outlines the chapter starting with a challenge for you to self-assess your reasons for entering secondary education. The growth of the secondary schools in America is then traced. A couple of the more important reform proposals are outlined, and then common elements of many reform proposals, including standards-based education, high-stakes testing, accountability, and improved teacher quality, are discussed.

If secondary schools are to meet the increasing demands of the 21st century, changes must be made. Many of the calls for reform focus on making the secondary schools more personal, having smaller high schools or schools within schools, developing personal learning plans for all students, better alignment between the high school and college, clear standards and high expectations for all students, and more qualified teachers.

In many respects, secondary schools have changed very little over the past 50 years. School days are still typically divided into six or seven periods, classes still meet largely in groups of 30 or so students, and most of the instruction is large-group instruction dominated by teacher talk (Ryan & Cooper, 2004). However, in some important respects, there have been some profound changes.

In recent years, the reform movements have focused considerable attention on high schools. Some of the assumptions and organizing principles of previous years have been challenged. The old distinctions between preparing individuals for higher education or for a career are beginning to disappear. The public recognizes that a rigorous preparation is necessary for success in both the world of work and higher education. New technologies are providing us with alternatives that can fundamentally change the way schools operate. As the outlines of education for the 21st century begin to emerge, it is quite clear that there will be significant changes in secondary education.

If you study the history of social change, you will discover that innovations can quickly change institutions in both positive and negative ways. Schools, as an important societal institution, will constantly be under scrutiny and will be influenced by the political, social, economic, and technological trends developing in the world beyond the school. As you look at historical and contemporary efforts to change education, you need to be aware that change is often based on a particular political philosophy rather than on hard evidence indicating an educational need. Politicians long ago learned that education is an important topic for most people and can be used for political gain.

Secondary schools today are caught up in waves of change that will transform our entire society. As an educator, you will confront and respond to changes of a magnitude and character that educators in years past could barely imagine. Many of these changes have the potential for great benefit or great harm to students. You will need the professional expertise to make these choices. In this text, we want to provide you with the foundation for this professional expertise. We will present you with both the challenges and the rewards of secondary education. We hope that you will become a reflective practitioner who will consider the material presented and how it can influence your attitudes, beliefs, and skills.

A good place to start your journey as a reflective teacher is with a self-assessment. What are your motives for seeking a career as a secondary school teacher? How do your priorities square with the realities of teaching at this level? These are interesting questions. In order to gain a personal perspective on these issues, spend a few minutes completing the self-assessment in Box 1.1. Your answers may tell you something about your priorities.

BOX 1.1 Self-Assessment

Priorities for Choosing Teaching

Individuals' reasons for choosing a career in secondary teaching vary. A few reasons that people sometimes mention are included in the statements that follow. What priority would you assign to each?

Priority

High	Medium	Low	
	✓		Making a contribution to society
✓			Enjoying freedom to work with few constraints
✓			Transmitting academic content
✓			Helping students develop as individuals
✓			Being rewarded for good performance

Reasons for Teaching

Now, let's look briefly at the five presumed characteristics of teaching noted in Box 1.1. that, many people believe, attract newcomers to the profession.

Making a Contribution to Society

Did you rate this option high on your list? If so, you have lots of company. Many people are motivated to teach because they believe they will be doing "something important." One study indicated that 52% of individuals polled cited this as a major reason for choosing teaching (Ornstein & Levine, 2003). Certainly, few people challenge the point that education is critical to health and survival of society. In addition, it is widely recognized that a quality teacher in the classroom is the key ingredient for quality education.

However, this by no means suggests that educators are members of a profession that enjoys an especially high status. In fact, you may be surprised at the number of your friends and acquaintances who will willingly assert that teaching demands quite low levels of intelligence and skill. For example, one of our students recounted being told, "You're a bright girl. Be something, don't be a teacher." You need to understand that not everyone will recognize the importance of the contributions you will make as a professional educator. In summary, teachers usually have a deep understanding of their importance. They know they are making an important contribution to society even though they may be criticized by segments of the general population. However, as a teacher you need to realize that you may need to rely on the personal satisfaction you get from knowing you are doing important work because it may not be forthcoming from others.

Enjoying Freedom to Work with Few Constraints

As a classroom teacher, you will enjoy a certain freedom of action. When you are in front of a classroom interacting with students, you are the one making the decisions, and you need to use all your knowledge and creativity in order to create a productive learning environment. The lesson is your personal creation. This can be both challenging and exhilarating. A teacher evaluator explaining the difficulty of evaluating teaching noted that one factor making it difficult is the personal investment that people have in their lessons. He noted that criticizing a lesson is like saying, "My, you have an ugly baby."

If you are someone who needs lots of structure and concrete guidance, if you have a high level of personal insecurity, if you have trouble making quick decisions, then teaching is probably not for you.

There are also limitations on what you can teach. You may teach in a state or school district that requires teachers to follow a detailed curriculum. Criticism of teaching in recent years has led to more emphasis on "scripted lessons" that teachers are expected to follow. The increased use of "high-stakes" standardized tests has placed pressure on teachers to teach to the test and require you to spend more time on content that will be tested rather than on content you may personally feel is important. Some school administrators require teachers to justify every lesson and to stick to a strict plan of content coverage. It is fair to say that contemporary teachers enjoy less freedom of action than just a few short years ago. This has caused considerable dissatisfaction in experienced teachers and has led some to leave teaching or to seek teaching positions in places where they do still enjoy considerable freedom of action.

Transmitting Academic Content

Are you excited about the subject or subjects you want to teach? Many secondary teachers choose to teach in the secondary school because they have such a high degree of enthusiasm and interest in their content area. This enthusiasm is a great asset in the classroom. Enthusiasm conveys to students that you believe what you are teaching is valuable and, even more important, that you derive some real satisfaction from knowing what you know. Your personal interest can ignite a commitment to your subject even among students who initially may express little enthusiasm for what you are teaching.

It can be very rewarding to work in a job that allows (even requires) you to continue to learn a subject that interests you. This is a key element of job satisfaction in any job. Some teachers find it exciting to be challenged to attend workshops, take additional course work, and engage in professional growth opportunities. It might be said that many individuals choose to be teachers because they enjoy being students. To them, this is one of the most appealing aspects of being a secondary school teacher.

On the other hand, when you begin working with a class of students, you need to understand that many of them may not share your interest in the subject. This can be discouraging to a teacher, especially a new teacher. The lack of student enthusiasm, even open hostility, toward a subject can be very discouraging. It is not rewarding to be working with a group of individuals who do not share your interest. One of the most common complaints that we hear from student teachers and new teachers is that the students they teach don't care about learning. That is why some new teachers are initially interested in teaching advanced placement types of classes because the presumption is that the students will be more interested in the subject.

Part of your role as a teacher is to motivate initially reluctant students to extend themselves to master the material. To do this, you need to develop ways that help all students respond "yes" to the Is-this-material-something-I-should-bother-learning? question. There are few things that are more rewarding to a teacher than sparking an interest in a subject in reluctant and unmotivated students. When you do this, you know you have made a difference. The self-confidence that accompanies the growing mastery of content is often a potent motivational force that, over time, can engender an enthusiasm that matches your own.

Helping Students Develop as Individuals

Sure, it can be fun to continue to grow in knowledge of your subject and discuss it with others. Yes, it is nice to be working in a profession where we are able to have considerable freedom. However, helping students grow and develop as individuals is the core of what education is all about. This was the most popular reason individuals gave for choosing teaching as a career. Helping children grow and learn was cited as a major reason for teaching by 90% of the respondents (Ornstein & Levine, 2003). This is how we make an important contribution to society. All of us want to know we have made a difference. We want to believe that what we are doing in life is important. Seeing individuals mature and develop, seeing them achieve success, and knowing you had a part is the reward of teaching.

Sometimes debates about school issues seem strangely disassociated from the real human beings the schools serve. Prescriptions for "improvement" tend to focus on test scores and other issues tied closely to the content-transmission goal of public education. The students, as human beings, when mentioned at all, often appear to be passive recipients who are waiting to be "improved" by the latest reform initiative. One of your challenges as a teacher will be to keep your focus on the growth and development of individual students. You will need to ask constantly, "But, is this good for students?"

Helping students grow and develop is one of the most rewarding dimensions of teaching.

When you begin to teach, you quickly learn that any suggestion that "students are pretty much the same" is a statement having no basis in reality. In fact, students represent as broad a diversity as exists in our entire society. Members of your classes will bring incredibly different sets of assumptions about "how the world is" with them to school, and they will vary hugely in terms of attitudes, aptitudes, and physical characteristics. One of your tasks as a teacher is to diagnose and respond to characteristics of students as individuals. Your challenge will be to find a suitable balance between the need to provide instruction tailored to characteristics of each student and the need to meet requirements to provide some common instructional experiences to all.

Being Rewarded for Good Performance

If you expect to work hard when you begin teaching, you will not be disappointed. Interacting with students, planning for instruction, participating in meetings, conferring with colleagues, and assuming other responsibilities will give you ample opportunity to demonstrate your commitment to the profession. You will find students, parents, guardians, and members of the general community who are appreciative of your efforts. However, you must realize that as a teacher you work in environments that have a high degree of anonymity. It seems strange that this would be true when you may be in front of 100 or more students every day. However, parents almost never see you teach. It is rare for other teachers or even school administrators to observe in your classroom. Secondary students will seldom compliment your teaching, simply because that isn't "cool."

It is a mistake to assume that everyone will applaud what you do. If you are expecting accolades from others, it probably won't happen with much frequency. You will need to rely on self-evaluations of your performance. You need to gather good and reliable data regarding your teaching success and be willing to reflect honestly on what you are doing and on your successes and failures. You may need to be satisfied with the personal satisfaction of knowing that you are doing a job well.

Another issue related to gaining recognition is that people vary enormously in their beliefs about what constitutes "good" educational practice. For example, you may be a strong believer in the worth of educational simulations as a way of engaging students' higher-level thinking skills. You might encounter a parent who thinks you should focus on preparing students for standardized tests by using the lecture method to cover a variety of factual material. No matter how hard you work developing and implementing high-quality simulations, this parent may not regard you as an effective teacher. What all this means is that different people apply different criteria in determining whether the job you are doing is acceptable. You need to understand that people who define quality instruction differently than you do may not be impressed by your instructional practices, no matter how hard you work to perfect them.

In summary, teaching is both highly rewarding and highly frustrating. It has incredible highs and dismal lows. It is a role that is recognized, as least verbally, by society as extremely important. There are few rewards greater than seeing students get excited about a topic and growing in competence. It is always rewarding and a bit sad to watch individuals you have seen grow and mature cross the stage at graduation time.

Yet society is quick to blame education and teachers for all sorts of ills. We are often accorded low status, and sometimes it seems as if all of us get labeled with the most incompetent of our profession. Decisions that impact our roles and the learning of our students are often made far from the classroom by individuals who appear to have little knowledge of the reality of secondary classrooms. It is as if our experience and judgments do not count and cannot be trusted. We hear politicians state the importance of education and then watch them cut budgets that hinder our ability to do our job. Many teachers struggle to make ends meet and end up finding ways of supplementing our incomes. Few people seem to recognize when we are doing a good job, and we tend to introduce ourselves as "I'm just a teacher."

Historical Development of Secondary Education

Secondary education is defined as education designed to serve students in the grades roughly from 7 through 12. Grade 6 may be included as a part of middle school. An understanding of the development of secondary education can provide you with an understanding of how organizational schemes and practices came to be and can provide perspectives for viewing changes and calls for reform. For example, many calls for reform seem to imply that at some point in our history there was a "golden age" of education when there were few problems. All schools had high achievement levels, all teachers were dedicated and qualified, and all students were motivated to learn. These critics contend that education has lost its way and needs to return to those days. An understanding of the history of secondary education can reveal the validity of that argument.

The Senior High School

The importance of a high school education is a relatively recent phenomenon. In the early colonial period of our nation, education was restricted to instruction in the basic skills. Education beyond the basic levels tended to be restricted to the sons of upper-class families. The curriculum was largely classical in nature, and the goal was to prepare these boys for leadership. However, this narrow application of secondary education was questioned.

Thomas Jefferson argued for a broader distribution of education by pointing out that democracy required an educated citizenry. In addition, as middle-class merchants and other practical occupations became more prevalent, they challenged the idea of a curriculum composed of Greek, Latin, and the classics. There were, however, some private secondary schools—such as the Franklin Academy; the Philips Academy at Andover, Massachusetts; and the Philip Exeter Academy at Exeter, New Hampshire—that emphasized the idea that secondary education was important.

The first public high school established in the United States in 1821 was the Boston English Classical School. The name was soon changed to the English High School. The program of study emphasized what was then defined as useful and practical subjects as opposed to subjects that appeared to have no clear connection to daily living. However, there was not an overwhelming response to the high school as an institution.

As late as 1860, there were only about 40 public high schools in the entire country (Barry, 1961). One of the barriers to the spread of the high school was money. Public financial support for elementary education dated back to colonial times. However, the high school was not viewed as useful for everyone. Those who attended secondary school still tended to be the upper classes and those preparing for higher education. There was doubt about the legality of using tax money to support secondary schools for this limited population. A landmark case in this area was the famous Kalamazoo case of 1874 (*Stuart v. School District No. 1 of the Village of Kalamazoo*, 30 Mich. 69 [1874]), which supported the right of state legislatures to pass laws permitting local communities to levy taxes to support secondary as well as elementary schools.

Once the legality of public funding was established, the number of secondary school increased rapidly. By 1900, there were over 6,000 high schools serving half a million students. However, in 1900, only 50% of the children were in school, and they received an average of only 5 years of schooling. Only 6% of the 17-year-olds were high school graduates (Bernard & Mondale, 2001).

Great debates developed concerning the purpose of secondary education. The debate centered on whether the secondary school should prepare students for the world of work or for the academic world of high education.

In the 1890s, the National Education Association's Committee of Ten issued a report suggesting that the high school should be almost exclusively devoted to preparing students for higher education. The committee recommended that all students take Latin, Greek, English, a modern non-English language, mathematics, the sciences, natural history, history, civil government, political economy, and geography (National Education Association, 1893).

However, this view came under attack as high schools grew to include a broader spectrum of the general population. By 1920, school budgets had grown, and high school graduation rates had climbed to 17% of the 17-year-old population. Child labor laws restricted the employment opportunities of youth, and laws were passed making school attendance compulsory. A report of the National Education's Committee of Nine issued in 1911 suggested that the high school had a responsibility to produce "socially efficient" individuals. This meant people who were committed to fundamental American values and were capable of making real contributions to the technical and social development of the nation (National Education Association, 1911).

Interestingly, English was not the only language of the schools. Because of the influx of immigrants in the early part of the 20th century, schools in many parts of the nation taught in the language of the major immigrant group. For example, many of the Germans who came to the United States were quite proud of their heritage and insisted that their language and traditions be taught in school. This persisted until World War I, when patriotic fervor led to an interest in an English-only curriculum (Bernard & Mondale, 2001).

In 1918, a compromise was reached by the National Education Association's Commission on the Reorganization of Secondary Education (National Education Association, 1918), and what has been widely regarded as a seminal document on the development of the American high school was issued.

The commission suggested that the high school should be "comprehensive" and should serve multiple purposes. These broad purposes were expressed in the Cardinal Principles of Secondary Education. These principles promoted that the following goals be developed:

1. Health
2. Command of fundamental processes
3. Worthy home membership
4. Vocational preparation

5. Citizenship
6. Worthy use of leisure time
7. Ethical character

These cardinal principles guided the development of secondary school throughout the 20th century. Even today, their influence can be seen in the purposes and the curriculum of the school.

The Junior High School

Junior high schools were not established until the early years of the 20th century. As large numbers of public high schools began to emerge, their academic programs were generally quite demanding compared to the basic education offered in the elementary schools. Some individuals saw the need for a school that would help prepare students for the rigors of high school.

Increased interest in child growth and development led others to conclude that children were not simply "miniature adults" but proceeded through developmental stages. This led some to the idea that a special school was needed that could respond to the unique physical and emotional needs of preadolescents and early adolescents. The views of those who saw the need for a school to prepare students for the rigors of high school often conflicted with those who wanted an institution that met the developmental needs of children. This debate has continued unabated since the first junior high school was established in Berkeley, California, in 1909.

The organizational pattern followed in Berkeley was copied by large numbers of school districts throughout the country. This was a 6-3-3 pattern that featured a 6-year elementary school, a 3-year junior high school, and a 3-year senior high school. Junior high schools in this pattern usually involved grades 7, 8, and 9. However, there were other patterns. A common one was a 2-year junior high school that served grades 7 and 8 and left grade 9 in the senior high school.

By the end of World War I, the debate over the purpose of the junior high school had been largely won by the partisans of academic preparation for high school. Most of the teachers hired for the junior high school had preparation that was oriented toward teaching in the high school. Many of the junior high teachers had aspirations to "move up" to the high school. Ever sensitive to negative comments that might come their way from teachers at the senior high school, many junior high school teachers worked hard to prove that there was nothing "academically soft" about junior high school programs.

As a result, attention was not focused on the specialized needs of junior high students. This continued to bring criticism from people concerned about the growth and development issues. Over time, they began to win support. Drawing on the work of developmental psychologists as an intellectual rationale, critics of the traditional high school began proposing in the 1960s the establishment of a school with a different emphasis. They proposed that this school be called a middle school, a term borrowed from European education.

The Middle School

The middle school concept began to catch on in the 1960s. In general, middle schools were organized to include at least three but not more than five grades that must include grades 6 and 7 (Lounsbury & Vars, 1978). What was more important was the middle school philosophy. The middle school was to be developed around the special emotional and developmental needs of students in the 11–14 age range. Since they first began to appear in the 1960s, middle school popularity continued to increase so that they are becoming the dominant type of intermediate school.

As originally conceived, middle schools were supposed to be schools heavily oriented toward serving the unique developmental needs of students. Many institutions called middle schools do reflect this philosophy. However, there are others that reflect the academic orientation that differs little from the junior high school programs that initially prompted the establishment of middle schools. It is common to hear middle school proponents refer to a school as "a middle school in name only."

Similarly, some junior high schools have developed student-oriented programs and curricula that are every bit as responsive to the developmental needs of students as similarly oriented middle schools. It is simply an overgeneralization to state that "middle schools care about students" and that "junior high schools care about subjects."

Junior high schools and middle schools have not enjoyed the same prestige as senior high schools. Most states do not have special certification for middle school or junior high school teachers, and most universities do not have preparations programs designed especially for those who want to teach at this level (McEwin & Dickinson, 1997). The pattern still persists that a large number of the teachers in the middle school have high school preparation.

There are many challenges as well as rewards in teaching students in the intermediate years. Individuals teaching at this level must have an appreciation of the special needs of students at this level. The students are active and can display great maturity one moment and tremendous immaturity the next. They are often not afraid to get

Active student engagement is essential for success in teaching middle school students.

MORE FROM THE WEB

The following are three Websites where you can explore issues and trends in secondary education.

Education Commission of the States

The Education Commission of the States has an extensive Website that covers a broad base of issues in education. Clicking on the issue "high school" brings up a wealth of information on reports, research, and contemporary issues in high school education. There are numerous other issues, such as testing and accountability, that are also linked to excellent reports and research.

Website: http://www.ecs.org

The National Middle School Association

This organization provides a wealth of information about middle school education. Current events, conferences, professional development opportunities, research summaries, and links to other sites are listed here.

Website: http://www.nmsa.org

National Association of Secondary School Principals

This site contains excellent information on issues, trends, research, and publications relating to secondary schools.

Website: http://www.nassp.org

excited about things and will often do things that are not "sophisticated" enough for high school students.

There is no doubt that these middle years are crucial years where many students either develop a positive self-concept and move toward success or begin the downward spiral toward failure. Because this age is the turning point for those who eventually drop out of school, the need for committed and understanding teachers at this level is great.

Reform Proposals

While reflecting on your personal priorities concerning teaching, you need to understand the nature of reform movements. In recent years, there has been an increased number of reports calling for the reform of secondary education. These movements have already altered the role of teachers and the nature of education. It is likely that change has just begun and that your role will be considerably different from the role of a teacher just a few years ago. In order to understand the movements shaping secondary education, you need to view them in light of previous efforts to change secondary education.

By the 1950s, there was tremendous growth in secondary education. Around 60% of the age-eligible students attended secondary schools (Bernard & Mondale, 2001).

However, there were great inequities based on gender, color, and ethnicity. African American students were segregated by law in 17 states. The opportunities for girls were limited, the average attendance for Mexican American students was 5.6 years, and 72% of the special education students were not even enrolled (Bernard & Mondale, 2001). So, while there were some groups that were doing well in secondary schools, a substantial segment of the population was not being well served.

A number of events quickly changed the educational scene. *Brown v. Board of Education of Topeka* in 1954 struck a blow at segregation. In the 1960s, advocates for the special needs of students followed the civil rights lead and began to lobby for their inclusion in public education. Toward the end of the decade, groups started lobbying for more inclusion of special education students. However, the Soviet launching of the earth satellite *Sputnik* in the fall of 1957 was a momentous event that triggered a massive wave of reform. The event was a severe blow to American pride, and people wanted explanations as to why the nation had lost its technical and scientific superiority.

Individuals who disagreed with the progressive school movement had been claiming that the schools were focusing too much on student needs and interests and attempting to make school "fun" and "meaningful." They seized on this event as evidence that American schools were too soft and had moved away from intellectual rigor. In 1958, the National Defense Education Act was passed and emphasized a discipline-centered curriculum. Science and mathematics, areas that were viewed as critical to national defense, were the first areas of the curriculum addressed by the new act. Much of the curriculum development was turned over to subject specialists and academics in the content areas. New curricula were developed for high school physics, biology, chemistry, and mathematics. A nationwide network of summer institutes for teachers was launched in an effort to improve the quality of instruction.

However, by the later 1960s, the United States was catching up in the space race. The development of the new subject-focused curricula did not seem to be having the desired impact, as there was little evidence that student achievement had improved or that more students were choosing to pursue science and mathematics in college.

Other social problems, such as widespread poverty, racial unrest, the Vietnam War, and a rebellious youth culture, shifted attention from the space race. Once again the schools became a target. This time a more liberal segment of the population depicted schools as joyless, oppressive, and inhumane places. This shifted the focus of the schools from the more conservative discipline emphasis that followed *Sputnik* to a student-centered, more open approach allowing high degrees of student freedom. A variety of alternative high schools were developed in many regions of the nation. Some of these allowed students to choose what they wanted to study and how they wanted to study it.

However, by the late 1970s, these trends were beginning to fade. They were brought to a halt with the publication in 1983 of the National Commission of Excellence in Education report *A Nation at Risk* (1983). Much like the reaction to *Sputnik* 25 years earlier, this report claimed that the schools were failing and that this failure threatened the survival of the nation. However, the threat at this time was not the scientific prowess of the Soviet Union but the economic prowess of nations such as Japan (Hlebowitsh, 2001). The economic success of other nations in the world and economic problems at home called for an explanation. Once again, fueled by questionable data drawn from student averages on the Scholastic Aptitude Test and international comparisons of educational achievement, education was identified as the problem.

Given that the challenge addressed by *A Nation at Risk* was an economic one and that many of those who crafted the report had business backgrounds, it is not surprising that the report signaled the ascendancy of a conservative philosophy emphasizing the application of business principles to education. The report called for higher graduation standards, more emphasis on the academic subjects, lengthening the school day and the school year, more emphasis on mathematics and science, national standards, increased accountability, and revised preparation programs for teachers to emphasize academic course work rather than education course work.

There were many who questioned the data and the recommendations of the report (Astuto, Clark, Read, McGree, & Fernandez, 1994; Berliner & Biddle, 1995). They pointed out that the American schools had been a great social achievement. More students from more diverse backgrounds had been educated to higher levels than any other society in the world (Ryan & Cooper, 2004). Significant improvements had been made in the educational attainments of minority populations, dropout rates were low, and more students were graduating from high school and contemplating higher education than ever before (Berliner & Biddle, 1995). For example, in California, with a tremendously diverse student population, the graduation rate in 2002–2003 was reported to be 86.9% (EdSource, 2004). However, *A Nation at Risk* was a public relations success, and large segments of society were convinced that education was failing. The reforms mentioned in the report continue to guide educational policy 20 years later.

No Child Left Behind

A direct descendant of *A Nation at Risk* is the *No Child Left Behind Act (NCLB) of 2001* (P.L. 107–110) signed into law in 2002. This act was a reauthorization of the Elementary and Secondary Education Act first passed in 1964 as a part of the Johnson administration's "war on poverty." The act focused on the establishment of state academic standards, assessment, accountability, and improved teacher quality. This legislation signaled a major change in the educational landscape. Although proponents of NCLB contend that it promotes local control, the law gives the federal government unprecedented power and control over state and local educational policy.

The primary goals of NCLB are as follows: all students will graduate from high school, all students will attain proficiency in reading and mathematics by 2014 (including students with disabilities and English-language learners), and all students will be taught by highly qualified teachers by the end of the 2005–2006 school year.

These goals are to be implemented and measured through a rigorous testing program that will test students every year from grades 3 to 8 in the subjects of reading and mathematics with the testing of science to be added by 2007–2008 for grades 3 to 5 and once more in grades 6 to 9. Each state is to establish a plan for defining adequate yearly progress for every school. The major factor in adequate yearly progress must be state test scores. High schools may also use graduation rates. Middle school can use one other factor, which could include scores on other tests and attendance rates.

Schools that fail to make annual yearly improvement face the following actions (Edsource, 2004):

- Year 1: The district must inform the parents of the school's status and must institute a series of actions that includes allowing students to transfer to another school and providing free transportation.
- Year 2: All the actions required in year 1 must be continued, plus supplemental services, such as tutoring and after-school enrichment, must be added.

- Year 3: Corrective action begins during this year that must involve at least one of the following: replace appropriate staff, implement a new curriculum, decrease the authority of the school principal, appoint an outside expert, extend the school day or year, or restructure the school.
- Year 4: The district and school must develop a plan for alternative school governance and allow parents to comment on the new plan. The plan must involve reopening the school as a charter school, replacing staff as appropriate, contracting with an outside agency to manage the school, or arrange for the state to take over the school.
- Year 5: Implement the new plan.

Quality teachers for the secondary level are defined as those who have a major or the equivalent of a major in each subject they teach. This requirement is extended to cover all teachers by the 2005–2006 academic year. This aspect of the legislation is a part of a long debate concerning appropriate teacher preparation and certification.

In several states, individuals preparing to be elementary teachers major in education. For decades, vocal opponents have claimed that this practice substitutes meaningless education courses for more substantive content courses and is therefore less rigorous than a major in a content area. The education major has long been cited by critics of education as a major reason for school failure. They contend that this allows the least academically talented individuals to enter the teaching force. At the secondary level, a substantial percentage of teachers are teaching courses in areas outside their college major. This has long been a target of those who propose reform in secondary education. They contend that a person cannot teach what they do not know. Of course, they are using a college major as an indicator of content knowledge.

Secondary teachers have commonly taught courses in their academic minor. In many smaller high schools, there simply is not enough teaching load to hire a teacher with a major for every class that is offered. The NCLB is a major attack on these practices and was an attempt to eliminate not only education majors but also individuals teaching in subjects outside their major.

The definition of teacher quality in NCLB has important implications for secondary teachers. Minors are no longer acceptable as preparation for teaching. However, some experienced teachers have been teaching in their minor for years with success. They now feel caught in the middle and will have to take additional courses in an academic subject or pass a rigorous subject matter examination in order to continue.

Middle school teachers are also finding the new regulations troublesome. Some middle school principals have hired teachers with elementary credentials in an effort to include individuals who have more emphasis on growth and development and more of a focus on the child. However, these teachers will now be required to either take additional course work to get the equivalent of a major or take the subject examination in each subject they teach. It appears, then, that NCLB provides support for the content preparation emphasis of the junior high school movement as opposed to the student-centered philosophy of the middle school. Unless adaptations are made, there is the possibility of a shift in the middle school emphasis and a possible dislocation of many middle school teachers.

There are also implications for where individuals choose to teach. Again, although NCLB claims to provide opportunities for students in low socioeconomic areas, those are the schools that have the most difficulty meeting annual targets and are the ones most likely to be given sanctions. It is possible that many individuals will be reluctant to teach in these schools because of the publicity and the sanctions.

As of 2004, concerns were being raised, and changes were already being made to NCLB. It is probable that significant changes will be made to the law as the consequences of the law begin to be felt in individual communities across the nation.

Breaking Ranks: Changing an American Institution

Another set of change proposals for secondary education was presented in 1996 when the National Association of Secondary School Principals released a report titled *Breaking Ranks: Changing an American Institution* (National Association of Secondary School Principals, 1996). This report was followed in 2004 by *Breaking Ranks II: Strategies for Leading High School Reform* (National Association of Secondary School Principals, 2004). Breaking Ranks II was intended to assist in the implementation of the first report. It identified seven cornerstones for bringing about reform in secondary education:

1. Identifying required core knowledge. This recommendation called for the identification of content that is essential for the learning of all students. This recommendation is similar to the establishment of standards required in NCLB.
2. Making connections with students. The report viewed the personalization of the high school as the key to school improvement. To accomplish this, the report called for smaller units within a high school so that all students would be known by faculty and staff. It was also suggested that the teaching loads of faculty be adjusted so that they would be responsible for contact with no more than 90 students during a given term.
3. Conducting personalized planning. Each student would have personalized planning. This would be accomplished by identifying a personal adult advocate for each student and developing a personal plan for progress.
4. Adapt the school to meet individual differences. Consistent with the notion of personalizing the school, teachers are encouraged to adapt to individual differences using a variety of instructional strategies and assessment tools.
5. Developing flexible schedules. The basic purpose was to have schedules more in tune with the way students learn and the requirements of different teaching approaches.
6. Changing the leadership structure of the school. This cornerstone called for the inclusion of students, teachers, family members, and the community in the leadership and decision making of the school. This would involve engaging the families as partners in the education of a student and working with local agencies to coordinate the delivery of health and social services to the students.
7. Providing continuous profession development. This cornerstone called for the professional development programs to be aligned with personal learning plans for faculty. The report recommended that faculty members have a broad base of academic knowledge with depth in at least one subject area.

These proposals are quite different from those included in NCLB, which promotes a businesslike, rather mechanical approach to school reform. *Breaking Ranks* emphasizes the personalization of the secondary school. The NCLB places the emphasis on "outputs," or results, rather than on "inputs," or approaches. The guiding principle behind NCLB is that schools will change only when they are threatened with serious sanctions or rewarded for meeting performance goals. *Breaking Ranks* takes a more optimistic approach, promoting the idea that schools can and will change if given the appropriate direction and tools. *Breaking Ranks*, like NCLB, has the same major goal of ensuring success for all students; however, the focus is more on how that goal might be achieved.

Educators generally find themselves in more agreement with the approach proposed by *Breaking Ranks*. However, *Breaking Ranks* would require widespread changes in the way schools are organized and would increase costs. In addition, NCLB has the voice of law and, therefore, a more immediate impact.

Reform Movement Trends

Reform proponents have noted that there are three basic components to successful reform: clear standards, well-crafted tests, and fair accountability (Ornstein, 2003). These three components reflect the business model of resource allocation and efficiency applied to education. Setting standards is the educational equivalent of setting production or sales goals, testing is providing concrete data reflecting on the accomplishment of the goals, and accountability assigns rewards or sanctions according to goal attainment.

Standards-Based Education

Policymakers became frustrated with previous educational reform efforts. States would adopt new books and curricula, and classrooms could continue pretty much as they had in the past. School districts would reorganize and develop new mission statements, and business would continue as usual. Money would be spent on professional development and technology and the same teaching practices continued. Finally, policymakers decided to get tough and focus on educational outcomes or standards. The basic premise is simple: identify clear, measurable descriptions of learning outcomes (standards); measure their attainment; and hold teachers accountable for how well their students perform. Standards-based education has become a foundation for educational reform movements across the nation. The modern standards movement owes much to the ideas of Diane Ravitch, a former U.S. assistant secretary of education, who promoted the approach in her 1995 book *National Standards in American Education: A Citizen's Guide*. Ravitch argued that "standards can improve achievement by clearly defining what is to be taught and what kind of performance is expected" (Ravitch, 1995, p. 25).

This is a positive aspect of clearly stated standards. Many secondary school teachers, even after having completed a college major in a subject, are left wondering what parts of that content need to be taught to a specific group of students. Clear educational standards can help teachers conceptualize the essential elements of a subject that should be taught to students. They can be very useful in planning for teaching. In the past, this decision was usually made with reference to the textbook provided by the school district. Textbooks, however, reflect the decisions of the authors as to what is important and can present an incomplete, limited view of a subject. Standards are viewed as a more comprehensive and reliable guide.

One argument that supporters of standards-based education make is that this places the focus on what students actually learn. Measurements of these educational outputs, in turn, provide a way to make meaningful comparisons among schools. Parents, guardians, and citizens can use this information to make judgments about individual schools and to apply pressure to improve those that do not prepare students well.

Proponents of standards-based education argue that, too often in the past, schools have been judged on the quality of inputs such as learning resources (textbooks, computers, laboratories, and so forth) that are provided to encourage students to learn. Critics of judging schools on inputs contend that it misses the central purpose of education: student learning.

Content standards describe what teachers are supposed to teach and what young people are to learn (Noddings, 1997). Many national subject-area organizations have developed a set of content standards defining what the organizations believe to be essential learning outcomes for their subjects. National content standards have been developed for such subjects as mathematics, English-language arts, history, civics and government, science, and geography. In addition, many states have developed content standards that are to guide curriculum development and assessment of learners' academic progress. These state standards are required in NCLB.

This focus on state standards represents a fundamental shift in the traditional ways educational decisions have been made. In the past, local control meant that curriculum decisions were made at the local level. The establishment and enforcement of state content standards on all districts in a state effectively removed control of the curriculum from local authorities. Proponents of standards point out that the high mobility of the population makes it important that there be some consistency of expectations across school districts. Stake (1999) acknowledges that whole states and the entire nation do have a legitimate interest in what every student is learning. However, he argues that this does not mean that every student should learn the same thing.

Stake's concern raises a critical question: Who should determine the content standards for the schools and therefore for all students? Should a group appointed by politicians, such as the president or governors, decide what students should know? Should business leaders or academic professors make this decision?

There have also been difficulties in creating standards that teachers will actually follow. One problem has been that national professional organizations have not always been careful about limiting the number of standards they have adopted and the length of the descriptive prose that accompanies them (Schmoker & Marzano, 1999). If you have an opportunity to view some standards developed by certain national subject-specialty organizations, you may well feel intimidated by the number and kinds of expectations for students these appear to be advocating.

In summary, it can be argued that the goal of the reform movement to have clear standards has largely been accomplished. Although there are many advantages to having clear standards, there are also potential problems. You will need to weigh the advantages of having clearly identified "targets" for your instruction against some possible negatives associated with (a) assessments that may not relate well to the content you teach, (b) concerns about turning over responsibility for establishing content priorities to people who may not have a good understanding of your students' needs, and (c) worries about the accuracy of school-to-school comparisons that may be made easier when standards-based programs are in place.

High-Stakes Testing

One of the most significant changes brought about by reform efforts is an increased emphasis on testing. The current reform movement changed the focus to student achievement, or the "outputs" of education. Testing was seen as a cost-effective way of measuring the outputs. Test results would provide understandable and concrete data by which the performance of schools and teachers could be measured. This information would provide parents and policymakers the basis for making decisions about schools and teachers.

This has led to a large increase in the volume of assessment and in almost every grade level and in nearly every subject learner achievement is being assessed (Stake, 1999). This brings up the issue of cost. There are some who point out that the use of tests might not be as inexpensive as thought. Over a decade ago, one study addressed the issue of the costs of assessment. It was estimated that in direct costs to testing companies and in indirect costs associated with the time and resources devoted to preparing for and taking the test, the cost to the nation was $20 billion (Sacks, 1999). Given the increase in testing just since the passage of NCLB, it is likely that the cost is now several times that amount.

High-stakes testing refers to attaching serious and important consequences to test results. The high stakes for students might be promotion to the next level or graduation. The high stakes for schools might be recognition and additional resources for good performance or sanctions and even the closing of schools for poor performance. High stakes for teachers include salary increments, the publicity of having class averages published in local newspapers, or even continued employment.

Proponents of high-stakes testing believe it is essential if change is to take place. They contend that only when there are serious consequences will educators and students take learning seriously.

The most prevalent approach to testing is the use of standardized tests. A standardized test is usually one that has been developed by a professional testing company. The test items are developed and tested on a group of students. Test items are revised as needed, and norms are established based on the scores of the group. Standards are then established for the administration of the test so that all students taking the test will do so under similar conditions. This process then allows for comparisons of student scores from across the nation based on the established norms or proficiency levels.

The testing associated with standards-based assessment presumes that the testing program will be well matched to the instructional program. In reality, this is not always the case. The simple fact that standardized tests are usually developed by large for-profit companies intent on selling tests to the widest possible audience means that tests cannot focus on the standards for different states. The result is that the test will not measure all the standards of a given state. In addition, it is likely that because of state-to-state differences, some of the content measured on a given standardized test may not have even been taught. In these instances, using test results as a valid measure of students' learning of content standards makes little sense.

High-stakes testing has fueled intense debate. Critics of high-stakes testing point out that such testing practices narrow the curriculum to those things included on the tests and that since lower-level content is easier to test, that is the content that will be emphasized. In addition, because the tests are so important, a great amount of instructional time is spent teaching to the test rather than teaching important content. Basing decisions solely on the content of a high-stakes test also runs the risk of misidentifying good teachers and good schools (Popham, 2001).

The issue of the alignment of the tests with content standards brings about another concern. Because there is seldom a strong alignment between tests and standards and because teachers are teaching to the tests, defining what should be taught is influenced more by those writing the tests than by those defining the standards.

Because of concern over the possible misuse and the negative consequences of high-stakes tests, several professional organizations have issued position statements. One such statement was developed by the prestigious American Educational Research Association (2000). This position statement included the following points:

1. Decisions that have important educational consequences should not be based solely on the basis of test scores.
2. The content tested must be incorporated into the curriculum and the materials prior to administering the test to students.
3. High-stakes tests should not be limited to the portion of the curriculum that is easiest to measure.
4. Sound procedures must be followed in establishing proficiency levels and passing scores.
5. The validity of the tests needs to be established and reported.
6. Attention needs to be given to language differences and students with disabilities.
7. The reliability or the precision of the test scores must be established.
8. The intended and unintended consequences of high-stakes tests needs to be subjected to ongoing evaluation.

In summary, many of the reform proponents have seen high-stakes testing as the only way to bring about educational reform. High-stakes testing is an important component of the reform movement and is likely to be a feature of education in the years to come. However, the goal of having well-crafted tests is one about which there is considerable debate. Most of the critics of high-stakes testing will contend that the majority of the tests are not well crafted and do not adequately indicate successful learning of standards. These individuals point out that high-stakes testing has the potential for serious harm. Educators need to understand the issues involved and be prepared to take a stand (Savage, 2004).

Accountability

The third component of educational reform is that of accountability. Accountability is directly tied to the standards movement and to high-stakes testing.

Accountability in education means holding schools responsible for what students learn. It is closely related to issues such as the financing and control of education. Accountability developed in response to several concerns. One was the cost of education. Educational expenditures are a significant portion of the budget of any state. As costs have increased, policymakers have insisted that schools be held accountable for spending money in ways that result in improved student learning.

In recent decades, especially following the release of *A Nation at Risk*, there has been an erosion of confidence in educators. Increasingly, members of the public want to make sure that schools are delivering a quality education to all students.

WHAT DO YOU THINK?

High-Stakes Testing

This is one of the most debated issues in contemporary education. There are intense feelings on both sides of the issue. There are those who believe that high-stakes testing is essential to the improvement of education, and there are those who see the movement as a serious detriment to quality education.

Questions

1. After reading the previous section, what is your position on high-stakes testing?
2. Do you agree that only high-stakes testing will motivate students and teacher to do better?
3. Which arguments do you find most compelling both for and against high-stakes testing?
4. What are the alternatives to high-stakes testing?

Few educators disagree with the concept of "fair accountability." However, several issues relate to questions of what teachers should be accountable for, what data are useful for accountability, and whether the accountability process is fair.

Is accountability fair if it is based on the results of one test that is given over 1 or 2 days once a year? Should teachers be held accountable only for how well students score on tests? Is it fair to hold teachers accountable when they have no control over a number of variables that influence student achievement, such as the quality of the learning materials, language differences, learning disabilities, and the home environment of the students?

Some experts point out that real educational reform is time consuming and costly. It requires reorganizing schools and classrooms, expanding tutoring programs, lengthening the school day and the school year, reducing class size, changing teaching and learning conceptions, and confronting the societal problem of poverty (Ornstein, 2003).

Other critics point out that there needs to be better data gathered from a variety of sources in order to reflect fairly on the accomplishments of the schools and teachers. They suggest that data on topics such as dropout and graduation rates, college acceptance rates, follow-up studies of high school graduates in the years following graduation, and teacher turnover rates are examples of data that need to be considered when making valid determinations of school and teacher accountability.

The problem is that the gathering of these data is difficult, time consuming, and expensive. However, if critics are interested in fair accountability and true educational reform, then a broader definition of accountability to include multiple data sources deserves to be considered.

In summary, accountability is an important concept that is here to stay. Teachers will need to gather data that indicate that students are learning. However, the idea of "fair accountability" is still an ideal. Educators must be knowledgeable and make sure that accountability does not continue to be defined in narrow terms that simplify the complexity of teaching and learning. Fair and useful accountability will mean that teachers, parents, and students all must be involved (Ornstein, 2003).

Improving Teacher Quality

The teacher is central to any attempt to reform secondary education. Thus, a focus on improving teaching quality is a component of nearly all reform proposals. Your own teacher preparation program may well include components that have been added in response to some of these improvement initiatives. Ideas put forward by the Interstate New Teacher Assessment and Support Consortium and the National Board for Professional Teaching Standards have been particularly influential.

Interstate New Teacher Assessment and Support Consortium (1999)

The Interstate New Teacher Assessment and Support Consortium (INTASC) was established about 20 years ago as an alliance among state education leaders, colleges and universities, and national groups with interests in promoting the educational improvement and development of high-quality educators. INTASC defines quality teachers differently than NCLB. It has promoted teacher preparation programs that ensure that teachers leave their preparation programs knowing both the subjects they will teach and the methods for transmitting content that will enable all students to learn. To achieve this end, INTASC has developed a guiding set of principles that are known as the INTASC Model Core Standards. They represent features of teaching and teacher performance that should be present regardless of subjects taught or the age and grade levels of students. Many state-level departments of education and teacher preparation programs in universities have used the INTASC standards as guidelines.

The Model Core Standards are listed in Box 1.2. At the end of many chapters in this text, you will find an exercise titled "For Your Portfolio." This provides you with an opportunity to put information you have learned into a professional-development portfolio. You will be asked to cross-reference materials you include to one or more of the Model Core Standards. To do this, you will want to refer back to the standards provided in Box 1.2.

National Board for Professional Teaching Standards

In 1987, the Carnegie Forum on Education and the Economy supported establishment of the National Board for Professional Teaching Standards (NBPTS), the governing board of which includes teachers, administrators, members of the public, and other stakeholders in education. The organization operates as a private, nonprofit group that receives financing from foundations, grants from large businesses, and certain federal sources.

NBPTS seeks to improve education by promoting the development of teachers who do the following:

- Are committed to students and their learning
- Know the subjects they teach and how to teach those subjects to students
- Are responsible for managing and monitoring student learning

BOX 1.2 INTASC Model Core Standards

The Interstate New Teacher Assessment and Support Consortium (INTASC) standards were developed by the Council of Chief State School Officers and member states. Copies may be downloaded from the Council's website at http://www.ccsso.org.

1. The teacher understands the central concepts, tools of inquiry, and structures of the discipline(s) he or she teaches and can create learning experiences that make these aspects of subject matter meaningful for students.
2. The teacher understands how children learn and develop and can provide learning opportunities that support their intellectual, social, and personal development.
3. The teacher understands how students differ in their approaches to learning and creates instructional opportunities that are adapted to diverse learners.
4. The teacher understands and uses a variety of instructional strategies to encourage students' development of critical thinking, problem solving, and performance skills.
5. The teacher uses an understanding of individual and group motivation and behavior to create a learning environment that encourages positive social interaction, active engagement in learning, and self-motivation.
6. The teacher uses knowledge of effective verbal, nonverbal, and media communication techniques to foster active inquiry, collaboration, and supportive interaction in the classroom.
7. The teacher plans instruction based on knowledge of subject matter, students, the community, and curriculum goals.
8. The teacher understands and uses formal and informal assessment strategies to evaluate and ensure the continuous intellectual, social, and physical development of the learner.
9. The teacher is a reflective practitioner who continually evaluates the effects of his or her choices and actions on others (students, parents, and other professionals in the learning community) and who actively seeks out opportunities to grow professionally.
10. The teacher fosters relationships with school colleagues, parents, and agencies in the larger community to support students' learning and well-being.

Source: Council of Chief State School Officers. (1992). Model standards for beginning teacher licensing, assessment, and development: A resource for state dialogue. Washington, DC: Author. http://www.ccsso.org/content/pdfs/corestrd.pdf.

- Think systematically about their practice and learn from experience
- Are members of learning communities (NBPTS, 1999)

Much of the work of NBPTS has been dedicated to identifying high standards related to what teachers should know and do to help students achieve. NBPTS has established a certification process for the purpose of identifying teachers who meet these standards. If you seek a National Board certificate after beginning your career as a teacher, you will undergo a rigorous set of assessments. You will be observed in your own classroom and in special situations that are developed for candidates at NBPTS assessment centers. You will also be required to prepare an extensive portfolio to document your instructional procedures and their effectiveness with learners.

National Board certificates do not replace teaching credentials, certificates, or licenses that states issue. What they do is provide formal recognition of teachers who have met much higher standards. National Board certificates provide evidence that holders have met rigorous criteria that clearly identify them as outstanding classroom practitioners.

Not everyone approves of NBPTS. A few critics argue that the practice of applying national standards and awarding certificates to people who meet them challenges the tradition of certifying teachers at the state level. Even though National Board certification does not replace state certification, some people suggest that it is a step in that direction. Supporters point out that the high NBPTS standards may encourage states to adopt more rigorous certification requirements that, in time, will improve the quality of teachers everywhere.

For additional information, you may wish to visit the National Board's Website at http://www.nbpts.org.

KEY IDEAS IN SUMMARY

- New challenges and trends are changing the face of secondary education. If you want to play a role in shaping your profession, you need to become familiar with arguments of both proponents and opponents of school change and reform proposals.
- The basic reasons people give for choosing teaching as a career include making a contribution to society, pleasant working conditions, transmitting academic content, helping students develop, and being rewarded for good performance. Of these reasons, helping students develop is cited by 90% of those preparing to be teachers as a major factor.
- The senior high school became a major component of education during the 20th century. In 1900, only about 6% of the 17-year-old population graduated from high school. However, in 2002–2003, approximately 87% of the population was graduating from high school in California. This graduation rate would be similar to that of the nation as a whole.
- The junior high school was originally developed as an intermediate-level school to prepare students for high school.
- The middle school is a recent development that has a philosophy that focuses on the unique developmental and intellectual needs of preadolescents. It is fast becoming the dominant intermediate school pattern.
- The *No Child Left Behind* Act continues the reforms initiated in the *A Nation at Risk* report released in 1983. The act established standards-based education with annual testing in many grades in reading and mathematics, implemented new requirements for teacher preparation, and mandates sanctions for those schools that do not meet annual yearly progress goals.
- *Breaking Ranks* is a proposal from the National Association of Secondary School Principals for change in secondary education. This report views the personalizing of

secondary education for students, accommodating individual differences, flexible scheduling, and changing the leadership structure as keys to educational reform.

- Standards-based education seeks to provide clear descriptions of what teachers should teach and students should learn. The idea is to provide clear "targets" for instruction.
- High-stakes testing is the use of standardized tests to measure student achievement of standards and the implementation of serious consequences for schools, teachers, and students who do not meet the standards.
- Accountability is a key ingredient in many reform proposals. It is the desire to hold educators accountable for students' learning. It changes the focus of education from "input," or what is put into education, to "outputs."
- Two important efforts to improve the competence of classroom teachers have been mounted, respectively, by the Interstate New Teacher Assessment and Support Consortium (INTASC) and the National Board for Professional Teaching Standards (NBPTS). INTASC has identified a list of capabilities that new teachers should have. Many teacher preparation programs now are designed with a view to preparing candidates who meet these standards. NBPTS has developed a system of issuing National Board certificates to experienced teachers whose performances measure up to rigorous standards.

REFLECTIONS

1. Have your reasons for choosing teaching changed as a result of the information contained in this chapter? If so, explain.
2. How does an understanding of the history of secondary education relate to some of the current issues?
3. What is your response to proposals to reform secondary education?
4. What is your reaction to high-stakes testing and teacher accountability based on student test scores?
5. Review the INTASC standards. Which ones do you think are your strengths? Which ones will require additional learning and experience?

LEARNING EXTENSIONS

1. Conduct a poll of secondary teachers on their reasons for choosing teaching as a career. Also ask them the extent to which teaching has met their expectations. Note any patterns that emerge from your poll. Is there a difference between high school and middle or junior high school teachers? Are there gender differences? Are there differences according to years of teaching experience? How do you account for the differences?
2. Together with several others in your class, organize a symposium on this topic:

   "The 10 Most Likely Changes in Secondary Education During the First Quarter of the 21st Century." Present findings to your class and invite follow-up comments at the end of the presentation.

3. Review professional journals for articles focusing on standards-based education, high-stakes testing, and accountability. List the claimed advantages and disadvantages. Define your own position based on the information you have gathered.
4. Interview some of the faculty in your teacher preparation program to determine how well your program matches the INTASC standards. Conduct a self-evaluation. Which of the standards do you think you can meet, and where do you need additional growth?

REFERENCES

American Educational Research Association. (2000, July). AERA position statement concerning high stakes testing in preK–12 education. http://www.aera.net/about//policy/stakes.html

Astuto, T., Clark, D., Read, A.M., McGree, K. & Fernandez, L. (1994). *Challenging the roots of reform: Challenging the assumptions that control change in education*. Bloomington, IN: Phi Delta Kappa Educational Foundation.

Barry, T. (1961). *Origin and development of the American public high school in the nineteenth century*. Unpublished doctoral dissertation, Stanford University.

Berliner, D., & Biddle, B. (1995). *The manufactured crisis: Myths, fraud, and the attack on America's public schools*. Reading, MA: Addison-Wesley.

Bernard, S., & Mondale, S. (2001). *School: The story of American public education*. Boston: Beacon Press.

Commission on the Reorganization of Secondary Education. (1918). *Cardinal principles of secondary education*. Washington, DC: U.S. Government Printing Office.

EdSource. (2004). 2004 resource cards on California schools. Palo Alto, CA: EdSource.

Hlebowitsh, P. (2001). *Foundations of American education: Purpose and promise* (2nd ed.). Belmont, CA: Wadsworth/Thomson Learning.

Interstate New Teacher Assessment and Support Consortium. (1999). Interstate new teacher assessment and support consortium. Washington, DC: Council of Chief State School officers. http://www.ccsso.org/intasc.html

Lounsbury, J., & Vars, G. (1978). *Curriculum for the middle years*. New York: Harper & Row.

McEwin, K., & Dickinson, T. (1997). Middle level teacher preparation and licensure. In J. Irvin (Ed.), *What current research says to the middle level practitioner* (pp. 223–230). Columbus, OH: National Middle School Association.

National Association of Secondary School Principals. (1996). *Breaking ranks*. Reston, VA: Author.

National Association of Secondary School Principals. (2004). *Breaking ranks II*. Reston, VA: Author.

National Board for Professional Teaching Standards. (1999). The five propositions of accomplished teaching. San Antonio, TX: Author. http://www.nbpts.org/nbpts.standards/five-props.html

National Commission on Excellence in Education. (1983). *A nation at risk: The imperative for educational reform*. Washington, DC: U.S. Department of Education.

National Commission on the High School Senior Year. (2001). *Raising our sights: No high school senior left behind*. Princeton, NJ: Woodrow Wilson National Fellowship Foundation.

National Education Association. (1893). *Report on the Committee of Ten on secondary school studies*. Washington, DC: Author.

National Education Association. (1911). *Address and proceedings*. Washington, DC: Author.

Noddings, N. (1997). Thinking about standards. *Phi Delta Kappan, 79*(3), 184.

Ornstein, A. (2003). *Teaching and schooling in America: Pre and post September 11*. Boston: Allyn and Bacon.

Ornstein, A., & Levine, D. (2003). *Foundations of education* (8th ed.). Boston: Houghton Mifflin.

Popham, W. (2001). *The truth about testing: An educator's call to action*. Alexandria, VA: Association for Supervision and Curriculum Development.

Ravitch, D. (1995). *National standards in American education: A citizen's guide*. New York: Basic Books.

Ryan, K., & Cooper, J. (2004). *Those who can, teach*. Boston: Houghton Mifflin.

Sacks, P. (1999). *Standardized minds: The high price of America's testing culture and what we can do to change it*. Cambridge, MA: Perseus Books.

Savage, T. (2004). Assessment and quality social studies. *The Social Studies, 94*(5), 201–206.

Schmoker, M., & Marzano, R. (1999). Realizing the promise of standards-based education. *Educational Leadership, 56*(6), 17–21.

Stake, R. (1999). The goods on American education. *Phi Delta Kappan, 80*(9), 668–672.

Stuart v. School District No. 1 of the Village of Kalamazoo, 30 Mich. 69 (1874).

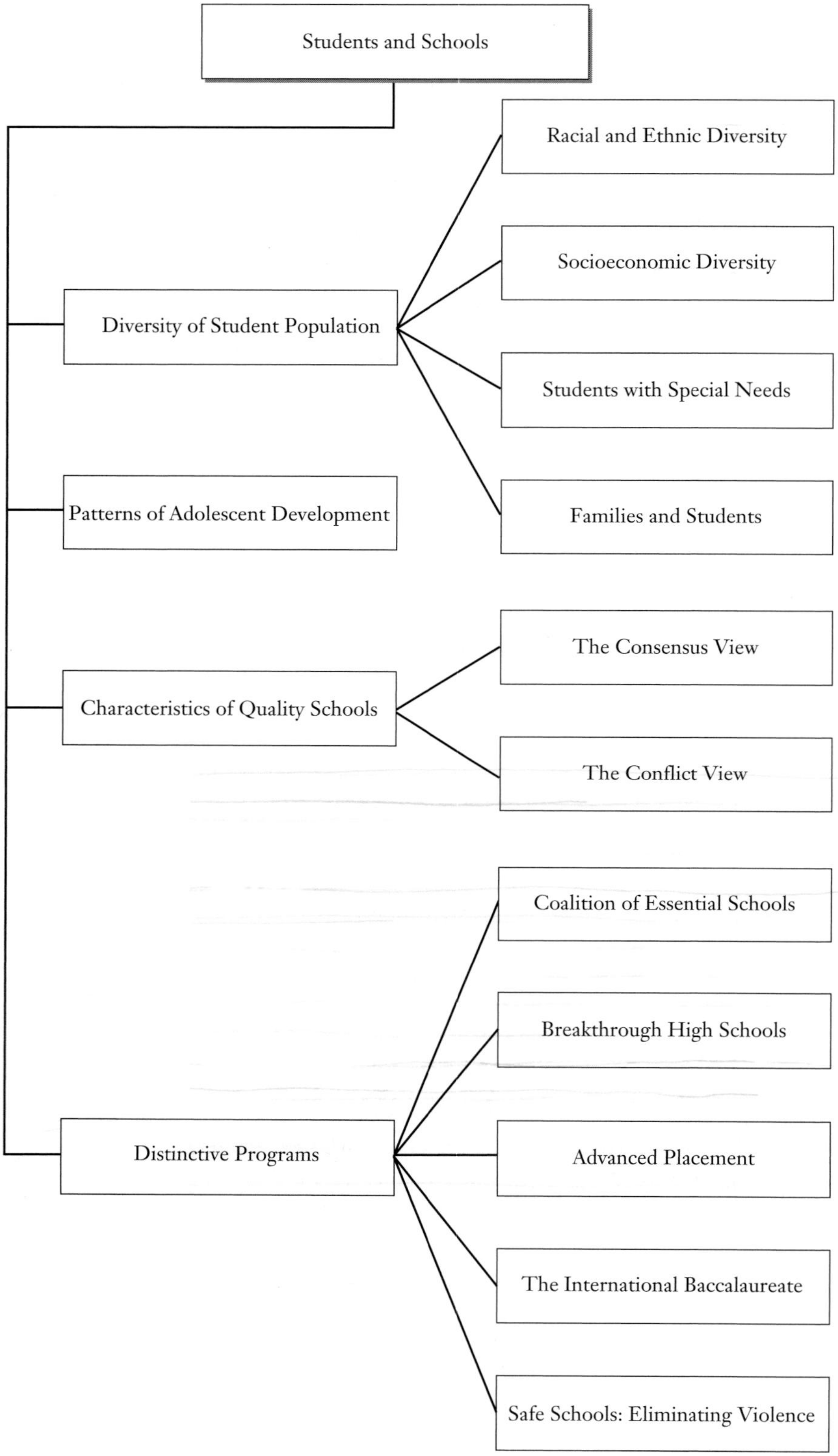

Figure 2.1
Graphic Organizer

CHAPTER 2

Students and Schools

OBJECTIVES

This chapter will help you

- identify the racial and ethnic characteristics of the current student population;
- describe the relationships between poverty and academic success;
- state the types of special needs students in secondary classrooms and the policy debates that have accompanied their inclusion in regular classrooms;
- suggest ways families influence academic achievement;
- explain patterns of preadolescent and adolescent development and how those patterns influence the behavior of secondary-level students;
- describe characteristic of quality secondary schools;
- define competing views of excellence in education;
- explain the elements of secondary education included in the Coalition of Essential Schools;
- compare the characteristics of "breakthrough high schools" with those of the Coalition of Essential Schools;
- define advanced placement;
- describe the International Baccalaureate program; and
- explain issues associated with the topic of school violence.

Introduction

"Contemporary students are really different from those of the past." "Students are basically the same as they have always been. The basic characteristics of adolescents have not really changed." You might encounter these two contradictory comments when hearing people discuss secondary students. Actually, there are elements of truth in both statements.

Certainly, it is true that there have been enormous changes in the world and in society. These changes do have an impact on students. Changes in technology, communication, and transportation provide opportunities and challenges that were not even considered just a couple of decades ago. Students have access to information that just a few years ago could be accessed at only the best research libraries. They encounter alternative lifestyles and value claims daily. Travel to distant and exotic places that used to be described only in books is now commonplace. The characteristics of the secondary age–level population has changed dramatically and become incredibly diverse. You will have students in your classes that come from all parts of the world. Some of your students will come from families where English is not spoken at home. The characteristics of the home have changed, and the probability is that both parents are working and, indeed, that a large percentage of the students you are teaching will be working. There will be students in your class who just a few years ago would have dropped out or would have been placed in a special school or special classroom. Indeed, the profile of a typical secondary school student is far different from what it used to be, and the students will exhibit a wider range of beliefs, values, and needs than those of past decades.

However, the basic characteristics of adolescents are not that much different from the way we were when we were in secondary schools. They exhibit the same patterns of intellectual and social development. Their basic social and intellectual needs are the same, and many of them echo the same concerns about themselves and their future that we expressed when we were progressing through this very difficult age.

In chapter 1, we noted that, although it sometimes appears to be forgotten, the students should be at center of education discussions. A large part of your success in teaching will depend on your understanding of the student. Be forewarned, however, that one of the "good news, bad news" aspects of secondary teaching is the unpredictability of secondary students. The good news is that each student and each group of students will be different and will react differently to your instruction. Secondary classrooms are unpredictable places, and you never know what may happen. Each day and each group will be different, and this keeps teaching interesting and exciting. The bad news is that the students are different and unpredictable, and you never know how they will react. This creates anxiety and tension. Understanding some basic characteristics of students can help you reduce some of the negative elements of the unpredictability and allow you to capitalize on the excitement and freshness that can come from being a secondary school teacher.

Diversity of the Student Population

One dimension where students today are considerably different from those of recent generations is in the composition of the student population. The student population today includes considerably more cultural, racial, and ethnic diversity than the secondary schools of the past. In addition, many of the students in the schools are living below the poverty level. Because of legislation, students with disabilities who in the past had been excluded from many secondary schools are now present in the classrooms. These various elements all contribute to a much more heterogeneous population than ever before. You are challenged to consider the assumptions you have made about the nature of the students you will be teaching in order to be better prepared to address the challenges of teaching.

Racial and Ethnic Diversity

One of the most dramatic differences in students is their diversity. The growing racial and ethnic diversity across the nation is impacting all geographical regions. This means that it will soon be almost impossible for a person to teach in a region where there is not a racial, linguistic, or culturally diverse student population.

An important component of the diverse population of the schools is the children of immigrants. The foreign-born population has increased 57% since 1990. In 2000, one out of every five children under the age of 18 had a least one foreign-born parent (Elmelech, McCaskie, Lennon, & Lu, 2002). Currently, immigrants make up over 5% of the public school population. Most of these students speak a language other than English at home. Estimates are that well over 2 million students in the United States are limited-English-proficient students. These data have significance for teachers because these students usually need extra academic instruction in order to achieve success, and approximately 20% of the high school students and 12% of the middle school students have missed 2 or more years of schooling (Garcia, 2002).

When you think of students with limited English proficiency, you may be inclined to think of students whose first language is Spanish. While Spanish is the most common first language among students with a home language other than English, schools today enroll students who speak many other languages at home as well. In fact, there are often more than 20 languages other than English spoken at home in even medium-size school districts. In metropolitan school districts, the number often exceeds 60.

Regardless of where your first teaching position is located in the country and regardless of whether your school is in an urban, suburban, or rural area, chances are high that many of your students will be members of racial or ethnic minority groups. Looking at the nation as a whole, nearly 40% of all students today are members of minority groups. Minority populations are growing at a more rapid rate than the general population. If present trends continue, minority group students will make up an even larger percentage of the secondary school population in the years ahead.

Students from nonwhite and Hispanic populations come from families that are in the lowest quartile of indicators of family "well-being" (Garcia, 2002). Many explanations for this have been proposed. The poor economic circumstances of many African American and Latino families are a contributing factor. There may be unintended cultural biases in modes of instruction and in testing procedures that fail to adequately measure what young people from ethnic minorities have learned. For some students who learned a language other than English as their first language, problems with English may contribute to difficulties at school.

This means that teachers are likely to face a growing number of students who might be classified as "at risk." Garcia (2002) notes that by eighth grade 40% or more of black and Hispanic students are performing one grade level or more below expected norms and achievement levels. When we view this in the context of the growth of this segment of the school population to 70% in the near future, this poses a daunting challenge for educators who are also facing higher academic standards, high-stakes testing, and accountability. Special efforts will be required if these students are to be provided with the educational foundations necessary for social and economic well-being. Critics of education and supporters of high-stakes testing have dismissed these concerns simply as excuses for poor performance.

Today especially, high percentages of minority students are found in central cities. In one recent year, African American students made up about one third and Latino students about one fourth of the central city student population (Wirt & Snyder, 1999).

You may be aware that many educators believe our increasingly multicultural society will be well served by a school system that brings together young people from diverse racial and ethnic backgrounds. However, as a result of the rapid increase in the total population of students who belong to racial and ethnic minorities, a pattern has developed showing that, within some schools in a given area, numbers of students from a single racial or ethnic group have grown significantly higher than numbers of students from other groups. Looked at as a whole, it appears that the schools are becoming more racially diverse; however, large numbers of individual schools are becoming less diverse. This pattern acts to increase isolation of members of one racial group from another. Recent data suggest, for example, that African American students in the border states and the South have less exposure to white students in their schools than they did 10 to 15 years ago. Similarly, Latino students in the schools have less exposure to white, non-Latino students in the South and the Northeast than they did 10 to 15 years ago (Wirt & Snyder, 1999).

One problem that seems likely to concern you throughout your career is the school dropout rate. Traditionally, members of some ethnic minorities, particularly African Americans and Hispanics, have dropped out of school at much higher rates than white students. Although calculating the actual dropout rate is difficult because of the way different states record data, one survey did identify the percentages of school dropout rates for individuals aged 16 to 24. In one recent year, 7.6% of the white students, 13.4% of the African American students, and 25.3% of the Latino students had dropped out (Wirt & Snyder, 1999). Over the past 30 years, dropout rates of African American students, though still higher than those of white students, have declined significantly; however, the number of Latino students dropping out remains very high. Dropout rates of Latino students who were born outside the United States are especially high—38.6% (Wirt & Snyder, 1999).

What can be done to improve this situation? There is some evidence that today's school programs are responding better to needs of ethnic minorities than in the past. One measure of this change is a record of improvement of minority students' scores on National Assessment of Educational Progress tests. Scores of African American and Latino students have greatly improved over the past 20 years on tests of reading, writing, mathematics proficiency, and science performance. While these scores still lag behind those of white (non-Latino) students, the gap has become much smaller. These differences in achievement levels greatly affect the rate at which minority students take sophisticated courses. For example, the percentage of white students taking calculus courses in high school is almost twice that of African American and Latino students (Snyder, 2000).

Poverty and Success at School

Chances are that many students you teach will come from families living below the poverty level. In 2002, one out of every six children below the age of 18 were living in families with incomes below the poverty line. More children are living in poverty today than 25 or 30 years ago, and the United States has a higher child poverty rate than 17 other wealthy nations (Children's Defense Fund, 2003). Although the poverty rates are higher for Hispanic and black students, there are actually more white non-Hispanic children living in poverty (Children's Defense Fund, 2003).

Young people from poor families face many challenges during the years they are in school. Among other things, these students are greatly at risk of dropping out before completing high school. Note some of these other differences between poor young people and nonpoor young people (Brooks-Gunn & Duncan, 1997):

- Poor young people are much less likely to enjoy excellent health than nonpoor young people.
- Poor young people are twice as likely as nonpoor young people to be in the lowest 20% of the student population in terms of their height.
- Poor young people are more likely to have a learning disability than nonpoor young people.
- Poor young people are twice as likely to repeat a grade in school as nonpoor young people.

- Poor, young, teen females are nearly three times as likely to give birth to a child out of wedlock as a nonpoor female teenager.

Students with Disabilities

More secondary students with disabilities of all kinds are now enrolled as members of regular middle school, junior high school, and senior high school classes. Federal legislation and supportive laws and regulations enacted by individual states have increased a commitment to inclusion, which means that these young people are included in regular class activities and that instructional services need to be delivered to them in an appropriate manner by regular classroom teachers.

Federal legislation requires states each year to report the numbers of special education students falling within each of the following 13 categories:

1. Specific learning disability
2. Speech or language impairment
3. Mental retardation
4. Serious emotional disturbance
5. Multiple disabilities
6. Hearing impairment
7. Deafness
8. Orthopedic impairment
9. Other health impairment
10. Visual impairment or blindness
11. Autism
12. Traumatic brain injury
13. Deaf-blindness

Today, more than 2 million secondary students fall into one of these categories. The number of special education students has been growing as a percentage of the total population of secondary school learners. The specific-learning-disability category has been growing fastest of all.

One policy issue you will face as an educator has to do with costs of services provided to special needs students. As the numbers of special education programs have increased, so have the costs associated with supporting them. To pay for these programs, it has been necessary for many school districts to divert funds from accounts traditionally used to support the general education program for all students (Parrish, 2000). The issue raises two questions: (a) how much money can be reallocated from general education to special education without undermining the quality of services provided to general education students, and (b) given the growth of special education programs and the need to support them, is it possible to increase the total amount of money available to support education so that increased costs of special education programs will not result in decreased support for general education? At present, there is little consensus on issues implied by these questions. You are certain to encounter arguments in support of many approaches to responding to these difficulties during your years in the profession.

Families and Students

Have you ever seen reruns of television shows from the 1950s? You know the ones that feature a "typical" happy family with a stay-at-home mother, a couple of kids, and a father who is welcomed happily into the group as he returns from a hard day at the office. All fathers on those shows seemed to be well-situated professionals. All families seemed to live in white houses in nicely maintained neighborhoods on tree-lined streets. All families seemed to have children who, if they had problems at all, tended to suffer from nothing so serious that it could not be nicely resolved within a single half-hour episode. For the most part, the portrait these shows presented of a "typical" American family was quite a stretch even in the 1950s. However, the depiction of two-parent families, including a stay-at-home mother, closely mirrored the national reality in the middle of the 20th century. Today, this kind of family arrangement is the exception rather than the rule.

Recent surveys reveal that mothers of over two thirds of school-aged children are employed. About 30% of children live as members of families headed by a single parent. This single parent is six times more likely to be the mother than the father (Wirt & Snyder, 1999). The nature of your students' families may have an effect on their performance in school.

One validated finding is that students with mothers who have more than a high school education perform better in school than students whose parents have received less formal education. Over the past three decades, there has been a tremendous increase in the educational attainment levels of students' mothers. For example, in the early 1970s, only about 18% of the mothers of these women had some college or university work or a college or university degree. Today, this figure has risen to about 49% (Wirt & Snyder, 1999).

Another interesting fact is that fathers' involvement in schools is closely associated with their children's academic performance. Fathers who do not live with their children tend to have very low levels of involvement with their children's schools. Fathers in two-parent families are much more likely to volunteer in schools, attend class events, participate in parent–teacher conferences, and go to general school meetings. The highest involvement levels at all are found among fathers who head households as single parents. However, single-parent households headed by males are very few in number (Wirt & Snyder, 1999). Some "pluses" for students with fathers who are highly involved in schools are reflected in these data for fathers from two-parent households.

Taken together, research on the influences families have on students' performance underscores a key point. That is, you need to take time to know your students well. The instruction you provide does not occur in a vacuum. Students' family situations vary greatly from individual to individual, and you need this kind of contextual information as you plan instructional experiences with the potential to respond to each student's particular circumstances.

Patterns of Adolescent Development

In addition to the multiple backgrounds of students you will face as a teacher, you will also be working with young people at a time when they are going through important personal developmental changes. You need to recognize these maturational patterns and seek ways to respond to students that are sensitive both to these "growing up" challenges and to the unique background characteristics each student brings to school every day.

However, you need to appreciate that descriptions of sequences of adolescent development are not meant to imply that all students experience exactly the same thing or that there is an iron-clad sequence of life events that ensures that every person will experience the same emotional, physical, and social changes at precisely the same age. These patterns are general ones, and there are enormous person-to-person differences in terms of when they occur and how much they influence individual young people.

You will see more profound physical differences among younger secondary school students than among older ones. Size differences among individual seventh, eighth, and ninth graders sometimes startle visitors to their classrooms. Some girls may look little different from much younger fourth and fifth graders. Some boys may not yet weigh 80 pounds, while others will have the height and bulk found more typically among high school seniors. During the adolescent growth spurt years, an individual might grow as much as 5 inches per year (Ormrod, 1998).

In addition to physical development, students are also undergoing personal, social, moral, and cognitive development. It is sometimes difficult for mature adults to understand that adolescents are qualitatively different from adults. It isn't that they simply lack experience; rather, they actually think and respond differently than more mature adults. This fact leads to many frustrations as adults try to relate to adolescents.

The school experience provides a setting where individuals are constantly interacting with teachers and peers and therefore plays a major role in these different types of developments. One aspect of personal development where schools play an important role is in the development of self-concept and self-esteem.

During adolescent development, social acceptance is a major issue. Some students feel isolated and left out.

All of us have general feelings about our self-worth. We are aware of our individual strengths and weaknesses and have come to recognize that there are some things we do well and some things we do poorly. These feelings about ourselves then lead us to the development of our self-concept or a belief in our feelings of self-worth and our view of ourselves as capable or inept, worthy or unworthy.

During the adolescent years, individuals are still searching for their strengths and their feelings of competence. It might be said that their self-concept is relatively unstable. A minor success might lead to great euphoria and a minor failure to the depths of despair. As the self-concept becomes more stable, reactions to success and failure become less extreme. The development of the self-concept during adolescence can influence a person for many years.

These factors led Erikson (1963) to define the adolescent years as the struggle between identity and role confusion. Individuals during this stage are trying to figure out their own identity and who they will be as an adult. They are trying to develop a sense of direction in their life, commit to political and religious beliefs, and decide on a career path. They are especially interested in separating their identity from that of their parents. As a result, they may "try out" several identities (much to the consternation of some parents and teachers).

However, this process will also lead to a certain amount of role confusion or mixed ideas and feelings about the way they will fit into society. They may see that some of the identities that they try out simply don't provide them with the satisfaction and the personal direction they need.

Self-concept and self-esteem play an important role in student behavior and achievement. Students with low self-esteem often demonstrate less productive or constructive behavior and therefore are likely to experience less success (Ormrod, 1998). Generally, the development of self-concept involves perceptions of self in at least three areas: cognitive competence, social competence, and physical competence.

Physical competence relates to students' beliefs about their ability to engage in physical activities such as sports. Because athletics is glorified in society and individuals with physical competence often command desirable resources such as money and attention, physical competence is often highly valued by adolescents.

Another dimension of physical competence that relates to the development of the self-concept during the adolescent years is physical attractiveness. Most of us can remember our adolescent days and our endless worry about our looks and appearance. We had to wear just the right clothes. We couldn't leave the house unless our hair was just right. Again, attractive individuals seem to command desirable resources in society, so physical attractiveness, as defined by the current standard, becomes very important to many adolescents.

Adolescents also give high priority to social competence. They are seeking to make friends and attain popularity. Any secondary teacher will tell you that talking and interacting with others is a high priority. Social competence relates to the beliefs individuals have about their ability to relate to other people, including the ability to make friends, being accepted by others, and gaining popularity. Individuals who have difficulty making friends or who do not relate well to others tend to develop low self-concepts.

Cognitive competence or the ability to do well academically is another important dimension of the self-concept. Actually, cognitive competence and helping students achieve success academically is the major goal of education. However, many secondary school students value physical and social competence more than cognitive competence. Therefore, teachers have a difficult challenge getting students to place a priority on cognitive competence.

Students usually begin to make finer distinctions about cognitive competence (Ormrod, 1998). They may see themselves as good at mathematics but a poor reader or as good at writing but poor in science. These perceptions will influence their motivation, study habits, and task persistence. The challenge for the secondary teacher is to help students develop cognitive competence by helping them understand the importance of the subject and by providing them with the types of successful experiences that will help them develop positive images of themselves as capable students.

The uneven patterns of physical, emotional, social, and academic growth and the constant quest of students seeking their own identity present unique challenges to teachers in the early adolescent years. If you are teaching seventh graders, on some days you will find a student acting as a mature adult might act. On other days, you may well see the same person doing something that would (or should) embarrass a fourth grader. As young people in this age-group strive to establish personal identities, they engage in a lot of behavioral experimentation. As this process develops, their behaviors swing wildly between surprisingly adult to disturbingly childish patterns. In general, these are some patterns you might expect to see if you're assigned to teach younger secondary school students:

- Students experience tension as they seek to establish a balance between a need to find their unique personal identities and a need to be an accepted member of a group.
- Students tend to shift their focus from their parents to their friends as they seek cues regarding acceptable attitudes and patterns of behavior.
- Students tend to place great emphasis on physiological changes they are experiencing and to worry whether their own rate of development is consistent with what others in their age-group are experiencing.
- Students begin to develop more sophisticated patterns of thinking; one consequence is that they begin to see their parents and other adults as less than perfect, a realization that leads to some disappointment and to an increase in a willingness to challenge adult authority.

Combining the cognitive development of secondary students as they move toward more abstract and complex thought, their preoccupation with self, and their search for personal identity can lead to some interesting patterns. This is often displayed in an excessive concern about what others think about them and makes peer pressure an especially important force. David Elkind (1981), a leading authority on developmental psychology, suggests that this combination of beginning to think more abstractly, coupled with concern for social competence and preoccupation with physical appearance, results in a unique form of adolescent egocentrism.

One aspect of this form of egocentrism leads many adolescents to behave as if an "imaginary audience" was closely observing their every action. Young people who have this attitude think others are closely watching everything they do. They are certain that every flaw or misstep will be noted by everyone. They may tend to "showboat" or be overly dramatic because it is as if they are on stage with everyone watching. You can sometimes see reflections of this attitude in students who seem to reject independent thought and fear to act or speak up until those perceived to be the "social leaders" identify the acceptable course of action. They are fearful that their words or actions will not be acceptable and may be ridiculed by their "audience."

Another interesting aspect of adolescent egocentrism is the "personal fable." Because individuals at this stage are going through so many changes, they view themselves as unique and surely beyond the understanding of anyone else, especially parents. This personal fable or powerful feeling of uniqueness often leads them to the conclusion that they are not subject to the normal dangers of life. They know that bad things happen, but they are convinced they always happen to others. They may then take foolish risks, such as driving recklessly, engaging in dangerous sexual conduct, or experimenting with drugs and alcohol (Ormrod, 1998). Over the years, concern about these social problems has led to programs of driver training, sex education, and substance abuse education. Those who are successful are those who take into account the personal fable and successfully engage students in discovering that they are not immune and that bad things can happen to them.

As students progress through their secondary school years, they tend to become more personally secure, more confident in their thinking abilities, and more accepting of the physiological changes that they have experienced (or are continuing to experience). High school students, particularly juniors and seniors, begin to reflect adult patterns of thinking and behaving. Though they continue to place a high value on attitudes of friends the same age, typically they are able to understand and appreciate the perspectives of people outside their own friendship group to a much greater extent than students in the early middle school years. However, it has become clear that the search for identity may last for many years beyond high school.

The following are characteristics you might expect to see among students if you are teaching at the upper high school level:

- Students often develop serious and intense relationships with members of the opposite gender.
- Students tend to begin reconnecting and recommitting to values and traditions of their own families and cultural groups, even when these may be at variance with views of their school friendship groups.
- Students' capacities for setting and pursuing long-term goals increase.
- Students develop more tolerance for accepting compromises and for delaying gratification of immediate wants.
- Students develop a strong sense of who they are—a pattern that is accompanied by more emotional stability and more self-reliance.

Characteristics of Quality Secondary Schools

Given the tremendous and overpowering changes that are taking place in the lives of adolescents, some have concluded that this is the worst possible time to try to educate someone. This may well be true, but teach them we must. It is true that many individuals make choices during the adolescent years that negatively impact their future prospects. This can certainly be one of the heartbreaking aspects of being a secondary school teacher.

Our challenge is to provide an educational environment that takes into account the nature of the students and provides maximum opportunities for them to develop levels of competence that will provide the foundations for growth into good, capable members of society.

What are the characteristics of a high-quality school? If you asked a cross section of people, you might or might not find patterns of agreement. If respondents spoke only about very general characteristics of good schools, you quite probably would find wide agreement on a number of points. For example, you might hear comments such as these:

"Good schools respect and respond to the dignity of individual students."

"Good schools help students develop tolerance for others."

"Good schools produce students who are committed to democratic decision making."

"Good schools promote the idea that citizens should work together for the good of the total community."

On the other hand, if you pressed people to elaborate on the meaning of phrases contained within these broad statements, you might be surprised at the different and often conflicting answers you would get. People with different life experiences, with different cultural backgrounds, and from different social groups bring widely varied perspectives to bear when they consider qualities associated with good schools (Oakes, Quartz, Ryan, & Lipton, 2000). Conflicting views about what constitutes excellence mean that different people apply different standards when they are asked to rate the relative excellence of a program at a particular school. These disagreements result because large numbers of people subscribe to one of two incompatible conceptions of the reality of the school:

- The consensus view of schools
- The conflict view of schools

The Consensus View

You will find that people who commit to this position believe that most Americans subscribe to a common set of values. They contend that people in this country agree about more things than they disagree about. Their view is that our present way of doing things is fair, good, and worthy of maintaining. There is a body of knowledge that everyone should know and that we know what that is. In their view, the purpose of the school is to provide the intellectual talent and skill needed to keep social institutions going in their present form.

There is an assumption that individuals start their school programs with relatively equal opportunities to succeed. Differences in their success as students come from individual effort. Economic rewards and high social status are thought to come to students who get good grades, qualify for admission to good colleges and universities, and develop the kinds of expertise our society appreciates. Good schools encourage students to achieve the kinds of academic success that, in their later years, will allow them to contribute to the nation's economic growth. Their success will help the entire country and result in improved standards of living for all.

Strong supporters of this position evaluate proposals for change in terms of their ability to promote and maintain existing social and political arrangements. For example, if there appears to be an erosion of economic competitiveness and workplace opportunities, then more rigorous science, mathematics, and technology courses are likely to be supported. If it appears that young people are apathetic about civic involvement, then there is likely to be calls for more history and civic education in an effort to develop more "patriotic" citizens.

On the other hand, if there is a suspicion that an innovation may alter some basic social arrangements, then individuals who commit to the consensus view will be less likely to support it. For example, certain topics, such as sex education or evolution, that are perceived to be a threat to the status quo of family or church are likely to be opposed.

Most of the recent reform proposals originating at the government level such as *A Nation at Risk* and the No Child Left Behind Act generally reflect the consensus position. The need for reforms is justified because of economic or social issues and an assumption that there is a body of knowledge that everyone must know. Change is promoted by either motivating or threatening students and teachers to teach and learn this knowledge.

The Conflict View

Those who subscribe to the conflict view reject the assumption of the consensus position that there is broad agreement that present social arrangements are good and should be maintained. They argue that many present arrangements act to benefit some groups and to disadvantage or marginalize others. They tend to see our society not as a harmonious collection of individuals sharing common values but rather as an arena where competing groups compete for benefits. This situation tends to produce winners and losers whose fate tends to be largely predetermined by the particular social, ethnic, or economic groups to which they belong.

People who subscribe to this position often see present school programs organized in ways that clearly provide more benefits to students from some groups than others. For example, secondary schools that offer classes in advanced mathematics may have adopted these programs to better serve the sons and daughters of highly educated parents who want to prepare them for positions in elite colleges and universities. Because school resources are limited, supporters of the conflict position contend that curricular decisions too often divert money away from needs of students from groups with little political or economic power. When this happens, school programs tend to perpetuate social differences across generations.

Proponents of the conflict position can be both receptive and resistant to change. Because of their view that many existing school programs do not deal fairly with all students, they often will listen attentively to suggestions for change. However, because their view of school conditions them to look for ways in which programs advantage some students and disadvantage others, they are inclined to look carefully at change proposals to see whether, when implemented, they will provide more benefits to some students than to others. For example, individuals who subscribe to the conflict view might see current reform proposals as directing resources away from multicultural and bilingual education that benefits marginalized groups to those programs that will benefit more privileged groups.

Distinctive Programs

Despite the difficulties associated with bridging widely divergent views about what constitutes excellent education, there have been several attempts to describe characteristics of high-quality schools. These descriptions have helped us identify features that individuals who identify with both the consensus view of schools and the conflict view of schools will support. Consequently, many of these discussions, combined with much of the research on quality schools, have prompted educators to recommend and/or develop a variety of distinctive programs.

Coalition of Essential Schools

One program that has received considerable attention is the Coalition of Essential Schools headed by Theodore Sizer. Sizer's plan has challenged the idea of the comprehensive high school. Sizer, a former headmaster of Phillips Academy in Andover, Massachusetts, and a former dean of the Graduate School of Education at Harvard helped found the Coalition of Essential Schools at Brown University in Providence, Rhode Island. Three of Sizer's books—*Horace's Compromise* (1984), *Horace's School* (1992), and *Horace's Hope* (1996)—have prompted spirited discussion among those interested in redesigning the high school.

Sizer argues that the comprehensive high school presents students with disjointed academic courses and that this arrangement stands in the way of deep and coherent learning. He points out that large high schools allow many students to go through their entire high school program without ever becoming well acquainted with individual teachers who could mentor them. Sizer also notes that present practices of evaluating students place a premium on displaying learned information on tests rather than on using learned information in ways that make sense in the world beyond the school.

In *Horace's School*, Sizer (1992) proposes some remedies. Here are some principles that Sizer believes should characterize a worthy successor to the comprehensive secondary school:

- All students would follow the same curriculum. Sizer argues that the present high school program with its multiple electives is designed to classify students. That is, so-called able students take college preparatory work, and so-called less able students take less challenging courses. Sizer contends that high schools should be about the business of providing a strong substantive education for all learners.
- Less is more. The comprehensive high school offers so many different subjects that students often sacrifice depth of preparation to breadth of exposure. Sizer contends that a program requiring students to take a smaller number of subjects and pursue them in more depth would better serve their needs. He favors organizing the curriculum around three key subject areas: (a) mathematics/science, (b) the arts, and (c) history/philosophy. Faculty members in all three areas would

share responsibility for developing students' language proficiency (reading, writing, and speaking), developing their inquiry skills, and promoting productive study habits.

- "Exhibitions" as evidence that knowledge can be used. As a replacement for conventional tests to show evidence that learning has taken place, Sizer proposes the use of what he calls exhibitions. These would be complex presentations of the products of learning that would demonstrate to students and to others in a highly convincing way that they could use newly gained knowledge. Students would be encouraged to keep portfolios of work indicating their progress toward preparation of presentation of their exhibitions.
- High schools subdivided into houses. Sizer (1992) argues that "everyone at school should be accorded the respect of being well known" (p. 143). To ensure that no student goes through high school without being known and appreciated as an individual human being, high school student bodies would be subdivided into "houses" of between 200 and 220 students. Twelve to 16 faculty members would lead each house, getting to know each student well and serving as academic and personal mentors.
- Extend the school year to provide adequate time for serious learning. The school year should be extended from 36 to 42 weeks.

Sizer's ideas are not just abstract discussion prompts. They are foundations for a serious high school reform initiative promoted by a group called the Coalition of Essential Schools. Several hundred schools are members. Contact information is provided here:

Coalition of Essential Schools
Website: http://www.essentialschools.org

Breakthrough High Schools

The National Association of Secondary School Principals proposed a "road map" for secondary school reform in its publication *Breakthrough High Schools* (2004). This publication identified 12 exemplary high schools. These schools had to meet the criteria of having at least 50% minority students and 50% students qualifying for free and reduced priced meals. In these schools, at least 90% of the students graduate and are accepted into college. They conducted an analysis of these schools and identified several patterns and consistent themes:

- Creating a safe and orderly school environment
- Having shared values and a vision focused on high achievement for all students
- Holding high expectations for students and staff members
- Supporting a personalized learning environment
- Shared leadership, decision making, and problem solving
- Making decisions based on data

Creating a Safe School The analysis of these successful schools found that there were consistent standards of behavior that were understood by everyone in the school. There was zero tolerance for some activities, such as gang-related behavior, and there were consequences for inappropriate behavior. However, students were given a voice regarding discipline codes, and structures existed to help students solve problems. Diversity was celebrated, and students felt free to risk taking more advanced courses. There was an attempt to develop a sense of family or community in the school. The result was that the school was a place where students felt safe.

Having a Common Message The importance of having a common message or a clear vision of the mission of the school is that it communicates expectations to the entire school community. Students are then socialized into a culture that supports the mission of the school. Many of these missions focus on the idea of high standards, high expectations, and success for all students.

High Expectations High expectations is a theme that runs through nearly all reform proposals. The effective schools studied in this report emphasized that the standards needed to be clear, easy to understand, and applied to all students. However, just having high expectations is not enough. Meeting the expectations needs to be the responsibility of the students, the staff, and the students' families. There needs to be a strong culture of support so that everyone can work to ensure high performance for all students.

Many of the schools in this study had International Baccalaureate programs that were open to any student willing to commit to the rigorous demands of the program.

Personalized Learning Making the secondary school personal has increasingly been emphasized in secondary school reform proposals. For example, the National Commission on the High School Senior Year (2001) noted that those in the bottom third of the class reported that no teacher, counselor, or other adult in the school environment knew him or her well. They called for individualized plans for each student in high school.

The *Breakthrough High Schools* report emphasized the importance of personalizing the secondary school. They indicated that much of success in secondary schools was related to establishing relationships. They pointed out that secondary students need to feel that they belong, are valued, and respected and that their opinions matter. Supportive relationships that help the students during this critical stage of development were viewed as essential. In addition, these supportive relationships also helped teachers identify warning signs of student trouble.

Shared Leadership, Decision Making, and Problem Solving It seems clear from recent studies of effective schools as well as effective management in general that the former model of autocratic leadership is no longer appropriate. Successful schools and businesses have recognized that there must be shared decision making. School principals need to be viewed as the leaders but must realize that they do not work in isolation. They need to be willing to involve others and give credit to others for success. Teachers and staff need to be empowered to suggest solutions to problems. Members of the community need to have a sense of ownership and input into decisions. This also allows the school to develop a culture of risk taking.

Basing Decisions on Data With the availability of modern technology, it is now possible for schools to gather, analyze, and quickly disseminate many types of data. In the *Breakthrough High Schools* report, data about attendance rates, in-school illness, and other school issues allowed school officials to quickly identify problems and allowed the school to respond in ways that corrected the problems. Finding ways of gathering data and getting it into classrooms and the students' homes helped support cooperative problem solving and shared decision making.

In summary, the Coalition of Essential Schools and the *Breakthrough High School* report have identified a number of dimensions of a quality secondary school. These are characteristics that are being used in successful schools today. They are not abstract proposals divorced from reality. Understanding these characteristics can assist you in evaluating secondary schools and provide a framework for you to analyze what you need to do in order to be a productive faculty member.

In addition to these broad portraits of successful schools, there are some specific school programs that are often viewed as important components of successful secondary schools. Those include Advanced Placement and the International Baccalaureate programs.

Advanced Placement Program

The College Entrance Examination Board has sponsored the Advanced Placement (AP) program since 1955. The program was initiated to provide additional opportunities for academically talented high school students. It gives hundreds of thousands of participating capable and motivated students opportunities to take rigorous college-level courses while still in high school. Nearly 14,000 high schools offer AP courses, and almost 3,000 colleges and universities give students college credit or award advanced academic standing based on AP examination grades. In one recent year, 700,000 students took more than 1 million AP exams (Advanced Placement Program, 2000). The American Council on Education accredits the Advanced Placement program.

If you teach approved AP program courses, you will have access to many special AP publications and will be eligible to attend AP summer teaching institutes that provide additional preparation for your work with AP students and academic subjects. The AP program has some resources available to provide financial support for some teachers who attend these professional development sessions.

Further information about the AP program can be found at the following:

AP Publications
Box 6670
Princeton, NJ 08541-6670
Website: http://www.collegeboard.org/apl

International Baccalaureate Program

The term "baccalaureate" in the phrase International Baccalaureate is not used in the American sense of a university degree awarded after a minimum of 4 years of college or university study. Rather, it is used in the French sense of an examination taken at the conclusion of a rigorous secondary school program, the results of which are heavily weighed in college and university admissions decisions. The program evolved over a number of years, beginning in the early 1960s. It was designed as a program for students in different countries that, if completed successfully, would qualify them for entry to top universities throughout the world. Today, International Baccalaureate programs are offered in more than 800 secondary schools in over 100 countries, including the United States. Instruction, depending on the location, is generally in English, French, or Spanish.

Students attending high schools that offer the International Baccalaureate program take a special set of courses during their last 2 secondary school years. These are selected from the areas of (a) their first language, (b) a second language, (c) individuals and society (including history, geography, economics, philosophy, psychology, social anthropology, organization, and management studies), (d) experimental sciences (including biology, chemistry, physics, and environmental studies), (e) mathematics, and (f) one of the following: art/design, music, Latin, classical Greek, or computing studies. In addition to these areas, students in International Baccalaureate programs take a course called Theory of Knowledge that challenges them to reflect critically on all experiences gained inside and outside the classroom. To qualify for the International Baccalaureate diploma, the student must also pass a series of rigorous examinations.

More information about the International Baccalaureate program can be found at the following:

International Baccalaureate Organization
North American and the Caribbean Region
200 Madison Avenue, Suite 2301
New York, NY 10016-3903
Phone: (212) 889-9242
E-mail: ibna@ibo.org
Website: http://www.ibo.org

Safe Schools: The Issue of Violence in Schools

One characteristic that is usually cited as an important dimension of a successful secondary school is a safe learning environment. In recent years, images of schools as safe havens for students and teachers have been shattered by several tragic incidents. Deaths of students and teachers have focused unprecedented attention on the issue of violence in the schools. Today, people in all parts of the country are engaged in efforts to identify and implement workable solutions to this problem.

As you think about this issue, it's important to keep the problem in perspective. While everyone wants to make schools safer places, you need to understand that, despite the high-profile school shootings that have been so widely reported in recent years, most people who spend their days in schools are not nearly so much at risk of experiencing violent behavior as are many others. Still, numbers are large enough to

CRITICAL INCIDENT

Would a High-Quality School Support This Approach to Teaching?

Pam Estaban, principal at Mossman Middle School, believes that she heads a particularly outstanding school. She believes her teachers do an excellent job of presenting content in ways that engage students' interests and build their general enthusiasm for learning. She is especially pleased with the work of teachers in the math department.

However, not everyone shares her pleasure. Rose Larsen, mother of sixth grader Judith Larsen, made these comments recently during a conversation with Edwin McKenna, one of Mossman's math teachers:

> Mr. McKenna, I'm quite unhappy about what is going on in your classroom. I have to admit that Judith doesn't share my concerns. In fact, you're one of her favorite teachers . . . and, I'll have to agree, you have done a good job of helping her develop a good attitude about mathematics.
>
> But your approach bothers me. I keep hearing about all the time students spend working in groups and helping one another. Now, I know Judith is capable, and I think she likes being looked at as "the expert" when you involve the class in cooperative work. But I don't think this is good either for Judith or for the other students in the long run. It is making the slower kids too dependent on the brighter ones. It tends to hold back the bright people because they have to spend too much of their time assisting those who "just don't get it."
>
> As you know, I'm an engineer. I hope Judith will think about this career when the time comes. I had to struggle through sophisticated mathematics courses to get my degree. Frankly, I had to do this by myself. In high school and college there is none of this group hand-holding business. I'm afraid that Judith is going to lack the personal study habits she is going to need once she gets to high school. In addition, because this group arrangement fails to encourage her to master content beyond what is expected of everyone in the group, she's not going to enter high school as intellectually equipped as she should be.
>
> I'm here to ask you to give up this cooperative business and get back to teaching these students as individuals. This emphasis on process at the expense of substance has got to go. These kids need more "meat."

■ ■ ■

What are some values that are especially important to Judith's mother? How do these values shape her views of what should go on at a high-quality school? What things do you think are highly important to her? Given her priorities, do her comments make sense?

What are some priorities that you can infer from the decision of Mr. McKenna to use a lot of group work in his classes? What might his motives for this approach be? What do his actions suggest about the kinds of things that are important to him?

Are there ways in which differences in the perspectives of Rose Larsen and Edwin McKenna can be bridged? Is there an accommodation that might be made that takes into account important values of each? What are some of your suggestions for responding to this situation? What do your proposed solutions reveal about your own values and priorities?

be of concern. In one recent year, about 149,000 teachers experienced an episode of violence at their work site (Warshol, 1998).

Your chances of being a victim of a violent crime in school are much less than the chances of people who work in retail sales. Police officers, taxi drivers, bartenders, gas station attendants, convenience store clerks, and mental health professionals are at more risk of experiencing a violent attack at work than are teachers at any level. Among teachers, middle school and junior high school teachers are at greatest risk. High school teachers are attacked at school only about half as often. Elementary school teachers experience the fewest attacks of any teacher group (Office of Safety and Health Administration, 1999). Though you should be concerned about the school violence issue, you also want to keep in mind that about 90% of the nation's schools that were recently surveyed reported that no violent crimes were committed on their campuses during the past school year (National Center for Education Statistics, 1998).

The type of violence a secondary school student is likely to experience at school is a physical fight. One recent survey found that over one third of students nationwide were involved in a physical fight one or more times during a single year. Students during the last 2 years of high school were much less likely to be involved in fights than younger secondary school students (American Medical Association, 1999).

Fears stimulated by physical fighting and other concerns have prompted some students to bring weapons to school. A recent study found that almost one fifth of the nation's students had brought a gun, knife, or club to school during the 30-day period preceding the survey (American Medical Association, 1999). There are particular concerns about young people who feel it necessary to carry guns for their own protection. They have been found to be three times more likely to commit a crime than students who do not own guns for the purpose of protecting themselves (Howell, 1998).

The fears some students experience lead them to seek safety by joining gangs. The culture of many gangs, in turn, supports physical confrontation and other approaches to violence (Howell, 1998). The paradox is that, in an effort to find safety and security by joining a gang, a young person often ends up embracing a subculture that prizes violence. Gang membership, too, increases the probability that a young person will have access to and abuse illegal drugs. Drug use, among other things, decreases the influence of traditional social controls, a circumstance that makes it psychologically easier for an individual to see violence as an acceptable behavioral option.

In response to concerns about weapon-bearing students, gang membership, and other conditions that increase the probability of violent behavior occurring in schools, educational leaders are developing plans to combat the problem. One active national organization, the National School Safety Center, helps schools in this country and elsewhere create safe school environments. More information can be found at the following:

National School Safety Center
141 Duesenberg Drive, Suite 11
Westlake Village, CA 91362
Phone: (805) 373-9977
Website: http://www.nsscl.org

The Safe Communities–Safe Schools model developed in Colorado is typical of approaches taken in many parts of the country to create violence-free school

MORE FROM THE WEB

If you are interested in learning more about some of the issues raised in this chapter, you will find dozens of excellent information sources on the Web. Some examples are provided here.

American Academy of Child and Adolescent Psychiatry

This site includes a tremendous number of links to information related to emotional, behavioral, and intellectual development of young people. There is an entire section titled "Facts for Families and Other Resources," which treats topics such as mental illness symptoms in teenagers, violence, and the psychiatry of adolescents.

Website: http://www.aacap.org

American Medical Association

The American Medical Association maintains this site. You will find here an extensive array of information sources featuring content related to youth safety and violence. Links allow you to easily access material from these sites. You will find content related to such issues as suicide, gun violence, and early indicators of potentially violent behavior and how you can help young people cope with disasters.

Website: http://www.ama-assn.org/adolhlth/special/school.htm

Adolescence Directory On-Line

This site provides an outstanding electronic guide to information related to adolescents. You will find links to topics including conflict and violence, mental health issues, and health and health risk issues and information for counselors of adolescents.

Website: http://education.indiana.edu/cas/adol/adol.html

environments. This model recommends that schools take actions related to five basic categories (Safe Communities–Safe Schools, 1999):

1. **Establish a Safe School Planning Team** The idea here is to involve a broad spectrum of people from the community in the process of planning for a safe school environment.
2. **Conduct a School Site Assessment** This activity seeks to identify any problems related to the school climate that might be negative enough to provide fertile ground for outbreaks of violent or unsafe behaviors.
3. **Develop Strategies and Implement Violence Prevention Problems to Address School Safety Concerns** This component is the heart of the model. It requires implementation of approaches designed to do such things as (a) ensure opportunities for all students to be involved in positive, rewarding activities; (b) identify

students who may be at risk of engaging in violent behaviors; (c) establish guidelines for behavior that spell out rights and responsibilities of all members of the school community; (d) identify procedures that students and others can use to quickly and anonymously report impending outbreaks of violence; and (e) identify and implement procedures for controlling access to the building and for screening visitors.

4. **Establish a Social Support Team** The purpose of the Social Support Team is to improve the social climate of the school. Members may include parents, teachers, administrators, students, counselors, mental health workers, and law enforcement officials.
5. **Develop a Crisis Response Plan** This plan describes precisely what teachers and staff members should do if an emergency situation develops. The idea is to prevent panic and help education professionals deal quickly, efficiently, and appropriately with a serious problem when it arises.

KEY IDEAS IN SUMMARY

- The word "diversity" applies well to today's secondary schools. Today's students reflect the spectrum of differences found throughout our society. Students vary in terms of their physical characteristics, aspirations, intellectual abilities, interests, and values.
- Today nearly 40% of students in the schools belong to racial or ethnic minorities. Percentages tend to be much higher in central cities. Educators today are challenged to develop school programs responsive to the needs of students in these groups who traditionally have not done as well at school as white, non-Latino students. The number of students whose native language is not English is increasing in secondary school classrooms. Though their achievement scores relative to white, non-Latino students have been improving, educators still have much work to do to close the gap.
- Young people from economically impoverished families face many difficulties during their school years. They are less likely than other students to enjoy good health. They are more likely to have a learning disability. They are twice as likely to repeat a grade in school as nonpoor young people.
- Today, more than 2 million secondary school students fall into one of 13 special education categories identified by the federal government. The category with the largest number of students includes young people with specific learning disabilities.
- Characteristics of students' families have changed over the years. Today, mothers of over two thirds of the total school population are employed. Nearly one third of the nation's children live in households headed by a single parent, usually the mother. The nature of families greatly influences how students perform at school. For example, young people with parents or guardians with more than a high school education do better than young people whose parents have had less formal schooling. Involvement of parents in school activities influence students' grade levels, general level of enjoyment of the school program, and level of participation in the extracurricular program.
- As they mature, secondary students experience sequential changes that affect their attitudes, interests, and personal concerns. For example, at certain stages of their lives,

secondary students are greatly concerned about how their rate of physiological change compares to that of others in their group. Over time, their abilities to engage in sophisticated levels of thinking and to seek long-term goals increases.

- It is difficult to define qualities of a "high-quality" school. This is true because people have different beliefs about what schools should do. For example, some people suggest that most Americans subscribe to a common set of values and that it is the job of the schools simply to pass them on intact to subsequent generations. Others contend that conflict rather than consensus more properly describes our society. People with this orientation tend to look somewhat suspiciously at individual school programs because they may serve the narrow interests of one group more adequately than another. Despite these difficulties, there have been attempts to define general characteristics of excellent schools.
- Not everyone likes the comprehensive senior high school model. Theodore Sizer and his followers have organized the Coalition of Essential Schools. Sizer argues that the comprehensive high school presents students with fragmented, disjointed academic experiences. He makes a case for less is more, arguing that students should pursue a more limited number of subjects in much more depth.
- The National Association of Secondary School Principals investigated 12 exemplary high schools. They identified several characteristics of these schools that they named "Breakthrough High Schools." Those characteristics included creating a safe school environment, having a common message, holding high expectations, personalized learning, shared leadership, and basing decisions on data.
- Another program designed to improve the comprehensive senior high school is the Advanced Placement program. Students enrolled in this program take rigorous college-level courses while still in high school, and many colleges and universities give these students college credit or award them advanced basic academic standing based on this work.
- The International Baccalaureate is an established program that enables students from different countries to qualify for entry into top universities throughout the world.
- Many people recognize that there are more dangers associated with public schools today than there used to be. Though incidences of school violence draw well-deserved attention, in general, violent crimes occur much less frequently in schools than in other places, for example, retail establishments. The most common kind of violence that occurs in school is the physical fight.

LEARNING EXTENSIONS

1. To help you learn more about today's diverse student body, invite a secondary teacher to your class who teaches a course that draws a typical cross section of students. (Classes that are required for high school graduation tend to do this.) Ask the teacher to describe the variety of interests, abilities, and attitudes of individuals in one of his or her classes. You might also wish to ask this teacher about specific instructional modifications that are made to respond to the needs of diverse learners.
2. Go to the Web, find a good search engine, and enter the term "school violence." Prepare a paper for your instructor that focuses on examples of what individual

school districts are doing to respond to this problem. If you uncover evaluations of these efforts, include this information in your paper as well.

3. Do some additional reading on Theodore Sizer's ideas for reforming secondary education. Your library will have some information. You might also consider writing to the Coalition of Essential Schools. (The address is provided in this chapter.) Once you feel you have a good understanding of Sizer's ideas, interview a secondary school principal. Ask him or her to comment on difficulties that might be encountered in an effort to incorporate Sizer's ideas into his or her school. Present a report of your interview to your instructor or to the class.

REFERENCES

Advanced Placement program. (2000). http://www.collegeboard.org/ap

American Medical Association. (1999). *Back to school: Safe schools and violence prevention*. http://www.ama-assn.org/adolthlth/special/school.htm

Brooks-Gunn, J., & Duncan, G. J. (1997). The effects of poverty on children. *Children and Poverty*, 7(2), 55–71.

Children's Defense Fund. (2003). *2002 facts on child poverty in America*. http://www.childrensdefense.org/familyincome/childpoverty/basicfacts.asp

Elkind, D. (1981). *Children and adolescents: Interpretive essays on Jean Piaget* (3rd ed.). New York: Oxford University Press.

Elmelech, Y., McCaskie, K., Lennon, M., & Lu, H. (2002). *Children of immigrants: A statistical profile*. New York: National Center for Children in Poverty, Columbia University.

Erikson, E. (1963). *Childhood and society* (2nd ed.). New York: Norton.

Garcia, E. (2002). *Student cultural diversity: Understanding and meeting the challenge*. Boston: Houghton Mifflin.

Howell, J. C. (1998, August). Youth gangs: An overview. *Juvenile Justice Bulletin*, 1–16.

National Association of Secondary School Principals. (2004). *Breakthrough High Schools: You can do it too!* Reston, VA: Author.

National Center for Education Statistics. (1998). *Violence and discipline problems in U.S. public schools: 1996–1997*. Washington, DC: Author. http://www.nsscl.org/studies/studies/nces98.htm

National Commission on the High School Senior Year. (2001). *The lost opportunity of senior year: Finding a better way*. Princeton, NJ: Woodrow Wilson National Fellowship Foundation.

Oakes, J., Quartz, K. H., Ryan, S., & Lipton, M. (2000). Becoming good American schools: The struggle for civic virtue in education reform. *Phi Delta Kappan, 81*(8), 568–575.

Office of Safety and Health Administration. (1999, August). *Workplace violence*. http://www.osha.gov/oshinfor/priorities/violence.html

Ormrod, J. (1998). *Educational psychology: Developing learners* (2nd ed.). Columbus, OH: Merrill/Prentice Hall.

Parrish, T. B. (2000, Winter). Special education—At what cost to general education? *CSEF Resource*, 2–3, 6.

Safe Communities–Safe Schools. (1999). http://www.colorado.edu/cspv/safeschools/model/htm

Sizer, T. (1984). *Horace's compromise: The dilemma of the American high school*. Boston: Houghton Mifflin.

Sizer, T. (1992). *Horace's school: Redesigning the American high school*. Boston: Houghton Mifflin.

Sizer, T (1996). *Horace's hope: What works for the American high school*. Boston: Houghton Mifflin.

Snyder, T. D. (Ed.). (2000). *Digest of education statistics, 1999*. Washington, DC: National Center for Education Statistics.

Warshol, C. (1998, July). *Workplace violence, 1992–1996*. Washington, DC: Bureau of Justice Statistics.

Wirt, J., & Snyder, T. (Eds.). (1999). *The condition of education, 1999*. Washington, DC: National Center for Education Statistics.

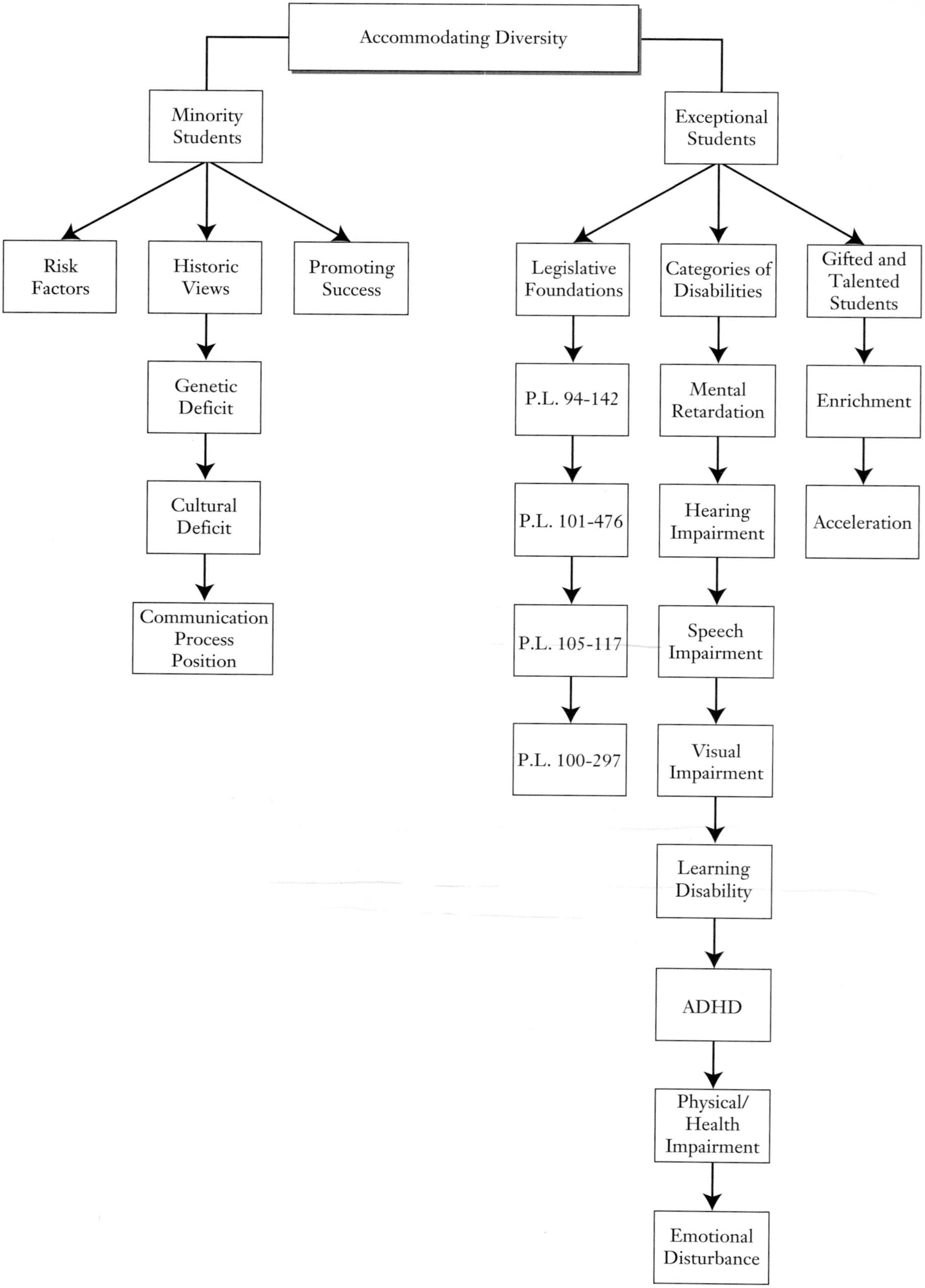

Figure 3.1
Graphic Organizer

CHAPTER 3

Accommodating Diversity

OBJECTIVES

This chapter will help you

- discuss the importance of responding to the special needs and perspectives of students from diverse cultural backgrounds;
- identify some planning perspectives that can be helpful in developing instructional programs well suited to needs of the different ethnic, cultural, and language groups enrolled in your classes;
- describe some teacher actions that can help students with different kinds of disabilities succeed in the classroom;
- explain changes in approaches to working with students who have disabilities and their implications for regular classroom teachers; and
- describe characteristics of gifted and talented students and suggest ways that the needs of these young people can be accommodated in the classroom.

Introduction

Diversity among students in schools today is greater than it has ever been. Present trends suggest that you will find even more differences among your students in the years ahead. In part, these changes result from alterations in the makeup of the general population. In part, they have come about because of legislative actions. The one certainty is that you will work with students from different cultural, ethnic, and language groups and with those who may be characterized by one or more "exceptionalities."

Demographers report steady increases in these populations and interesting predictions for the future. For example, Sobol (1990) reports that by 2020, one of every three people in the United States will belong to a group currently labeled minority. Martin and Midgley (1999) add that by 2050, Latinos, Asian Americans, and African Americans will constitute 48% of the U.S. population. These figures pose interesting perspectives as we consider the increase in the ethnic populations in our nation's classrooms. It is not unusual today for classrooms in large urban districts to be populated with over 90% ethnic minority (many of whom will be English learners), raising the question, Which group is the minority? Student populations in cities such as Los Angeles, California; Detroit, Michigan; Miami, Florida; and Brownsville, Texas, are just a few examples that fall into this category. These changing dynamics necessitate changes in the preparation for teachers entering the profession. You must arm yourself with knowledge about different ethnic and cultural groups as well as teaching methods that are particularly appropriate for them.

In addition to the increase in ethnic group populations, you will encounter larger groups of exceptional students. These students include those with a variety of personal circumstances, including specific learning disabilities, speech or language impairments, mental retardation, hearing impairments, visual impairments, physical and health impairments, emotional disturbance, and other conditions. Increasingly, these learners are being served as members of regular classrooms. Over the past 25 years, there has been an increase of over 50% in the number of students participating in federal programs for learners with disabilities (Condition of Education, Indicator 45, 1998).

As we explore these student populations, keep in mind two points. First, the groups are not mutually exclusive. Some English learners are also gifted; some will have learning difficulties. Second, this chapter is not a methods chapter. Chapter 7 will familiarize you with teaching strategies that are appropriate for helping all students succeed in your classroom.

Minority Students

Whether you are a member of the cultural and ethnic majority or a member of a cultural or ethnic minority, as you prepare to work with students, you need to recognize that there are no universally applicable generalizations about teaching people from different personal backgrounds. You must take the time to learn about the cultural backgrounds of the individual students enrolled in your classes. If you fail to do this, problems can arise. For example, some teachers have erroneously assumed that all Asian students are "model minorities" who are bright, psychologically secure young people who are motivated to do well at school. Differences among individual Asians are as significant as between Asians and other groups. If you stereotype these young people as members of a model minority who need only a minimal amount of your special attention, you may find that Asian students in your class who experience academic difficulties develop negative self-images. You may also encourage other students to act irresponsibly toward these students out of a mistaken belief that the Asians are dull, academic grinds whose outstanding school performance requires others in the class to work too hard to keep up (Pang, 1995).

Risk Factors

Unfortunately, compared with the achievement of white students, many minority students have not done well in school. Experts who have studied achievement of students in schools have identified a number of risk factors that are characteristic of students who do not do well no matter what their ethnicity or background. Among these risk factors are the following:

- Lives in a single-parent family
- Family receives public assistance
- Primary language other than English
- Brother or sister who dropped out of school
- Mother not a high school graduate
- Has attended five or more schools during lifetime
- Less than 1 hour per week spent on homework
- Spends no time each week reading for fun
- Watches television more than 5 hours per night

- Little communication with parents about things studied at school
- Is overage for grade level by at least 1 year (Gleason & Dynarksi, 1998).

Individuals having a single risk factor may not necessarily experience difficulty in school. Researchers, however, have determined that students having two or more risk factors are particularly likely to do poorly. Minority students are much more likely than white students to be in this situation.

Historic Views of Minorities

Several educators have identified historical perspectives that delineate explanations for minority group failure. An early explanation for minorities' failures to excel in school was the genetic deficit view (Freeman & Freeman, 2001; Savage & Armstrong, 2004). The premise of this position was that some minority groups do better than others because of genetic makeup. This was ascribed to their status as sons and daughters of individuals who were not particularly bright. Hence, it was argued, an insufficient capacity to learn was passed on to their children. This mistaken belief provided a perfect rationale for schools to do little or nothing to improve instruction directed at minority students. Why, it was argued, should the schools commit scarce resources to programs designed to serve individuals who lacked the capacity to learn from them?

The genetic deficit view had fallen from favor by the middle of the last century. In the 1960s, a new deficit view, the cultural deficit position, enjoyed some currency for a time (Erickson, 1987). Individuals who were impressed by this idea felt that school problems of minority group students could be traced to their homes. They alleged that the homes provided an intellectually sterile background that failed to give them attitudes and aptitudes needed for success in school. The cultural deficit argument allowed school leaders who were reluctant to commit serious resources to programs designed to help minority students to blame the home for failure of these young people to learn. Because many minority students came from impoverished home backgrounds, some argued that the hope that special programs for minority students might improve their performance in school was illogical.

Still another variant on the blame-the-students, the-schools-can-do-nothing theme was the communication process position. Proponents of this view blamed poor minority student performance on language differences separating students and their teachers, alleging that these differences were so profound that minority students could not understand what was said in the classroom or what was expected of them at school. Their failure was attributed to this communication gap. Critics of this position pointed out that some minority students did extremely well in school despite economic and social backgrounds very similar to those of minority students who did poorly.

Though you may occasionally hear support for the genetic deficit, cultural deficit, and communication deficit positions, most educators now reject these views. All three arguments have been recognized as weak attempts to excuse the school from being accountable for minority students' learning. Today the view is that minority students' failures in school have often resulted from the lack of a serious commitment on the part of educators to plan and deliver programs designed to help these students learn. The rhetoric of concern has been there for many years, but a willingness to develop an intellectual and a financial commitment to help minority students in schools is relatively recent.

MORE FROM THE WEB

Meeting Diverse Learners Needs

Challenges educators face in providing instruction that is responsive to the needs of an increasingly diverse student population have prompted the development of many Websites with practical information for teachers. We have selected a few you might want to visit.

Defining Multicultural Education

Not all educators agree on components and purposes of multicultural education. At this site, you will find information related to this issue from a number of leading authorities in the field. You will find details related to definitions of the term "multicultural education" and to components, assumptions, goals, and principles of multicultural education programs.

Website: http://curry.edschool.virginia.edu/go/multicultural/initial.html

Bilingual Education: Focusing Policy on Student Achievement

This site is maintained by the Association for Supervision and Curriculum Development, a group dedicated to improving school programming for all learners. If you explore either "Education Topics" or "Issues," you will find information here about various approaches to meeting needs of bilingual students, particularly with respect to some controversies they have engendered and to some research-based findings about approaches that have worked well with students whose first language is not English.

Website: http://www.ascd.org

Teaching Diversity: People of Color

Some members of the American Historical Association (AHA) have been concerned that many studies of American history have failed to include references to contributions of certain racial and ethnic groups. In response to this situation, the AHA Committee on Minority Historians has commissioned an essay series. At this site, you will find references to available essays, including topics such as "Teaching U.S. Puerto Rican History," "Teaching Asian American History," "Teaching Asian American Women's History," "Teaching African American History," and "Teaching American Indian History."

Website: http://www.theaha.org/pubs/diversity.htm

The Council for Exceptional Children

The Council for Exceptional Children is a leading professional organization for educators with interests in serving the needs of students with disabilities. You will

find much information here about useful approaches to inclusion and to many other topics related to serving these students well in the classroom.
Website: http://www.cec.sped.org

Federation for Children with Special Needs

The Federation for Children with Special Needs is an advocacy group dedicated to supporting efforts to serve students with disabilities well. You will find links to information sources maintained by state and federal agencies. This is a good source for details about inclusion and other topics related to students with disabilities.
Website: http://www.fcsn.org/resource.htm

National Association for Gifted Children

The National Association for Gifted Children advocates in support of programs for gifted and talented students. There are good links at this site to other Web locations where information is available related to meeting the educational needs of these students.
Website: http://www.nagc.org

The National Association for Multicultural Education

This site provides the organization's definition of multicultural education as well as information about issues in multicultural education. You will also find links to state Websites.
Website: http://www.name.org

The National Association for Bilingual Education

This association is dedicated to important issues in bilingual education. You will find discussion of policy and legislative issues as well as links to other important sites that are concerned with bilingual education.
Website: http://www.nabe.org

Guidelines for Promoting Academic Success

A number of guidelines have been suggested to promote better learning and better attitudes toward school on the part of minority group learners. We have included here some recommendations that are reflected in many of these proposals:

- Assume that all students can learn
- Provide good teachers
- Insist that teachers become aware of their own cultural perspectives
- Encourage teachers to avoid favoritism in the classroom

- Include students from varied ethnic and cultural backgrounds in each group when members of a class are divided into groups for instruction
- Vary teaching methods to accommodate different learning styles
- Organize curricula around relevant themes
- Develop close working relationships with students' families
- Emphasize development of higher-level thinking skills
- Use conversations to uncover ways to contextualize instruction

Assume That All Students Can Learn As a teacher, you will find minority group students (and, indeed, students in general) very sensitive to how you view them. If students feel that you have little confidence in their abilities to learn, minority group students will be inclined to "live down" to your expectations. Under the best of circumstances, the middle school, junior high school, and senior high school years are emotionally trying for young people. The last thing you want to do is to reinforce any feelings of personal inadequacy your students might have. Your students will not be motivated if you fail to convince them of your sincere belief in their ability to learn.

In addition to the negative impact on students' self concepts that can result if your actions suggest to them that they cannot learn, such an attitude can affect how you interact with these young people. There is evidence that teachers' beliefs about the learning potential of students influence their commitment to prepare good lessons and deliver high-quality instruction. In other words, your conviction that your instruction can make a difference motivates students to do their best. In the absence of this motivation, the quality of your instruction is likely to suffer, and as a result, your students will not achieve a high level of academic success.

When you think about your students, remember that there is great diversity within any group of people. You want to avoid concluding that information that may well describe certain individuals who are African American, Latino, Native American, or Asian generalizes to all people who belong to one of these groups. This kind of stereotyping distorts reality.

For example, your African American students are likely to be descendants of people who came from widely separated areas in Africa, from the Caribbean, or from South America. Families of some of these students may have come to this country relatively recently. Others may be descendants of African Americans who have lived here for generations (Lee & Slaughter-Defoe, 1995). Characteristics of your African American students may also vary depending on socioeconomic levels of their families, religious orientations, rural versus urban family backgrounds, and many other factors.

These differences imply a need to understand students well and to vary your instruction to meet their needs. You need to keep in mind the folly of searching for a single teaching approach that will respond well to the characteristics of every student you teach. This mistaken approach is akin to a futile search for an instructional holy grail. "It risks becoming a sacred calling that consumes resources in the search for an illusory panacea for complex social and educational ills" (Lomawaima, 1995, p. 342).

Provide Good Teachers Good teachers help students develop better attitudes toward school and learn more than do mediocre teachers. It is particularly critical that minority students be taught by individuals who are sensitive to their special ethnic and cultural perspectives, respectful of them as individuals, and strongly committed to the view that they can and should learn. Regrettably, individuals who lack these important characteristics teach large numbers of minority students.

In many places with large minority student enrollments, turnover rates of teachers are high. This means that many minority students are taught by teachers who are either relatively new to the profession or relatively new to the school where they are presently employed. Many of these teachers also are people who are teaching outside their major field of preparation. Minority students, further, have a higher-than-average probability of being taught by teachers holding only an emergency teaching credential.

Teachers Must Be Aware of Their Own Cultural Perspectives If you are a member of the white majority, you may well live in a world where perspectives of your own group are so dominant that you may fail to recognize that you have a worldview that may differ from that of members of other cultural and ethnic groups. In truth, all people are to a great extent conditioned to make sense of the world in ways consistent with the perspectives of the people with whom they interact. If you have had few relationships with people from cultures other than the dominant white majority, you may not immediately understand that some of your minority group students come from groups whose ideas about how the world is and how people should behave vary from your own. This means that you need to think clearly about your own assumptions and to reflect on how actions you take might be viewed by students in your classes with different views about how the world operates. You need to consider answers to such questions as these:

- What are my views about what the curriculum ought to be?
- How do I think individuals learn in the classroom?
- What do I consider to be appropriate behavior in the classroom?
- What assumptions am I making about the previous experience and the background my students bring to school?
- To what do I attribute lack of school success of students who are members of certain groups?
- Where did I get my ideas about good educational practice?
- How are my ideas influenced by the community I lived in and the schools I attended when I was a student?

Honest answers to these questions can help you think about the appropriateness of decisions you make about working with students from cultural and ethnic groups that differ from your own. To enhance your success, consider drawing on some practices of cultural anthropologists—become a participant-observer in the community where you teach. Take part in cultural events sponsored by different ethnic and cultural groups. Note carefully the worldviews, the values, the norms, the cultural practices, and the rituals of the individuals you teach, then use this information to develop programs that will provide a culturally responsive education for your students.

If you fail to recognize that there are multiple perspectives on these issues and erroneously assume that your own worldview is the only one (or at least the only "correct" one), you may have difficulty communicating with people from other social and cultural orientations. This has proved to be particularly true if you are a white teacher and find yourself teaching large numbers of minority students. For example, as a member of the dominant white culture, you may conclude that a person who avoids eye contact with you when being addressed is "shifty," "guilty," or "ashamed." Your conclusion would make sense, given the cultural orientation of the white majority.

However, not all cultures view eye contact in the same way. In some minority cultures, young people are taught that it is not polite to look adults in the eye. Hence, a student who looks away from you when you are speaking may feel he or she is politely recognizing your position as a high-status, intelligent adult. You would be making an error if you concluded this behavior was an indication of a student who "has something to hide." Over time, errors of this kind can strain your relationships with students, thereby negatively affecting students' attitudes and motivation to do assigned work.

Avoid Favoritism in the Classroom By the time they arrive in secondary schools, many minority group students may have had experiences in school and elsewhere that have led them to conclude that sometimes members of minority groups are treated differently than members of the white, non-Latino majority. Additionally, nearly all

CRITICAL INCIDENT

"Mr. Hobbs, Your History Is Irrelevant."

Nolan Hobbs teaches U.S. history at Lee High School. He also occasionally is called on to teach economics classes and sociology classes. Recently, he shared these comments with Rafaela Sanchez, Lee High School's vice principal for academic programs.

> Things have gone just great this year. Well, that's generally the case, but there is a student in my fifth-period class who has become a bit of a thorn in my side. I'm talking about Cassiella Birdsong. You'll remember she was in talking to you a few weeks ago about getting some bulletin board space in the hall for the African American Students Association.
>
> Well, anyway, Cassiella has convinced herself that I have absolutely nothing to teach her. She told me this morning that our history book was "filled with a bunch of junk about dead white guys." Even though I go out of my way to include information about contributions of African Americans, she still has it in her head that my whole course is dedicated to imposing a point of view she wants no part of.
>
> I know she's bright, and I am concerned that she's just not working up to her potential. I'm getting pretty frustrated with her telling me every day how "irrelevant" everything in my course is. Her attitude is beginning to have a bad influence on some of the other students as well.

■ ■ ■

How might you explain Cassiella's point of view? What do these views tell us about her values? Is her reaction something Mr. Hobbs should be concerned about? What does Mr. Hobbs believe to be important? What should he do next? In addition to the vice principal, who else might he consult for advice? What specific advice would you provide to Mr. Hobbs and/or to Cassiella?

students are concerned about the general issues of consistent and appropriate treatment. Your credibility definitely will be at risk if your students suspect you are not fair.

One way to demonstrate fairness is to avoid favoritism in the classroom. It is particularly important that minority group students sense that, as individuals and as a group, they are being treated as well as others in the class. If your minority students suspect that you single out individuals for negative treatment or comments in a way that seems tied to ethnicity or race, you may find it difficult to maintain their interest and cooperation.

Students often measure fairness by looking at how teachers handle episodes of misbehavior. The general rule you should follow is to respond to a given kind of misbehavior in the same way regardless of who the offender is. That is, your high-achieving students shouldn't get off more lightly than your low-achieving students, your white students shouldn't get off more lightly than your minority group students, and so forth. When students feel that you dispense justice equitably and hold all to the same standard, their motivation levels increase, your discipline problems diminish, and students' achievement levels improve.

Include Students from Varied Ethnic and Cultural Backgrounds in Each Group When you plan group work, it is important that your groups not serve as a vehicle for resegregating students on the basis of race or ethnicity. For one thing, individual groups sometimes are asked to do different things (e.g., you may assign some groups to work on more challenging academic tasks than others).

There is evidence that some groups are organized by teachers so that racial minorities are concentrated within a few groups (Rist, 1985). This is a mistake. Learners must not see group instructional techniques as subtle covers for an instructional program designed to provide different (and perhaps lower-quality) instruction to minority group students.

Additionally, a key purpose of secondary education is to help students adjust to living in a multicultural society. Given this priority, it makes sense for you to organize groups to encourage personal contacts among students from varying cultural and ethnic backgrounds. Such practices break down group-to-group isolation and provide a way for students to become more familiar with perspectives different from their own.

Respond to Different Learning Styles Students vary in terms of their preferred learning styles. This means that some individuals learn better when they read about new information. Others learn better when they listen to someone explaining new content. Others are visual learners—people who master new content best when they are presented with examples they can see. Still others need opportunities to touch, handle, and otherwise manipulate physical objects. Kinds of preferred learning settings also vary. For example, some individuals prefer to learn alone, while others do much better when they are organized into groups.

Researchers have found that students' cultural backgrounds affect their learning styles (Grant & Sleeter, 1994). This does not mean that individuals with similar cultural backgrounds do not vary. Rather, it suggests that more people from one cultural group may have a given learning style than people from another cultural group.

There is evidence that students from African American and Latino backgrounds do better when they are presented with a broad general overview of a situation first and then asked to think about how specific information relates to the general situation (Bowman, 1991). (For example, it would be better for you to provide general information about the Civil War and then go on to ask about the relationship of the

Battle of Gettysburg to the war in general.) Non-Latino white students, however, have been found to do well when complex situations are first broken down into small parts. These small parts are learned one at a time, and only in the end does a general picture emerge. (Given this orientation, you might have your class study individual battles of the Civil War one at a time and conclude with a description of their cumulative effects on the war in general.)

Organize Curriculum Around Relevant Themes Students should have an opportunity to study a topic in depth. The more diverse the student population, the more important this idea becomes (Garcia, 2002). Conceptually, this varies from the normal school day where classes are divided into time periods and taught without connections among subjects. Freeman and Freeman (2001) point out that one benefit of this approach is that students more easily develop their academic language. Typically, this approach has been more common in elementary classrooms. However, as middle and high school environments change to adapt to new dynamics, the opportunity to develop integrated, thematic instruction is becoming more common.

Develop Close Working Relationships with Students' Families To the extent possible, you should establish relationships with members of minority group students' families. Although many relatives of minority students are positively disposed toward the school and its programs, this attitude is not universal. Some of them did not have particularly good experiences in school themselves and may be inclined to lump educators into a category that includes indifferent city hall bureaucrats, law enforcement officials, and other establishment figures who, in their view, have not always treated minorities fairly. People with these views may be reluctant to come to the school on open house nights or on other occasions, and you need to make special efforts to contact them.

Students' priorities and general attitudes are strongly influenced by those of their parents, grandparents, and other relatives, especially those living in the same household. If you can establish a common ground with a student's family members that results in a consensus regarding what the student should be doing in school, the student may benefit. In fact, Ogbu (1973) found that "school learning is most likely to occur when family values reinforce school expectations" (p. 27).

Emphasize Development of Higher-Level Thinking Skills If you have some minority group students in your classroom who are not doing well, you need to avoid the temptation to lower your instructional expectations. Their academic performance may result from circumstances having little or nothing to do with their real ability levels. Students gain nothing when they are provided with unchallenging classroom instruction. What you need to do is fit instructional tasks to students in such a way that they will be intellectually "stretched" but not to the extent they will be unable to succeed. For learning to take place, Vygotsky (1978) suggests that it must take place in a student's zone of proximal development (ZPD). He defines the ZPD as "the distance between the actual developmental level as determined by independent problem solving and the level of potential development as determined through problem solving under adult guidance or in collaboration with more capable peers" (p. 86). Over time, instruction that pushes students to develop sophisticated thinking skills gives them the tools needed for dealing with more complex subject matter. These academic successes build students' confidence and stimulate their interest in the school program.

Use Conversations to Uncover Ways to Contextualize Instruction As you seek to "connect" with your students, you need to develop instructional activities that members of your class see relate to their own lives, their families, and their communities (Tharp, 1999). Your aim is to contextualize your instruction, creating teaching episodes that tie closely to the personal experiences of the people who will receive it—your students. Providing good contextualized instruction requires you to know your students well. One useful approach for gaining insights into your students' personal backgrounds involves engaging them in conversations. If you listen carefully and respectfully to what students say, they will reveal a great deal about their personal, family, and community backgrounds. All this information can be useful as you design lessons that are responsive to the individual circumstances of your students.

Exceptional Students

There are great differences among exceptional students. Sometimes the term "special education student" is used as a general descriptor for individuals who have learning disabilities, physical problems, or emotional and behavioral difficulties that deviate markedly from the norm. Exceptional students also include those identified gifted-and-talented learners whose intelligence and/or skill levels have been found to be well above those of their age or grade peers. And, as mentioned earlier in this chapter, English learners can fall into either of these categories. (Unfortunately, too often they are placed automatically and erroneously into special education programs.)

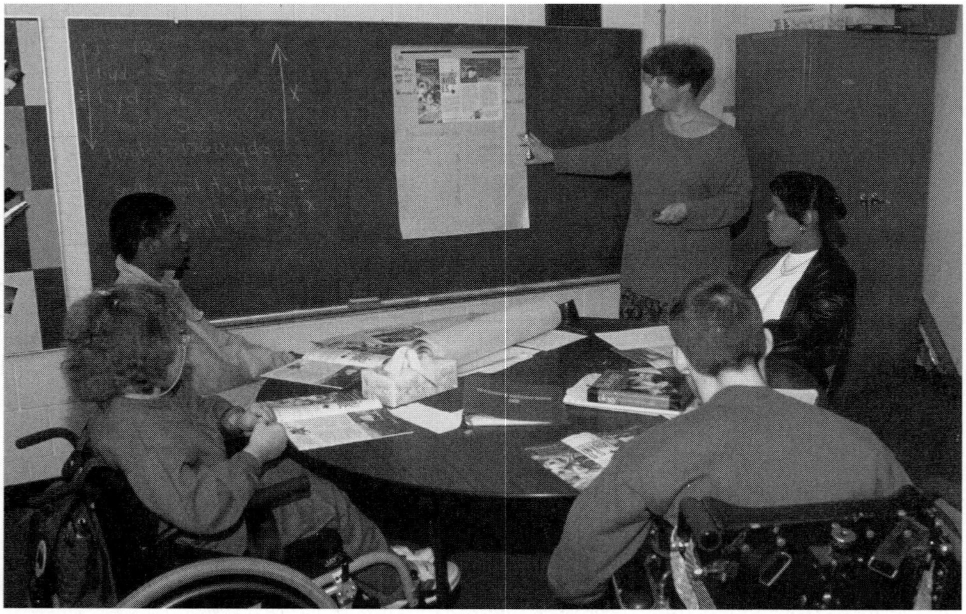

The contemporary classroom includes students from diverse backgrounds as well as students with a variety of exceptionalities and disabilities.

Legislative Foundations of Programs

Several complex regulations govern the education of exceptional students. Among these laws are (a) the Education for All Handicapped Children Act, which was first passed in 1975 as Public Law (P.L.) 94-142 and renamed the Individuals with Disabilities Education Act in 1990 (P.L. 101-476); (b) the Individuals with Disabilities Education Act of 1997 (P.L. 105-117); and (c) the Jacob K. Javits Gifted and Talented Students Act of 1994 (P.L. 100-297).

When the Education for All Handicapped Children Act was enacted in 1975, both supporters and critics predicted that it would change the face of education in the United States (Heward, 1996). This proved to be true. The updated version of this legislation, the Individuals with Disabilities Education Act, mandates the following six basic principles first articulated in the original 1975 legislation.

- *Zero Rejects*. Schools must enroll every child regardless of the nature or severity of the disability. Implementing this principle has been expensive. Many school districts have had to increase their budgets to provide funds to provide educational services for some students who previously were excluded from schools.
- *Nondiscriminatory Testing*. Multiple indicators must be used to determine whether an individual has a disability and whether special services are needed.
- *Appropriate Education*. Schools must develop and implement an individualized education plan (IEP) for each student with a disability.
- *Least Restrictive Environment*. A student with a disability is to be educated in the setting that is the least restrictive for that individual. Often this has involved placement (or mainstreaming) of students with disabilities in regular classrooms for at least part of the school day. This provision has changed the nature of the student population served by regular teachers in traditional classrooms. Students with disabilities, who formerly were segregated into special education classrooms, now are interspersed with so-called regular students in traditional classrooms.
- *Due Process*. The rights of students and their parents in planning and placement decisions must be protected by due process procedures.
- *Parental Participation*. Parental participation in the decisions made regarding the education of the student is mandated.

The Individuals with Disabilities Education Act of 1990 added an important new principle. It required schools to provide transition services for students with disabilities (Heward, 1996). Transition services are identified as a coordinated set of services designed to help the student make the transition from high school to postschool activities such as college, vocational training, employment, and independent living or community participation. This addition to the original legislation was adopted in response to studies that revealed educational programs were doing a poor job of preparing students with disabilities for life after high school.

Public Law 105-117, the Individuals with Disabilities Education Act of 1997, tremendously broadened existing requirements to serve learners with disabilities in regular classrooms. In part, this expansion stemmed from a strong legislative support for the principle of *inclusion*. Inclusion represents a commitment to the idea that students, regardless of unique personal characteristics (including disabilities of all kinds), not only have a legal right to services in a regular classroom but also are welcomed and wanted as members of these classes. Some schools now pride themselves on being *full-inclusion* environments. In these schools, you will find almost a total absence of special classrooms for learners with disabilities. Virtually all services are provided to these students in regular classrooms.

Advocates of inclusive education claim several key advantages for this approach (Smith, Polloway, Patton, & Dowdy, 1996). Among their points are the following:

- It is possible for special education students to receive an appropriate education in the regular classroom.
- Educating special students in the regular classroom reduces the stigma that sometimes has been attached to them when they have been taught in separate "special education" classes.
- Because teachers in regular classrooms expect students to have varied abilities, there is less likelihood of any individual student being permanently mislabeled as a "special education" student and provided with an instructional program inappropriate to his or her needs.
- In a society that includes incredible diversity, there are benefits for both special education students and regular classroom students when they are taught together. This kind of association can promote tolerance of individual differences and recognition of the point that all people have personal strengths and weaknesses.
- All students benefit when teachers make efforts to individualize their instruction to meet individual student needs. When special education students are included in regular classrooms, there is a greater incentive for teachers to individualize their teaching.

The Individuals with Disabilities Education Act of 1997 put important new legal muscle behind the view that learners with disabilities should be taught, to the fullest extent possible, as members of regular school classes. Some important new requirements of this legislation include the following:

- A student's regular classroom teacher *must* be involved in the development of a student's IEP and must participate in IEP planning.
- Parents and guardians have the right to be involved in *all* decisions regarding their children's eligibility for and placement in programs designed to serve them.
- Information about learners with disabilities' achievement must be included in regular public reports on test scores.

The Jacob K. Javits Gifted and Talented Students Act of 1994, unlike the others discussed in this section, did not mandate specific services but provides incentives for state and local education agencies to address the specific needs of individuals with this exceptionality. It allocates money for the identification of gifted students and the professional training of teachers. Money made available as a result of this legislation also supports the National Center for the Education of the Gifted. The Javits Act was adopted out of a recognition that gifted and talented students have special needs and that they may require additional support and services if they are to reach their potential.

Students with Disabilities

Students with disabilities include individuals having many different kinds of characteristics. In general, these are people who have a mental or physical condition that prevents them from succeeding in programs designed for people not having this condition (or these conditions).

Categories Various descriptions have been developed for categorizing disabilities. These descriptions, listed here, are discussed in the sections that follow:

- Mental retardation
- Hearing impairment
- Speech impairment
- Visual impairment
- Learning disability
- Attention-deficit disorder
- Physical and health impairment
- Emotional disturbance

Mental Retardation Mental retardation is a term that is difficult to define with any degree of precision. In general, people are described as mentally retarded when their intellectual development is (a) significantly below that of age-mates and (b) their potential for academic achievement has been determined to be markedly less than that of so-called normal individuals.

In the past, IQ scores were often used to determine whether a person could be categorized as mentally retarded. A problem with using IQ for this purpose, however, is that people who may appear to be mentally retarded on the basis of an IQ test may be perfectly capable of functioning in a normal fashion under other conditions. For example, people with low IQ scores may succeed in some job roles after leaving school. Because of this, the American Association of Mental Deficiency (AAMD) has long advocated that mental retardation be identified using broader and more diverse measures than a simple IQ test score. The AAMD suggests that people who are mentally retarded cannot function within the typical range of life situations. Individuals capable of functioning within this range should not be classified as mentally retarded regardless of their IQ test scores.

Several levels of mental retardation have been described. These include the categories of (a) educable, (b) trainable, and (c) severely or profoundly retarded. The type of student with mental retardation who is most likely to be assigned to spend part of the instructional day (or the entire instructional day) in a regular classroom is someone in the educable category.

It is difficult to speak authoritatively about what educable students can do because there are tremendous differences among individuals in this category. In general, educable students can derive some benefits from the school program. It is your responsibility to diagnose specific characteristics of educable students and, in cooperation with parents and other school officials, devise appropriate learning experiences for them.

Educable students often have short attention spans. They may become easily frustrated. By the time they reach their secondary school years, many have a history of failure in school. Often, they lack confidence as they begin a new task. Frequently, they experience difficulty grasping abstract ideas or complex sequences of ideas.

The following principles make sense as you plan instructional programs for educable students:

- Lessons should be short, direct, and to the point.
- Material should be introduced in short, sequential steps.
- Content introduced in prose form should be reinforced by additional visual and oral examples.
- It may be useful to assign a student who is not mentally retarded to work with the educable student as a peer tutor.
- Directions should be delivered clearly, using vocabulary that educable students understand.
- Lessons should not place educable students in highly competitive situations, particularly those requiring them to compete against non–mentally retarded students.

In addition, educable students often require more time to complete tasks than do their non–mentally retarded fellow students. You need to avoid imposing tight, restrictive deadlines when giving them assignments. It is better for these students to succeed at completing fewer tasks than to fail a larger number of them. Successful task completion is an important builder of self-esteem for these young people.

Hearing Impairment Students who are hearing impaired fall into two key categories: (a) students whose hearing loss is so profound as to greatly inhibit their ability to acquire normal use of oral language (classified as deaf) and (b) students whose hearing loss is serious but not serious enough to prevent them from acquiring normal speech patterns (classified as hard of hearing).

There are great differences among students who are hearing impaired. Some of them are unable to hear certain pitches. Others require different levels of amplified sound. Some have had a hearing loss since birth; others may have suffered a hearing loss after they were old enough to have acquired some oral-language proficiency. Despite individual differences, students who are hearing impaired generally experience difficulty developing great proficiency with the spoken language. School programs for these students place a heavy emphasis on helping them improve their oral language proficiency.

Many students who have severe hearing losses have been taught to pay close attention to visual clues. Many know how to read lips. Because of their dependence on visual signals, you need to provide these students with lessons that enable them to take advantage of their visual learning skills. For example, you should face these students directly when you give directions and present new information. It helps if you write information on an overhead transparency rather than on a chalkboard. (When you write on an overhead, you face students, thus enabling hearing-impaired students to watch your lips. When you write on the chalkboard, students can't see your lips because you face away from them.) It is also a good idea for you to remain relatively stationary when speaking to hearing-impaired students. Trained lip-readers find it difficult to understand a person who is in motion.

Assignments and other directions need to be provided in written form. (They can be oral as well, but the written information can help eliminate possible confusion among hearing-impaired students.) When you deliver a lecture, it helps to provide class members with a general printed outline that includes at least major topics and subtopics to be covered. Additionally, it is a good idea to provide students with lists of important (and potentially confusing) words before the lecture begins. This is particularly true when terms with multiple meanings are to be introduced. (Consider the term *"market"* as it is understood in everyday conversation and how specialists in economics use it.) A discussion of special vocabulary before the lecture begins may help students who are hearing impaired (and other students as well) better grasp the material.

All students do better when instruction is well organized and when point-to-point transitions are clear and smooth. Clarity in planning and delivering instruction is even more critical for hearing-impaired students than for the general population of secondary school learners. Students who are hearing impaired lack the multiple communication channels that other students sometimes use to make sense out of disorganized lessons.

Some hearing-impaired students wear hearing aids or other mechanical devices. You need to know how they work. For example, you should learn how batteries are replaced in hearing aids. It may be a good idea to keep a supply of batteries on hand. Many school districts employ specialists in the education of students who are hearing impaired to provide additional guidance regarding how you can best serve these young people in your regular classroom.

Speech Impairment Identifying students who have serious speech impairments is difficult. The process demands a great deal of personal judgment. In general, individuals are thought to suffer from impaired speech when their speech differs significantly from that of others in the same age-group. Speech problems encompass a range of difficulties. These relate to such things as voice quality, problems in articulating certain sounds, and stuttering.

Because speech impairments do not represent the obvious obstacles to learning as hearing impairments and visual impairments do, you may not immediately appreciate their seriousness. You need to be aware, however, of an important side effect of speech impairment, one that occurs in a distressingly high number of students suffering from this problem: low self-image. Because of the frustration they feel at not being able to speak normally, some of these students conclude that they are inferior or even incompetent. The dropout rate of students with speech impairments is high.

Often students with speech impairments profit from work with a trained speech therapist; thus, school districts have these specialists on staff to provide support. There are also things you can do in your classroom to help these students. In general, students with speech impairments need emotional support. Avoid placing them in situations that call unnecessary attention to their condition.

In classroom discussions, it makes sense to call on students with speech impairments only when they raise a hand and indicate a willingness to volunteer a response. When such students begin to speak, they should be allowed to finish what they have to say without interruption or correction. Praise and other kinds of reinforcement should be provided when these students volunteer a remark in class.

You need to provide opportunities for speech-impaired students to speak with you on a one-to-one basis. These occasions allow you to boost students' morale by making sensitive, supporting comments to them. Additionally, these one-on-one discussions give students a chance to talk about course work (and other matters) without feeling that they will be embarrassed by a communication difficulty that might draw ridicule from others in the class.

Visual Impairment The term "visual impairment" is used to describe a variety of conditions related to the sense of sight. Some visually impaired individuals have no sight whatever. However, most students in this category have some sight. Some see a world that is blurred, dim, or out of focus; others may see only parts of objects. About 1% of the school-age population is visually impaired.

Whenever assignments are written on the chalkboard or written information is distributed, you need to make special arrangements to ensure clear communication with your students who are visually impaired. Sometimes oral explanations will suffice. At other times, you may find it useful to provide these students with audio recordings of information. Your students can play back the tapes later to ensure they have the needed information.

Personal mobility is an important problem for students who are visually impaired. Over time, many of these students develop good mental pictures of places they visit frequently. They require some experience in a new environment before a good mental picture develops. You need to make time for visually impaired students to visit classrooms when classes are not being held. This will give them an opportunity to become familiar with placement of furniture and with other room features. If you change room arrangements later, you need to give visually impaired students time to become familiar with the new configuration.

Learning Disability A student with a learning disability exhibits a disorder in one or more of the basic psychological processes involved in understanding or using spoken or written language. The problem may be revealed in such areas as listening, writing, reading, spelling, or computing. Sometimes learning disabilities are referred to by such terms as perceptual handicaps, minimal brain dysfunction, and dyslexia. Students who have learning disabilities have difficulty processing sensory stimuli.

People with learning disabilities often find it hard to follow directions. They may appear disorganized. You will often find that these students have difficulty getting started on assigned tasks. Often they have a low tolerance for frustration. They may become tense and appear incapable of doing anything when they feel you are pressuring them. Their handwriting often appears disorganized. Letters within words may be inconsistent in size, and there may be letter reversals. Some students with learning disabilities have unusual speech patterns. For example, words may be spoken out of their proper sequence.

Most students with learning disabilities need special help with organization. These students often find it difficult to distinguish between important and unimportant information. You need to take time to highlight key ideas for them and to provide ways of organizing information into meaningful patterns. In addition, learning-disabled students often have a hard time dealing with alternatives. Sometimes they become anxious when they are forced to make choices. It makes sense for you to limit options available for these students.

By the time they reach their secondary school years, many students with learning disabilities have experienced years of frustration and failure in school. As a result, their self-esteem is low. You need to do whatever you can to help these young people develop more self-confidence. In a supportive classroom environment, these students can learn.

Attention-Deficit/Hyperactivity Disorder Attention-deficit/hyperactivity disorder (ADHD) might be thought of as a specific type of learning disability. It bears special mention because students with ADHD have been declared eligible for services under the Individuals with Disabilities Education Act "when ADHD impairs educational performance or learning" (Lerner & Lerner, 1991, p. 1). Students with ADHD have difficulty staying actively engaged on assigned tasks and in pursuing, paying attention to, and completing their school work. Sometimes they appear to be hyperactive, racing from one idea to another and producing extremely sloppy work as a result of a compulsion to finish quickly. At other times, these students give the impression that they aren't listening to what is being said (Lerner & Lerner, 1991). ADHD is common. It accounts for fully half of all referrals of children to outpatient health clinics. More male students than female students have been diagnosed with ADHD by a ratio of 9:1 (Edwards, 2005).

In working with these students, you need to modify the learning environment and the nature of assigned tasks. Students with ADHD are easily distracted by noise. They have problems with tasks that are too difficult or when others in the class establish the learning pace. These students do better when tasks are self-paced.

In general, students with ADHD require more structure in their lessons than other students. To help these students pay attention, it is a good idea to increase the potential for holding their interest by adding color, shape, and texture to learning materials. These students do better in small classes than in large ones, and they tend to profit more from direct instruction than indirect instruction (Lerner & Lerner, 1991).

Physical and Health Impairment Physical and health impairment is a broad category. In general, it includes students who have limitations related to physical abilities or medical conditions that may interfere with their school performance. About half of the students in this group have suffered from a crippling disease.

The range of conditions in this category makes it impossible to provide recommendations appropriate for every student with a physical or health impairment. In working with these students, the first thing you should do is to gather complete information regarding the specific nature of the condition of each person who falls into this general category. Counselors and parents often are able to provide specific descriptions of each student's special circumstances. Once you have this information, you can decide on modifications of your programs that need to be made for each student with a physical or health impairment.

These modifications will vary greatly from case to case. For example, some conditions may make it impossible for affected students to complete tasks as quickly as others in the class. This may mean adjusting the time allowed for these students to complete the assigned work. If you have learners who require walkers or crutches, you may find it necessary to rearrange classroom furniture to make it easier for these students to move about the room.

In general, students with physical and health impairments are fully capable of meeting the intellectual challenges of regular classroom instruction. Your major adjustment comes not in devising unique methods of instruction but in identifying appropriate responses to accommodate special limitations imposed by particular physical and health conditions of these students. When the special needs of these students are met, most of them do extremely well in the regular classroom.

Emotional Disturbance Emotionally disturbed students are characterized by patterns of behavior that vary significantly from age-appropriate norms. These patterns negatively affect their personal and social development. Some emotionally disturbed students may be defiant, rude, destructive, and attention seeking. Others may be fearful and withdrawn.

Most emotionally disturbed students find it difficult to cope with their environments. As a result, they often experience difficulty making the kinds of adjustments needed to stay focused on school-related tasks. As a result, academic problems are common among these students and frequently lead to low self-concepts. Many of these students become caught up in a negative cycle featuring poor academic performance, leading to diminished self-esteem, and resulting in poor attitudes that contribute to additional academic performance problems and a renewal of the same distressing sequence.

You need to attend to four key principles in working with emotionally disturbed students:

- Design success-oriented activities. Students must sense that they have a reasonable chance of succeeding.
- Communicate behavior expectations with exceptional clarity, and enforce them consistently.
- Minimize distractions to reduce the probability of students' being distracted from their assigned work.
- Ensure that students understand that there is a clear and definite relationship between their behaviors and consequences flowing from these behaviors.

By the time many emotionally disturbed students enter their secondary school years, they have experienced so much failure that they doubt they can master anything that is taught in school. Additionally, many of them suspect that school learning isn't particularly useful. As a result, some of these students go to great lengths to avoid serious engagement with academic tasks. Specifically, they lack motivation. This means that you must work hard to convince them that mastery of school subjects will yield important personal benefits. These benefits need to be characterized by immediacy. It does little good to tell an emotionally disturbed student to "do this because it will help you get a better job in 10 years."

Your instruction needs to be designed to maximize these students' potential for success. It helps to cut large, complex tasks into smaller parts that appear less intimidating. As individual parts are mastered, provide positive feedback to encourage students to stay on task. Additionally, you should take steps to help these students develop appropriate self-regulatory behaviors. With help, these students can be taught self-monitoring techniques that will help them behave in ways that will facilitate learning and assist them to develop more positive self-concepts.

In working with emotionally disturbed students, you need to understand that the problems these young people experience will not disappear overnight. In many cases, emotional disturbance is a condition that has developed over many years. Change may take months or even years.

Action Requirements for Teachers Suppose you find yourself with a number of students with disabilities in your classroom. To help them learn, first of all, you must have an accepting attitude toward these young people. You don't want to approach teaching these students with a mistaken preconception that working with learners with disabilities will be a frustrating and unrewarding experience. On the contrary, you are likely to derive considerable satisfaction from helping these special young people as you see them begin to exercise self-control, make academic progress, and overcome emotional problems.

The world of teaching has changed dramatically in the past few years. As a secondary teacher, you are increasingly likely to be involved with groups of professionals. For example, your school may have specialists who work with language minority students as well as students with disabilities. In some schools, there are intervention assistance teams whose members will be available to help you adapt and deliver instruction for exceptional students. A resource teacher may also be available for some portion of the day to assist you in working with students with disabilities. This team approach requires that you prepare yourself to work with all the individuals interested in the welfare of your students. You may well find yourself involved in such collaborative activities as the following:

- *Participating in the IEP Meetings.* As a classroom teacher, you will be expected to attend and make contributions during these meetings and to understand the specific objectives for the student as prescribed in the IEP.
- *Communicating with Specialists in the Education of Students with Disabilities Concerning the Objectives and the Content of the Classroom.* Discrepancies between expectations and the abilities of the students are a major cause of failure of students with disabilities who are taught in regular classrooms (Smith et al., 1996). Discussions you have with professionals who have special training in working with students with disabilities can help you work effectively with these young people.
- *Informing the Special Student About Behavioral and Academic Expectations.* A lack of understanding on the part of students regarding the expectations and demands in the regular classroom is frequently the cause of much frustration and anxiety and can lead to acting-out behavior. You need to take care that these students understand what they are to do.
- *Monitoring Student Progress.* It is especially important that you assess the progress of exceptional students frequently. This helps the team make adjustments in the delivery of services to the special education students. In addition, celebrating success is important in building students' self-esteem.
- *Communicating Openly with Specialists Any Concerns and Fears You Have About Teaching These Young People.* If you do not deal with these concerns and fears, you

may communicate nonacceptance to the students with disabilities who are members of your classes.

- *Learning the Unique Characteristics of Each Student.* It is important to find out from specialists in the education of students with disabilities information about such issues as the distractibility of individual students, including details about such issues as learning rates, specific difficulties in processing information, and the nature of any special learning aids you need to provide.

Your objective is to provide opportunities for students with disabilities to succeed. This requires modifying your instruction so that these young people have a legitimate opportunity to learn and grow (Smith et al., 1996). At the same time, you need to guard against making too many accommodations. Many of these young people can do much of the work teachers ask of students without disabilities. You want to be sure that students with disabilities feel that they are a legitimate part of the regular classroom group. You should encourage them to participate and interact with regular students so they will not be isolated and separated from the normal activities of the classroom.

Your work with specialists in the education of students with disabilities should not be restricted to planning for classroom instruction. For example, together you may also want to spend time identifying appropriate post–high school academic or vocational training opportunities for these young people. Students with disabilities represent a group that particularly benefits from adult support as they think about what to do with their lives. Teaching self-advocacy is a key to helping students with disabilities make the transition to life after high school.

Part of your efforts should be directed to helping special needs students think about what they need to do to live independently. You can help them make this transition by pointing out practical applications of what you teach in the classroom. Helping students understand how to be organized, how to handle and solve problems, how to establish and maintain social networks, and how to deal with issues such as drug abuse are among the topics that you can deal with in the context of your lessons.

Gifted and Talented Students

In a status report prepared more than 20 years ago, the U.S. Commissioner of Education pointed out that only a few specific programs for the gifted and talented existed in the nation's schools. Stimulated by the considerable interest generated by this report, Congress established the Office of Gifted and Talented within the U.S. Office of Education. Some time later, the Jacob K. Javits Gifted and Talented Students Act of 1994 (P.L. 100-297) provided funds to support programs to identify gifted students and to prepare teachers to respond to their special needs. This legislation also established funding for a National Center for the Education of the Gifted.

At one time, students were selected for gifted and talented programs almost exclusively on the basis of their scores on standardized intelligence tests. Critics charged that gifted and talented people had a wide range of abilities and that intelligence test scores did not appropriately identify many of these. Further, fears that standardized intelligence tests were culturally biased and, hence, tended to screen out minority group students drew additional negative attention to selection based only on test scores.

WHAT DO YOU THINK?

Students Should Be Placed in Ability Tracks

A critic of present secondary school practices recently made the following comments:

> The presence of less academically able students in secondary classrooms results in a waste of academic talent. Teachers have to gear instruction to the lowest common denominator, which slows down the progress of brighter students and leads to boredom. If we want significant reform in education, we need to remove this handicap and encourage our gifted and talented students. One way we can do this is to follow practices established in some other countries.
>
> Students could be tested as they enter high school and assigned either to a general track or a college track. Less able students would take general-track courses and not be asked to compete with brighter students in the college track. Students in the college track could be provided more challenging work. This system would simplify teachers' jobs. They would not have to plan for such a wide range of academic talent as they now must do in classrooms open to all.

Questions

1. Would everyone benefit from this plan? Why or why not?
2. Describe possible negative effects of this idea.
3. What track would you have been in if you had been assigned to either a general track or a college track at the time you completed the sixth grade? Point out any major flaws in this proposal.

Through the years, educators and researchers have broadened the conception of characteristics of gifted and talented people. The work of Renzulli (1978), a leading expert in the education of these students, was especially important in gaining acceptance for the idea that selection should be based on multiple criteria. Renzulli argued that evidence should be gathered in three distinct categories of student characteristics when decisions were being made regarding who should be admitted to gifted and talented programs:

- Intelligence
- Task commitment
- Creativity

Information related to intelligence should be gathered not just from standardized test performance. We should consult other sources, such as grades and comments from individuals who have had opportunities to observe academic work of students.

Task commitment refers to a person's ability to see through a project or activity to the end. People who are gifted and talented tend to finish things, even when there are frustrations along the way. They are not apt to bounce from one project to another, leaving a lot of loose ends along the way.

Creativity refers to the ability to engage challenges and solve problems in unusual ways. Gifted and talented students tend to look at dilemmas in nontraditional ways and to use innovative (and sometimes surprising) techniques to respond to them.

What are gifted and talented students really like? Certainly there are popular misconceptions. Consider, for example, how some films portray bright students as eccentric misfits. Contrary to this view, most studies have found that gifted and talented students are well accepted by their peers. It is true that these students face some special kinds of pressure from other students. In particular, they may be pressured to do less and thereby keep the teacher from setting expectations too high for the class as a whole (Brown & Sternberg, 1990).

Some gifted and talented students have parents who expect too much of them. This leads some of these students to set unrealistic expectations for themselves and to feel bad when they fail to live up to them. You can help these students by focusing them on their accomplishments, not their shortcomings (Baum, 1990). Teach them that everybody has strengths and weaknesses and that there is nothing to be ashamed of when they are less than outstanding in a given area.

Enrichment and Acceleration Enrichment and acceleration are the two basic orientations of programs for gifted and talented students. Enrichment programs assume that students will remain in the same classes and go through school at the same rate as other nongifted and talented students. However, there is an expectation that enriched programs will be provided for them that go well beyond the academic fare served up to the other students.

Acceleration programs increase the pace at which gifted learners complete their schooling. In an accelerated program, a gifted learner might complete the entire high school program in just 2 years. There is no attempt to keep gifted learners in classes with learners who are in the same age-group. This often means that gifted learners are in classes where most of the others are older than they are.

Though there are loyal supporters of both, today enrichment programs are much more common than acceleration programs. This is true because enrichment programs can be implemented with fewer administrative changes. In addition, the possibility that some gifted and talented students in accelerated programs will be in classes with students who are much older than they are is a source of concern to some parents and educators and, hence, is a force working against the popularity of the acceleration approach.

When you work with gifted and talented students, you have to take care to ensure that what these students are asked to do is truly different from what is required of other students. It is particularly important that you do not simply ask them to do more of the same. (For example, if you ask most of your students to do 10 homework problems, it is a mistake to ask your gifted and talented students to do 15 problems from the same set.) If you do this, you will communicate to gifted and talented students that their condition is a burden for which you are punishing them by asking them to do more school work than their classmates. Students are likely to see this as unfair. One result can be a diminished interest in school and a disinclination to stretch academically.

It is important to encourage development of gifted and talented students' creativity. To accomplish this, you can do the following:

- Let your students know that you encourage risk taking
- Suggest ways your students might put to use information they might gain as a result of taking risks

Avoid placing unnecessary limits on gifted students' creativity by laying out hard-and-fast rules regarding how learning will be assessed. You should communicate to these young people that innovative, creative responses will be all right. You want to challenge them to develop unusual approaches that will stretch their imaginative and creative powers.

Establishing the Personal Importance of Learning It is important to provide gifted and talented students with opportunities to pursue some issues they select themselves. They should be encouraged to redefine tasks you provide in ways that will make them more personally important. Gifted and talented students often are not motivated to stretch themselves in pursuit of uninspiring academic goals that seem little connected to their own needs or interests. They may see such pursuits as "a stupid game" and simply refuse to play.

However, when these bright young people are encouraged to play an active part in identifying (or at least redefining) the learning task, they often will commit their intellectual and emotional resources to it with great enthusiasm. This kind of commitment is essential. Without it, they may fail to fully develop their outstanding creative, imaginative, and intellectual powers.

KEY IDEAS IN SUMMARY

- Ethnic and cultural diversity among the population of secondary students is becoming more pronounced. In responding to particular needs of minority group students, teachers need to guard against assuming that all students from a given ethnic, racial, or cultural group share common characteristics. There are important within-group differences, and the proper approach is to focus on the characteristics of the individual student rather than on the presumed characteristic of the group to which he or she belongs.
- A number of risk factors have been identified that commonly characterize students who drop out of school. These include (a) living in a single-parent home, (b) being a member of a family receiving public assistance funds, (c) speaking a primary language other than English, (d) having a brother or sister who dropped out of school, (e) having a mother who is not a high school graduate, (f) having attended 5 or more schools during his or her lifetime, (g) spending less than 1 hour per week on homework, (h) spending no time each week reading for fun, (i) watching television more than 5 hours per night, (j) rarely communicating with parents about things studied at school, and (k) being overage for his or her grade by 1 year or more.
- In times past, poor performance levels of minority students were attributed to such "causes" as genetic deficit. According to this now discredited view, minority group children lacked the necessary intellectual resources to succeed academically; hence, it made little sense to worry too much about their failure to do well in school. Another outdated view suggested that minority students suffered from a cultural deficit (from

intellectually sterile home environments) that failed to prepare them to do school work. Still another view was that minority students suffered a communication process problem. It was suggested that they had language characteristics that made it virtually impossible for them to grasp what teachers expected them to do. The genetic deficit, cultural deficit, and communication process views are now largely regarded as blame-the-victim excuses that allowed schools to avoid their responsibilities to provide quality educational services to minority group students.

- A number of guidelines have been developed to help teachers promote better learning and better attitudes toward schooling among minority group students. These include (a) assuming that all students can learn, (b) providing minority students with good teachers, (c) insisting that teachers become aware of their own cultural perspectives, (d) encouraging teachers to avoid favoritism in the classroom, (e) including students from varied ethnic backgrounds in each group when students are divided into groups for instructional purposes, (f) varying teaching methods to accommodate different learning styles, (g) organizing curriculum around themes, (h) developing close working relationships with students' families, (i) emphasizing development of higher-level thinking skills, and (j) using conversations to uncover ways to contextualize instruction.
- Provisions for meeting the needs of students with disabilities have changed in recent years. One approach has been that of defining a continuum of services and placing exceptional students in the least restrictive setting. Increasingly, there has been a commitment to the principle of inclusion. Inclusion presumes that (a) to the extent possible, these students should be taught in regular classrooms and (b) their membership in these classrooms should be expected and welcomed.
- Recent changes in the delivery of services require that secondary teachers collaborate with teachers who are specialists in the education of students with disabilities. Among other things, this cooperation can help students with disabilities make the transition to experiences they will face after completing high school.
- There are several legislative mandates that must be followed in delivering instruction to students with disabilities. These mandates provide very specific guidelines that school authorities must follow in preparing, delivering, and assessing instructional programs for these students.
- Teachers today encounter many students with disabilities in their regular classrooms. This means that all classroom teachers need to have some familiarity with various categories of student disability and be able to develop, in cooperation with others, programs of instruction that will be appropriate to the special needs of these learners.
- Gifted students tend to be selected on multiple criteria. Often, these include measures of intellectual abilities, creativity, and task commitment (persistence). Despite some popular misconceptions, most gifted and talented students are well adjusted and get along well with other students. These students tend to be served either by enrichment programs or acceleration programs. Currently, enrichment programs are more common than acceleration programs.

REFLECTIONS

1. What does the term "exceptional student" mean? What are some categories of exceptional students found in secondary schools?

2. What are some risk factors associated with dropping out of school? Are these more or less common among minority group students than among the school population as a whole?
3. What are some historic views of minority group students, and how might they have influenced school practices in the past?
4. Why is it important for teachers to appreciate the cultural context minority group students bring with them to school?
5. Why is it desirable for teachers to approach their instructional tasks with the assumption that all students can learn?
6. Open communication between regular classroom teachers and teachers with special training in the instruction of students with disabilities is critical to the development of lessons that will respond well to these students' needs. What are some kinds of information that regular teachers and these specialists need to share?
7. What is meant by full inclusion, and how is this concept changing what regular classroom teachers do?
8. What categories of mentally retarded students are you likely to encounter in your classes, and what are some things you can do to help these young people learn?
9. In what ways can you help students with (a) learning disabilities, (b) attention-deficit disorders, (c) physical and health impairments, and (d) emotional disturbance problems?
10. Why has selection of gifted and talented students sometimes posed problems? What are some criteria commonly used today to identify these young people?

LEARNING EXTENSIONS

1. Interview a central office administrator from a school district that enrolls a culturally and ethnically diverse group of students. Ask this person to comment on high school graduation rate differences among the major cultural and ethnic groups enrolled. In addition, solicit comments about any special programs the district has to encourage minority group students to stay in school. Share your findings in an oral report to your class.
2. Read some reports in professional journals (perhaps supplemented by other sources suggested by your instructor) that describe programs that have increased high school graduation rates of minority group students. From these articles, develop a list of features that seem associated with the success of these programs. Distribute these lists to others in your class and use them as a basis for a discussion focusing on the topic "Keeping Minority Students in Our Secondary Schools: What Works."
3. Many teachers who work successfully with students from diverse cultural and ethnic groups have taken time to familiarize themselves with how members of these

groups see the world. Compile a list of journal articles, books, and other sources of information that might be helpful to non-Latino white teachers interested in learning more about the cultural perspectives of members of selected minority groups. Share your list with others in the class.

4. Invite a panel of five or six secondary school teachers to your class. Have them discuss experiences they have had in working with students with disabilities who are enrolled in their regular classes. In particular, urge them to share ideas about how instruction has been modified to meet these students' special needs.
5. Organize a class debate on this topic: "Resolved that programs for the gifted and talented divert scarce educational resources away from other, more deserving students."

REFERENCES

Baum, S. (1990). The gifted/learning disabled: A paradox for teachers. *Education Digest, 55*(8), 54–56.

Bowman, B. (1991). Educating language minority children: Challenges and opportunities. In S. L. Kagan (Ed.), *The care and education of America's young children: Obstacles and opportunities* (pp. 17–29). Nineteenth Yearbook of the National Society for the Study of Education. Part I. Chicago: National Society for the Study of Education.

Brown, B. B., & Sternberg, L. (1990). Academic achievement and social acceptance. *Education Digest, 55*(7), 57–60.

Condition of Education. (1998). Education of students with disabilities. Retrieved from http://www.nces.ed.gov/pubs98/condition98/c9845a01.html

Edwards, C. H. (2005). *Teaching and learning in middle and secondary schools: Student empowerment through learning communities*. Upper Saddle River, NJ: Merrill/Prentice Hall.

Erickson, F. (1987). Transformation and school success: The politics and culture of educational achievement. *Anthropology and Education Quarterly, 18*(4), 335–356.

Freeman, D. E., & Freeman, Y. S. (2001). *Between worlds: Access to second language acquisition* (2nd ed.). Portsmouth, NH: Heinemann.

Garcia, E. (2002). *Student cultural diversity: Understanding and meeting the challenge*. Boston: Houghton Mifflin.

Gleason, P., & Dynarksi, M. (1998). *Do we know whom to serve? Issues in using risk factors to identify dropouts*. Princeton, NJ: Mathematica Policy Research, Inc.

Grant, C. A., & Sleeter, C. E. (1994). *Making choices for multicultural education: Five approaches to race, class, and gender*. New York: HarperCollins.

Heward, W. (1996). *Exceptional children: An introduction to special education* (5th ed.). Upper Saddle River, NJ: Merrill/Prentice Hall.

Lee, C., & Slaughter-Defoe, D. (1995). Historical and sociocultural influences on African American education. In J. Banks & C. Banks (Eds.), *Handbook of research on multicultural education* (pp. 348–371). New York: Macmillan.

Lerner, J. W., & Lerner, S. R. (1991). Attention deficit disorder: Issues and questions. *Focus on Exceptional Children, 24*(3), 1–17.

Lomawaima, K. (1995). Educating Native Americans. In J. Banks & C. Banks (Eds.), *Handbook of research on multicultural education* (pp. 331–347). New York: Macmillan.

Martin, P., & Midgley, E. (1999). Immigration to the United States. *Population Bulletin, 54*(2), 1–44.

Ogbu, J. H. (1973). *Minority education and caste*. New York: Academic Press.

Pang, V. (1995). Asian-Pacific-American students: A diverse and complex population. In J. Banks & C. Banks (Eds.), *Handbook of research on multicultural education* (pp. 412–424). New York: Macmillan.

Renzulli, J. (1978). What makes giftedness: Re-examining a definition. *Phi Delta Kappan, 60*(3), 180–184, 261.

Rist, R. C. (1985). On understanding the process of school: The contributions of labeling theory. In J. A. Ballentine (Ed.), *Schools and society: A reader in education and sociology* (pp. 88–106). Palo Alto, CA: Mayfield.

Savage, T. V., & Armstrong, D. G. (2004). *Effective teaching in elementary social studies* (5th ed.). Upper Saddle River, NJ: Merrill/Prentice Hall.

Smith, T., Polloway, E., Patton, J., & Dowdy, C. (1996). *Teaching students with special needs in inclusive settings*. Boston: Allyn & Bacon.

Sobol, T. (1990). Understanding diversity. *Educational Leadership, 48*(3), 27–30.

Tharp, T. (1999). Vision of a transformed classroom. *Talking Leaves, 3*(3), 1–2.

Vygotsky, L. (1978). *Mind in society: The development of higher psychological processes*. Cambridge, MA: Harvard University Press.

PART 2 *Preparing for Teaching*

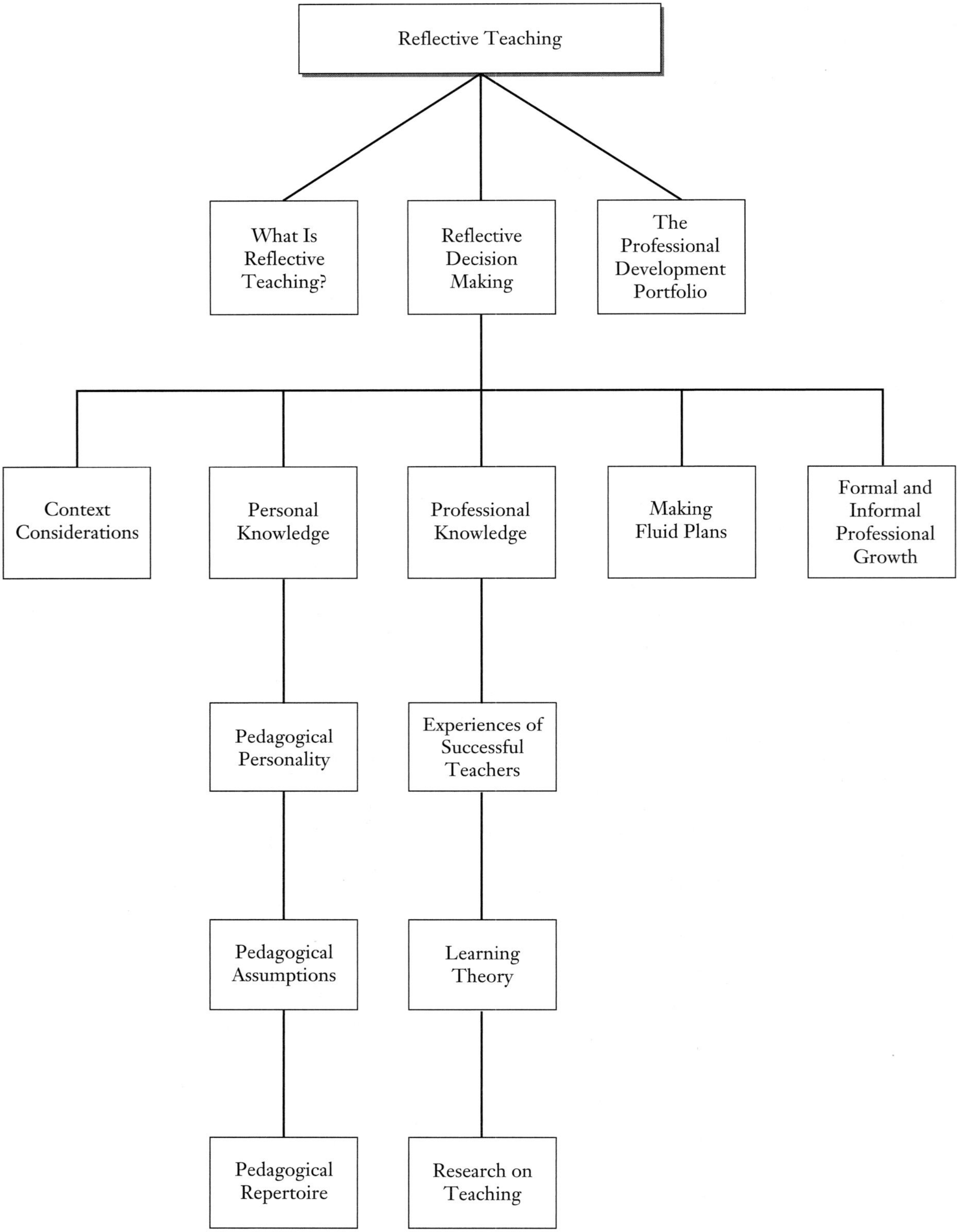

Figure 4.1
Graphic Organizer

CHAPTER 4

Reflective Teaching

OBJECTIVES

This chapter will help you

- define reflective teaching;
- define constructivism;
- describe the four elements of the decision-making processes of reflective teachers;
- point out how the following affect a teacher's classroom performance: pedagogical personality, pedagogical assumptions, and pedagogical repertoire;
- describe strengths and weaknesses of various sources of information about effective teaching and learning;
- point out some limitations of learning theories as sources of information teachers can use as bases of lessons for students in specific classes;
- describe how teachers' expectations of students may influence their instructional practices;
- define fluid planning and state why it is necessary; and
- explain how professional development portfolios can help teachers be more effective.

Introduction

Since you are interested in a career as a secondary school teacher, let's focus on teaching. Suppose you have just been employed to teach 10th-grade world history (or math, English, or science—choose your own subject). Where will you begin? How will you approach your task?

Some of you may smile and say to yourself, "I'm a history major. In high school, I had an outstanding world history teacher. I'll begin by following his or her example." Being knowledgeable in the subject is certainly an important prerequisite for teaching success, but it doesn't help you make decisions about where to start, what to include, and how to make your subject meaningful to a particular group of students. What if they don't share your interest and enthusiasm?

Your intent to follow the example of one of your own outstanding teachers may be a good start, but this approach presents you with certain problems. For one thing, you and your model teacher are different people. You do not share the same experiences, personality, or knowledge. In addition, the students in your classroom may be quite different from those taught by your model. Even in the unlikely event that you were able to follow patterns established by this teacher perfectly, students you teach may not react to your instruction as you remember yourself and others reacting to your model's instruction. They have different experiences and live in a different time, and their interests are influenced by their social and cultural backgrounds.

If you decide not to follow the example of one of your own teachers, you may decide simply to follow suggestions provided in the teacher's guide that accompanies the text supplied for your class. This approach presumes that teaching is simply a matter of finding the right "recipe." Once it is located, all you need to do is follow the steps, and all your students will learn. Unfortunately, this is not reality. The individuals who wrote the text had no information relating to your specific group of students and their backgrounds, interests, strengths, and weaknesses. Veteran teachers will tell you that what works in one period of the day may not work another period of the day. Classrooms simply vary too much for a prescription written by someone far removed from the classroom to work. The ideas may be helpful, but they should not be seen as a prescription.

When confronted with prescriptive teaching approaches, it might be useful to remember that teaching has little in common with work on an assembly line. Students are not inert, raw materials who will eagerly and passively await your attempts to "mold" them into predetermined final products.

If teaching were like manufacturing, you would reject raw materials (students) with flaws that prevented them from benefiting from your actions. That is not how education functions. As a teacher, you have to accept all students. It is a violation of professional ethics to deny instruction to anyone who fails to conform to your expectations. If they have learning problems or lack maturity, it is your responsibility to do whatever you can to ignite student interest and provide conditions that give every member of your class a legitimate chance to achieve success. In some instances, you may need to enlist outside help.

Because of differences among students and because of your obligation to respond to the needs of all of them, simply following suggestions in a teacher's guide will not suffice. Despite these difficulties, there have been numerous attempts throughout educational history to develop "teacher-proof" programs or prescriptions that, if followed religiously by teachers, would all but guarantee high levels of student learning. Not surprisingly, educational history contains many examples of failures because the differences between teachers, students, and contexts were ignored.

It is important to understand that teaching is not a technical act but a professional one. The challenge of becoming a teacher requires that you decide what you value, how you will conduct yourself with students, and the type of teacher you want to be (Goethals, Howard, & Sanders, 2004). It requires that you engage in decision making based on knowledge that takes into account unique circumstances. You must consider the nature of the students you are teaching and their previous knowledge, aspirations, motivations, and attitudes. In addition, you need to understand alternative approaches to teaching and when and how to use them. When confronting these needs, new teachers are frequently overwhelmed by the number of decisions and the importance of the decisions they must make on an everyday basis.

Reflection becomes an integral component of professional growth. Taking time to reflect deeply regarding your values, beliefs, and aspirations; conducting honest self-assessments of your knowledge and skill; and seeking feedback are essential steps in your journey to becoming a teacher (Goethals et al., 2004).

The graphic organizer at the beginning of this chapter illustrates that the chapter has three major components: (a) a definition of reflective teaching, (b) the process of reflective decision making, and (c) the uses of professional development portfolios in the process of reflection. The process of reflective decision making includes the five areas of professional knowledge, personal knowledge, context considerations, making fluid plans, and formal and informal professional growth. Developing personal knowledge is accomplished by considering the experiences of other teachers, learning theory, and research on teaching. Personal knowledge is developed by reflecting on your pedagogical personality, your pedagogical assumptions, and your pedagogical repertoire.

What Is Reflective Teaching?

Reflective teaching is based on the psychological model of constructivism. Constructivism holds that human beings build knowledge. Knowledge does not consist of a set of facts or concepts to be shoved into predetermined file folders somewhere in the brains of students. Knowledge is created and stored when people seek to bring meaning to their experience (Zahorik, 1995). This means that learning how to teach cannot be reduced to a set of procedures that you can apply effectively in all situations. You bring a set of personal filters related to your knowledge, beliefs, attitudes, and values through which you process information related to the task of learning how to teach. How you interpret information about teaching will be different from those around you. What you see as relevant may be perceived as irrelevant by another. In order for you to develop as a professional, you need to be able to reflect on your beliefs and theories and check their validity.

Preparing to teach, then, does not involve collecting a list of "how to's." Rather, your task is to master techniques that will help you make sense out of your experiences. New information you learn should present you with alternatives and should challenge you to test your assumptions and beliefs. If you are open to new information and are willing to engage in reflection, then professional growth is possible.

Because humans construct knowledge, it is conjectural and fallible and grows through exposure. This means that knowledge is never stable. Indeed, it is constantly changing. Your understanding of teaching will be continuously altered as you learn from new experiences. This process of nonstop professional renewal energizes teachers. Members of our profession never "know all there is to know" about teaching.

Reflective teaching builds on the concept of reflection. As applied to education, reflection refers to your ability as a teacher "to reflect thoughtfully on the conditions at hand and respond appropriately in the best interest of the learner" (Rogers & Freiberg, 1994, p. 349).

Henderson (1996) suggests that decision-making processes of reflective teachers include four elements:

1. Decisions are sensitive to the context of the situation. Learning does not take place in a vacuum. It occurs in the context of a specific school in a particular community during a certain time of the year. Schools and parents have expectations. Your students may come from families with few resources or abundant resources. The peer groups within the school have certain norms and sanctions for those who choose to ignore them. The students may be concerned in the fall with trying to become a part of a group, while in the spring they might be consumed with thinking about summer vacation. Their moods change according to things they are experiencing in their personal lives. They simply do not leave all their experiences and emotions at the classroom door.
2. Decisions are guided by a cycle of fluid planning. As a teacher, you face an interesting dilemma. On the one hand, you have to plan to achieve success. On the other hand, you are working with unpredictable human beings. Even your best plans, those that worked last period, may not necessarily work this period. What is the solution? It is certainly not to give up planning. Rather, you have to engage in fluid planning. This means that you have to be ready to modify plans when unexpected conditions arise. It sometimes is difficult to see that this is something excellent teachers do routinely. What you are likely to see in a visit to their classrooms

is a seamless flow of orderly instruction. What you ordinarily don't see are the minute-by-minute decisions that the teacher is making.

3. Decisions are informed by professional and personal knowledge that is critically examined. In order to make good decisions, you need to have a good knowledge base. You need to be aware of the possible reasons learning occurs. You need to know about alternative approaches to teaching your content and the possible consequences of these approaches. However, beyond just having a lot of background about teaching and learning, you have to constantly reflect on or examine your decisions. What were your reasons for making a particular decision? Were they valid? Did you overlook important information that should have been considered? This means that you subject your personal and professional knowledge base to an ongoing critical examination.
4. Decisions are enhanced by both formal and informal professional growth opportunities. As a reflective teacher, you function as a lifelong learner who is constantly seeking new knowledge. You need to discover sources of information that will help you grow professionally. These might be formal opportunities such as additional course work, or they might come to you in informal ways. For example, you might gain important insights into your local community by cooperating with area residents on an important neighborhood project.

Judy Eby (1998) proposes a model of reflective teaching based on Dewey's (1933) ideas of reflective thinking. This model focuses on active, persistent, and careful thinking that takes into account evidence that is synthesized into action (Eby, 1998). Specifically, Eby suggests that successful reflective teachers are characterized as follows:

- Active people who energetically seek solutions to problems rather than passive people who ignore them or rely on tradition and imitation as guides to their instructional practices
- Persistent people who are undaunted in their search for successful responses to instructional challenges and who are not satisfied with superficial or simple solutions
- Careful practitioners who reflect a commitment to the ethical and moral dimensions of teaching as they keep an unwavering focus on students' needs rather than their own
- Thoughtful individuals who consider evidence as they review, study, and reconsider what has occurred in the classroom for the purpose of revising practices in ways that will better serve students' needs

As a reflective teacher, you function as a hypothesis tester. Based on your own past experiences and your knowledge and intuition about capacities of your students, you devise an instructional strategy. As you implement it (and after), you check the accuracy of your assumptions. You might ask yourself questions such as these:

- Were my preconceptions about what might be effective correct? If not, why not?

- Were there parts of the lesson that worked particularly well? If so, how might I capitalize on these successes in preparing other lessons?
- Were there a few weak spots in a generally good lesson? If so, how might I fix them?

This kind of systematic review helps you keep focused on student understanding. Researchers have found that effective teachers spend considerable time thinking about impact-on-student issues as they reflect on their own instructional practices. Less effective teachers tend to focus on issues associated with relatively superficial events that interrupt the flow of their instruction (e.g., announcements coming in unexpectedly over a speaker system) rather than on components of classroom instruction that provide important learning benefits to students (Reynolds, 1992). In other words, effective teachers use more important, student learning–related criteria as they assess the adequacy of their instruction.

A key to your development as an effective reflective teacher is to "do something" with your conclusions once you have thought carefully about how well a lesson has served your students. You want to put new insights to work as you plan new learning experiences for members of your class. It does no good whatsoever to think carefully about what has happened and then simply repeat instructional practices that did not work particularly well the first time.

A department head one of the authors knows mentioned a comment she made to a particularly ineffective teacher who went through the motions of thinking about how her lessons were being received by students (generally not well) and then making absolutely no modifications in her instructional program. In a conversation with the department head, the teacher said, "I should be getting better. After all, I've had five years' teaching experience."

The department head replied, "No, you haven't. You just repeated your first year five times!" This comment may have been a bit harsh, but it underscores the point that simply thinking about how your lessons have gone is not enough; to grow as an effective, reflective practitioner, you have to act on your conclusions. Such action over time adds to your professional knowledge base and is a key element in your professional growth (Reynolds, 1992).

Reflective Decision Making

Combining James Henderson's (1996) reflective-teaching decision-making processes with Judy Eby's (1998) reflective-teaching dimensions results in a framework for putting reflective teaching into action. This framework suggests that as you seek to become a more effective reflective teacher, you need to commit to the following:

- Considering the context
- Using personal knowledge
- Applying professional knowledge
- Making fluid plans
- Taking advantage of formal and informal professional growth opportunities

Context Considerations

In order to achieve success, you need to actively and carefully consider elements of the context that will influence how you teach and how your students learn. Successful teaching requires more than just walking into a classroom and implementing a generic set of lesson plans. The most significant variable of all is the nature of your students.

Students are not empty vessels or blank slates who walk into your classroom eager to be filled with knowledge (Henderson, 1996). Young people in a typical classroom are incredibly diverse. You can expect some who are eager to learn and some who are not. Certain individuals will have a previous history of success and others a history of failure. Many students will view your subject as relevant; others will think it is boring. Some students may come from homes where they have been provided with considerable support and assistance; others will come from homes where indifference seems to rule. You may have some students for whom English is a second language.

As you begin planning, you need to think about answers to these questions:

- What are your students' hopes, dreams, and aspirations?
- What is their history of success?
- What is their prior knowledge of the subject?
- What are their attitudes toward the subject?
- How powerful are the peer groups, and what are the prevailing norms of the peer group about education in general and this subject in particular?
- What are their interests, and what motivates them?
- What are their cultural backgrounds?

Actively pursuing the answers to these questions means that you must spend considerable time and energy observing students, speaking to them, diagnosing their previous knowledge, conducting interest surveys, reviewing records, and talking with other professionals in the school. You will not be able to gather all this information before you begin teaching. You will need to continue gathering this information throughout your career. Your students will change from year to year. You will even see important student differences in the various classes you teach during a given year.

Another key context variable is the school itself. Characteristics of individual schools vary enormously. Even those in the same district with similar student populations might often provide quite different contexts for teaching and learning. One way to understand these differences is to think about each school as having a unique culture.

Individual schools have their own attitudes, norms, values, beliefs, sanctions, myths, ceremonies, and traditions that influence both the teachers and the students. Barth (2001) notes that every school has a culture. Some are toxic, and some are hospitable. He states that the culture in a school wields astonishing power in shaping how people think and act and that the culture is incredibly resistant to change.

Marzano (2003) reviewed research on effective schools and identified several school level factors that appear to be important in enhancing student achievement. He identified a guaranteed and viable curriculum, challenging goals and effective feedback, parent and community involvement, a safe and orderly environment, and collegiality and professionalism as the school-level factors that make a difference.

CRITICAL INCIDENT

"Somehow, I'm Not Connecting"

Jared North, a first-year social studies teacher at Cotton Mather Senior High School, poured a cup of coffee and slumped into a chair in the departmental office. He looked wearily across the room at Ramona Reyes, the longtime head of the social studies department.

"Rough day?" Ramona asked.

"Not one of my greatest," Jared admitted. "You just wouldn't believe some of the answers I got on my short essay question."

"Right," Ramona acknowledged with a grin. "All of us get strange answers from kids all the time."

"Well, OK," admitted Jared, "this may not be all that unusual. But it's discouraging. We've been studying the Civil War and the campaign leading up to the Battle of Gettysburg for a solid week. I just can't understand where some of these kids are coming from. Some of their answers don't make any sense at all."

"Give me a 'for instance,'" asked Ramona. "Maybe that will shed a little light on what's going on."

"OK," Jared replied. "I asked a pretty straightforward question: 'Why did Lee take the army into Pennsylvania?' I got some just crazy answers. One kid said that Lee went there because the other Confederate generals were busy elsewhere. Another one said Lee knew that Quakers who opposed war had settled Pennsylvania and that he felt no one there would fire a shot at his troops once they crossed the Pennsylvania border. Another person said that Lee might have had relatives in Pennsylvania and that he had personal reasons for going there. Someone else actually wrote that fodder for horses was known to be good in Pennsylvania, and that's why Lee took his men there."

"And I take it," Ramona asked, "that these answers don't have much to do with what you were discussing in class?"

"Absolutely nothing!" replied Jared.

"OK, let's think about these answers. But first of all, tell me something. How did you give your students the question? I mean, did you give it to them orally, or was it written on the board or on a paper that you gave to each student?" asked Ramona.

"I wrote it on the board. The students wrote their answers in class on paper I gave them," answered Jared, shaking his head and wondering why Ramona was interested in this issue.

"All right, let's think about this," Ramona continued. "You know, Jared, written language doesn't communicate as clearly as spoken language. It lacks the inflections and emphases we give individual words when we speak that add to the clarity of what we're trying to say. When your students read your question, they probably put their own inflections on your written words. These could have given your question a different meaning than you had intended. There are many ways your question might have been spoken. Let's look at some of these. Now help me out, the exact wording of your question was 'Why did Lee take the army into Pennsylvania?' Is that right?"

"Yes," Jared acknowledged. "That's exactly what I put on the board."

"Here are some different ways individual students might have read your question: 'Why did Lee take the army into Pennsylvania?' A student who read the question this way probably would have focused on the reasons, motives, and so forth for Lee's actions. This is probably what you wanted.

"But another student could have read the question as 'Why did Lee take *his* army into Pennsylvania?' Read in this way, the question seems to be asking why Lee as opposed to someone else took the army into Pennsylvania. A student who interpreted the question in this way would tend to focus on other people who might have taken the army and why, in the end, Lee led the army to Pennsylvania.

"Still, another student could have read the question as 'Why did Lee take his army into *Pennsylvania*?' Read in this way, the focus of your question seems to focus on special characteristics of Pennsylvania that convinced Lee to take his army there. Again, this interpretation would prompt a student to answer your question in a certain way."

"That just blows me away, Ramona. I thought I was asking a really simple question. So how do I keep this kind of problem from happening again?"

"There's no simple answer. There is no 'silver bullet' out there that will slay every instructional problem. That's one of the difficulties we have in this business that seems to elude politicians and other simplistic reformers. People keep forgetting that we deal with individuals and keep looking for a one-fits-all approach to teaching. What you need to keep in mind is that each of your kids has a special set of prior experiences. You need to be careful about dismissing an answer that you get that seems 'strange,' 'bizarre,' or 'totally off base.' Often there is an internal logic to what students tell us in their answers. But we can't know what this logic is until we really know our students well. That's the real key—know your kids, how they think, what is important to them, and how they 'make sense of the world.' When you do that, you'll be a lot less astounded by the responses you get on your tests."

■ ■ ■

What steps should Jared take next? How can he go about finding out more about each of his students? Are some students likely to have values that lead them to think that some things are not as important (or, in some cases, more important) to them as they are to Jared? If so, what use might Jared make of this information? What does he need to do to make his instruction more responsive to his students' needs? Where should he seek information about possible instructional responses he might make? Who are some other people whose advice he might seek?

A guaranteed and viable curriculum is one in which the school has a central focus on teaching and learning. Teachers are given clear guidance regarding what is expected, and students are provided the time to learn the content.

Challenging goals and effective feedback refers to a clear specification of goals that are challenging for students accompanied with a high expectation that the students will achieve them. In addition, the attainment of the goals is monitored, and effective feedback is provided.

Parent and community involvement focuses on how involved and supportive the parents and the community are in supporting the school. This factor can be identified by considering the effectiveness of the communication between the school and the parents—actual participation of parents and others in the daily operation of the school and governance structures that allow parents and the community some voice in school decisions.

A safe and orderly school environment is one where both the students and the teachers feel safe. This is related to a clear set of school-wide rules governing student behavior. There is an emphasis on teaching self-discipline and responsibility to students, and rules are consistently enforced.

The final factors, collegiality and professionalism, focus on the professional climate of the school. It relates to the manner in which faculty members and administrators interact with each other. Fullan and Hargreaves (1996) define this as authentic interaction that includes openly sharing failures and mistakes, demonstrating respect for each other, and constructively analyzing procedures and practices.

As you reflect on the type of teacher you want to be, you need to consider the context factors and how they will impact you. This can assist you in finding a school with a professional context that can help you achieve success and grow as a professional. Some questions you might consider are the following:

- Does the school have a clearly stated set of goals and expectations?
- What is the extent of parent and community participation?
- Is the environment an orderly one that is conducive to learning?
- How do teachers and administrators interact? Is there obvious respect?
- Do teachers in the school believe that they can achieve success with their students?
- What are community perceptions of the school?
- What resources are available for teachers to use to supplement and support their classroom instruction?

Clearly, some answers to these questions can highlight conditions that may make it difficult for you to be successful. For example, it is hard for students to concentrate on learning if they are worried about their safety. If access to the Internet is difficult, then there are constraints on teachers' abilities to plan lessons that depend on information available only through the Internet. The physical environment of the school can also undermine your well-intentioned efforts to serve students well. In places where there are out-of-date textbooks, leaking roofs, poor lighting, and overcrowded classrooms, students' performance levels are likely to suffer. Finally, if faculty members do not get along or if there is tension between teachers and administrators, issues associated with smoothing difficult interpersonal relations problems may divert attention from providing optimal learning experiences for students.

In addition to the parent and community involvement, you should also attend to the community context. Community priorities and values affect the entire educational enterprise. In response to this reality, it makes sense for you to learn as much as you can about the community where your school is located. This task will require some real effort, particularly if you find yourself teaching in an urban school that may be located in an area far removed from your personal residence. Students attending your school may manifest behavior patterns and reflect attitudes that will make sense to you only if you understand the residential patterns, demographics, religious preferences, norms, values, and other characteristics that go together to create the local community culture. You might begin by seeking answers to questions such as these:

- What is the ethnic and socioeconomic composition of the community?
- What are the major opportunities and challenges in the community?
- What opportunities are provided in the community for the students to be involved in local activities?
- What are the expectations of the community for the school?
- Do community members view the school as supportive or threatening?

Careful consideration of these questions can contribute to understandings that will help you understand some of the student attitudes and behaviors you will see in your classes. This information can assist you in the process of making instructional decisions that are appropriate to the needs of your students. Instructional decisions that are made in light of information about community characteristics enhance students' chances for learning. In turn, students who learn feel good about themselves, reflect positive attitudes back to the community, and act to enhance your credibility as a professional educator.

Personal Knowledge

Decisions you make as a teacher are filtered through your own values, beliefs, and understandings. You will have developed some of these as a consequence of your fundamental personal values. Others will be associated with some of your general personality characteristics. Still others will tie closely to the particular store of knowledge you have acquired.

Palmer (1998) places great emphasis on personal knowledge. He notes that we often ask the "what," "how," and "why" questions but seldom ask the "who" question. The most important question, he says, is "Who is the self that teaches?" It is imperative that we ask this most fundamental question about teachers and teaching. Palmer further emphasizes that good teachers possess a capacity for connectedness and weave a complex web between themselves, their subjects, and their students. Thus, in becoming a good teacher, it is essential to ask the "who" question.

What should you know about yourself as you consider your role as a teacher? One authority who has investigated this question suggests you should think about information related to these three categories (Millies, 1992):

- pedagogical personality
- pedagogical assumptions
- pedagogical repertoire

Pedagogical Personality Pedagogical personality is a term used to refer to your self-concept, confidence, and biases in terms of how these characteristics affect your interactions with students. To gain an appreciation of your pedagogical personality, ask yourself these questions:

- What do I believe about myself and my abilities as a teacher?
- What do I fear?

- What do I find fulfilling?
- What is my view of what a teacher "ought to be like"?

Pedagogical Assumptions The phrase "pedagogical assumptions" refers to the basic values and beliefs that guide teachers' practices in the classroom. Questions that focus on this dimension include the following:

- What do I believe is the purpose of education?
- What do I believe about teaching?
- How do I feel about students from different social, economic, and ethnic groups?
- What learning principles are most important and should guide my instruction?

Answers to these questions will help explain how you organize for instruction and interact with students.

Pedagogical Repertoire The term "pedagogical repertoire" refers to teachers' knowledge of and appreciation for alternative approaches to managing students and introducing content. Questions such as these provide insights into the nature of your own pedagogical repertoire:

- What are the best approaches to managing students in the classroom?
- What alternatives are available to me to teach this content?
- In which instructional approaches do I have the most confidence?
- What are some of my ideas for motivating members of this class?
- With which instructional techniques am I not comfortable?

The act of answering questions associated with pedagogical personality, assumptions, and repertoire can help you think through alternative approaches to teaching specific content to specific students. Thinking about possible responses challenges assumptions and encourages thought about choices you might make when several options seem to have promise. The hope is that, over time, this process will increase your understanding of yourself and provide the foundation for continual professional growth.

Professional Knowledge

In addition to personal knowledge, reflective teaching requires you to have professional knowledge related to basic principles of teaching and learning. There are several sources of information about this kind of professional knowledge:

- Experiences of successful teachers
- Learning theory
- Research-on-teaching studies

Experiences of Successful Teachers You can sometimes learn about these experiences by consulting directly with a successful teacher. This kind of exchange may well

MORE FROM THE WEB

Developing Your Personal and Professional Knowledge Base

These Websites provide you with some opportunities to add to your personal and professional knowledge base. On these sites, you will have the opportunity to interact with others, locate notices of professional development opportunities, and find sample lesson plans.

Teachers Helping Teachers

This site is regularly updated with new information. Among other things, you will find advice posted for newcomers by experienced teachers. Lesson plans are available. There are excellent links to other educational resources.

Website: http://www.pacificnet.net/~mandel

Discovery School

This is an excellent site that features many links to resources for teachers. There are links to tips for teaching individual subject areas, evaluation tools, special education resources, and upcoming professional development seminars.

Website: http://discoveryschool.com/schrockguide

take place during your student teaching when you have the opportunity to work with one or more especially effective teachers. While you can learn much from the experiences of successful teachers, it is a mistake to rely only on professional judgment as you seek to broaden your knowledge of teaching. For example, some outstanding teachers have developed patterns gradually over the years that have become so embedded in their own personalities that they may be unable to tell you how they operate in the classroom. In response to the question "Why did you do that?" they may just respond, "I can't really tell you; it just felt right."

Another obvious limitation on professional judgment as a source of information is that each person has a unique personality and style. Something that works splendidly for another teacher may be a disaster when you try it.

Finally, professional judgment sometimes is just plain wrong. Behaviors that may seem right to a given individual and that may even have a lot of intuitive logic behind them may be undesirable. For example, common sense would seem to dictate that the more praise a teacher gives to a student, the better that student's academic performance will be. Researchers have found that this is not true. In fact, praise that is not tied clearly to a specific correct accomplishment with a given academic task may have little or no impact on students' learning (Good & Brophy, 2004).

In summary, you need to critically examine and reflect on the advice and practices of other teachers. Uncritical acceptance can lead to frustration and difficulties.

Learning Theory Learning theory is another source for information on teaching and learning. Individual learning theories explain relations among variables in the teaching–learning process.

Teacher reflection is encouraged through peer coaching.

Bigge and Shermis (1999) classify current learning theories into two broad families: the behaviorist family and the cognitive interactionist family. For the behaviorists, learning is defined as a change of observable behavior that occurs as a result of a relationship between stimuli and responses. A great emphasis is placed on making sure that desired responses are reinforced and that wrong or undesired responses are ignored so that there is a strengthening of the bond between the stimuli and the desired responses. This increases the probability that the correct or proper responses will occur when the individual is confronted with stimuli.

Cognitive interactionists, on the other hand, view learning as a process of changing insights or thought processes. They see learning as taking place inside the student. They are more interested in helping students reorganize or change their perceptual or cognitive fields in order to gain insight.

It is obvious that your reflections will be guided by your learning theory. If you lean toward the behaviorist approach, you would be interested in the observable actions of the students, and your problem solving will be directed toward understanding how to reinforce desirable responses and identifying and removing what might be reinforcing inappropriate responses.

If you lean toward a cognitive interactionist approach, you will be more concerned with identifying how the student views or understands the world and how to help them constantly reorganize this information in order to gain understanding.

Learning theory is not always as helpful as you might think. The theories themselves are grounded in a body of research and analysis that attempts to frame general principles consistent with this scholarly work. However, when dealing with the rapid-paced environment of the classroom filled with unpredictable human beings, it is not always clear which principles apply. Bigge and Shermis (1999) outline three choices that teachers might make:

1. A teacher might try to adhere to one systematic theory as much as possible.
2. A teacher might eclectically borrow ideas from the different theories and fit them together into a mosaic that can be drawn on when needed.
3. A teacher might develop his or her own new or synthesized theory by selecting and modifying ideas from other theories.

Therefore, not only are your reflections guided by your learning theory, but your reflections result in the reinforcing or changing of your personal learning theory.

Research-on-Teaching Studies Individual research studies represent another source of information about teaching. There has been an enormous increase in research focused on classroom instruction over the past couple of decades. Organizations such as the American Educational Research Association publish reviews of research in specific areas. One journal that summarizes research on topics of interest to teachers in each issue is the *Review of Educational Research*. It is available in most university libraries and many public libraries as well.

Regrettably, research rarely speaks with a united voice on a given issue. It is not uncommon for several studies of the same question to come up with quite different results. You need to be especially wary when someone prefaces a defense of a particular instructional practice with the phrase "Research proves." Research rarely proves just one thing. It is important to know how much research has been done and what the general trend of the findings is. (Generally, a trend is all you can hope to find. All studies of a given question almost never yield common results.)

In spite of the frustrations you may encounter as you try to find consistent patterns of findings, we highly recommend that you become familiar with professional research literature. This research can be very helpful to you as you reflect on your teaching and can help guide your reflections to useful solutions for instructional problems.

To give you some sense of trends uncovered by specialists who conduct research on teaching, we have selected some findings that can provide you with information that can be useful when you reflect on your instructional decisions. Information in this section has been divided into these five categories:

- Beliefs about students
- Stimulating student interest
- Using student contributions
- Making wise use of time
- Presenting good lessons

Beliefs About Students The most important variable teachers work with is student characteristics. It makes no sense for you to plan instruction without good information about the backgrounds, abilities, interests, and general behavior patterns of your students. Decisions you make in response to this information will greatly influence the overall impact of your instruction.

Teachers' expectations of individual students are strongly tied to their beliefs about what students can do (Good & Brophy, 2004). These findings suggest that students for whom you hold high expectations will achieve more than students for whom you have lower expectations.

Teachers' expectations result from their analyses of several key variables. These include student appearance, intelligence and achievement test scores, and behavior patterns. Some evidence suggests that some teachers even form opinions about how an individual student will perform on the basis of how their older brothers and sisters did in school. If you are not aware of these perceptions and their limitations, you may find yourself interacting with some class members in ways that do not support their maximum personal and intellectual development. Braun (1987) described a cycle of behavior that some teachers develop as a result of their beliefs about what individual students can do:

1. The teacher establishes a level of expectation for a student on the basis of what he or she believes to be true of this individual.
2. Student behaviors are interpreted in light of this expectation.
3. As a result of how the teacher reacts, the student begins to develop a self-concept that is consistent with the teacher's beliefs.
4. As a result, the student's performance begins to reflect the teacher's expectation. This means that students for whom the teacher has higher expectations do well and that students for whom the teacher has lower expectations do poorly.

How should you deal with the possibility that your perceptions of individual students may affect how you interact with them? There is no easy answer. It is human nature to make inferences about others. However, self-monitoring efforts can help you check the accuracy of the inferences you are making and ensure that you are not

WHAT DO YOU THINK?

Have a Teacher's Expectations Ever Influenced You?

Without realizing they are doing so, teachers sometimes communicate to some students that they have little confidence in their abilities. At the same time, they may communicate to others in the class that they expect great academic work from them. Reflect on some of your own experiences as a secondary school student as you respond to these questions.

Questions

1. Can you recall times when a teacher's actions prompted you to do more? To do less? What happened in each case?
2. Do you recall any students who could have done better work but were turned off by what they perceived to be a lack of teacher confidence in their abilities?
3. If you remember times when teachers seemed to have preconceived notions about what individuals could do, how do you think their impressions affected these students' abilities?

prompting irresponsible patterns of behavior. Periodic efforts to take stock of what is going on often are helpful. As part of ongoing reflection, you need to think seriously about any biases you might have that are resulting in unproductive patterns of working with certain individuals.

Stimulating Student Interest Disinterested students tend to misbehave and disrupt the learning of others. The key to prompting student interest is to plan learning experiences that connect students' past experiences and views to what is important in the school curriculum. This implies a need for you to know your students well. You also must know your subject matter well enough so you can adapt and explain it to students in an understandable way (Reynolds, 1992).

It is important to remember that planning for motivation does not occur only at a lesson's beginning. You need to plan for motivation during three distinct phases of a lesson: (a) at the beginning, (b) during the lesson development, and (c) at the conclusion of the lesson.

Motivation often occurs when students' curiosity is aroused. Frequently, this happens when they are introduced to something unique or novel (at least unique or novel to them). Sometimes students react positively to information regarding the personal importance of mastering the content that is about to be introduced. Variety during the lesson also tends to prompt continued student interest. The same can be said about encouragement. It is especially important for you to take time at the end of a lesson to highlight what students have learned.

Students' confidence grows as they realize they have encountered and understood substantial amounts of new material. Feelings of success and accomplishment build students' levels of self-esteem. As a result, they become more highly motivated to study material introduced in subsequent lessons. Additional information related to motivation is introduced in Chapter 9.

Using Student Contributions How should you use student contributions? No answer to this question fits every occasion. The key principle is that your reaction to students' contributions should encourage their continued participation, provide them with appropriate feedback, and, at the same time, ensure that you do not lose the central focus of the lesson.

When should you challenge students' ideas? In general, if a challenge to an idea will cause the student to do more thinking about the issue and develop more sophisticated reasoning skills, the challenge may make sense. However, if the student is likely to see your challenge as a put-down, little good will come of it. This is a good time to consider another approach. When you decide that challenge is appropriate, you want to deliver it in a tone of language that implies, "I may disagree with what you have said, but I still think highly of you as a person."

Making Wise Use of Time Time available for instruction is limited. As a result, you need to use it wisely. Researchers have identified what is called "opportunity to learn" as one of the most significant variables that accounts for student achievement (Freiberg & Driscoll, 2000). Opportunity to learn refers to the amount of time available to students to learn the content. Not surprisingly, when students have more time to learn the content (more opportunity to learn), they have higher achievement. Unless you plan carefully, administrative tasks such as roll taking, distributing and collecting materials, and making announcements can significantly reduce the opportunity to learn. Carefully planning administrative tasks so that you spend only a few minutes each day on them will provide you with many additional hours of instructional time over the academic year.

As you consider time management issues, consider three types of time that can help you keep students on task and increase opportunity to learn.

The first, allocated time, is the amount of time you set aside for students to learn specific material. Researchers have found that different teachers allocate very different quantities of time for teaching the same content (Good & Brophy, 2004). Why is this so? In part, this situation arises because of class-to-class differences in students. Interestingly, another determinant seems to be the teachers' varying levels of personal interest in and feelings of competence with the topic being taught. Teachers tend to allocate more instructional time to topics they like and about which they believe themselves to be particularly well informed. For example, some English teachers who really enjoy teaching literature allocate much more time to teaching literature than to teaching writing. Consider the long-term implications for students who need to master skills in both areas.

To properly make time-allocation decisions, you also need to consider the relative importance of each topic as it relates to the major aims of the course. You need to provide sufficient time for students to learn material associated with each topic but not so much time that they become bored. Just because you allocate a given amount of time for students to work on an assigned task does not guarantee that they will do so.

A second type of time, student engaged time, refers to the portion of allocated time that the students are actually engaged in studying the assigned material. Researchers have observed great classroom-to-classroom differences in the amount of engaged time (Good & Brophy, 2004). Student engaged time is a better indicator of opportunity to learn because it is the time the students are actually interacting with the content. In general, your intent should be to increase the total amount of engaged time.

Finally, a third type of time, academic learning time, is the portion of student engaged time when the students are not only interacting with the material but also experiencing success. Sometimes even though students are engaged in studying material, they are not experiencing success. Thus, they are not really learning. Our goal then is to maximize academic learning time. One place to begin is to make sure you know your students well. This allows you to match your assignments to the prior knowledge of the students, their interests, and their abilities. You will also need to monitor student progress carefully so that you can quickly step in and help them when they begin to experience difficulty. Then you need to be ready to reteach the lesson or parts of the lesson in order to help students achieve success.

Presenting Good Lessons Good planning is a basic characteristic of successful secondary school teachers. Well-planned lessons feature the following:

- Clarity
- Feedback to students
- Good modeling

Clarity Clarity requires a clear and precise use of language and a presentation style that moves logically and smoothly from point to point. There are many threats to clarity. For example, your students may be confused if you use vague and ambiguous terms or if you use vocabulary that is unfamiliar to them. One of the problems you will encounter in teaching secondary school is that specific subjects have content-specific vocabulary that has special meaning. New teachers often assume that students understand these terms. When they do not, confusion and frustration result.

Internal summaries also enhance clarity of lesson presentation. These are stopping points during a lesson when you pause to review with students what you have already covered. These summaries help students focus on key points and see interrelationships among important ideas.

Clarity is improved when your lessons feature a well-organized conclusion. A good conclusion summarizes what you have covered and draws students' attention to important ideas. You often will want to repeat key content ideas during this phase of a lesson to help your students retain the new material.

Feedback to Students Feedback to students involves specific actions you take to communicate information to students about the appropriateness or correctness of their responses. This information helps your students avoid errors and focus on important dimensions of content.

Praise is often used as part of feedback. Researchers have found that, to be effective, praise should be specific and genuine. Further, it should be used in moderation (Good & Brophy 2004). The term "*specificity*," as applied to appropriate use of praise, means that you need to tell your students what they have done that you have found praiseworthy. The praiseworthy behavior you cite should relate to content you are teaching. If you give general praise that has no clear connection to a desirable academics-related behavior, this action will have little impact on student performance.

Criticism also has its place when you provide feedback to students. Proper criticism focuses on helping a student resolve an academic difficulty. It is designed not simply to indicate student errors but also to suggest appropriate ways of correcting mistakes. Good criticism never demeans students as people. It focuses on enhancing their self-esteem by helping them master content.

Good Modeling Providing a model for learners during a lesson acts to improve student performance. For example, your personal enthusiasm for a topic often is catching and most likely will increase levels of student interest. Students also benefit when you model thinking processes that are appropriate for a particular task. For example, you might solve a problem similar to ones your students will be asked to solve by thinking out loud with members of the class. ("Now if I found myself faced with this situation, the first thing I would look at would be. . . . Next, I would compare ________ and ________. If they seemed consistent, I probably would decide to . . .")

You sometimes may find it useful to develop an example of a product of learning similar to what you expect to receive from students. For example, if you want your students to write a short paper comparing and contrasting the positions of two individuals, you might prepare a sample of such a paper. When making your assignment to the students, you can share this material, drawing their attention to various features you hope to see in the papers they will be preparing. An example of this kind greatly reduces the possibility your students will fail to understand your expectations.

Making Fluid Plans

Armed with thoughtful information carefully gathered about the context and your personal and professional knowledge, you will be ready to make fluid plans. Fluid plans are flexible and responsible. They are general designs that you prepare carefully, but they do not lay out an inflexible instructional path. They function as guides that you will use to begin your lessons and that you will be expected to modify, as needed, as your teaching unfolds. As a user of flexible plans, your teaching is adaptive. It does not consist of a set of preplanned, totally scripted instructional acts.

Formal and Informal Professional Growth Opportunities

Your preparation for teaching does not end when you are awarded an initial teaching certificate or license. You will need to continue to develop your personal and professional knowledge throughout your career. You can best do this by pursuing activities that will help you learn what you need to know. Your specific actions will vary depending on your own diagnosis of your personal professional needs. For example, if you need additional knowledge in your content area, you might decide to take additional courses in your subject. If you need to develop a better understanding of your community, you might consider one or more informal approaches to gaining this information. For example, you might think about volunteering for some community events or taking other actions that will bring you into closer contact with local people, organizations, and neighborhoods.

The Professional Development Portfolio

By definition, reflective teaching demands reflection. As a means of organizing information to consider as you engage in serious thought about teaching and learning, you may find a professional development portfolio useful. This kind of a portfolio often includes ideas and thoughts about information or instructional techniques you would like to include in your lessons. In addition, you may also want to include materials you actually use in lessons along with your thoughts about how effective individual lessons were and what you might have learned that will improve your teaching of subsequent lessons. Keeping a professional development portfolio can be an important aid to your development as a teacher.

Professional development portfolios can be formatted in a variety of ways. Often, they include (a) information or materials that prompt you to reflect and (b) written summaries of your reflections.

Individual teachers vary in terms of specific items they put in professional development portfolios to prompt reflection. After considering your options, you might decide to include entries such as these:

- Descriptions of procedures for implementing new instructional techniques
- Explanations of special features of your teaching context (nature of the students, noise levels in your classroom, adequacy of learning materials, and so forth)
- Copies of lesson plans you have developed
- General information from a variety of sources that you think might facilitate your development as an effective teacher

- Comments of any observers who may have seen you teach
- Examples of student work

Written summaries of your reflection may take different forms. For example, you might decide to frame your written reactions as answers to questions you might pose:

- How might I actually incorporate some new instructional techniques into my lessons, and what is my rationale for wanting to do so?
- To what extent have context variables helped and hindered the effectiveness of my lessons, and how might I change what I have been doing in light of this information?
- Do lesson plans I have used really emphasize what I want to highlight with my students, and is the presented information optimally organized and sequenced to facilitate learning of all my students? What specific changes would I want to make when teaching these lessons again?
- How can I move from a knowledge-level understanding of new information I have learned about effective teaching to converting this information to part of my active teaching repertoire?
- How congruent are comments noted by people who have observed my teaching with my own perceptions about how I have been performing? What thoughts do I have about changing what I have been doing as a result of thinking about their observations and suggestions?
- How pleased am I with the quality of work I am getting from students? What can I do to increase the numbers of students who are achieving high levels of academic success and deriving personal satisfaction from their involvement in my lessons?

Whether you decide to use questions to prompt written summaries of your reflections or to use a different approach to recording your thoughts is a matter of personal preference. The critical point is that a professional development portfolio must include some record of your own reflections about the basic information that is included. Otherwise, preparation of the portfolio amounts to little more than construction of a scrapbook. To have real value as an aid to your professional development, you need to engage the content, mull it over carefully, and give written expression to your reflections. It is the intellectual engagement, not the simple gathering together of included materials, that makes professional development portfolios credible vehicles for developing teachers' expertise.

You may wish to start a professional development proposal as you work through this text. At the end of chapters in this text, you will find a "For Your Portfolio" exercise. This provides you with an opportunity to put information you have learned into a professional-development portfolio. Once you have started a portfolio, you need to review it regularly. You might ask yourself some general questions as you conduct these periodic status checks. Some examples include the following:

FOR YOUR PORTFOLIO

This is a good time to begin assembling your personal portfolio. This portfolio will be useful to you in establishing a foundation for reflection, providing information about your growth, and providing evidence of your knowledge.

One of the first steps in developing a portfolio is to establish an organizational framework. One we suggest is to establish your portfolio using the INTASC standards. There are 10 standards, so you can begin by establishing 10 sections for your portfolio. In each section, you should provide some material related to each standard as well as your personal reflections about the material you have included.

The content of this chapter relates specifically to INTASC Standard 9. (A professional educator is someone who is a reflective practitioner.) Select two or three items that you will include in your portfolio related to the content of this chapter. You might consider entries that focus on areas such as your pedagogical personality, your pedagogical repertoire, or your personal learning theory.

1. How does this information relate to your ability to reflect and self-evaluate?
2. Write a reflection stating why you chose each entry and what you think it indicates about your ability to be a reflective practitioner.

- Does my portfolio reveal that I have been actively engaged in seeking answers for questions and in growing professionally?
- Have I been persistent in seeking knowledge and in finding ways to respond to the challenges of teaching?
- Have I been thoughtful and careful in drawing my conclusions, and have I considered the moral and ethical dimensions of my actions?
- Have I adequately considered the impact of my ideas on my students?
- Are criteria I have been using to judge my success as a teacher worthwhile and important?
- Does my portfolio reflect changes I have made as I have learned new things about my students, my teaching context, and my subject?

Professional growth portfolios can provide you with a basis for understanding yourself and for promoting your professional development. You may find yourself looking back at sections of your portfolio completed early in the academic year and observe with real satisfaction some of the changes you have made in working with your students. Portfolio-based documentation of your increasing expertise as a teacher can be a tremendous confidence builder. A record of past successes will function as an excellent motivator as you begin thinking about ways to become more effective in areas that, you believe, still need work.

KEY IDEAS IN SUMMARY

- Reflective teaching is an orientation to instruction that will call on you to reflect thoughtfully on the conditions at hand and to vary your teaching responses so as best to serve the needs of students. Eby (1998) points out that the reflective teacher needs to be active, persistent and careful and to consider available evidence while engaging in reflection. The foundations of reflective teaching are found in constructivism, the idea that knowledge does not exist in any abstract sense but that it is "constructed" by individuals as they interact with and attempt to make sense of their environment.

- Reflective teaching involves (a) a sensitivity to content, (b) a willingness to be informed by personal and professional knowledge, (c) an understanding that good instruction is best guided by fluid planning (planning that quickly adjusts to changing circumstances in the classroom), and (d) a commitment to career-long informal and formal professional development.
- Your decisions as a teacher will be influenced strongly by your own personality, biases, and general worldview. This means that you need to develop an awareness of your own personal perspectives. Such awareness will help you avoid making decisions that are too strongly tied to your biases—decisions that, in some cases, may not be best for your students.
- Researchers have found an important connection between teachers' expectations of students and students' levels of performance. In general, your students will do better when you hold high expectations for them.
- When you teach, you may find yourself gathering information for decisionmaking from many sources. Personal experiences of other teachers may provide some useful information. However, because of differences in individual teacher personalities, students to be served, and other variables, these experiences may not be wholly useful to you. Learning theory offers some guidance. However, principles derived from learning theory may not be applicable in every instructional situation. Individual research studies also provide some useful information. Again, studies may yield insights that may not be applicable to the special features of your own teaching setting.
- Relating the school curriculum to students' needs and interests enhances their levels of interest. Ideally, motivational activities should occur during three distinct phases of a given lesson: the beginning, as new information is presented, and at the end. Researchers have found that using student ideas during a lesson helps maintain student interest and involvement. Ideally, you should react to students in ways that (a) encourage their continued participation, (b) provide them with appropriate feedback, and (c) help them maintain a focus on the central content of the lesson.
- Effective teachers manage time wisely. It is particularly important to maximize the amount of classroom time actually devoted to instruction. This is referred to as "opportunity to learn." As students are provided with more time or more opportunity to learn, achievement increases. Researchers who have looked at the issue of teachers' use of time have identified three important time concepts. Allocated time refers to time set aside for instruction. Engaged time refers to the time students are actually working on an assigned task. Student success rate is the actual time by students working on a task with success.
- Good lessons do not happen by accident. They tend to feature recurring patterns of effective teacher behavior. These include (a) efforts to ensure clarity of communication, (b) attempts to enhance student achievement through provision of appropriate feedback, and (c) modeling.
- Understanding your teaching context requires you to gather information about your students, the culture of your school, and the nature of your community. Information about these dimensions can help you reflect on the opportunities and challenges you face in the classroom and assist you as you seek to design more successful lessons.
- Continued professional growth is a characteristic of successful teachers. This professional growth is best enhanced when you actively pursue formal and informal professional development opportunities.

REFLECTIONS

1. Do you consider yourself a reflective person? How do you think this will influence your teaching?
2. What personal knowledge do you have about yourself that you think is related to your potential success as a teacher?
3. How would you describe your pedagogical personality?
4. What is your theory about teaching and learning? What are the roots of this theory?
5. What are some research findings on teaching that you find especially useful? Why?

LEARNING EXTENSIONS

1. Several books have been written relating teachers' classroom experiences. Read several teachers' accounts from one of these sources. As you read these accounts of classroom teachers, consider how they address the context, the personal and professional knowledge base, fluid planning, and professional growth. Prepare a report on your reading to share with your class.
2. Much is being published today about reflective teaching. Read four or five journal articles that focus on this subject. Summarize your findings in a short paper. Include comments comparing and contrasting information from these articles to information about reflective teaching introduced in this chapter.
3. Do an informal needs assessment of your personal and professional knowledge. Identify what you want to know about yourself and what you want to know about teaching and learning. Use this assessment to guide you as you proceed through this book and your teacher preparation program.
4. Teach a lesson to other members of your class and arrange to have someone videotape your presentation. Review the videotape privately, identifying aspects of your lesson that you think could have been done better. Prepare a written summary explaining precisely what you would do another time to improve your overall presentation.
5. Spend some time as an observer in a secondary school. Try to identify and characterize the elements of the school culture. How does this culture seem to influence both teachers and students?

REFERENCES

Barth, R. (2001). *Learning by heart.* San Francisco: Jossey-Bass.

Bigge, M., & Shermis, S. (1999). *Learning theories for teachers* (6th ed.). New York: Longman.

Braun, C. (1987). Teachers' expectations. In M. Dunkin (Ed.), *The international encyclopedia of teaching and teacher education* (pp. 598–605). New York: Pergamon Press.

Dewey, J. (1933). *How we think* (Rev. ed.). Lexington, MA: D. C. Heath.

Eby, J. W. (1998). *Reflective planning, teaching and evaluation K–12* (2nd ed.). Upper Saddle River, NJ: Merrill/Prentice Hall.

Freiberg, H., & Driscoll, A. (2000). *Universal teaching strategies* (3rd ed.). Boston: Allyn & Bacon.

Fullan, M., & Hargreaves, A. (1996). *What's worth fighting for in your school?* New York: Teachers College Press.

Goethals, M., Howard, R., & Sanders, M. (2004). *Student teaching: A process approach to reflective practice* (2nd ed.). Upper Saddle River, NJ: Merrill/Prentice Hall.

Good, T, & Brophy, J. (2004). *Looking in classrooms* (9th ed.). Boston: Allyn & Bacon.

Henderson, J. C. (1996). *Reflective teaching: The study of your constructivist practices* (2nd ed.). Upper Saddle River, NJ: Merrill/Prentice Hall.

Marzano, R. (2003). *What works in schools: Translating research into action*. Alexandria, VA: Association for Supervision and Curriculum Development.

Millies, P. (1992). The relationship between a teacher's life and teaching. In W. Schubert & W. Ayers (Eds.), *Teacher lore: Learning from our own experience* (pp. 25–42). New York: Longman.

Palmer, P. (1998). *The courage to teach: Exploring the inner landscape of a teacher's life*. San Francisco: Jossey-Bass.

Reynolds, A. (1992). What is competent teaching? *Review of Educational Research, 62*(1), 1–35.

Rogers, C., & Freiberg, H. J. (1994). *Freedom to learn* (3rd ed.). Upper Saddle River, NJ: Merrill/Prentice Hall.

Zahorik, J. A. (1995). *Constructivist teaching (Fastback 390)*. Bloomington, IN: Phi Delta Kappa Educational Foundation.

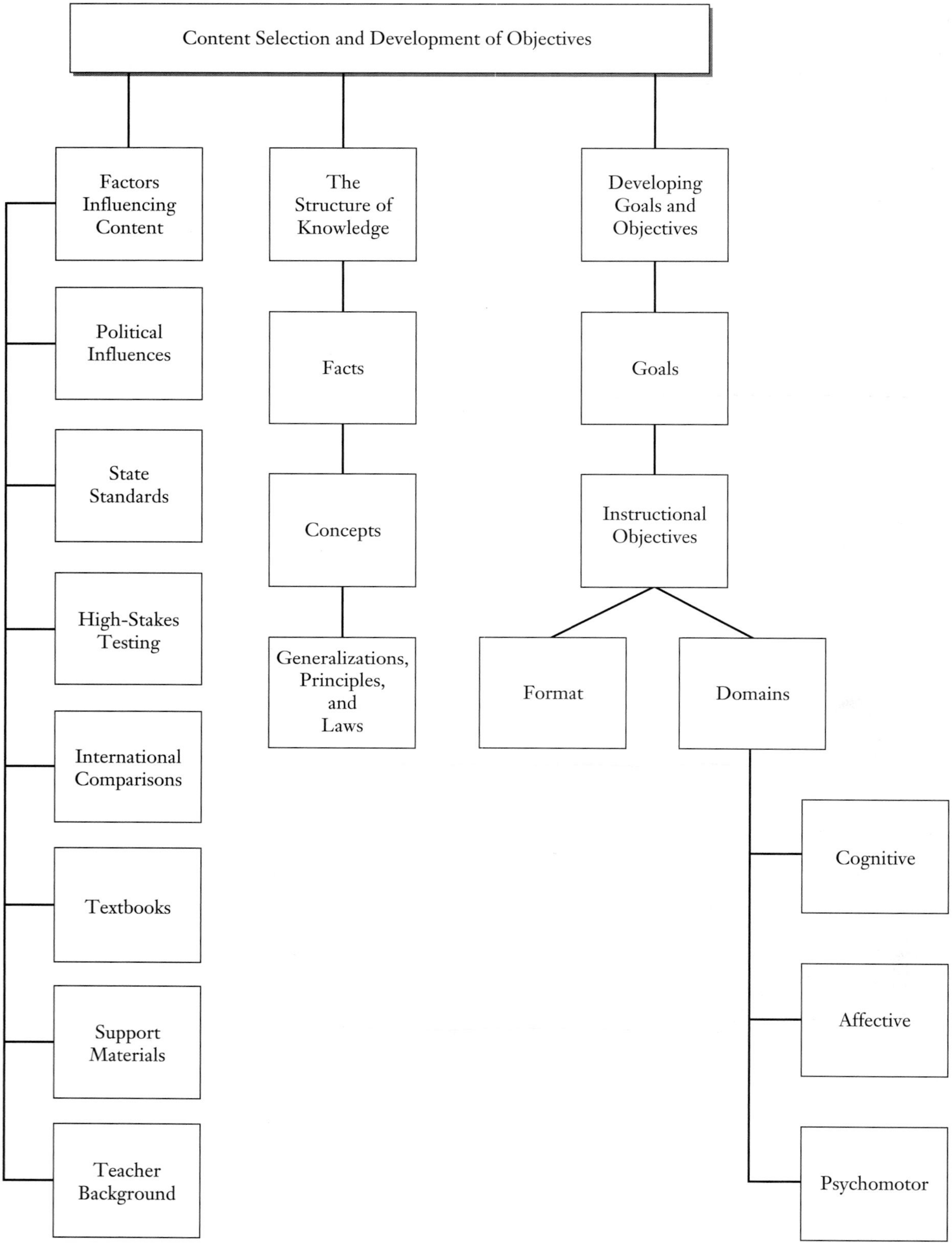

Figure 5.1
Graphic Organizer

CHAPTER 5

Content Selection and Development of Objectives

OBJECTIVES

This chapter will help you

- describe some issues you need to consider when selecting content to introduce to students;
- explain how political influences, standards, and frameworks; textbooks; availability of support materials; and teacher background influence your content selection decisions;
- state how the structure of knowledge can help you decide what content to include and exclude in your instructional programs;
- define goals and instructional objectives; and
- describe the cognitive, affective, and psychomotor domains of learning.

Introduction

Who decides what is taught in the school curriculum? What difference does it make? Should the content of the curriculum be decided by politicians? What about publishing companies? Should those who write standardized tests determine the content? We hope this chapter will give you some insight into the complex issues you will face as you select content to teach your students.

Generally, those preparing to be secondary school teachers have given little thought to the content of the curriculum. They often assume that there is a well-defined body of content to be taught about which nearly everyone agrees. In the past, the only time that the content of the curriculum came into question was when a new set of textbooks was adopted.

Historically, decisions about what should be taught in the schools have been left in the hands of state and local school district officials. The assumption was that local officials were the ones elected by the parents and were likely to be most responsive to the needs of both society and the students. However, as education has become more of a national political issue, the question of what should be included in the school curriculum has become a hotly debated topic. Much of the power to determine the curriculum has been moved from the local level to the state and national levels and has been influenced by a variety of factors.

Factors Influencing Content Selection

Political Influences

Across the nation, the battles rage. We have the history wars, the math wars, and the science wars. These are battles over the content of the curriculum, and not too long ago, such discussions seldom made it out of state- and district-level curriculum committees. However, times have changed, and the content of the school curriculum regularly makes the news. This news is usually related to standards that are developed and adopted by various professional organizations and state boards of education that define what should be taught. For example, the debate over history standards developed by a national panel reached such a peak during the presidential campaign of 1996 that Robert Dole, the Republican presidential candidate, declared that those who developed the new history standards were worse than the external enemies of the nation (Wineburg, 2001)!

Similarly, high-level and often acrimonious debates over the science curriculum are taking place in many states as they respond to calls to include "intelligent design" as an alternative theory to evolution. The situation is no different in the mathematics area as groups battle over whether the emphasis should be on problem solving and mathematical reasoning or on traditional computation and basic skills. In California, the recommendations of teachers and educators regarding the math curriculum were rejected by the state board of education in favor of programs supported by politicians (Jacob, 2001). There is no doubt about it: the school curriculum has become a hot political issue.

State Standards and Frameworks

In response to pressure from legislation such as the *No Child Left Behind Act*, most states have now adopted specific content standards that specify the content to be included in the curriculum of secondary school courses. Some local school districts have developed similar requirements and have developed curriculum documents outlining the district response to the state standards. These are legal guidelines that place limits on your decision-making authority. You are required to teach the mandated curriculum. However, you are free to go beyond that which is mandated.

It is important that you know the content standards in the state where you will teach. To view state content standards for your state, visit http://www.aligntoachieve.org. This site provides links to all state content standards documents. Alternately, you might also visit the Website maintained by your state department of education.

High-Stakes Testing

Results of standardized tests are now regularly reported in local news media and are used as indicators of school quality. Many of these are what have been termed "high-stakes tests." In other words, they are tests to which important decisions such as promotion, retention, teacher evaluation, or even the availability of resources are attached. Schools and teachers whose students score poorly on these tests may come under public criticism or even face the loss of students and money. As a result, administrators in your school district or building may urge you to think about the types of information assessed on standardized tests as you make decisions about which content to emphasize.

Popham (2001) contends that this emphasis on high-stakes testing is doing serious educational damage to students. He claims that such testing has resulted in a curricular reductionism that has eroded a rich curriculum and is robbing students of important things they should be learning. He concludes that this has led to a distortion of the intellectual fabric of the curriculum and restricts not only the content of the curriculum but also the cognitive operations of the students. When the curriculum is determined by what is tested, the decisions about the curriculum are left to those invisible and unknown individuals who write the tests (Armstrong, 2003). In addition, the tendency is to emphasize content that can be easily measured rather than that which is most important.

We by no means are suggesting that you take a purely reactive stance when confronted with a situation when standardized test scores are considered very important. It may be that the tests being used are not doing an adequate job of sampling important kinds of content. As a professional educator, you have an obligation to participate in the process of enlightening the general public about the limitations of standardized test scores. Professional educators today work for the adoption of student assessment programs that go beyond standardized testing to embrace diverse measures of student learning.

CRITICAL INCIDENT

Teaching to the Test

On a Monday afternoon, Betty Lewis waited with her math colleagues in the faculty lounge for a mathematics department meeting with Ms. Walker, the high school principal. Ms. Walker called this special meeting on short notice, and there had been a good deal of talk all day about the agenda.

When a grim-faced Ms. Walker entered the room, it became obvious that she was in no mood for pleasantries. She got right down to business:

> "We just received our standardized test scores from the state for the mathematics test our students took in the spring. Our school's average score is down 6 points from last year. To make it worse, average scores in the other high schools in the district went up. The superintendent has called me on the carpet. He was blunt. He said the scores were an embarrassment to the district and that members of the school board want to know what is wrong with our math department.
>
> "The superintendent let me know in no uncertain terms that he expects some immediate action to be taken. In response to his request, I am going to require that each of you teaching students who will be taking the test this year spend a minimum of 15 minutes in each class period drilling students on material likely to appear on the test. I have files of tests from previous years in my office. I want you to study them carefully and identify sample test items you can use to help your students practice for the test they will take in the spring. I will expect a weekly report from each teacher identifying precisely what has been done in every period to focus students' attention on content likely to be included on the standardized test."

Betty Lewis and the other teachers were stunned as they heard this announcement. One veteran teacher looked at Ms. Walker and commented, "Don't you think this policy is a somewhat drastic reaction to a 1-year dip in our students' scores? Besides, if we do what you're asking, how will we cover the required course content?"

Another teacher said, "What about our academic freedom? As certified professionals, isn't it our responsibility to teach students what we consider to be important?"

Still another teacher protested, "I question the ethics of taking items from past tests and teaching the students to respond to them correctly. This is 'teaching to the test,' not teaching students how to understand the subject matter. It seems to me this is just plain wrong."

In response to these questions, Ms. Walker said, "I hear what each of you is saying. Let me make some particular comments about the issue of ethics. I would ask you whether it is ethical for our school to be evaluated on the basis of one standardized score. That is precisely what our community is doing to us. We depend on our community for support. We may not like the game that is being played, but that is the reality we are faced with. Basically, the curriculum is what the community demands. If this means that your academic freedom sometimes has to be compromised, that is just how it is. None of us is happy about all this. But I assure you, the superintendent and board of education members are extremely concerned about the decline in our scores. If our students don't do better next year, even more drastic changes may have to be made."

■ ■ ■

How do you respond to the issue of teaching to the test to raise scores? What are pluses and minuses of this practice? What are some values expressed in Ms. Walker's comments? What values are reflected in reactions of some of the teachers? Are there ways in which these divergent views about what teachers should do might be reconciled?

What would you do if you were a member of this mathematics department? Do communities unfairly judge schools based on standardized test scores? If so, what might be done about this situation? What is the proper course of action when there is a conflict between community desires and decisions that teachers as professionals want to make?

International Comparisons of Student Achievement

Another factor fueling the debate concerning the curriculum is the result of international comparisons of student achievement. Many of the international comparisons appear to reflect poorly on the accomplishments of American students. The *Third International Mathematics and Science Study* (TIMSS) was one of the most extensive and rigorous international comparisons of student achievement ever undertaken. Data were collected on academic achievement of fourth Graders, eighth graders, and students in their last year of secondary schooling. In Grade 4, U.S. students were found to be achieving above the international average in both mathematics and science (National Center for Education Statistics, 1997). In Grade 8, students were above the international average in science but below the international average in mathematics (National Center for Education Statistics, 1996). High school seniors in the United States performed below international averages in both mathematics and science (National Center for Education Statistics, 1998).

Although the sample, the methodology, and the conclusions of the TIMSS study have been called into question, these data are still cited by many as the basis for needed changes in the school curriculum. One of the conclusions cited in the study was that as U.S. students progress through school, their performance compares less favorably with students in other countries. What explains this pattern? Some people have argued that it is a product of underfunding of education in the United States by citing that the percentage of the gross national product that goes to education in the United States is less than nearly all other industrialized nations. Others suggest that, particularly at the high school level, schools in the United States enroll a higher percentage of age-eligible young people than many other countries.

While these interpretations are clearly open to debate, there are two variables that seem to account for some of the performance differences. First, the TIMSS results revealed that a high percentage of American middle school and senior high school teachers were familiar with research-validated methodologies associated with effective mathematics and science instruction. However, relatively few of them were implementing these approaches. These techniques were found to be much more prevalent in classrooms of countries where students outscored their U.S. counterparts.

Second, the content of the curriculum, particularly the mathematics curriculum, at Grades 8 and 12 in U.S. schools was found to be less sophisticated than that in schools of many nations whose students' achievement scores were higher (National Center for Education Statistics, 1999). Some authorities argue that reports of poorer performance of U.S. students do not necessarily mean that teaching in U.S. schools is inferior. Many of these scholars have focused on a variable called "opportunity to learn" to explain lower scores of American students. Researchers who have studied opportunity to learn have concluded that student achievement tends to go up when (a) a given aspect of content is treated and (b) sufficient time is allocated for students to master this aspect of content (Good & Brophy, 2004).

The opportunity-to-learn variable provides a logical explanation for failure of American students to do as well as students in other countries on tests of comparative performance. One such study compared mathematics achievement of 11-year-olds in California and England (Barr, 1987). Students in England achieved higher scores than students in California. Close analysis of backgrounds of students who took these tests revealed that much of the achievement test focused on topics that were treated in English schools 1 or 2 years earlier than in American schools. In this case, differences in scores could be explained by content selection differences rather than by lower-quality teaching in California schools.

These international comparisons suggest that the curriculum is important. All educators need to focus on what is taught and when it is taught. Teachers have an ethical obligation to make sure that all students are provided with the opportunity to learn important content. Students cannot learn what they are not exposed to and what they are not encouraged to learn.

Textbook Selection

Teachers have long based curricula decisions on the content included in textbooks. The assumption is that the people writing textbooks and preparing curriculum guides are experts who have the knowledge to make the key content selection decisions. However, there are several factors that call this assumption into question.

First, textbooks are developed by for-profit companies. They are interested in selling the most textbooks and therefore develop books that are likely to appeal to the widest audience. The content of a book usually addresses the content standards of a few "textbook adoption" states that purchase large numbers of textbooks. In reality, the standards of different states are political documents that are derived through compromise. Thus, the political leanings of a few states may play a large role in what appears in textbooks. This may not be the best curriculum for all students.

Second, if you examine several textbooks in a subject you want to teach, don't be surprised if you find that textbook authors do not agree about the content to include or how the content should be divided and sequenced. Your examination may also uncover errors in content. Regular critiques of textbooks point out numerous errors

Reviewing resource material is useful in selecting content to be taught.

of fact as well as errors of omission. Finally, you will probably find that the individual texts vary considerably in terms of the depth of treatment given to individual topics. All these issues call into question the notion that textbooks are the best source of information for curriculum content.

Relying on the text to define the content of the curriculum for you can also lead to instructional difficulties. The characteristics and the prior knowledge of students in every class you teach will differ from the assumptions of the textbook and curriculum document writers. If your students have different prior knowledge than that assumed by the textbook writers, the students may have trouble comprehending the text or may reject the content as unimportant.

In summary, as you consider the text as a source of content, you must weigh all these issues. You must also ask yourself whether you want to place the decision making for your curriculum content in the hands of a few publishing companies and authors.

Availability of Support Materials

The availability of instructional support materials will have an influence on your content decisions. If you have to make a choice between two topics, one of which is supported by abundant learning resources other than the textbook and one of which is supported by few such materials, you may well feel compelled to select the one supported by plenty of support resources.

Though the kinds of materials available can represent a problem, you need to guard against a temptation to view instructional resources as being more limited than they really are. For example, you no longer need well-stocked school libraries to provide your students with access to large quantities of information to supplement what is provided in course textbooks. Modern computer technology, particularly the Internet, makes it possible to draw information into schools in even in the poorest and most remote locations.

Teacher Background

It is widely accepted that the teacher is the most important variable in providing quality teaching. Much attention has been paid in recent years to make sure that high school teachers have strong subject matter knowledge in the subjects they teach. For example, subject matter preparation of teachers is a key element of the *No Child Left Behind Act*. Although the freedom of teachers to make content selection decisions has been eroded somewhat in recent years with the implementation of state standards and high-stakes testing, you still have an important role to play in content selection and organization. You need to remember that you are the person closest to the students and that you are most aware of their prior knowledge, their motivations, and their academic strengths and deficiencies. While you will need to consider the standards or frameworks of your individual state, the nature of your standardized testing program, and the influence of textbooks, in the end, *you* are the one in position to make content decisions that influence what students will learn.

The focus on teachers' background raises the question of the usefulness of those college courses you completed in identifying the content that should be taught to secondary level students. How about those notes from your college courses? A nice thought, we agree, but this too is no solution. For one thing, the scope of many college and university courses is narrower than the typical secondary school course you will teach. For example, only a small portion of the content presented in a university-level comparative anatomy course is relevant for students in an introductory high school biology course. Further, the intended audience for university professors' lectures differs considerably from the students enrolled in typical secondary school classes.

Debate over the content of the curriculum is an indicator of the extent to which education has become politicized. Individuals of all political persuasions realize the importance of what is taught in school; however, many of them believe that decisions about the curriculum should not be left to the discretion of the teacher. In fact, there are some programs being adopted that call for teachers to adhere to a predetermined schedule and a script when teaching.

Your subject matter background is an important dimension in selecting content. Your background will help you prioritize the content, evaluate instructional materials, and identify important questions. The importance of your subject matter background is not just to help you select the facts and the content to be covered but also to help you know important questions to ask.

In summary, you can no longer assume that what should be taught in school is a given about which there is universal agreement. In fact, selecting the content of curriculum has become a political minefield. You need to be aware of the issues relating to the selection of content in your teaching field. The following questions might guide you as you consider these issues:

- What are the goals and objectives for teaching my subject?
- What content is best to accomplish these objectives?

MORE FROM THE WEB

Content Standards

Content standards are an important consideration when selecting content to be taught. The following sites will provide you with more information about standards.

Integrating New Technologies into the Methods of Education

This site is sponsored by the University of Northern Iowa. It provides a summary of the background of the standards movement and links to national content organizations and national content standards.

Website: http://www.intime.uni.edu/model/content/cont.html

Oregon Department of Education

This site includes content background and resources matched to Oregon content standards. The topics are organized by subject and can give you an understanding of the relationship between standards and content selection.

Website: http://www.ode.state.or.us/cifs/learning resource

- What can I do if the textbook coverage is inadequate?
- What should I do if my students can't read the textbook?
- How concerned should I be about what my students will be asked on standardized tests?

These difficult questions vex even many experienced teachers. How to select important content that is well matched to students' capabilities is one of the challenges you will face throughout your career.

Understanding the Structure of Knowledge

A beginning step in responding to the many pressures regarding curriculum content is to understand the basic structure of knowledge. Textbook writers, developers of curriculum guides, and others who attempt to organize content for instructional purposes seek to break down subject matter in a systematic manner. One approach they use derives from the work of learning theorists Jerome Bruner (1960) and Hilda Taba (1962). This structure-of-knowledge framework provides an understanding of how knowledge is organized and can help you make selections of content for your subject. It is a very useful tool for planning your units and lessons and gives you a way of evaluating and responding to the curriculum "wars."

The structure of knowledge framework is built around the relationship between specific facts and concepts that organize facts into specific categories and generalizations or principles that point out the relationship between concepts. It is based on the premise that the major focus of the curriculum should be on important concepts and generalizations rather than the acquisition of a body of facts.

There are three types of information in the structure of knowledge:

- Facts
- Concepts
- Generalizations, principles, and laws

Facts

Facts refer to a specific circumstance or situation. They have limited transfer or explanatory power. For example, that Mexico City has more people than New York City is an interesting fact. It might suggest a reason for asking your students to seek an answer to a question such as "Why has Mexico City grown so large?" However, simply knowing this fact does not help a person understand the general reasons why cities grow or the economic, political, and social problems of cities. The real value of facts is that they can stimulate questions and hypotheses or can be used to verify hypotheses. In essence, they provide concrete examples around which concepts and generalizations can be formed.

Appropriate selection of facts has long been an issue of concern to curriculum developers. Curriculum specialist John Jarolimek (1990) recommended that in planning instruction, you should select from among these three types of facts:

- Facts that are likely to remain important over a long period of time
- Facts used frequently in everyday living
- Facts needed to develop or elaborate on important ideas and generalizations

The basic point is that facts do have some value. As teachers, we should recognize that there are some facts that need to be included in the curriculum. However, just the attainment of facts does not mean that a person will be "knowledgeable" and can use their knowledge base to understand and respond to new situations. Therefore, the facts that are included in the curriculum need to be chosen for a specific purpose.

Concepts

Concepts are major ideas or categories that help organize information. They are often defined as terms or phrases that denote a category of items with common characteristics. For example, the term "mammal" defines a classification of animals that have common characteristics making them different from "reptiles." The phrase "division of labor" defines an economic or organizational scheme that has certain characteristics regardless of the setting. Therefore, concepts have wide transfer value. This means that a concept, once learned, can be applied to understanding new situations.

The defining characteristics of a concept are called attributes. Less complex and simpler-to-learn concepts have relatively few attributes. However, an abstract concept such as "democracy" has a large number of attributes.

The fewer the number of attributes and the more concrete a concept is, the easier it is for students to learn. More complex concepts require more teaching time than less complex concepts. Thus, a simple concept, such as "*triangle*," with very few well-defined attributes that can be illustrated using concrete examples, might be learned quickly. However, a complex concept like "*democracy*" might require several lessons.

Bruner (1960) stated that any child at any stage of development could learn concepts. He saw differences in learning as based on the "concreteness" of the concept, not on the ability to see relationships that form the foundation of concept learning. Younger children or those with little previous experience in a subject need to begin with concepts that have relatively few attributes and that can be illustrated using concrete examples. Additional attributes can be added and more abstract applications made as the student learns. Therefore, teaching a complex concept like "democracy" to novice learners requires that they begin by encountering very concrete and relatively simple examples of this form of government.

Concepts are wonderful intellectual tools. Once they have been learned, they help us quickly relate new learning to previous learning. For example, there are hundreds of breeds of dogs. These are animals of various sizes, shapes, and colors. However, they all share certain attributes that distinguish them from cats or other animals. Thus, once the critical attributes are understood, an encounter with a dog we have never seen before helps us quickly place the animal in the appropriate category and provides us with a large measure of understanding about that specific animal and what we might expect or predict. We are spared the intellectual task of learning a whole new range of facts and information. Similarly, a person who understands the major concepts of economics, such as supply, demand, market, transportation, and division of labor, can enter an entirely new business and in a relatively short time understand the business.

Because of their ability to transfer to a wide variety of new situations and because they form the foundation of a subject, the major concepts of a given subject should be a major emphasis in the curriculum. Thus, in selecting content for the curriculum, considerable thought needs to be given to identifying the key concepts of the subject.

This is where your content background and the notes from your college courses might be useful. You might want to review your notes, not for specific facts but in order to identify the key concepts that form the foundation for the subject and that have wide application and transfer.

Similarly, textbooks frequently identify what the authors believe are the central concepts by highlighting them or including them in vocabulary lists. The information they include in the chapter is usually intended to illustrate or develop these key concepts.

Understanding that teaching key concepts is an important focus and that most textbooks are written to try to explain concepts can be very useful. Once you have identified the key concepts, if students are having difficulty with the text, you can think about alternative ways of presenting the concepts that might be more interesting and compatible for your students. Students who are not interested in a particular topic and therefore are not motivated might be energized by learning the key concept in a context that does interest them.

Concepts are organized in the mind into a hierarchy, or schema, that individuals use to store and retrieve information. Some concepts, such as "reptile," are broad terms that help organize vast quantities of subordinate information. These large-scale concepts help organize more narrow, related concepts, such as snake, turtle, and lizard, which are much limited in scope. Awareness of concept hierarchies and the connections between broad and related, narrower concepts can help you plan and sequence material for students.

Generalizations, Principles, and Laws

The next level of the structure of knowledge goes by several names, including generalizations, principles, and laws. Though they represent a common content type, there are some differences among these types. In general, laws and principles are based on somewhat stronger evidence and are more universally applicable than generalizations. Some academic disciplines tend to use one of these terms more frequently than others. For example, there are many laws in physics. Findings of social scientists often are reported as generalizations. Specialists in art and music often cite principles of composition.

Wiggins and McTighe (1998) labeled this level of knowledge "enduring understandings." They define this type of knowledge as understandings that go beyond discrete facts or skills and that are applicable to new situations. Therefore, this level of learning has great transfer value that crosses time and place boundaries. If something applies to just one specific instance or place, then it is not a generalization or an enduring understanding.

Generalizations, principles, and laws are statements that summarize the relationship between two or more concepts. Often, the generalizations will have an "if-then" dimension. In other words, the statement will state that if A happens, then B will be found. To give you a feel for the nature of generalizations or principles, the following are some examples drawn from a variety of subject areas. You might try to identify those with an "if-then" characteristic:

- Inherited characteristics of living organisms do not occur randomly; rather, they follow predictable patterns.
- Increased specialization in production leads to interdependence among individuals, communities, states, and nations.
- Descending temperatures result in contraction of objects; ascending temperatures result in expansion of objects.
- Areas and perimeter measurements of polygons do not occur in a random pattern; they can be determined by computations involving linear and angle measurements.
- Compositions of chemical compounds follow predictable patterns that can be discerned through the application of appropriate analytical procedures.
- A force equal to the weight of the dispersed fluid buoys up a body immersed in a fluid.
- Because natural resources are limited and human wants are unlimited, every society has developed a method for allocating scarce resources.
- Different moods of paintings featuring common subjects and symbols result from differences in the sensory and compositional features of the individual work.

In any given subject, there are a limited number of key generalizations or principles that summarize the knowledge in the field and that provide the impetus for new research. A person who is considered an "expert" in a subject is one who has clear understanding of the major generalizations or principles in the subject. For example, a psychology professor stated that in child growth and development, there were only about 25 to 30 basic principles or generalizations. If these principles are clearly understood, a person would have a very solid understanding of child growth and development.

Scholars doing pioneering work in their individual specialties constantly challenge existing generalizations, principles, and laws. Therefore, they should not be introduced to students as definitive answers. Your students need to understand that the search for new knowledge continues and that many of them can look forward to active participation in this exciting process.

Because generalizations, principles, and laws summarize the content of a subject and organize tremendous quantities of information, they function well as content organizers. These broad explanatory statements encourage students to place facts in context and to recognize the importance of understanding relationships among concepts.

Since generalizations, principles, and laws describe relationships among concepts, students must grasp the concepts before generalizations, principles, and laws can be understood. Consider this social science generalization:

As a society becomes more educated and industrialized, its birthrate declines.

If your students are unfamiliar with the concepts of society, education, industrialization, and birthrate, this generalization will make little sense. You have to ensure that your students understand the concepts related to the generalizations you select as a focus for your teaching.

Again, your academic preparation and those class notes can help you select the content to be taught by assisting you in identifying important generalizations or principles that are central to the subject you are teaching. Unfortunately, this may require some digging on your part. Too often, college-level instructors tend to fill lectures and tests with facts. As students strive to pass the course, they tend to focus on the facts and may miss the basic principles or generalizations. You may have to step back from the specific content of your notes and ask yourself, "What is the main idea?" "What does this specific information illustrate?"

Textbooks are often written with a generalization in mind. However, textbooks are often less specific in identifying generalizations than they are about identifying the concepts. You can usually identify the key generalizations that formed the foundation for the textbook by reading the material and asking yourself, "What are the main ideas or relationships that are being discussed?"

The structure of knowledge can help you evaluate and respond to the curriculum wars. For example, during the controversy over the history standards, critics of the standards claimed that the new standards were flawed because they did not include certain facts. One such assertion was that the standards did not call for students to know that George Washington was the first president of the United States. However, the developers of the standards pointed out that the new standards asked students to examine major issues confronting the new nation during this era. This would certainly require them to know that Washington was the president (Wineburg, 2001). In other words, the critics of the standards were looking for the inclusion of specific facts, whereas the developers were focusing more on concepts and generalizations. Too often, the curriculum wars have become battles over which set of facts to teach rather than on what concepts and big ideas should be learned.

Understanding the structure of knowledge can help you become a creative teacher. When you understand that concepts and generalizations rather than specific facts are the focus, you can begin to brainstorm different ways and different content selections that you can use to teach them. If you are teaching in Wyoming, you might choose different examples for teaching the concepts than someone in Chicago. However, in both places the key concepts and generalizations could be the same. In addition, when students have difficulty, you don't need to get caught in the trap of just having students review the same set of facts over and over in hopes that they will somehow now remember them. You can provide them with alternative examples that might be more understandable to them.

When presented with the structure of knowledge, one of the first questions asked by teachers focuses on the issue of testing. Teachers understand the wisdom of focusing on concepts and generalizations, but they point out that standardized tests tend to focus on facts. There is some truth to this assertion, although good tests will try to measure the understanding of concepts and principles. Another strong argument for focusing on concepts and generalizations is that research indicates that individuals begin forgetting facts in a matter of minutes unless those facts are tied to something meaningful. Concepts and generalizations can help make facts more meaningful and therefore enhance retention. In addition, understanding the key concepts and generalizations can often help someone figure out the correct answer when confronted with a new question.

It could be argued that the priorities of those who are interested in improving student achievement have been misdirected. Rather than spending more time on drilling students with factual content that will soon be forgotten and often will need to be retaught, spend time on making the facts meaningful. If you do this, you will enhance retention, and students will ultimately need less time to learn.

Some teachers have found that focusing on concepts and generalizations during the year with a week or two of review of basic facts is an effective strategy for preparing students to take standardized tests.

Developing Goals and Instructional Objectives

Once you have identified the content to be taught in your classroom, you need to identify your learning outcomes, or what the students should know as a result of your teaching. The learning outcomes take the form of goals and objectives.

Goals

Goals are broad statements that identify what students should learn as a consequence of their exposure to the content. Goals often address the "why" question. If you are teaching students a semester course in biology, why should they learn this content? What do you expect them to know when they have completed the course? The goals might be focused on students understanding and applying the key concepts and generalizations or principles. Other goals might include skills and attitudes you hope the students will acquire as a result of your instruction.

For example, a goal in the skills area might be that the student can identify and use resources on the Internet or in the library or can give an oral presentation on a topic. An attitude goal might be that the student will develop a positive attitude toward the subject and will be motivated to further study.

In summary, goals are the broad purpose statements that give you a sense of direction and focus and help you select the content and plan lessons for a unit of study. However, they tend to be somewhat abstract and offer you little day-to-day guidance.

Instructional Objectives

Instructional objectives are specific statements that focus on the daily outcomes of your teaching. They are narrow purpose statements that focus on what students will learn as a result of a given lesson. The basic question you need to ask each day as you prepare your lessons is, "What should students be able to do as a result of this lesson?"

In districts with well-developed curriculum guides, new teachers sometimes find that major course topics, generalizations, and concepts have been identified for them. Only rarely, though, are teachers provided with preestablished lists of instructional objectives. Typically, teachers write these themselves.

A well-written objective identifies a specific, observable student behavior that will be an indicator that the student has learned. This behavior should be one that builds student competence toward a broader goal. No specific number of instructional objectives is right or correct for a given goal statement. You must exercise your own judgment in this matter.

Instructional objectives help you in two ways. First, they serve as guideposts for instructional planning. Once a set of instructional objectives for a given unit of work has been prepared, subsequent instructional planning ties to these objectives. For example, selection of instructional materials is influenced by the expectations of student learning stated in the objectives. If a film has potential to help students grasp understandings associated with an objective, a good case can be made for including it in the instructional sequence. If the film has little relationship to the objectives, then you have a basis for eliminating it from further consideration. For example, we can remember some teachers who would order films that had no relationship to the objectives. They were selected because the teacher liked them or because they would serve as a "filler" so that the teacher would not have to plan a lesson. This is professionally irresponsible and is a waste of valuable instructional time.

A second advantage that instructional objectives provide teachers is associated with student learning. The use of instructional objectives helps you to be organized and purposeful. There is less confusion about your expectations. This is particularly true when you share instructional objectives with students and make sure they understand what it is they are supposed to be learning (Good & Brophy, 2004).

Development of instructional objectives is a key step in the planning process. It is preceded by identification of topics, concepts, generalizations, and goals. After instructional objectives have been prepared, use them as reference points as you make decisions about instructional techniques, learning materials, evaluation, and other elements. These planning "parts" often are gathered together into systematic instructional units.

An illustration of the relationship of instructional objectives to major concepts, a generalization, a goal, and a topic is presented in Box 5.1. Note the effort to ensure that identified major concepts have been referenced in at least one instructional objective.

BOX 5.1 The Relationship Between Learning Objectives and the Structure of Knowledge

Topic: Solving Equations

General Goal:

Students will understand the relationship that exists between multiplication and addition as they are exposed to methods for applying this relationship to solving equations.

Generalization:

The distributive principle states that the product resulting from the multiplication of a given number and the sum of two others equals the product of this given number multiplied by the first of these two numbers plus the product of this given number multiplied by the second of these two numbers. Algebraically, the equality suggested by the distributive principle is depicted as follows:

$$a \times (b + c) = (a \times b) + (a \times c)$$

Major Concepts

- Simplification
- Equation
- Addition process
- Subtraction process
- Multiplication process
- Division process
- Distributive principle

Instructional Objectives

1. Each student will respond correctly to 8 of 10 true/false questions related to the nature of the distributive principle.
2. Each student will solve correctly at least 7 of 10 equations requiring them to use a combination of the addition and multiplication processes.
3. Each student will solve correctly at least 11 of 14 problem equations requiring the use of combinations of the addition, subtraction, multiplication, and division processes.

A Format for Preparing Instructional Objectives Of the many formats available for preparing instructional objectives, one we have used for some time is the ABCD format. This scheme presumes that a complete instructional objective includes four elements. Reference must be made in the objective to the audience (A) to be served, to the behavior (B) to be taken as an indicator of appropriate learning, to the condition (C) under which this behavior is measured (e.g., kind of assessment procedure to be used), and to the degree (D) of competency to be demonstrated before mastery of the objective is assumed. In the next sections, we will look at these components of a complete instructional objective one at a time.

A* = *Audience The A component of an instructional objective identifies the person or persons to whom the instructional objective is directed. Some individuals leave out this dimension of the objective. We like to include it because it identifies the nature of the individuals who are to be involved in learning. This is especially useful if instruction has been differentiated in the classroom so that different students might be working on different objectives. It can also be useful when other teachers are considering using a teaching approach. The definition of the audience can help them determine if this objective would be appropriate for their class. The audience for a particular objective could be an entire class of students, a group even larger than a class, a small group of students, or even a single student.

Typically, the audience component of an instructional objective will appear as indicated in the following examples:

"Each student will . . ."

"The literature circle group will . . ."

"All students in fourth period U.S. history will . . ."

"Joanne Smith will . . ."

B* = *Behavior The B component of an instructional objective describes the observable performance that will be taken as an indicator that learning has taken place. This is the heart of an objective. The behavior in an instructional objective must be described in observable terms. This suggests a need to select verbs that describe performance in precise and specific ways and a need to avoid verbs that describe less readily observable kinds of phenomena. To illustrate this distinction, consider the following choices:

"Each student will appreciate foreign policy differences of the Republican and Democratic presidential candidates by . . ."

"Each student will describe foreign policy differences of the Republican and Democratic presidential candidates by . . ."

In the first example, it is unclear to both the teacher and the student what kind of behavior will be taken as evidence that mastery has occurred. It is not clear what kind of performance signals "appreciation." A student, given an instructional objective with a behavior statement of this kind, might well be confused as to how he or she should study the material.

The use of the verb "describe" in the second option is much more precise. "Describe" suggests a behavior that is much more observable and specific than does "appreciate." A student presented with an instructional objective calling on him or her to describe foreign policy differences can expect to be assessed on his or her ability to

BOX 5.2 Kinds of Verbs Suitable for the Behavior Component of an Instructional Objective

What Do You Think?

Below is a list of verbs that might be used in writing instructional objectives. Look at the list. Identify those verbs that (a) you think would be suitable for use in an instructional objective and that (b) you do not think would be suitable for use in an instructional objective. Be prepared to defend your decisions.

compute	apply	appreciate	understand
describe	conjecture	comprehend	note
select	solve	demonstrate	judge

provide some clear indication of a familiarity with key policy points of each candidate. The use of the verb "describe" in the instructional objective suggests to students a need to study carefully specific positions of each candidate. It is true that the verb "appreciate" might suggest a similar activity to some students. But the meaning of "appreciate" is much less precise than "describe." For example, some students might take the "each student will appreciate" directive to mean that they are to do nothing beyond developing a general knowledge that, indeed, both candidates have differing foreign policy views. For a student who had this impression, there would be no deeply felt need to become thoroughly familiar with foreign policy positions of each candidate.

In summary, a good deal of ambiguity is removed when verbs used in the behavior component of an instructional objective reference a relatively specific and an observable kind of student performance (see Box 5.2).

The following fragments of complete instructional objectives indicate how the behavior component might look:

- Cite specific examples of . . .
- Describe characteristics of . . .
- Distinguish between . . .
- Name . . .
- List . . .
- Demonstrate . . .

C* = *Condition The C component of an instructional objective describes the condition of assessment. That is, under what condition will the student demonstrate the behavior? Will the student demonstrate the behavior using notes? Will students have to perform something from memory? Will they be expected to demonstrate the behavior under different conditions? For example, students might be able to correctly select the right response on a multiple-choice question when there are only four choices, but can they actually apply the information when not being prompted to do so?

In some instances, the condition might be responding to a formal test of some kind. In other instances, a less formal procedure may be described. The condition component conveys to the student information regarding how his or her learning will be assessed at the conclusion of the instructional sequence. Typically, the C component of an instructional objective will appear as indicated in the following examples:

- During an oral presentation
- During an open-book test
- On a multiple-choice examination
- On a project completed by a small group
- On a formal paper, 6 to 10 pages in length, footnoted properly
- During a game situation

D* = *Degree The D component of an instructional objective details the minimum level of proficiency that will be acceptable as evidence that the objective has been achieved. The basic question that needs to be asked here is, "How proficient does the student need to be?" You might expect students just learning the content to perform tasks at a lower level of proficiency than more advanced students. Some tasks require a higher level of proficiency than others. For example, you might require that someone learning basic mathematical operations perform the operation correctly nearly every time so that he or she will be able to continue with more advanced operations. However, a social studies teacher might not require that a student identify the causes of the Civil War with 100% accuracy since this knowledge is not critical for additional learning, and individuals still argue about the causes of the Civil War.

You can establish the degree or the proficiency level using several different methods. One is to indicate the percentage of the total number of items on an assignment or test that must be responded to correctly. Clearly, this procedure does not work for all tasks. On some tasks or assignments, such as an essay item, the degree frequently might include the number of points made in the essay or the number of errors in the essay.

There is a good deal of teacher artistry involved in describing the degree of competence a student must demonstrate as minimal evidence a given objective has been achieved. Establishing a proficiency level is a matter of professional judgment. It should be based on the nature of the content you are teaching as well as the prior knowledge and success of the students. In addition, as you gain experience, you will gain additional insight into proficiency levels that are appropriate for students.

Typically, the D component of an instructional objective will appear somewhat as indicated in the following examples:

- Show correct form on at least 8 of 10 . . .
- In an essay in which specific references are made to (a) motivations for immigration, (b) domestic resistance to immigration, and (c) psychic rewards of immigration . . .
- Answer correctly 85% of the items on a quiz
- Will have fewer than five mistakes

Putting It All Together: The ABCD Format

Recall that all complete instructional objectives include references to A, the audience; B, the behavior; C, the condition; and D, the degree.

A couple of instructional objectives are listed here. Individual components of each objective have been underlined and labeled:

A B D C

1. Each student (A) will solve (B) 8 of 10 problems on a weekly quiz (D) featuring questions about right triangles. (C)

A C B D

2. The Swedish immigration group, (A) in an oral presentation to the class, (C) will cite (B) at least five reasons supporting and five reasons opposing 19th-century Swedish migration to the American South. (D)

Note that the ABCD components may appear in a variety of orders. The order is not critical. What is important is that all four be considered when writing an objective.

In summary, the ABCD format is an easily learned procedure. Instructional objectives containing all four components are capable of conveying a good deal of information to students about a teacher's expectations. For the teacher, they provide a reminder to keep instruction on track in such a way that learning experiences provided will clearly be consistent with the kinds of expectations reflected in the assessment procedures followed at the conclusion of a given instructional sequence.

Domains of Instructional Objectives For some years now, educational outcomes have been divided into three basic categories or "domains": (a) the cognitive domain, (b) the affective domain, and (c) the psychomotor domain. In very general terms, the cognitive domain includes what we might call academic or intellectual kinds of learning. The affective domain includes learning related to values, beliefs, and attitudes. The psychomotor domain includes learning related to the sensorimotor system and fine- and large-muscle control. See Box 5.3 for samples of objectives for each domain.

Because the general area of concern of each domain has certain unique features, it is not surprising that instructional objectives in each domain tend to be organized in slightly different ways and to be directed toward different purposes. In the sections that follow, some of these differences are introduced.

Instructional Objectives in the Cognitive Domain The cognitive domain is concerned with rational, systematic, or intellectual thinking. When we think about subject matter content and our expectation that students will learn it, we have in mind the cognitive domain. The organization of objectives in the cognitive domain stems from the work of Benjamin Bloom and others who, in the mid-1950s, set about the task of developing a system for identifying categories of learning. Out of their deliberations came a groundbreaking educational document, *Taxonomy of Educational Objectives: Handbook I: The Cognitive Domain* (Bloom, 1956). Commonly referred to as "Bloom's taxonomy," this document suggested that there exists a six-step hierarchy of thinking ranging from the most elemental thinking processes to the most sophisticated.

BOX 5.3 Samples of Instructional Objectives

The following are some sample instructional objectives relating to the different domains of learning.

Cognitive Domain

Comprehension

Each student will provide literal translation from Spanish to English for 10 sentences making no errors in at least 8 of the sentences.

Application

Using a tape measure and a 22-inch globe, ninth-grade geography students will correctly compute the distances between 10 pairs of world cities with less than a 50-mile error allowance.

Evaluation

Each student will compare, contrast, and critique the plays of Racine and Corneille in terms of their adherence to the "rules" of classical drama.

Affective Domain

Receiving

When opportunities develop, students will seek additional information on a controversial political issue.

Valuing

Students who take a stand on an environmental issue will demonstrate a commitment to that issue by joining an environmental organization, spending time volunteering, or making a monetary contribution to an organization furthering that issue.

Organization

Each social studies student will identify at least two value priorities that were given precedence over others by the signers of the Declaration of Independence.

Psychomotor Domain

Awareness

Each student will describe to the teacher the correct finger placement on a violin for chord named by the teacher.

Performance of Individual Components

In front of the instructor, each student will demonstrate with 100% accuracy the proper body posture and the steps for a beginning dive.

Integration

Each art student with no assistance from another person will raise a clay pot of at least 8 inches using the potter's wheel.

Ordered in terms from simplest to most complex, the elements of Bloom's taxonomy are as follows:

1. Knowledge
2. Comprehension
3. Application
4. Analysis
5. Synthesis
6. Evaluation

For teachers, proposed learning experiences can be categorized by comparing their intellectual complexity with the types of thinking referenced in Bloom's taxonomy. In general, a task demanding "knowledge-level" performance requires a different type of thinking, often considered "low level," than a "synthesis-level" task that is considered "high level." In thinking about instructional planning, teachers find it useful to know something about the kinds of thinking implied by each level of the taxonomy. When they have made a decision regarding the kinds of intellectual demands they wish to include in their program, they then need to prepare instructional objectives that are clearly directed toward encouraging student performance at the targeted taxonomical level (knowledge, comprehension, application, analysis, synthesis, and evaluation). Let us look briefly at characteristics of each level of the taxonomy.

Knowledge Knowledge is defined as the recall of a piece of previously learned information. The recall might involve a wide range of material, including the recall of a specific fact or the recall of a whole theory or complex operation. However, regardless of the complexity of the recall, all that is required is bringing to mind the relevant information. The student is not required to do anything with the information. No manipulation or interpretation is required. The knowledge level is usually considered the lowest level of learning outcomes in the cognitive domain.

Comprehension Comprehension is a slightly more complex mental operation than knowledge. Comprehension refers to what many call "understanding." Comprehension is defined as the ability to understand the meaning of the material. Demonstrating that understanding might be shown by translating the information from one form to another, explaining or summarizing the information, or predicting the consequences of future effects. Comprehension requires that the student do something with the material. Therefore, it is more complex than the knowledge level.

Application Application refers to the ability to use learned material in a new situation. This is really one of the primary goals of all education. We expect the students to be able to apply what they learn in school to new situations they encounter in the world outside the classroom. The application might include the application of such things as methods, concepts, generalizations, and theories. The application level is considered more complex than comprehension because it involves knowing the material well enough to know when and to what situations the information can be applied.

Analysis Analysis requires students to understand the composition of the material well enough that the component parts and the organizational structure are understood. This might include identifying the various parts of something and the relationship between the parts. The analysis category is considered "higher-level thinking" because it does require that the student perform some manipulation of the material and to go beyond surface features, such as facts, to get to the underlying structure of the material.

Synthesis Synthesis requires students to take a number of separate pieces of information and combine them to create knowledge that is new (or, more accurately, knowledge that is new to the student). Synthesis is often viewed as one of the central thinking processes in creativity. This level might include production of something new and unique, like a theme or a speech. Synthesis is considered more complex than analysis because it involves not just understanding the underlying structure of something but also rearranging structure to create a new pattern or a new structure.

Evaluation Evaluation is the ability to judge the value or worth of something. This level does not just call for opinions. At this level, students are called on to make judgments in light of clearly identified criteria. The criteria for the judgment might come from the student or be given to them. To be at the evaluation level, it is essential for both the element of judgment and the element of established criteria to be present. Evaluation never calls on students to engage in simplistic sharing of unsupported personal opinion.

Instructional Objectives in the Affective Domain The affective domain, as noted previously, concerns people's values, feelings, and attitudes. Clearly, in schools we are concerned about the total development of our students, not just with their mastery of academic content. Therefore, we need to consider the issue of students' values, feelings, and attitudes as the instructional planning process goes forward.

One framework that has been used to classify objectives in the affective domain is a companion piece to *Bloom's taxonomy*. This is the *Taxonomy of Educational Objectives: Handbook II: Affective Domain* (Krathwohl, Bloom, & Masia, 1964). This taxonomy was developed on a continuum relating to the internalization of an attitude or a belief. It begins with the level of simply being aware of an issue or phenomenon to the place that the value or belief becomes a part of the individual's outlook on life.

The affective taxonomy identified five levels according to the level of internalization:

1. Receiving (or attending to something)
2. Responding
3. Valuing
4. Organization
5. Characterization by a value or a value complex

Receiving (Attending) Receiving refers to the willingness of a student to attend to a particular stimulus. Individuals cannot begin internalizing a value unless they are first willing to attend to something new. For teachers, this is the task of getting or directing the student's attention. Receiving might range from just an awareness that something exists to selective attention on the part of the student. For example, it might be getting them to attend to a book, a music selection, or a value position that may be different from their own. Receiving does not require any overt response on the part of the student other than attending to something. Receiving is the lowest level of the affective domain.

Responding The next step in the internalization process requires that the student have some active participation. At this level, the person is not only attending to a phenomenon but also reacting in some way. For example, if we were interested in developing student interest in reading literature, at this level the student would respond by actually reading a piece of literature.

Valuing At this level, the student has moved beyond just being aware of something or engaging in some form of active participation. The student attaches some worth or value to a particular object, activity, or behavior. At this level, we would expect the student's overt behavior to demonstrate internalization of the value. For example, they would choose to spend their time, energy, or money to further their interest.

Organization Once individuals have attached value to something, they then need to bring together different values, reconcile conflicts between values, and develop a hierarchy of values. In other words, they need to organize an internally consistent value system. This is a complex and sophisticated task that requires analyzing, comparing, and synthesizing values.

Characterization by a Value or a Value System The highest level of internalization of a value is when values have become so ingrained that they influence behavior in ways that others can see. The behavior is so pervasive and consistent that others can identify what the individual values or believes. In contemporary jargon, this individual doesn't just talk but also "walks the walk."

It is best to view the cognitive and the affective domains together. There are several ways they overlap. Success in the affective area often associates with success in the cognitive area; in other words, students who like and feel good about what they are doing in school tend to do better in their academic courses than do those who are unhappy in school. Those students who have developed a clear value are more likely to be motivated and pursue additional cognitive learning in the area.

Teachers who demonstrate concern for students' values, feelings, and attitudes direct their energies toward helping students develop an emotional as well as an intellectual dimension to what they are learning in school. The goal of supporting each student's growth toward self-confident and mature adulthood is consistent with an instructional program that makes heavy cognitive demands on students. The critical variable is not the difficulty of the work but, rather, whether the instructional system has been designed in such a way that each youngster has a realistic chance for success. As long as students feel that they are succeeding, their attitudes toward school and the teacher generally will remain positive. Success in academic work can itself be an important contributor to students' developing sense of self-worth.

The affective domain involves all areas in which the general emphasis is on values, attitudes, and feelings. But when planning instructional objectives, there are some special concerns.

Recall that instructional objectives identify observable student behaviors. This aspect of objectives can be something of a problem when we are dealing with the affective area. There is a heavy-handed, possibly authoritarian ring to the suggestion that a given instructional program is dedicated to shaping students' values in a given way. Certainly in a society that values open discussion and democratic decision making, we have no business establishing instructional objectives that seem to say to students that certain values, attitudes, and feelings are right whereas others are wrong. A teacher who tries to do this is asking for trouble.

When developing instructional objectives in the affective domain, we must ask ourselves this question: "In what area(s) do teachers have a legitimate need to know about students' values, attitudes, and feelings?" Perhaps there are several answers to this question. But the one that has always made the most sense to us is that teachers have a need to know how students are feeling about the instruction to which they are being exposed. For example, do they like the topics selected? How do they feel about the various school subjects? If we accept the premise that students who feel disposed toward what is going on in their classes will do better in those classes and, hence, may grow in terms of their own feelings of competence and self-worth, then we have every reason to make some deliberate efforts to gather information that will tell us something about these kinds of student feelings.

Instructional Objectives in the Psychomotor Domain The psychomotor domain includes behaviors that require coordination of the body's muscular system. Specific behaviors in this area can range from activities such as running that require intensive use of large muscles to precision-drawing activities that require good control of the body's fine-muscle systems. The degree to which an individual teacher may have a need for instructional objectives in the psychomotor domain depends on the extent to which intended learning outcomes require students to demonstrate motor control (control of the body's muscular systems).

Even though the psychomotor domain has received less attention than the cognitive and the affective domain, there have been several attempts to define it. The framework that we have used successfully contains four stages:

1. Awareness
2. Performance of individual components
3. Integration
4. Free practice

Awareness The simplest of these stages is the level of awareness. Somewhat akin to the cognitive level of knowledge, awareness demands only that a student be able to describe correctly the movements that need to be made to properly complete a muscular activity.

Performance of Individual Components At level 2, the student is able to correctly demonstrate individual parts of a complex muscular activity.

Integration At level 3, the level of integration, the student can perform the entire muscular activity, including all necessary components, with some teacher guidance.

Free Practice Finally, at level 4, the student can perform the muscular activity correctly, in numerous settings, and without any prompting from the teacher. In general, students who achieve level 4 psychomotor objectives can be thought of as having complete mastery of the targeted muscular behavior.

FOR YOUR PORTFOLIO

Knowledge of content standards, the content you will teach, and the ability to write objectives are often topics that are discussed in job interviews. In addition, INTASC Standard 1 states that the professional educator understands the central concepts, tools of inquiry, and the structures of subjects taught. Therefore, this chapter provides key information about materials you should select for inclusion in your portfolio.

1. Select up to three items to be included in your portfolio. Develop a rationale explaining your reasons for including these specific items and how they relate to INTASC Standard 1.
2. What materials can you include in your portfolio that will demonstrate your understanding of the central concepts of your subject? How can you display these materials so that you clearly communicate your understanding to others?
3. What can you include in your portfolio that illustrates your understanding of the content standards in your content area?

Teachers who wish to prepare objectives in this area need good diagnostic information about students' levels of psychomotor development. If students are asked to perform at levels that are far in excess of their ability levels, many will refuse to try out of a belief that they are "beaten before they start."

In summary, developing your curriculum requires that you identify the content that you will be teaching and your learning targets. Your learning targets include long-term goals and short-term objectives. Your instructional objectives should include aspects of both the cognitive and the affective domain and, where appropriate, the psychomotor domain. It is also important to understand the hierarchy of levels in each of these domains so that students are provided with instruction that goes beyond the lowest levels of learning.

KEY IDEAS IN SUMMARY

- The content of what is taught in schools has been the focus of intense debate in recent years. Far from being a topic about which there is general agreement, a variety of forces are shaping what is being taught in the schools.
- Some of the key forces shaping the curriculum are standardized tests and state standards. These are replacing the textbook and teacher decisions about what should be taught.
- Selection of course content for a given group of students should start with an understanding of the structure of knowledge. The structure of knowledge consists of three levels: facts, concepts, and generalizations. A major focus of instruction should be on learning the major concepts and the key generalizations of a subject rather than just on the acquisition of facts.
- Once decisions have been made about the content to be taught, instructional targets need to be developed. Goals are long-range targets that state what students should learn over an extended period of time. Instructional objectives are specific statements of observable student behaviors that are the focus of an individual lesson.
- Well-written instructional objectives help teachers focus on what they are teaching and serve as indicators that learning has occurred. They are useful to students because they clearly communicate learning expectations and what they will be expected to do. Four dimensions can be addressed in writing clear instructional objectives: the audience, the behavior, the conditions, and the degree of learning.
- There are three domains of learning that should be considered when selecting content and developing goals and objectives: cognitive, affective, and psychomotor. Each of these domains is organized into different levels, moving from simple to more complex behaviors.

LEARNING EXTENSIONS

1. Obtain a current textbook in your subject area. Analyze its content. Is the content consistent with what you think should be taught? Can you identify the key concepts and generalizations? In general, how could the content selection and sequencing be improved? Present your reactions to your instructor in a short paper.
2. Obtain the content standards developed by the national organization in your content field and the content standards adopted in your state. Perform a content

analysis of the two documents and identify the differences and similarities between the two sets of standards. Compare these standards to the content included in the textbook you selected.

3. Interview a secondary school teacher about how he or she selects specific content to be taught. Ask this teacher whether he or she places more emphasis on certain topics than others and, if so, why. Ask how standardized testing has impacted the content selection decisions of the teacher.
4. Select some content that you would like to teach. Write some instructional objectives for that content, including at least three different levels of the taxonomy in at least two of the domains.

REFERENCES

Armstrong, D. G. (2003). *Curriculum today*. Upper Saddle River, NJ: Merrill/Prentice Hall.

Barr, R. (1987). Content coverage. In M. Dunkin (Ed.), *The international encyclopedia of teaching and teacher education* (pp. 364–368). New York: Pergamon Press.

Bloom, B. (Ed.). (1956). *Taxonomy of educational objectives: Handbook I: The cognitive domain*. New York: David McKay.

Bruner, J. (1960). *The process of education*. Cambridge, MA: Harvard University Press.

Good, T., & Brophy, J. (2004). *Looking in classrooms* (9th ed.). New York: Longman.

Jacob, B. (2001). Implementing standards: The California mathematics textbook debate. *Phi Delta Kappan, 83*(3), 264–272.

Jarolimek, J. (1990). *Social studies in elementary education* (8th ed.). New York: Macmillan.

Krathwohl, D., Bloom, B., & Masia, B., (1964). *Taxonomy of educational objectives: Handbook II: Affective domain*. New York: David McKay.

National Center for Education Statistics. (1996). *Pursuing excellence: A study of U.S. eighth-grade mathematics and science teaching, learning, curriculum, and achievement in international context*. Washington, DC: Author.

National Center for Education Statistics. (1997). *Pursuing excellence: A study of U.S. fourth-grade mathematics and science achievement in international context*. Washington, DC: Author.

National Center for Education Statistics. (1998). *Pursuing excellence: A study of U.S. twelfth-grade mathematics and science achievement in international context*. Washington, DC: Author.

National Center for Education Statistics. (1999, March). *TIMSS: The third international mathematics and science study*. Washington, DC: Author.

Popham, W. (2001). *The truth about testing*. Alexandria, VA: Association for Supervision and Curriculum Development.

Taba, H. (1962). *Curriculum development: Theory and practice*. New York: Harcourt Brace and World.

Wiggins, G., & McTighe, J. (1998). *Understanding by design*. Alexandria, VA: Association for Supervision and Curriculum Development.

Wineburg, S. (2001). *Historical thinking and other unnatural acts*. Philadelphia: Temple University Press.

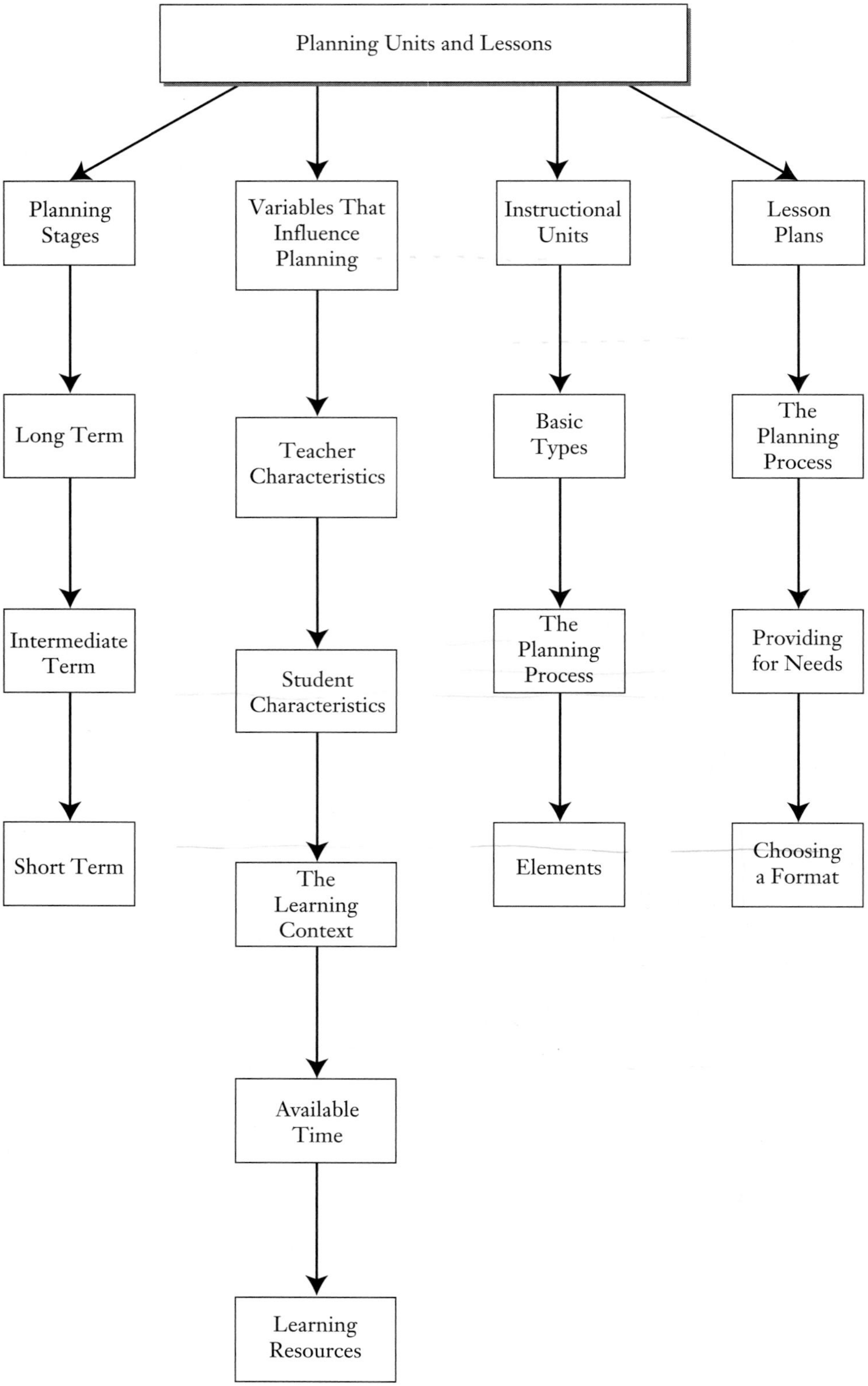

Figure 6.1
Graphic Organizer

CHAPTER 6

Planning Units and Lessons

OBJECTIVES

This chapter will help you

- identify the three basic stages in instructional planning;
- describe the importance of unit and lesson planning;
- point out some variables that will influence what you do in planning instruction;
- explain differences between single-subject and interdisciplinary units;
- describe how you might go about initial planning for an interdisciplinary unit;
- explain some components of unit and lesson plans;
- describe components of several models for planning lessons;
- point out some basic issues that need to be addressed in preparing a lesson plan; and
- develop a usable format for preparing unit and lesson plans.

Introduction

When you look over tables of contents in secondary school textbooks or contents of school curriculum guides, you may conclude that most instructional planning has already been done. These resources can help you. However, because of the unique characteristics of your own teaching situation, you will find it necessary to assume responsibility for planning effective instructional programs for your own students.

Researchers have found that effective teachers spend considerable time planning for what they do in the classroom. One study found that outstanding teachers devote 10 to 20 hours a week outside of the classroom to instructional planning (Clark & Yinger, 1979). What you decide to do as a result of your instructional planning may vary from actions taken by other teachers in your building. For example, you may decide to write out highly detailed descriptions of what you intend to do each day. Others with whom you work may be comfortable with a few brief notes in a plan book or even on a single sheet of paper.

In general, as a newcomer to the profession and as a teacher who may well have two or more separate subject preparations each day, your best initial course is to commit to providing considerable detail in your written plans for instruction. Careful planning of this kind can give you a good focus for your overall instruction and provide important cues that will help you move smoothly from point to point as you teach your students.

Planning Stages

Instructional planning can be divided into three basic stages:

- Long term
- Intermediate
- Short term

Long-Term Planning

Long-term planning focuses on an extended period of time: a grading term of several weeks' duration, a quarter, a semester, or even an entire school year. It focuses on identifying and sequencing major topics or themes that you will teach during the period being planned. You may find that outsiders have made some of your long-term planning decisions. For example, local or state curriculum guidelines often specify what topics you must teach in a certain course during one semester.

Sometimes external influences will pressure you to emphasize particular content at certain times. For example, some standardized testing programs feature large numbers of questions about certain topics and relatively few about others. If you are in a district where improving standardized test scores is a high priority, your planning decisions may be influenced by a desire to provide learning experiences that will help students perform better on these assessments. Science fairs, history fairs, and other events that are scheduled at certain times of the year may also encourage you to focus students' attention on particular topics at specific times during the school year.

When long-term planning decisions are converted to written form, the resultant documents often do not contain much detail about how you will introduce content to students. Rather, the emphasis ordinarily is on broader issues. For example, long-term planning documents you prepare may include more general information and include such components as statements of philosophy, descriptions of overall goals and aims of individual courses, and listings of major topics you will be teaching.

Intermediate-Term Planning

Intermediate-term planning begins to introduce more specificity into the planning process. Ordinarily, your focus here is on shorter periods of time that are embedded within the longer time periods that are the focus of long-term planning. For example, your planning might focus on four 4-week periods within a 16-week semester. The written expression of intermediate-term planning decisions often is a document called an *instructional unit*. Instructional units are designed for varying time periods; many organize instruction for a 1- to 5-week time period.

Sometimes school districts, state authorities, publishers, and others will provide you with unit plans. However, because conditions vary so much from place to place, you will need to modify these units to fit your own specific instructional environment. You must rework these externally developed units to take into account what your students already know, their interests and aptitudes, and the availability of learning resources you have available to support instruction. Because of the many special characteristics of individual students, classes, and schools, units you prepare yourself for use in your own classroom generally are better able to respond well to local conditions than those developed by outsiders.

Short-Term Planning

Short-term planning focuses on quite short periods of instructional time. The most common written expression of short-term planning is the *lesson plan*. Some lessons begin and end during a single instructional period. Others may cover a slightly longer period of time. Lesson plans function as a basic script for instruction. They contain information that help you keep instruction on track and moving smoothly from point to point.

Lesson plans include more specific information than instructional unit plans. In addition to instructional objectives (discussed in detail in chapter 5), they often provide details regarding instructional techniques used, how transitions are to be handled, specific learning materials used, and ideas for monitoring and assessing students. Lesson plans are context specific. Hence, they are best prepared by you personally.

Variables That Influence Planning

Several variables interact to influence planning decisions made by individual teachers, including the following:

- Teacher characteristics
- Student characteristics
- The learning context
- Available time
- Learning resources

Teacher Characteristics

You and your teaching colleagues vary greatly in terms of your educational philosophies, beliefs about students and how they learn, academic background in the subjects taught, general interests, and mastery of individual teaching techniques. These variables interact to affect instructional decisions. Researchers have verified this observation. For example, there is evidence that teachers who have a poor personal academic grounding in the content they are expected to teach ask more low-level (recall and memory) questions and encourage fewer questions from students than teachers with better academic preparation in their subjects (Kauchak & Eggen, 1989).

To better identify personal characteristics that may unconsciously be shaping instructional decisions, it is useful to ask yourself self-diagnostic questions such as these:

How important do I think this content is?

How well am I prepared to teach this information?

What, in general, do I believe to be the most important outcomes of schooling?

What teaching approaches do I like, and which ones don't I like?

Student Characteristics

Students have vastly different interests, abilities, and academic backgrounds. Successful planning requires you to know your students well. Lessons that are based on unwarranted assumptions about students' mastery of prerequisite information (and about other critical student characteristics) will fail. In thinking about the student characteristics variable, you should consider asking yourself questions such as these:

What previous knowledge and background in this topic do these students have?

What are these students interested in?

Do some of these students have special needs? If so, how can they best be accommodated?

Are there ways to take instructional advantage of some special characteristics of students in this class?

The Learning Context

There are enormous differences among the nation's secondary schools. The character of individual schools is shaped by the general nature of the communities they serve, the characteristics of their students, the actions of school administrators, and state and local school policies. Taken together, these variables help give each school its own learning context.

Because of differences in the learning context, expectations of teachers sometimes vary considerably from school to school. For example, some administrators may be extremely sensitive to public reaction to students' standardized test scores and may pressure teachers to pay particular attention to content likely to be sampled on these tests. In other buildings, teachers may have to carefully document what they do, and administrators may require every teacher to submit detailed lesson plans for every class session that is taught.

Another component of the learning context is the requirements imposed by state standards. You may be required to design lessons and units that adhere very specifically to standards established in your state. Administrators will guide you in the often complex details that define your content.

The learning context in the school where you teach almost always will be more supportive of some kinds of teacher behavior than others. For this reason, in deciding whether to accept a position that has been offered to you, you should ask yourself questions such as these:

What does the community expect of teachers and the schools?

What will I need to do in this school to please administrators?

Do state standards dictate curriculum?

How are teachers evaluated in this school?

Is my teaching style compatible with what people expect here?

Available Time

Time affects planning in several ways. The most important time consideration in planning for instruction is the amount of time you have—days and class periods—actually available for instruction. You may teach in a school that uses block scheduling so that you meet students for extended periods of time but fewer days per week. Or you may teach each group of students for approximately 50 minutes each day. No matter the format, you must make difficult decisions about how this precious time should be allocated among the many topics that may merit attention.

The planning process itself takes time. Do not be surprised if you feel some stress as you try to strike a balance between a need to plan new instructional experiences, correct student work, attend to committee obligations, and still maintain some semblance of a family and social life. Over time, your planning proficiency will grow, and you will find yourself better able to juggle unit and lesson planning and other aspects of your personal and professional life.

Learning Resources

You may find yourself in a teaching situation where the resources available to support your instruction will place limits on what you can plan and deliver to students. You need to take a realistic inventory of available learning resources before getting very far into the instructional planning process.

Learning resource problems sometimes pose serious difficulties when state regulations or even local administrative policies change suddenly. For example, a guideline requiring all science teachers to spend at least 40% of their time in class doing laboratory work will produce nothing but frustration if appropriate laboratory facilities and other materials are not in place to support this kind of teaching.

CRITICAL INCIDENT

Challenges of the Web

Sam Buelton walked into Jody Chu's classroom shaking his head. Jody, the chair of the social studies department, was at her desk using time at the end of the day to deal with some administrative paperwork and prepare for the next day.

"Hello, Sam. How are things?" Jody asked, glad to be diverted from the memo she was reading with yet another warning from the principal's office about the excessive amount of copying paper the department was using.

"It's been one of those 'good news, bad news' days," Sam replied as he took a seat at a vacant student desk at the front of the room.

"How so?" asked Jody.

"You'll remember how I mentioned at the last department meeting that this semester I was going to insist that student term papers include citations to some sources on the Web."

"Yes, I remember we all thought that would be a good idea."

"Well," Sam continued, "the papers came in a couple of days ago, and I just began correcting them today during my planning period. You'll remember that I wanted them to choose some topic related to the American Revolution. To get them started, I gave them a list of some Web addresses. Apparently, where I went astray was in telling them to look for links to other sites when they visited these sites."

"What happened?" inquired Jody. "It seems to me that instruction makes good sense. I mean, one of the advantages of the Internet is that it gives students a chance to access information in quantities that you and I never could have reached when we were in school."

"Well, you're certainly right about that," Sam acknowledged, "but there was a downside to this I hadn't thought about. My list of Websites included some impeccable sources of information, such as the Library of Congress. What I hadn't counted on was students following links that led to other sites that led to more links that led to more sites and on and on and on. What happened is that some of them found sites with information that, in some cases, goes beyond unreliable to simply outrageous."

"Such as?" asked Jody.

"Well, one of the papers I got has lots of beautifully footnoted references to 'information' put up on the Web by an outfit called Real Truth in History. From what I've been able to determine, this is a fringe group consisting of UFO aficionados and people who reject most mainstream historical scholarship. Among other things, there are assertions that extraterrestrials who, for unexplained reasons, became progressively angrier with Great Britain in the late 18th century were responsible for fomenting discontent among residents of the American colonies. According to this student's term paper, Sam Adams, Patrick Henry, George Washington, and the rest of the bunch were all getting advice from non-earthlings."

"How funny," said Jody, shaking her head and laughing. "That kid is breaking new scholarly ground!"

"I know at one level, it is just hilarious," acknowledged Sam. "But Jody, this kid really believes this stuff. He told me that the authorities wouldn't allow inaccurate information to be put up on the World Wide Web."

"Well Sam, that is funny," said Jody. "But you do have a problem. It's what those of us who've been in the business refer to as the 'mysterious they' belief."

"Mysterious they?"

"Yes," Jody went on. "Lots of our students innocently believe in the existence of some 'mysterious they' who police publications and broadcasts to keep untruths from being disseminated. All of us in the profession continue to be amazed at how widespread this belief is. Listen carefully to discussions in your class, and you're sure to hear comments such as 'They won't allow it.' 'They always get the upper hand.' 'They keep people like us down.'"

"You're right," said Sam. "I've heard lots of comments like that."

"Well, to get back to the Web source problem, it seems to me you've got to deal with a couple of issues. You've got to deal with the 'mysterious they' issue, and then you've got to provide some specific instruction on characteristics of reliable information sources."

"Makes sense," said Sam. "But, I'm not quite sure where to begin."

■ ■ ■

Do you think the situation Sam is encountering is a common one that secondary school teachers face? What are some alternative steps Sam might take? If you were Sam, how would you deal with the individual student who wrote the term paper he discussed with Jody? As you think about your response, remember that the student had done an excellent job of following citation-formatting guidelines and followed Sam's directions about using the World Wide Web to find information. What does this situation suggest to you about the level of detail that you need to provide in your instructions to students?

Instructional Units

Organizing instruction into well-planned units has several advantages. When you group lessons together and systematically sequence them in an instructional unit, each lesson can build on content you have introduced previously. Interrelated lessons can help you develop an instructional scheme that promotes students' abilities to see relationships and draw conclusions from analyses based on large quantities of information.

The process of unit planning will alert you to the need to gather certain kinds of learning resources. For example, as you plan a unit, you may determine that you need certain videotapes and maps that must be ordered from a centralized media facility several weeks in advance. Because usually you will plan a unit some time before you teach it, typically you will have enough time to obtain the learning materials needed to support your instruction.

When you plan units, you must be sensitive to the special characteristics of the learners you will teach. Information about students will help you identify an appropriate place for beginning instruction. This information can come from your personal knowledge of students' past performance and from other sources, such as diagnostic test results.

Unit plans give you a sense of direction and security as you deliver instruction. They eliminate uncertainty about "what I should do tomorrow." They help establish a sense of order and routine that conveys to students that you know what you are doing.

Basic Unit Types: Single Subject and Interdisciplinary

Many units treat topics that relate to a single academic subject, such as American history, geometry, biology, or English. Others are interdisciplinary units. The idea behind interdisciplinary units is to provide information in ways that help students grasp "the connectedness of knowledge and life" (Palmer, 1995, p. 55). Proponents of this approach believe that interdisciplinary teaching can help your students perceive reality as a whole, not as something that has been artificially divided into packages that bear names of the individual academic subjects (Pate, McGinnis, & Homestead, 1995).

The Planning Process

Some educational methods textbooks and teacher education programs recommend a linear approach to instructional planning. Linear planning begins by (a) identifying the unit generalizations and objectives, (b) identifying appropriate content for achieving the objectives, (c) designing and sequencing learning activities related to the objectives, (d) identifying and gathering needed learning resources, and (e) identifying evaluation procedures.

Though this approach seems to make certain logical sense, researchers have found that few teachers follow this sequence. When you teach, more typically you will find yourself moving back and forth among unit planning elements and continually making adjustments until all pieces seem to fit together (Yinger, 1979). Often you will begin your planning process by identifying examples of content that you need to teach. Once you have these in mind, you can move on to identify some guiding generalizations or some key questions. You are likely to make some modifications to your selected generalizations, content samples, and key questions as your unit planning process goes forward.

Wiggins and McTighe (1998), in their book *Understanding by Design*, describe a process that is becoming quite popular in school settings. This "backward design process" begins by identifying desired results, then determining acceptable evidence (How do you know students have achieved these results?), and finally planning learning experiences and instruction to help them get there. This planning sequence is centered on identifying "enduring understandings" or the big ideas that we want students

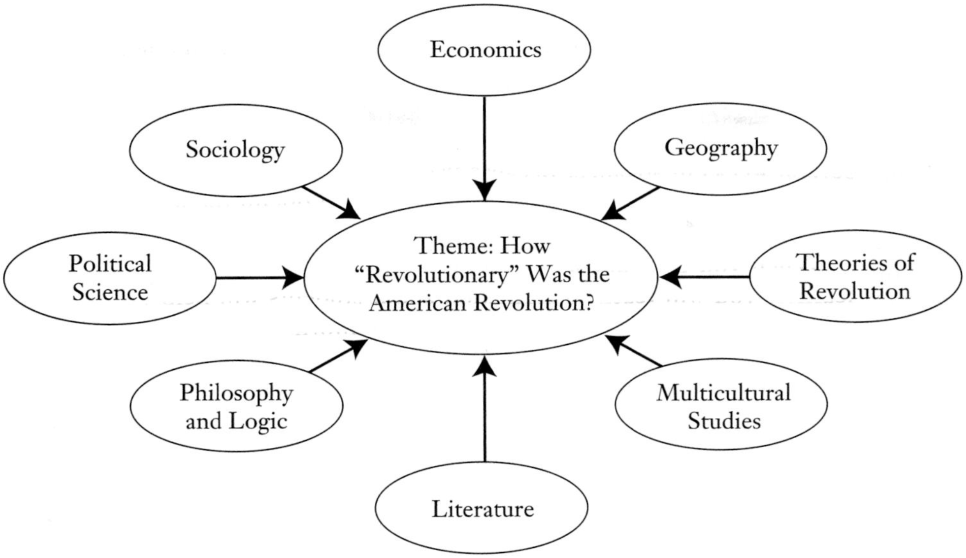

Figure 6.2

"to retain after they've forgotten many of the details" (p. 10). It is a process that can work well for interdisciplinary planning purposes as well as single-subject planning.

Figure 6.2 illustrates a basic planning framework for an interdisciplinary unit. Note that this unit is guided by a theme that is stated in the form of a question ("How 'Revolutionary' was the American Revolution?"). Themes, which may or may not be stated as questions, frequently provide a focus for interdisciplinary units. This unit proposes to draw content from eight separate subject areas. For each of these, the unit planner will identify a generalization, some content samples, and a key question.

Figure 6.3 displays results of initial unit planning for this interdisciplinary unit. Note the list of suggested resources at the end of this material.

This is a list that will be expanded and modified as the unit planning goes forward. Information displayed in Figure 6.2 is used to guide decisions that result in a complete unit, including components such as those introduced in the next section.

Elements

Instructional units can be formatted in many ways. Many of them include these parts:

Unit title
Rationale and major goals
Major generalizations and concepts
Instructional objectives and a tentative time line for teaching content related to each
Instructional strategies for each objective
Plans for the beginning and ending
Evaluation procedures
List of needed learning resources

ECONOMICS

Generalization: Wars put financial strains on economies and require actions to divert more resources to military uses and to raise additional revenues, often through new taxes.

Content Samples

- Mercantilism
- Financial consequences for England associated with the defeat of France in French and Indian War and how these influenced policies toward the colonies
- Financial problems of the colonies in the war—the case of the hyperinflated "Continental"

Key Question: How did economic circumstances in both England and America contribute to the war, and how extensive were economic changes during and after the war?

SOCIOLOGY

Generalization: The groups and classes to which people who lived in the former colonies belonged affected the levels of their interest in and support for the cause of the Patriots during the Revolutionary War.

Content Samples

- The relative strength of personal identity as "English" or "Colonials"
- The relative strength of personal identity as "Virginians" or "New Yorkers" compared with their identity as "Americans"
- The degree to which political and social events surrounding the war affected the personal and economic lives of individuals and groups

Key Question: How were individuals in different social classes affected by conditions that led to the war, and to what extent did these prompt them to become active participants? How changed were these people's lives as a result of the war?

GEOGRAPHY

Generalization: Issues associated with such variables as the relative location of a place, its human characteristics, and its special physical features affect its interactions with other places.

Content Samples

- Regional attitudes toward the war
- Demographic differences among the former colonies
- Cultural and economic priorities in various regions of the former colonies

Key Question: How did special characteristics of individual regions affect attitudes toward the war, and did the war itself act to bind these regions more closely together?

POLITICAL SCIENCE

Generalization: Decisions relating to the exercise of political power are often reflected in documents issued by formal bodies that presume they have the authority to make such decisions.

Figure 6.3

Content Samples

- Declaration and Resolves of the First Continental Congress (1774)
- Declaration of Causes and Necessity of Taking Up Arms (1775)
- Virginia Declaration of Rights (1776)
- Declaration of Independence (1776)
- Political arrangements in the former colonies during the war
- Legacies of British governance systems and the impact of the war on oligarchic power

Key Question: What arguments were made in official documents asserting American authority over British authority, and what political arrangements were sought during and after the war that either were (a) consistent with traditional British practices or (b) changed from traditional British practices?

THEORIES OF REVOLUTION

Generalization: Revolutions are puzzling phenomena; various theories have been developed that have tried to identify the defining characteristics of a revolution.

Content Samples

- Crane Brinton's theory
- Martin Lipset's theory
- Theda Skocpol's theory
- Louis Gottschalk's theory

Key Question: What criteria should be applied to determine whether a given set of events is truly revolutionary, and do these criteria suggest that the American Revolution was a "real" revolution?

PHILOSOPHY AND LOGIC

Generalization: Different rules for identifying assumptions, framing arguments, and otherwise building a case in support of a particular position are associated with specific philosophical and logical orientations.

Content Samples

- The Age of Reason as a context for thinking at the time of the American Revolution
- The Declaration of Independence as an example of Age of Reason logic
- Categorical syllogism as a framework for arguments in the Declaration of Independence
- The power of the categorical syllogism form to make arguments in the Declaration of Independence appear strong to educated 18th-century Europeans

Key Question: Is it true that the organizing and sequencing of an argument can add strength to the specific evidence that is presented, and did the special kind of logic used in the Declaration of Independence make a compelling case in support of revolution?

MULTICULTURAL STUDIES

Generalization: Members of minority ethnic and cultural groups chose their sides based on such things as their status as free persons or slaves, their perceptions of the relative long-term

Figure 6.3 *(continued)*

benefits of becoming aligned with one side or the other, and their emotional ties to such enemies of Britain as Spain.

Content Samples

- In 1777, Lord Dunsmore promised freedom to any slave who would fight for the British.
- African Americans fought on both sides during the Revolutionary War.
- The status of African American troops depended heavily on whether they had been slaves or free people at the time of their enlistment.
- Latinos were heavily involved in actions in areas along the Gulf of Mexico and the lower Mississippi River, particularly under the leadership of Marshall Bernardo de Galvez, governor of Spanish Louisiana.

Key Question: To what extent did experiences of cultural and ethnic minorities during the Revolutionary War lay the groundwork for actions taken in later years to achieve more widespread involvement in our nation's economic, social, and political affairs?

LITERATURE

Generalization: Themes reflected in particular literary works often reflect social, economic, and political events of the times in which they are written.

Content Samples

- John Dickenson's *Letters from a Farmer*
- Philip Freneau's "The Northern Soldier" and "To the Memory of Brave Americans"
- Patrick Henry's "Speech before the Virginia Convention of 1775"
- Thomas Paine's *Common Sense*

Key Question: How did selected literature of the Revolutionary War period reflect conditions of the time, and to what extent did these works contribute to change?

• • •

Examples of Resource Materials

American Revolution: Resources at the New York Public Library. Available at http://www.nypl.org/research/chss/subguides/milhist/rev.html

Brinton, C. (1965). *The anatomy of revolution.* New York: Vintage Books.

Brookhiser, R. (1995). *Founding father.* New York: Free Press.

Cole, R. (1995). The role of African Americans in the American Revolution. Available at http://www.ilt.columbia.edu/kl2/history/blacks/blacks.html

Dickenson, J. (1767, 1926). *Letters from a farmer. Letter/III.* In F. L. Pattee (Ed.), *Century readings for a course in American literature* (pp. 81–84). New York: The Century Company.

Dickenson, J. (1768). The liberty song. In F. L. Pattee (Ed.), *Century readings for a course in American literature* (p. 73). New York: The Century Company.

Forbes, E. (1943). *Johnny Tremain: A story of the Boston revolt.* Boston: Houghton Mifflin.

Freneau, P. (1786, 1926). The northern soldier. In F. L. Pattee (Ed.), *Century readings for a course in American literature* (p. 145). New York: The Century Company. From revolution to reconstruction. (1994). Available at http://grid.let.rug.nl/~welling/usa

Figure 6.3 *(continued)*

Hispanics in the American Revolution. (1995, 1996). Available at http://www.clark.net/pub/jgbustam/galvez/galvez.html

Lee, S. P., & Passell, P. (1979). *A new economic view of American history.* New York: Norton.

Medvedev, S. M. (1995). American Revolution: A revolution? Available at http://grid.let.rug.nl/~welling/usa/revo1.html

Meltzer, M. (1987). *The American revolutionaries: A history in their own words.* New York: Crowell.

Olson, K. W. (1995). An outline of American history. Available at http://grid.let.rug.nl~welling/usa

Ward, H. M. (1991). *The American Revolution: Nationhood achieved, 1763–1788.* New York: St. Martin's Press.

White, L. M. (1975). *The American Revolution in notes, quotes, and anecdotes.* Fairfax, VA: L. B. Prince Company.

Figure 6.3 *(continued)*

Unit Title Your unit title should communicate the essence of the content you propose to cover. Unit titles ordinarily are short. Sometimes even one word suffices. Examples of unit titles include "The Halogens" (chemistry), "The Lake Poets" (English), "Factoring" (mathematics), and "The Progressives" (history). Figure 6.4 explores title selection in more depth.

It isn't easy to select good unit titles. Each unit represents a segment of a course. The unit should bring together content elements that share common features. Often unit titles reflect a theme that functions as a useful organizer. If too much content is included in one unit, students may be overwhelmed. On the other hand, if information is divided into too many units, content can become excessively fragmented. This also poses difficulties for students.

Suppose you were assigned to prepare units for one semester's work in a middle school, junior high school, or senior high school. (You choose the course.) There are about 16 instructional weeks in a semester. Identify titles of five or six units you would use and indicate how much time you would devote to each.

1. How did you decide on unit titles?
2. What are other ways you might have divided the semester's work into units?
3. How did you decide on time allocation?
4. What might be some alternative time recommendations?

Unit Titles	Time Allocation

Figure 6.4

Rationale and Goals A *unit rationale* is a statement designed to establish your unit's importance. Writing the rationale helps you explain why the unit's content needs to be taught. The rationale can be used to convince others that the material you propose to cover is important. This is particularly important as you prepare to answer student questions such as "Why do we need to know this stuff?"

Goals in unit plans are statements that describe general learning outcomes. Sometimes they describe relationships between unit content and the entire school subject of which they are a part. Goal statements provide other teachers, administrators, parents, students, and others with an appreciation of the basic purposes of instruction associated with the unit. Suppose you were teaching high school English and were preparing a unit titled "The Epic Hero Theme." You might produce a goal statement something like this:

This unit seeks to introduce students to the form, extent of use, and the purposes of "epic hero themes" as vehicles for communicating a culture's values.

Major Generalizations and Concepts Generalizations in instructional units succinctly summarize the key ideas your students should master as a result of their exposure to unit content. (Chapter 5 provides more information about generalizations.) Recall that concepts are terms. Generalizations take the form of a statement of relationship among concepts. Hence, to understand a generalization, students must also grasp the concepts associated with it. Consider this generalization from sociology:

When urbanization occurs rapidly in a country, differences in status among people in various social classes become more pronounced.

This generalization would be impossible to comprehend by a student who did not know the meaning of such concepts as urbanization, country, status, and social class. One of your tasks in planning units is to identify concepts associated with guiding generalizations that your students are unlikely to know. You must include instructional experiences that will help them grasp meanings of these concepts.

Instructional units containing large numbers of generalizations with complex concepts require more instructional time than those dealing with less complex concepts. This reality requires you to consider the sophistication of the content you expect your students to learn and think about how much instructional time you should allocate to teaching the unit.

Objectives and Suggested Time Lines Objectives describe what you want students to be able to do as a result of instruction. They also describe the competence level your students are expected to gain as a result of their exposure to instruction. They tie in closely to the generalizations and related concepts you select to guide overall unit planning. The number of objectives will vary from unit to unit. You need to strike a balance between providing too many (which means each covers a very restricted range of content) and too few (which may stretch a single objective across an excessively large and complex body of information). In a unit designed to cover about 3 weeks, there might be between 6 and 10 objectives. At this point, you might want to review proper formatting of objectives in chapter 5.

An objective related to a unit on the Revolutionary War might look something like this:

On an essay examination, students will compare and contrast American and British advantages at the time the Revolutionary War began. Each essay must include references to at least two American advantages and two British advantages.

The time you will allocate for instruction associated with each objective will vary with its sophistication. If the objective asks your students to demonstrate only low-level knowledge and comprehension levels of thinking, you will need to schedule relatively short periods of instructional time. On the other hand, if one of your objectives proposes to have students engage in sophisticated analyses of complex information, you will have to commit considerable instructional time preparing students to succeed at this challenging task.

Time required to teach an individual unit also varies for reasons other than complexity of the objectives. The nature of students in your class will influence your pacing decisions. In addition, there often are differences depending on the time of the school year the unit is taught. Often units introduced early in a school year, when your students are getting reacclimated to doing school work, will take up more of your instructional time than those you introduce later in the year.

Instructional Strategies An *instructional strategy* consists of systematically organized instructional techniques that are directed toward helping students master an objective. You need to identify an instructional strategy for each objective included in your unit. Because some objectives require more sophisticated student thinking than others, some of your instructional strategies will be more complex than others. The "worth" of any instructional strategy is determined in terms of its ability to help students master the objective to which it relates.

Typically, instructional strategies are not described in great detail in instructional unit plans. A sentence or two describing the general instructional approach to be taken for each objective will suffice. You will describe your instructional strategies in much greater detail in your lesson plans. Lesson plans provide guidance for what you intend to do in the classroom on a given day, and it is appropriate that you include detailed information about instructional strategies you plan to use in these important documents.

Suppose you were teaching a high school physics course. When referring to an objective focusing on student comprehension of the coefficient of expansion principle, you might write the following information about an intended learning strategy in a unit plan outline:

Conduct an inquiry lesson on the unequal rate of expansion in response to heat of different metals using the bimetallic knife.

You would develop this strategy into a series of clearly defined steps in a related daily lesson plan.

Plans for the Beginning and Ending Your unit plans often will feature detailed descriptions of how you intend to introduce the unit to students. The introduction is critically important to the success of the unit. If your initial activity captures your students' interest, it will be easier for you to sustain their enthusiasm as you go on to introduce the new body of content.

Good unit introductions accomplish several purposes. They stimulate initial student interest and give students a general overview of unit content. They also provide them with a clear idea about what you expect them to do.

Conclusions or suggested culminating activities often are written into instructional unit plans. Their purpose is to help students pull together the key ideas that have been introduced. Often these activities will ask your students to engage in application activities that require them to use some of the information they have learned. A good culminating activity can build students' confidence by providing them with opportunities to verify for themselves that they have mastered challenging new material.

Evaluation Procedures It is necessary to include information about your approaches to evaluating student progress in your instructional unit plan. You need to think about evaluation procedures not just for the culminating assessment at the conclusion but also for interim assessments that you will make from time to time as you teach the material.

Selected evaluation procedures must be consistent with the unit's objectives. For example, if the language of your objective implies that students should be able to engage in analysis-level thinking, you must select an evaluation procedure that has the capacity to assess this kind of thinking.

Many evaluation procedures are available. For more information about the general issue of assessment of students, refer to chapter 13.

List of Needed Learning Resources Well-designed units are supported by a variety of learning resources. You need to identify these resources as you plan your units. You may wish to reference such items as supplemental readings, software, video- and audiotapes, Internet addresses, compact discs, maps, laboratory equipment, and resource people who may be invited to the class. You may also want to list learning materials you have designed yourself that will supplement the text and other basic instructional resources.

Today, budgets rather than materials' availability place more limits on the kinds of learning resources you can obtain. Catalogs containing an incredible variety of support materials regularly arrive at school district offices, at individual buildings, and in faculty mailboxes of classroom teachers. These catalogs taken together with district- and building-level library, media, and instructional resource centers will help you develop a feel for the range of available materials. If you are fortunate enough to be employed in a well-funded school district, you may be allowed to purchase substantial quantities of instructional support materials for units you develop. If you work in a less affluent setting, it is probable that budgetary limitations will severely restrict your purchases of these materials.

Figure 6.5 introduces an example of a single-subject instructional unit that includes these basic components.

Lesson Plans

Instructional unit plans describe the general flow of instructional activity over a period of several weeks. Shorter-range instructional decisions are expressed in lesson plans. A lesson plan might be looked at as a script you can follow while teaching students during a given period (or, in some cases, over one, two, or three successive periods—some individual lessons take more than 1 day to teach).

Title
The American Revolution

Rationale and Unit Goal

The American Revolution was a key event in American history. An understanding of the Revolution helps explain the nature of Americans' basic beliefs and values. The goals of this unit are to help students grasp forces that led the American colonists to band together and to help students appreciate American values, beliefs, and institutions that, in large measure, are traceable to the American Revolution.

Focus Generalizations (or Enduring Understandings)

Revolutions often occur when people believe that legitimate authority is insensitive to and unresponsive toward their needs.

Related Concepts

- Revolution
- Legitimate authority
- Wants and needs
- Responsive government

Revolutions challenge people to rethink their assumptions about the nature of the proper relationship between citizens and their government.

Related Concepts

- Role of citizenship
- Individual rights
- Role of government
- Governmental rights
- Loyalty
- Rebellion
- Independence

The values and beliefs of a given group of people have their roots in the pivotal events in the history of the people.

Related Concepts

- Values
- Beliefs
- Continuity and change over time
- Pivotal event
- Historical antecedents

Objectives and Suggested Time Allocation

- Each student will identify events leading to the American Revolution. Suggested time allocation: 1 day
- In an essay, each student will compare and contrast American and British advantages and disadvantages at the time of the outbreak of hostilities. At least two advantages and two disadvantages should be cited for each side. Suggested time allocation: 2 days

Figure 6.5

- Each student will identify American approaches to financing the war. Suggested time allocation: 1 day
- Each student will identify key military developments of the Revolutionary War and explain their importance. Suggested time allocation: 3 days
- Each student will analyze the results of the war with specific reference to its (a) political effects, (b) social effects, and (c) economic effects. Suggested time allocation: 4 days
- Students working in groups will identify values and beliefs that became important during the time of the American Revolution that are still highly valued and influential in the United States today. Suggested time allocation: 2 days
- Each student will profess an interest in learning more about the American Revolution. Suggested time allocation: No specific allocation. The instruction of the entire unit should be directed toward this objective.

Suggested Teaching Strategies

Beginning the Unit: Bring in newspaper accounts of an ethnic or civil conflict occurring somewhere in the world. Ask students questions such as these:

- What do you think causes people to become so angry that they will fight and kill one another?
- What happens to a country when this kind of conflict occurs?
- Are there circumstances when it is right for people to rise up against the legal government?
- What about our own Revolutionary War? Did the colonists have legitimate reasons for rebelling against England, or were they just trying to serve their narrow, personal interests?
- In what ways do you think the Revolution might have changed ways people thought and acted?

Show parts of the filmstrip series *The American Revolution: Two Views*. Point out to students that questions noted previously and those raised in the filmstrip will be investigated by the class over the next three weeks. Explain that the basic purpose will be to identify some reasons revolutions take place and to think about the nature of the proper relationship between a government and the citizens it serves. Suggested time allocation: 1 day

Recommended Teaching Approaches for Each Objective

Objective 1: Divide the class into several groups. Ask members of each group to conduct research and to report on how each of the following events contributed to the eventual outbreak of the Revolutionary War:

- Proclamation of 1763
- Sugar Act of 1764
- Stamp Act of 1765
- Declaratory Act of 1766
- Townshend Acts

Show the film *Prelude to Revolution.*

Objective 2: Divide the class into four groups. Assign each group to develop one of these lists:

- List of British advantages and disadvantages
- List of American advantages and disadvantages
- List of possible British arguments in support of and against going to war
- List of possible American arguments in support of and against going to war

Each group will share its list with the whole class. Allow students to work with the computer-based lesson titled "Revolutionary War: Choosing Sides." Discuss.

Figure 6.5 *(continued)*

Objective 3: Write the following information on the chalkboard: "It costs a great deal of money to conduct a war. How can this money be raised?"

Involve students in a brainstorming activity designed to provide answers to this question. Debrief. Go on to discuss ways money has been raised for recent conflicts (Operation Desert Storm, Vietnam War, Korean War, and so forth). Assign students to read material explaining problems Americans faced in raising money to pay for the Revolutionary War and how money was actually obtained.

Objective 4: Lay out a time line for the years 1775 to 1781 in the front of the room.

- Assign groups of two or three students to conduct research on key events of the Revolutionary War.
- Ask them to place the event at its proper place on the time line and to write a description explaining what occurred and why the event was important.
- Ask students to view the videocassette titled *The American Revolution.*
- Discuss key events of the war.

Objective 5: Provide students with information about the Treaty of Paris of 1783. Divide class members into four teams. Ask each team to gather information about one of these questions:

- What were the issues of interest to France, and how did the treaty affect France?
- What were the issues of interest to Spain, and how did the treaty affect Spain?
- What were the issues of interest to Americans, and how did the treaty affect the former colonies?
- What were the issues of interest to the British, and how did the treaty affect Britain?

Conclude with a discussion of benefits and losses conferred by the treaty on the parties involved.

Objective 6: As a concluding activity, conduct a brainstorming activity in which students are challenged to identify basic values and beliefs held by the colonists during the Revolutionary War.

- Discuss the list generated by the class.
- Then ask groups of students to take one of the identified values or beliefs.
- Find examples of how it still influences the behaviors of present-day Americans.

Objective 7: Administer an interest survey on the last day the unit is taught to identify which aspects of the unit topic were most interesting to students. The survey should also elicit information about how students feel about learning more about the American Revolution.

Suggested Evaluation Procedures

Procedures for Individual Objectives

Objective 1: Use a matching test. Students will be required to match events leading up to the Revolution with a description of the event (knowledge and comprehension-level evaluation).

Objective 2: Each student will be asked to prepare a written speech that might have been delivered by a colonist before the outbreak of the Revolutionary War. The speech may make a case either in support of or opposing going to war with the British. The written speech will be evaluated in terms of the quality of the arguments made, the correct identifications of potential advantages and disadvantages for each side, and its general persuasiveness (analysis- and synthesis-level evaluation).

Objective 3: Each student will respond correctly to 8 of 10 true-or-false items focusing on American attempts to finance the Revolutionary War (knowledge-level evaluation).

Figure 6.5 *(continued)*

Objective 4: Each student will respond correctly to at least 80% of multiple-choice items on a series of short examinations focusing on key events and other important developments associated with the Revolutionary War (knowledge- and comprehension-level evaluation).

Objective 5: Each student will prepare an essay focusing on social and economic consequences of the Revolutionary War. Each paper must include specific references to at least two social and two economic results of the war. Evaluation of the essay will take into account the quality of information cited and evidence that thinking goes beyond a recitation of material covered in class (analysis-level evaluation).

Objective 6: Each student will participate as a member of a team of four in a group activity that results in a product of some kind that illustrates and explains issues and values raised during the Revolutionary War that continue to be relevant for us today. These products or projects can take many forms, including artwork, original plays, panel discussions, radio or television scripts, debates, and symposiums.

Objective 7: Administer a simple attitude inventory on which students are asked to respond on a 1 to 3 scale (1 being highest or most positive and 3 being lowest or least positive) that asks them to record their interest in or feelings about various topics covered during the unit. Students need to be informed that their responses on the attitude inventory will have no bearing on their grades. Some teachers may prefer to give the same attitude inventory at both the beginning and the end of the unit. This will allow the teacher to look for shifts in interest in individual topics that may have resulted because of what students experienced as the unit was taught.

Suggested Learning Resources

General Reference Books

Bliss, G. A. (1980). *The American Revolution: How revolutionary was it?* New York: Harper & Row.

Fritz, J. (1981). *Traitor: The case of Benedict Arnold.* New York: Putnam's.

Gephard, R. E. (Ed.). (1984). *Revolutionary America.* Washington, DC: U.S. Government Printing Office.

Meltzer, M. (1986). *George Washington and the birth of our nation.* New York: Watts.

Meltzer, M. (1987). *The American revolutionaries: A history in their own words.* New York: Harper & Row Junior Books.

Meltzer, M. (1988). *Benjamin Franklin: The new American.* New York: Watts.

Meltzer, M. (1991). *Thomas Jefferson: The revolutionary aristocrat.* New York: Watts.

Miller, J. (1959). *Origins of the American Revolution.* Stanford, CA: Stanford University Press.

Student Texts

Boorstin, D. J., & Kelley, B. M. (1986). *History of the United States.* Lexington, MA: Ginn.

Bragdon, H. W., McCutcheon, S. P., & Ritchie, D. A. (1996). *History of a free people.* New York: Glencoe/McGraw-Hill.

Paine, T. (1776, 1975). *Thomas Paine's Common Sense: The call to independence.* Woodbury, NY: Barron's Educational Series.

Patrick, J., & Berkin, C. (1987). *History of the American nation.* New York: Macmillan.

Figure 6.5 *(continued)*

Ritchie, D. A., & Broussard, A. (1997). *American history: The early years to 1877*. New York: Glencoe/McGraw-Hill.

Ward, H. M. (1991). *The American Revolution: Nationhood achieved, 1763–1788*. New York: St. Martin's Press.

World Wide Web

American Revolution: Resources at the New York Public Library. (1995). Available at http://nypl.org/research/chss/subguides/milhist/rev.html

Cole, R. (1995). The role of African Americans in the American Revolution. Available at http://www.ilt.columbia.edu/k12/history/blacks/blacks.html

Hispanics in the American Revolution. (1995, 1996). Available at http://www.clark.net/pub/jgbustam/galvez/galvez/html

Medvedev, S. M. (1995). American Revolution: A revolution? Available at http://grid.let.rug.nl/~welling/usa/revo1.htm

Olson, K. W. (1995). An outline of American history. Available at http://grid.let.rug.nl/~welling/usa

Fiction

Collier, J. L., & Collier, C. (1976). *The bloody country*. New York: Scholastic.

Forbes, E. (1943). *Johnny Tremaine: A story of the Boston revolt*. Boston: Houghton Mifflin.

Snow, R. (1976). *Freeland Starbird*. Boston: Houghton Mifflin.

16-mm Film

Prelude to revolution.13-minute film available from Encyclopedia Britannica Educational Corporation, 425 N. Michigan Ave., Chicago, IL 60611

Videocassette

The American Revolution. Available from Guidance Associates, Communications Park, Box 3000, Mt. Kisco, NY 10549

Filmstrip

The American Revolution: Two views. Four-color filmstrips and accompanying cassette tapes available from Social Studies School Service, P.O. Box 802, Culver City, CA 90232-0802

Computer Software

"Revolutionary war: Choosing sides." Computer-based role-playing exercise. One diskette available in either Apple or MS-DOS format from Social Studies School Service, P.O. Box 802, Culver City, CA 90232-0802

Posters

"American patriot posters." A set of 10 color posters of Revolutionary-era patriots available from Social Studies School Service, P.O. Box 802, Culver City, CA 90232-0802

Figure 6.5 *(continued)*

Typically, you are likely to put more detail into your lesson plans earlier in your career than you will after you have taught for several years. Once you gain experience, you will be able to keep details related to your lesson in your head and will not require as many written prompts as will a beginner who is still getting used to managing students and moving smoothly from one instructional point to another.

There are no precise rules governing how much detail a "good" lesson plan should contain. In general, there should be enough information to enable a substitute teacher to deliver your lesson without too much difficulty.

The Planning Process

As is true for unit planning, the process followed in developing lessons varies from individual to individual. You may decide to begin by focusing on learning activities; some of your colleagues may begin by thinking first about the objectives they are trying to achieve; still others on your faculty may start the lesson-planning process by thinking about the kinds of evaluation tools they will be using. Regardless of where you decide to begin the planning process, you have to answer some key questions. Among them are the following:

What is the lesson objective? The answer to this question is important. For one thing, it requires you to weigh the importance of what you are contemplating and to determine that the purpose is a worthy one. Thinking about the objective sometimes also prompts ideas about possible teaching approaches.

What is a good entry point for instruction? To answer this question, you must have good information about the students to whom you intend to teach the lesson. The entry point of any lesson should tie in clearly to prior lessons and to what students already know.

What state standards will I address? If you teach in a state that has mandated standards, you must identify the ones you will include in each lesson. Some administrators require that teachers highlight these standards on each lesson plan and in some instances write these on the board each day.

How can I gain students' attention? This question prompts you to think about how students can be motivated at the beginning of a lesson. If an initial interest can be established, your students are more likely to stay with you for the duration of the lesson.

What is the best way to sequence lesson content and activities? This is a difficult question because there is no answer that is right for all situations. In some cases, logic of the subject matter dictates the response. For example, in a mathematics lesson, less complex content must precede more complex content. In other subjects, however, the sequencing decision is much more a matter of your personal professional judgment.

How can students become actively involved in the lesson, and what should they do to demonstrate they have learned? Lessons requiring students to actively manipulate the new content tend to be more successful than those that require them only to read or listen passively. Additionally, learning theorists say that new information is better remembered when people have had an opportunity to use it in some way. For this reason, it is important to include application activities in lesson plans whenever possible (Good & Brophy, 2004).

How should students be grouped during the lesson? You need to decide whether your students will be taught as members of one large group or as members of a number of small groups. If the decision is to have them divided into groups, specific thought must be given to deciding how group members will be selected and how students will move smoothly (quickly and quietly) from the large group into the small groups. If it is important for groups to have leaders, you must decide how they are to be selected and how they will report to you. You also must plan ways to distribute materials quickly and efficiently to all group members.

How can needs of students at different ability levels be met, and what should be done to monitor the progress of individual students? Because all classes have individuals with vastly different levels of ability and interest, your plans must assume that some students will need different learning materials than others and that some will finish more quickly than others. You also should devise a system for keeping track of how individual students are doing.

What kind of practice assignments need to be developed? It is important to think carefully and to prepare in advance lesson assignments that call on students to apply what they have learned. Good assignments of this kind almost never can be created on the spur of the moment. You need to design them carefully before starting to teach your lesson.

How should the lesson be concluded? It is as important to plan a sound lesson conclusion as well as a highly motivating lesson beginning. Your conclusion should help students draw together major points that have been introduced. It is particularly important for you to build in time for the conclusion phase of a lesson. You do not want to just stop. Your ending needs to be a carefully executed component that you treat as an essential feature of the lesson.

What materials are needed? Some lessons fail because teachers have not thought about needed materials. Books, handouts, paper and pencils, and other needed items are not available for students to use. You should consider preparing a "needed-materials checklist." When you have such a list, you can check off the availability of individual items as you prepare to teach the lesson. This ensures that any problems you experience with the lesson will not be caused by lack of available materials.

What rules and management guidelines should be adopted for this lesson? Some lessons include activities that are designed to promote very active student involvement. To ensure that students maintain a focus on the planned academic activity, you have to think through your expectations regarding what kinds of student behaviors are appropriate and about how your expectations will be communicated to students. Additional thought needs to be given to possible actions that will ensure student compliance with these expectations.

How much time should be allocated to each part of the lesson? Time is a scarce commodity in the classroom. This resource needs to be expended wisely to ensure the maximum possible learning benefit for students. Some parts of lessons clearly deserve more attention than others. Careful planners take time to make decisions about how much time they intend to devote to each part of a lesson.

MORE FROM THE WEB

Units and Lessons

A tremendous number of Websites include information about instructional units and lesson plans. You will find instructions about different formatting approaches as well as numerous examples of completed units and lessons. You should have little difficulty in finding material related to the subject(s) you will be teaching. Here are some sites that are representative of what the Web has to offer if you are looking for information related to units and lessons.

Lesson and Unit Ideas

This site, sponsored by the U.S. Department of Education, provides a searchable database of literally thousands of lesson and unit ideas.

Website: http://www.thegateway.org

This site, sponsored by the International Reading Association and the National Council of Teachers of English, provides excellent lesson ideas primarily for language arts teachers.

Website: http://www.readwritethink.org

Frank's Teachers' Software

More and more software is becoming available to help you construct units and lessons. At this site, you will find information about something called "Frank's Unit Maker," an inexpensive software package that will help you write instructional units on your computer.

Website: http://www3.sympatico.ca/frank.e.stokes

EMT 669 Sample Instructional Units

This site is one of many that feature examples of instructional units related to a specific academic subject. Here you will find a number of examples of instructional units for mathematics. Examples of titles are (a) Projective Geometry Unit, (b) Transformational Geometry, (c) Maximum and Minimum Values of a Function, and (d) Circles: Their Lines and Segments.

Website: http://jwilson.coe.uga.edu/emt669/units.html

Lesson Plan Outline

There are many existing lesson plan formats. You will find one example in this chapter. Here is another.

Website: http://www.geneseo.edu/~stuteach/lesplan.html

Providing for the Needs of Special Groups of Students

Students in today's classrooms are more diverse than they have ever been. You need to prepare lessons that will meet the needs of exceptionally bright students as well as students with any one of a number of special conditions that range from emotional problems to physical challenges of various kinds to mild and moderate mental retardation. Today, federal and accompanying state legislation require all students to spend as much of the school day as possible in regular classrooms rather than in isolated classrooms where they have little contact with "typical students." This means that your lesson plans must make provisions to meet the special needs of a variety of students. A single approach to teaching a class of 20 to 30 students will not do. Chapter 7 will provide additional information to help you plan lessons for *all* students who are in your classrooms.

Choosing a Format

There are many acceptable ways to format a lesson plan. What is important is that you give serious thought to the organizational scheme and prepare your plan carefully once you decide on an arrangement. Your district may provide you with the required format, or you may have the opportunity to choose your own. Numerous Websites

GENERIC LESSON PLAN MODEL

Lesson Title ______________________________

Unit Title ______________________________

Objective(s) ______________________________

Standards Addressed ______________________________

Needed Prerequisite Knowledge or Skill ______________________________

New Terms and Key Ideas ______________________________

Procedures for Accommodating Students with Special Needs ______________________________

Time ______________________________

LESSON SEQUENCE

1. Gaining attention/informing students of objective
2. Presenting new material
3. Checking understanding/monitoring
4. Eliciting behavior/practice/feedback
5. Providing for independent practice/application/extension
6. Providing for closure

Assessment Plan ______________________________

Materials Needed ______________________________

Teacher Evaluation of Lesson Effectiveness ______________________________

Figure 6.6

provide lesson plan templates that allow you to design and edit your lessons. One such site can be found at http://www.lessonplanbuilder.org, a site sponsored by the California Department of Education. Here you can create a lesson, have it peer-reviewed, and subsequently edit it as often as necessary. No matter which scheme you adopt, the format should allow you to refer quickly to the completed plan to keep on track and to ensure that no planned parts of the lesson inadvertently are omitted. Because of the need to use lesson plans while instruction is being delivered, you do not want them to be too long. In addition, you want to avoid formats that make individual items difficult to find. Figure 6.6 presents a generic example of a lesson plan

FOR YOUR PORTFOLIO

1. INTASC Standard 7 focuses on instructional planning. What materials and ideas you learned in this chapter related to instructional units and lesson plans will you include as "evidence" in your portfolio? Select up to three items of information to be included. Number them 1, 2, and 3. To which other INTASC standards might these materials also relate?
2. Think about why you selected these materials for your portfolio. Consider such issues as the following in your response:
   - The specific purposes to which this information can be put when you plan, deliver, and assess the impact of your instruction
   - The compatibility of the information with your own priorities and values
   - The contributions this information can make to your personal development as a teacher
   - The factors that led you to include this material as opposed to some alternatives you considered
3. Prepare a written reflection in which you analyze the decision-making process you followed. In addition, mention the INTASC standard(s) to which your selected material relates. (First complete the following chart.)

Materials You Selected and the INTASC Standards

Put a check under those INTASC standards numbers to which the evidence you have selected applies. (Refer to chapter 1 for more detailed information about INTASC.)

Item of Evidence Number	INTASC Standards									
	S1	S2	S3	S4	S5	S6	S7	S8	S9	S10
1										
2										
3										

format. This format can be modified to suit your individual instructional needs. In addition, you might want to compare it to the online format at the lesson plan builder site mentioned previously.

KEY IDEAS IN SUMMARY

- Because of the unique characteristics of individual teaching settings, you need to do much of your own instructional planning. Researchers have determined that effective teachers devote a great deal of time to planning.
- As you prepare for instruction, you will engage in long-term, intermediate-term, and short-term planning. Long-term planning embraces a time period of a semester or a full academic year. Intermediate-term planning focuses on time periods ranging from about 2 to 6 weeks in length. Instructional unit plans represent the written expression of intermediate planning. Short-term planning focuses on what goes on during one (and sometimes two or three) class periods. Short-term planning decisions are written in the form of lesson plans.
- Many variables affect specific decisions you make as you prepare instructional plans. Among variables that must be considered are (a) your own personal characteristics, (b) characteristics of your students, (c) the general learning context, (d) state mandates, (e) available time, and (f) available resources to support learning.
- Some instructional units draw content from a single academic subject. Others are interdisciplinary in nature. In planning interdisciplinary units, you often will begin by identifying relevant generalizations or enduring understandings associated with each source subject, samples of content associated with each source subject, and a key question related to each source subject.
- There are different ways to format instructional units. Many of them contain these key content categories: (a) unit title, (b) rationale and major goals, (c) major generalizations and concepts, (d) instructional objectives and an indication of time to be devoted to instruction related to each, (e) instructional strategies for each objective, (f) plans for beginning and ending the unit, (g) evaluation procedures, and (h) a list of needed learning resources.
- Lesson plans include details regarding instructional decisions that will guide teaching for a relatively short period of time. They might be thought of as scripts teachers follow during a given period, sometimes a time as short as a single class period. Many different lesson plan formats have been developed.

REFLECTIONS

1. As a teacher, why do you have to do so much instructional planning of your own when so much excellent information is available in curriculum guides, textbooks, and other learning materials?
2. What are some characteristics of long-term planning?
3. What are some similarities and differences between intermediate-term and short-term planning?
4. What is the importance of the learning context in instructional planning?

5. What are some typical components of instructional units?
6. How might you go about the process of constructing an interdisciplinary unit?
7. Why is it probable that you will include more details in your lesson plans early on in your teaching career than during your later years in the profession?
8. What are some questions you should ask yourself as you plan lessons?
9. Why is it important to carefully plan conclusions for your lessons?
10. What are some sources of information that can be helpful to you in planning meaningful lessons for special groups of students?

LEARNING EXTENSIONS

1. Review some district- or state-level curriculum guides. How many parts of the instructional unit format introduced in this chapter are included in the guides? What would need to be added to this material to make an instructional unit complete?
2. Interview a teacher about the process he or she follows in preparing an instructional unit. How does this person start this task? What goes into his or her decisions about sequencing content? Where is information about available materials found? What kind of format is used?
3. Visit two or more schools and compare how teachers in each approach a common subject. What differences are attributable to teacher variables and student variables? What differences seem to be caused by differences in the teaching context?
4. Get together with several others who are preparing to teach the same secondary school subject. Develop an instructional unit following the format introduced in this chapter. Share your unit with your instructor and request a critique. Be prepared to participate in a class discussion focusing on special difficulties you encountered and how you overcame them.
5. Write a lesson plan focusing on a topic you would like to teach. Be prepared to share answers to these questions with others in the class: How long did it take you to prepare the lesson? Do you think you would be able to accomplish this task more quickly were you to prepare another lesson? How comfortable would you feel in teaching this content?

REFERENCES

Clark, C., & Yinger, R. (1979). *Three studies of teacher planning* (Research Series No. 55). East Lansing: Michigan State University, Institute for Research on Teaching.

Good, T. L., & Brophy, J. E. (2004). *Looking in classrooms* (9th ed.). New York: Longman.

Kauchak, D., & Eggen, P. (1989). *Learning and teaching: Research-based models*. Boston: Allyn & Bacon.

Palmer, J. M. (1995). Interdisciplinary curriculum—Again. In J. A. Beane (Ed.), *Toward a coherent curriculum* (pp. 55–61). 1995 Yearbook of the Association for Supervision and Curriculum Development. Alexandria, VA: Association for Supervision and Curriculum Development.

Pate, P. E., McGinnis, K., & Homestead, E. (1995). Creating coherence through curriculum integration. In J. A. Beane (Ed.), *Toward a coherent curriculum* (pp. 62–70). 1995 Yearbook of the Association for Supervision and Curriculum Development. Alexandria, VA: Association for Supervision and Curriculum Development.

Wiggins, G., & McTighe, J. (1998). *Understanding by design*. Alexandria, VA: Association for Supervision and Curriculum Development.

Yinger, R. (1979). *A study of teacher planning: Description and theory development using ethnographic and information processing methods*. Unpublished doctoral dissertation. Michigan State University, East Lansing.

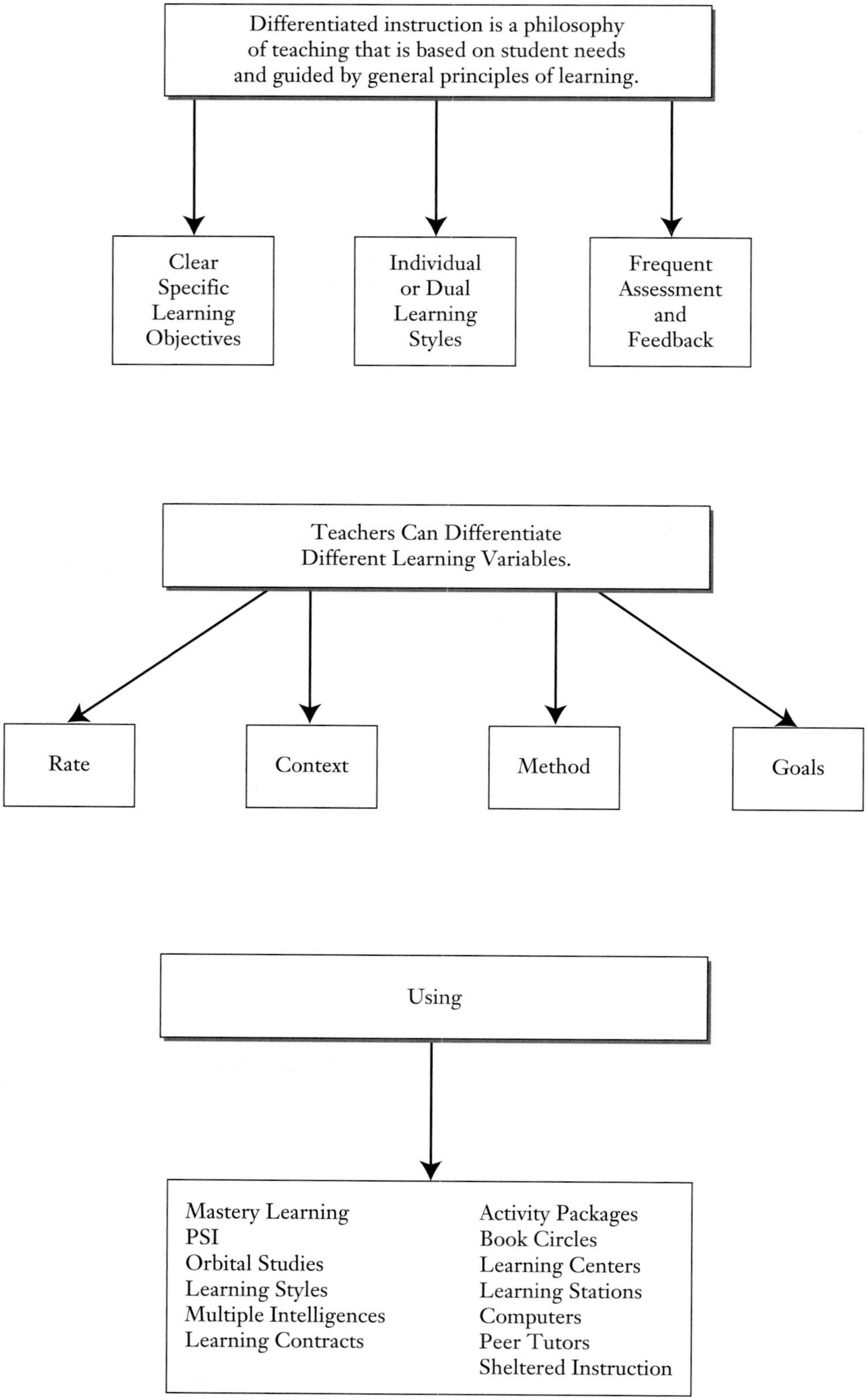

Figure 7.1
Graphic Organizer

CHAPTER 7

Differentiating Instruction

OBJECTIVES

This chapter will help you

- describe some alternative views of differentiated instruction;
- identify variables that can be altered to accommodate individual differences;
- explain some assumptions made by proponents of the mastery learning approach and describe features of the Personalized System of Instruction;
- point out some arguments for and against attempting to individualize instruction in ways that accommodate individual learning styles;
- describe typical features of a learning contract;
- explain components in an activity package;
- identify types and purposes of learning centers;
- describe features of learning stations;
- describe process for using book circles;
- suggest ways in which computers can be used to support differentiated instruction programs;
- distinguish between the two major types of peer-tutoring programs; and
- identify specific techniques for differentiating instruction for English learners.

Introduction

Now that you know that students from many backgrounds will be on your class rosters when you start teaching, what should you do? The first rule is to avoid panic. Teachers throughout the country face and respond to the student-diversity challenge every day. The rich variety of young people in your classes provides a context that allows you to introduce individual students to perspectives that, absent the ethnic, language, and cultural diversity common in secondary schools today, would not be possible. To exploit this opportunity, you need to know something about *differentiated instruction*. This general term refers to the idea that you need to vary lesson approaches in every class you teach in ways that will both accommodate and take advantage of the student-diversity variable (Lefrancois, 1994). Differentiated instruction, even though it includes many individual approaches to instruction, is not the individualized instruction of the 1960s and 1970s where individual students were isolated in study carrels to progress through boring workbooks. It requires, instead, teachers who are in touch with the students they teach and are willing to "attend to both student similarities and student differences" in an effective and engaging manner (Tomlinson, 1999). Differentiated instruction is not a teaching strategy; it is not a set of activities. It is a philosophy based on a set of beliefs—namely, that each student is unique with different learning styles, interests, and experiences. As such, they require teachers who provide a learning environment that meets them where they are and challenges them to grow (Tomlinson, 2000).

Instructional specialists for years have promoted the use of differentiated instruction (Good & Brophy, 2004). In practice, teachers in elementary schools have been quicker to adopt various differentiated instruction approaches than teachers in secondary schools. In one study, Larry Cuban (1984), an influential education scholar, found that less than one fifth of secondary teachers made any attempt to individualize their teaching.

Why have relatively few secondary school teachers committed to differentiated instruction? For many, there are probably personal reasons or reasons connected to some special features of their school and students. Often we hear "I have 150 students every day" or "I don't have enough materials" or sometimes even "I must teach to the standards." It may also be that proponents of differentiated approaches sometimes have talked in global terms about the benefits of this kind of teaching without providing detailed information about how to implement it. Sometimes, too, enthusiasts have provided overblown descriptions of the alleged benefits of differentiated instruction, raising doubts among experienced teachers who are appropriately wary when panacea-like qualities are claimed for any instructional methodology. These are certainly valid realities for any secondary teacher. However, they should not preclude you from designing instruction that meets the needs of each student whom you teach each day. This does not mean that you differentiate everything for every student each day. Instead, based on both formal and informal assessment, you choose times in your instructional sequence to differentiate (Tomlinson, 1999).

As you plan lessons in a differentiated classroom, remember that the key ingredient in a differentiated classroom is good teaching. You must begin by determining what common insights or understandings you want all students to gain as a result of your instruction. As you reflect on your options, give careful consideration to your own teaching context and your answers to questions such as these:

- Who are the students?
- What do you expect them to do when they have mastered the new material?
- Given the nature of the lesson you want to teach, what constraints are imposed by the kind of content you will be teaching?
- What materials are available?
- What is the level of your own knowledge about the topic and about procedures for "packaging" information in a way that will individualize the lesson for different students in the class?

Reflection on these questions can help you make a decision regarding the appropriateness or inappropriateness of selecting a differentiated approach to introduce specific content to specific students. In this chapter, you will find material that will broaden your understanding of processes and procedures associated with differentiated instruction, information that will help you make informed decisions about this approach as you consider adapting the approach to your own purposes. The graphic organizer at the beginning of the chapter visually depicts the ideas associated with differentiated instruction.

Defining Differentiated Instruction

The term *differentiating instruction* is interpreted by different people in various ways. For some, differentiation suggests a program where all students work independently on the same assignment. In this type of situation, every person does the same thing; only the rate of progress varies. This view of individualization is sometimes labeled *continuous progress learning*. The words *continuous progress* imply that the rate of academic development of one student will not be held up because others in the class may learn at a slower rate.

Others see differentiation as focusing not on the rate of learning but on the content of instruction. These people see differentiated programs as those where individual students study different topics, with the teacher acting as an overall learning manager. Differentiated programs of this kind place a great deal of responsibility on students.

Another conception of differentiation focuses on identifying modes of engaging students that are well suited to their individual characteristics. For example, there is considerable interest in multiple intelligences (Gardner, 1999). Individuals who subscribe to this theory contend that different individuals have varying forms of intelligence (e.g., visual-spatial, bodily-kinesthetic, logical-mathematical, musical-rhythmic). As a teacher, you are more likely to succeed if you provide particular students with instruction framed in a way that capitalizes on the kinds of intelligence where they have particular strengths. This perspective underscores the folly of assuming that any single learning activity will be universally appropriate for all students. For example, some of your students will do better when you introduce new content using a *narrational approach*—an entry point to instruction that features learning new information through stories of various kinds (Gardner, 1999). Others may do better if you use an *aesthetic approach*—a mode of instruction that focuses on students' receptiveness to artistic principles or to "materials arranged in ways that feature balance, harmony, and composition" (Gardner, 1999, p. 171). Still others may respond more positively to you if you use a *hands-on approach*—an entry point to instruction that gives students opportunities to build or create something tangible (Gardner, 1999). If you would like to learn more about approaches related to the multiple intelligences theory, you might enjoy reading one of Howard Gardner's books, *Intelligence Reframed: Multiple Intelligences for the 21st Century* (1999).

Approaches to differentiation based on multiple intelligences and on other theoretical underpinnings reflect a general orientation to teaching, not a specific set of procedures. When you say you are interested in "differentiating instruction," what you are committing to is an intent to think about teaching in a particular way. You are suggesting that you place a great deal of value on "personalizing" learning. In practice, this requires you to design your lessons in ways that will fit your teaching to the special needs of individuals in your classes and that will avoid forcing students to endure instructional approaches that are ill suited to their personal attitudes and aptitudes.

Altering Variables to Accommodate Individual Differences

What does a commitment to differentiating instruction mean in practice? Among other things, it requires you to give serious thoughts to variables you can alter to accommodate individual student differences. As you plan instruction, you will be in a position to make changes associated with the following:

- The rate of learning
- The context of learning
- The method of learning
- The goals of learning

Altering the Rate of Learning

The term *rate of learning* refers to the pace at which your instruction occurs. When you expose all students in a class to exactly the same instructional program, you assume that everyone is capable of learning at the same rate. This assumption rarely stands up to close inspection. Individuals learn at different rates. When your instruction fails to respond to these differences, students who generally learn faster often get good grades, and those who learn more slowly get poor grades and sometimes even fail.

Some experts contend that all students can learn or master the same educational goals if they are given sufficient time to do so (Lefrancois, 1994). They argue that students who fail often do not do so because of lack of aptitude for learning; rather, they fail because they are given insufficient time. They further suggest that "student aptitude" really refers to the amount of time a student needs in order to learn. Students with higher learning aptitude learn faster than those with lower aptitude. This means that, given enough time, all students can be successful.

When you manipulate the learning-rate or pacing variable, the basic content remains the same, as do basic assignments for students. What you alter is the time allowed for individual students to complete assigned tasks. You make arrangements that allow brighter students to move quickly through the material. This scheme permits your less able learners to use more time to finish their work.

Altering the learning rate makes the most sense in situations when you believe it is essential for all your students to master a given body of content. This form of differentiation is reflected in a number of formal instructional approaches, such as *mastery learning*. Mastery learning presumes that differences in students' levels of achievement result not from differences in student intelligence or aptitudes but rather from variations in time required by individuals to learn assigned content (Bloom 1976, 1980).

The *Personalized System of Instruction* (PSI) represents an example of an application of the mastery learning idea (Guskey, 1985). Similar to other mastery learning programs, it features the following:

- Clearly specified learning intentions
- Diagnosis of students' entry-level capabilities
- Numerous and frequent assessment measures
- Specification of mastery levels to be attained
- A structured sequence of facts, principles, and skills to be learned

- Frequent feedback to learners about their progress
- Provision of additional time that allows students who fail to achieve mastery to study some more and master the content

Essentially, the PSI approach requires you to break down a course into small units of instruction with support materials provided for each. In PSI, your students take as much time as they need to learn each unit. You permit individuals to take a mastery quiz whenever they feel they are ready. Each quiz has a cutoff point (usually 80% to 90% correct) that is used to indicate mastery of the content. If a student does not pass the quiz, he or she is allowed more time to study the content with other students until the quiz can be passed successfully. When students are successful, they move on to the next small unit. At the end of the course, you administer an examination that covers all the material. This means your unit quizzes are not used to assign grades to students. Instead, their function is to help individuals determine whether they need more time to learn the content. Students who pass the quizzes the first time spend less time on the material than do those who have to recycle (Slavin, 1994).

Mastery learning approaches such as PSI have positive as well as negative effects. On the positive side, researchers who have studied the impact of PSI at the college level have found the approach to be quite effective. In general, they have discovered that the mastery approach increases achievement (especially among less able students), results in less variation of achievement, and seems to have a positive impact on student attitudes toward school (Lefrancois, 1994).

PSI also has its critics. In certain situations, use of the approach has not resulted in increased student motivation and achievement. Some students don't like the format. Their complaints often center on the lack of opportunities to work with others. This may explain the finding that students in mastery learning approaches were observed to have lower completion rates in college courses than students who were enrolled in non-PSI versions of the same class (Lefrancois, 1994).

Other criticisms of mastery learning approaches have focused on procedural and contextual matters. For example, the additional time required to meet the needs of each student may not be available in most secondary schools. Schools operate within relatively fixed time constraints (Slavin, 1994). Any effort to implement mastery learning more widely probably would require restructuring of the school day and the school year. Perhaps those who learn quickly could leave school earlier in the day and would not have to stay in school for the 180 or so days that are usually required in a school year. When they mastered the content, their school year would be over. Other students who need more time to master the content might be in school for considerably longer than the present typical school day or the school year.

There is some question regarding whether the additional time required for the corrective instruction might be better spent covering more material. This concern arises because the amount of content covered is positively related to increases in achievement (Slavin, 1994).

Because mastery learning programs often divide large tasks into small pieces, if you adopt this approach, you will find yourself confronted with the need to keep on top of a great deal of paperwork. This feature, along with the frequent testing that goes on, often creates work for teachers that, in the view of some, goes beyond what they face in more traditional instructional programs (Good & Brophy, 2004). The potential for greatly increased record-keeping responsibilities has led many secondary teachers to steer clear of mastery learning approaches. In addition, some secondary teachers have found that time spent monitoring students and keeping them on task increases when they use mastery learning.

Some critics of mastery learning have also challenged the assumption that frequent testing is desirable. They argue that frequent testing results in assessments that focus on isolated pieces of content. Such tests may encourage students to lose sight of the larger dimensions of the subject. Some teachers have found that students may do well on mastery tests but experience difficulty in applying what they have learned to different settings (Good & Brophy, 2004).

In summary, mastery learning programs work best when they focus on a relatively narrow band of content that is required of all students. They demand content that lends itself easily to division into numerous smaller pieces that can be organized for purposes of teaching and testing. Under these circumstances, mastery learning programs can motivate some of your students who have experienced chronic failure in more traditional instructional programs. Success will depend on your ability to monitor students carefully to assess levels of progress and encourage them to stay on task. It is particularly important that those students who have experienced only limited academic success in the past develop confidence in their own abilities to succeed. When you use a mastery learning approach, you have to work hard to ensure that this happens.

Altering the Context of Learning

Instead of focusing on the issue of pacing, you might want to individualize your instruction by altering the context of learning. When you do this, you do not change the goals of instruction. Rather, your focus is on identifying means for getting students to reach those goals in ways that are compatible with their own aptitudes and interests.

If you decide to alter the context of learning, you may wish to use an approach such as orbital studies (Tomlinson, 1999). In orbital studies, you assign students to follow different paths, based on their individual differences, that lead them to acquire information about a common topic or subject. For example, if you are teaching mathematics, you might assign students with interests in cars to study some topics in the context of how they are applied in car design. If you have others who are interested in urban design, you might ask them to study the same concepts as they might be applied in laying out city parks and other features of cityscapes.

Whether you use orbital studies or another approach to altering the context of learning, your basic assumption is that your students will be more motivated when they study materials that they find interesting. Supporters of this approach point out that many traditional programs fail to consider students' personal priorities. Content in traditional texts often contains examples that fail to connect with students.

From a management standpoint, there are some attractive features of differentiating by altering the context of learning. For one thing, you still maintain the focus of the entire group on a common set of skills or concepts. This means that you can be quite flexible in organizing your day-to-day instructional program. For example, on some days, you may individualize content related to your major subject focus and assign students to work with different kinds of materials based on their particular aptitudes and interests. On other days, you may choose to have the entire class work with the same learning materials.

Differentiating by altering the context of learning does present certain difficulties. For example, you may be challenged to find learning materials that are well suited to the diverse interests and aptitudes that may be represented among your students.

Even if you can locate the kinds of materials you will need, the expense of acquiring them may be beyond what your school's budget can handle. In recent years, this problem has become less serious because of the proliferation of computers in the schools. Computers connected to the Internet can access almost unlimited information. In addition, more and more computers in schools now have multimedia capability. You can now find extensive learning materials available on fairly inexpensive CD-ROMs. These new electronic technologies make it easier for you to fill gaps in your on-site supplies of learning materials as you attempt to establish an appropriate "fit" between these items and the backgrounds of individual students.

It may take you some time to develop a high degree of comfort with an approach to teaching that regularly features altering the context of learning. The approach takes time to master, and time constraints during teacher preparation programs often mean that new teachers receive limited training in procedures for implementing instruction that is organized in this way. Initially, you may wish to try the approach in a single class, perhaps during instruction focusing on a topic that you will be teaching over a period of several weeks. This experience will help you gain some insights into challenges associated with implementing and managing the approach. Once you have successfully altered the context of learning for a short period of time in a single class, you may want to implement it in other classes and for longer periods of time. Use the exercise in Figure 7.2 to practice planning teaching scenarios that alter what students study.

Standardized testing is one force that sometimes hinders teachers' efforts to use differentiated programs that vary the context of learning. There is a trend for school quality to be assessed in terms of students' scores on these tests. When your students study material in contexts well suited to their personal needs, some of them may not come into contact with the kinds of contexts used to present items on standardized tests. This situation may cause you to feel pressured to expose all your students to

One variable you can manipulate in a differentiated program is the context of learning. When you do this, all your students seek to master a common set of objectives, but you provide them with means of doing so that take advantage of their individual strengths and interests. The idea is for you to provide options that are well matched to individual student interests.

As an exercise, identify a specific objective for a subject you would like to teach. Identify three separate interests that might be represented among students in your class. Suggest kinds of learning options that might help students with each of these interests to master the material.

Objective:

____

Interest A:

Suggested Learning Experiences:

Interest B:

Suggested Learning Experiences:

Interest C:

Suggested Learning Experiences:

Figure 7.2

information in contexts closely paralleling those commonly assumed by developers of standardized assessments. There is no simple solution to this problem. In general, you need to seek a balance between your need to present content to students in ways they will find personally meaningful and your need to introduce it in a context that will not be startlingly different from what they will confront when they have to take standardized tests.

Altering the Method of Learning

Differentiated programs that focus on altering the method of learning attempt to respond to different learning styles of students. These programs presume that people vary in their aptitudes for specific tasks and in their preferred modes of learning. This is what is called *attribute–treatment interaction*. The basic premise for this type of instruction is that your instructional methods should be matched to the particular learning styles of your individual students (Lefrancois, 1994).

Advocates of the learning-style approach contend that just as individuals differ in personality, so too do they differ in the way they learn (Slavin, 1994). One approach to learning-style instruction focuses on the modalities of learning. Modalities refer to the sensory channels through which individuals receive and give information. These modalities include visual, auditory, kinesthetic, and tactile. Some people learn more efficiently when they are presented with visual material, others when they hear it, others when they touch or feel objects, and others when they are physically involved in doing something (Guild & Garger, 1985).

Another dimension that you will want to think about when considering learning styles relates to field dependency and field independency. Field-dependent individuals see patterns as a whole and have difficulty separating out specific aspects or parts of what they encounter. However, field-independent people tend to focus on the parts that make up the whole.

Learning styles also are sometimes classified according to an abstract–concrete dimension. Some people deal better with abstract than with concrete phenomena; others deal better with concrete than with abstract phenomena. Similarly, people vary in how they respond to random versus sequential information. Some deal better with information that appears in an ordered, sequential fashion. Others deal better with information that comes in a random, nonsequential way. Scholars who have studied the preference for abstract or concrete experiences and the preference for sequential or random information have found that (a) some people have concrete-sequential learning styles, (b) some people have abstract-sequential learning styles, (c) some people have concrete-random learning styles, and (d) some people have abstract-random learning styles (Gregorc, 1982). A number of learning-style inventories are available for use in your classroom. You might want to locate one via a Web search and administer it to your students.

In recent years, leading instructional specialists have done much to popularize approaches based on learning styles. They have identified four basic types of stimuli that influence learning: (a) environmental, (b) emotional, (c) sociological, and (d) physical. Rita Dunn and Shirley Griggs (1988) identified 18 different elements associated with these four sets of stimuli and devised a learning-style inventory to help individuals identify their preferred learning style.

When you attempt to individualize by altering the methods of instruction, the learning intentions and content of learning remain the same for all students. Your task is to devise ways for students to process new information in ways that are compatible with their individual learning styles. To make this happen, you may decide to provide students with several options for learning new material. For example, some of your students might choose to read information from a textbook, and others might choose to view a sound clip from a CD-ROM with information about the same topic.

Altering the method of instruction based on learning style poses several problems. For one thing, a staggering variety of options are at least theoretically available to you as you attempt to accommodate different learning styles. Just diagnosing the learning styles of the number of secondary students taught in a normal day can be a formidable task. Current measures of learning style include many dimensions and often are lengthy and difficult to administer (Lefrancois, 1994). There is no standard test you can give that will reliably identify the preferred learning style of each of your students.

Some critics of this approach challenge the assumption that if you simply allow your students to choose a method of learning that seems right for them, they will choose one that is appropriate for their individual needs. They point to evidence that this might not be the case. For example, some research indicates that lower-ability students tend to perform better when they are in highly structured classroom environments and that higher-ability students tend to perform better in more loosely structured classroom environments. However, when students are asked for their preferences, lower-ability students express a preference for permissive unstructured classes, and high-ability students express a preference for highly structured classrooms. These decisions run counter to what research suggests would be the "wise" choice for each group (Lefrancois, 1994).

In addition, the research base on learning styles and the effectiveness of matching teaching methods or styles to learning styles is thin. Existing studies have yielded inconsistent and contradictory findings (Slavin, 1994). Though the theoretical rationale for this practice is well grounded, research on matching instructional methods to individual student characteristics is in its infancy. In addition, there are practical issues to be addressed and resolved before altering the mode of instruction to fit individual student characteristics becomes a common feature of secondary school programs.

As a practical matter, you may find it difficult to implement a large number of different instructional approaches if you determine that your students have a wide range of preferred learning styles. For example, you may not know much about the kinds of instructional processes that are appropriate for students with some learning styles. In addition, you may lack access to some instructional resources you need to provide choices that are optimally suited to the learning styles of some members of your class. The bottom line is that you need to reflect on the nature of your students, the nature of your own background, and the nature of your particular instructional context as you decide how far you can (or want to) go down the path of altering the methods of learning.

Altering the Goals of Learning

In differentiated instructional programs that feature altering the goals of learning, the purposes of instruction are varied to accommodate characteristics of individual students. Such programs are controversial and rare. They tend to exist primarily in private schools that are not bound to the bureaucracy of state and district regulations.

Much of the debate about the approach results from the great latitude it can give to students. In a few altering-the-goals-of-learning programs, students are permitted to make many decisions about what they want to learn. If you find yourself teaching in such a situation, your work will be primarily that of a facilitator. You will listen to students and help them clarify their personal goals. This approach presumes that your students are the best judges of their own educational needs. There also is an assumption that, when given the freedom to do so, your students will make intelligent choices.

Some examples of highly student-controlled programs of this type were implemented in a small number of schools during the late 1960s and 1970s in response to those who charged that schools were imposing too many restrictions on students. More recently, educational critics have been making quite a different argument. Many of them have suggested that schools provide students with too many electives and that authorities should require a larger number of core courses for all students. These recommendations have acted to eliminate most of the highly student-controlled differentiated learning programs of the type that appeared in some schools 20 to 30 years ago.

Some more common examples of altering-the-goals-of-learning approaches to differentiated instruction feature goals that are negotiated between teacher and students. One scheme of this type that has been used by many teachers is the *learning contract*, an agreement that you negotiate with an individual student. Its terms are variable. Typically, you as the teacher retain the final word as to what the contract will include. Often learning contracts specify a specific agenda of personalized tasks that a student must complete in a specified period of time (Tomlinson, 1999).

The following items illustrate contents often found in learning contracts:

- A description of what steps the student will take to accomplish the learning intention
- A list of learning resources that will be used
- A description of any product(s) the student will be required to produce
- An explanation of criteria that will be used in evaluating the student's work
- A list of dates when different tasks are to be completed and submitted to the teacher for review

When you use a contract approach, both you and the student sign the agreement. Its provisions become the student's differentiated curriculum. When its terms are satisfied, you and the student develop a new contract or agenda. Completed contracts document what the student has done and learned.

As a prelude to initiating a learning contract approach, you need to become a proficient learning diagnostician. This means that you have to know your individual students well enough to recommend inclusion of learning experiences in any contracts you negotiate that are appropriate for the needs of the individual who will do the work. You also must know a great deal about the kinds of support materials that are available for students to use. It makes little sense to negotiate contract terms that call on a student to work with learning resources that are not easily accessible.

CRITICAL INCIDENT

Success Is Killing Me!

LaShandra Diaz is a middle school teacher who recently developed a learning contract for one of her students, Cody Wong, who was having difficulty in her classroom. This student had done nothing for her, so she was willing to try anything to get him involved in the learning process. He responded well. His work improved, as did his test scores. Now, Cody's parents are so pleased that they have shared their son's success with other parents whose children are in LaShandra's classroom. Many of them now want her to design learning contracts for their kids.

Even though Ms. Diaz is thrilled with the positive public relations, she just can't figure out how to design 28 learning contracts given the time it takes to lay out the objectives, find appropriate materials, and prepare individual assessment instruments. The parents are coming to see her on Thursday, and she doesn't know what to do.

■ ■ ■

What should LaShandra say when she meets with the parents? Are there others from whom she should seek advice before they arrive? Would it be possible to develop learning contracts for these students without placing an irresponsibly heavy burden of work on LaShandra? How might school administrators feel about all this?

Committing to Differentiated Approaches

Successful implementation of differentiated instruction requires you to make a serious commitment to this approach. In addition to the blocks of time you must allocate to preparing and monitoring individual instructional programs, you have to accept the responsibility of managing a huge volume of paperwork. Further, you must be prepared for the reality that some of your students may not be pleased when they first encounter an approach to teaching that they may not have experienced before. This can be a particular problem if you make a common mistake: assuming that differentiated instruction requires students to work alone. It does not. What you are trying to do is establish approaches that take advantage of students' individual strengths. Your analyses of student characteristics often will lead you to plan differentiated lessons that require groups of students with similar interests and aptitudes to work together.

Teachers in today's secondary schools use many kinds of differentiated approaches successfully. You may be interested in some of the examples introduced in the sections that follow.

Activity Packages

One approach you might take in responding to the need to individualize your instruction involves preparation of activities packages. These are highly structured, self-contained guides to learning that break content into a series of small steps. Your students must accomplish each step before you allow them to go on to the next. Often you will develop a summary test that students will take after they have completed all material in a package.

Activity packages are an especially flexible format for delivering differentiated instruction. You can construct packages to address possible needs to vary (a) the rate of learning, (b) the context of learning, (c) the method of learning, and (d) the goals of learning. Your decisions regarding an appropriate focus will be based on your own analyses of the needs of students in your classes. Regardless of what you decide to emphasize, your activity package probably will include components such as those discussed in the sections that follow:

- Title
- General description and rationale
- Objectives
- Premeasure of understanding
- Learning program
- Postmeasure of understanding

Title Titles play both a motivational and a descriptive function. Because you want to spark student interest in the content of the activity package, you need to think creatively about the title you select. For example, suppose you are teaching music and want to prepare a short activity package exposing students to some basic music theory principles. Simply titling the activity package "Music Theory" is unlikely to prompt much student excitement. You might decide on something a bit more evocative, such as "Beethoven to Heavy Metal: Explorations in Music Theory."

General Description and Rationale This section of your activity package lets your students know what they must do to complete the work. You often will provide some indication of the approximate time required to do this. Often, too, you will briefly describe some important new terminology that students will be encountering as they work with the material. In addition, you will provide an explanation about why students should attach some importance to learning the new content.

Objectives In this part of the activity package, you will make clear to students exactly what it is they are expected to learn. You will include information that tells them what they will have to do to assure you that they have grasped the new material. The idea here is to give them some learning "targets" and to remove any misconceptions they might have regarding your expectations.

Premeasure of Understanding Typically, you will want students to take a pretest or engage in some other kind of exercise to provide you information about what they know about the topic before they begin working with the instructional material in your activity package. Results on these premeasures can tell you whether students have the needed prerequisite knowledge necessary to succeed on the tasks they must accomplish as they work through the activity package. In addition, this information can help you spot students who may already have mastered some of the material in the package. When this situation develops, you can direct these students to skip sections introducing material they have already mastered.

Learning Program The heart of your activity package is the learning program. Often, you will divide this component into several sections. You will provide separate instructions for students regarding what they must do to complete each section. For example, you may include references to pages to be read, CD-ROMs to be viewed, software to be run, and papers to be written. You also will include any forms you want students to complete as they work with the new material.

If you have divided the activity package into sections, you typically will provide assessment activities at the conclusion of each. For example, you may decide to include short practice tests. When students do well on tests associated with individual sections, typically they also do well on the more comprehensive post-measure of understanding they will take when they have completed the entire activity package. If your students do not perform well on a section test, they can go back and review the material again and retake the section test before moving on to new material.

Postmeasure of Understanding You usually will develop some kind of postmeasure of understanding for students to take once they have completed all the work associated with a given activity package. You may decide to use short-answer or forced-choice test items. You may decide to have students prepare a paper or a project of some kind. You will design the postmeasure to reflect both the specific content of the activity package and the nature of students who will be working with the material.

Book Circles

Book circles have become a very popular approach to differentiate instruction in content classrooms. These are modeled after the popular book discussion groups that are hosted by local book stores and celebrity TV hosts such as Oprah Winfrey. The book circle approach allows you to differentiate using several chosen books that relate to content being taught. Your books might be selected because they offer different reading levels for your students. Thus, students read a book that is most appropriate for their current reading level but one that is related to the major ideas you are currently teaching.

The key ingredient for book circle success is structure. Most teachers use a structure suggested by Harvey Daniels (2001), a structure that assigns roles (e.g., discussion leader, artist, word watcher, narrator) to each student. Not only does this give students a purpose for reading, but it also creates an opportunity for them to participate in each discussion session. Because they know ahead of time what is expected, they can be prepared for each session. Most teachers have students rotate roles each week so that each student has an opportunity to experience a variety of roles. Once the small-group process is complete, the students come together for whole-class activities that allow them to share books with their classmates.

If you are interested in learning more about book circles in the secondary classroom, you might want to read Harvey Daniels's book *Literature Circles: Voice and Choice in Book Clubs and Reading Groups* (2001) or one of any number of books now available on this topic. A Web search will generate a list of 10 or more. These books will assist you with topics on teaching your students the process, procedures for selecting books, project ideas, and assessment techniques.

Learning Centers

A learning center is a place you designate within your classroom where a student goes to pursue either required or optional activities related to a single topic. It functions as a self-contained environment for learning all required information about a given subject. Centers typically include these features:

- General information about the topic
- A list of options students may pursue in mastering the material
- Needed learning materials
- Information about tests or other assessment alternatives

For example, if you were teaching a world history course, you could set up a center focusing on this topic: "Reasons for the Outbreak of World War I." Your center might allow students to gain information about this subject in a variety of ways. You could decide to include such options as the following:

- Reading some material from one or two textbooks
- Reading a transcript of a lecture on this topic
- Working with an appropriate CD-ROM
- Listening through headphones to a discussion of this issue on a cassette tape
- Reading items posted on Internet newsgroups that focus on World War I.

Sometimes you might decide to set up several centers in your classroom. Usually, when you do this, each center has an independent focus. Successful completion of work at one center is not a prerequisite for work at another.

You can make centers as simple or complex as you want. For example, you can do something as simple as setting up a bulletin board display in a corner of your room that features a topic title, an instruction sheet, and descriptions of activities students will complete prior to taking a test on the content. More complex centers you prepare may require space for media equipment such as computers, sound equipment, and electronic display panels. You may also find a need to provide special shelving for books, globes, reprints of articles, CD-ROMs, computer software, and other kinds of learning materials. A sophisticated center may require a considerable commitment of classroom space.

Learning centers can be used for different purposes. Among the major types are the following:

- Alternate-materials center
- Enrichment center
- Reinforcement center

Alternate-Materials Center The alternate-materials center focuses on content that you want all students in the class to learn. It responds to individual student needs by including a wide variety of learning materials related to the common topic. Your students are allowed to select materials that are consistent with their own interests and abilities.

In your classes, you may find that many of your students are not highly proficient readers. As a result, some of them may have a hard time dealing with information that is presented to them in the course textbook. An alternate-materials center responds to this dilemma by providing other learning options for students who are not good readers. For example, you might provide less difficult reading materials, audiocassettes, relevant CD-ROMs, easy-to-use software and computers to run the programs, and other alternatives that treat information similar to that in the course text.

Enrichment Center The enrichment center is designed to challenge those of your students who are capable of doing more sophisticated work than many others in your class. Enrichment centers focus on a topic that is being studied by the entire group. However, only your more able students are assigned to work at centers of this type, and you include assignments that motivate them and encourage them to stretch their mental powers. Sometimes you may wish to use enrichment centers to maintain the interest of brighter students who finish regular assignments more quickly than others in the class and who need to be assigned to an additional productive learning activity.

Reinforcement Center Reinforcement centers focus on a topic all students in your class have been studying. Their primary purpose is to provide your students opportunities to review what they have learned. Hence, you will typically set up reinforcement centers toward the end of a given instructional unit. Activities provide your students opportunities to work again with difficult concepts that have been introduced and to practice new skills.

In preparing reinforcement centers, you will often want to focus on aspects of content that students have found difficult. Sometimes, when you have been working with a particularly large and difficult topic, you may wish to develop several reinforcement centers. You will design each of these to deal with a particular area of the general topic.

Learning Stations Learning stations, unlike learning centers, divide a single topic into several components. Each learning station you prepare will provide experiences for students related to one part of a more general topic. Individual stations are interrelated, and your students must complete work at each of them.

In terms of their basic organizational features, individual learning stations are much like learning centers. They typically include general information, learning alternatives, needed materials, and details about what students must do to demonstrate what they have learned. Depending on the focus of the content, you may want your students to work through learning stations in a prescribed sequence. If you decide that it is important for teachers to complete the sequence in a particular order, you can assign numbers to each station and instruct your students to work through them in numerical order. In other cases, when the material does not have to be presented in a sequential fashion, you can begin the exercise by randomly assigning students to individual stations and telling them to work through them in any order.

Because this approach always requires you to develop several interrelated stations, you will find that total preparation time is longer than what will be required of you when you develop a single learning center. In addition to deciding on which elements of a larger topic will be featured in each station, you also must think about how to manage student movement from station to station.

In planning a series of learning stations, your first task is to divide a proposed unit of work into a number of subtopics. Each of these becomes the focus for an individual station. Next, you need to decide on the physical locations for each station and develop appropriate sets of instructions. You also have to gather together needed learning materials, support equipment, and assessment devices. Finally, you have to think through some important management issues, especially procedures you want students to follow to signal to you that they have completed work at a given station and are ready to move to another.

Planning for this last issue is important. Your rules should ensure that individual stations do not become overloaded with students. To prevent this from happening, you might want to establish a no-more-than-four-students-at-one-station guideline. If such a rule is to succeed, you have to develop productive work for students who have completed work at one station and who are waiting for someone to vacate a position at another one. You might want to provide printed instructions to cover this situation that begin with this phrase: "If you have finished all work at this station and there are too many people at the next station, do this until there is a vacancy at the next station: [Specific instructions follow]."

Successful learning station instruction requires you to keep good records. These records help you keep track of the progress of individual students as they pass through the various stations. You can use this information to identify problems of individual students and to pinpoint any design deficiencies at a station that may be causing difficulties for a large number of your students. Figure 7.3 shows an example of student instructions for learning stations.

Both learning centers and learning stations have typically been more common in elementary and middle school classrooms than in high school classrooms. The context in which you teach will determine whether you will be able to use them. If you travel from classroom to classroom as some new teachers do, you probably will not be able to use centers or stations effectively. If, however, you teach in the same classroom all day and teach the same subject several times a day, you might want to try this approach to differentiated instruction. It can be an exciting change of pace for students.

Computers and Differentiated Instruction

One of the fast-growing approaches to differentiating instruction in secondary schools is computer-based instruction. Over the past 15 years, the number of computers in schools has increased at an explosive rate. Today, there are at least a few personal computers in virtually every middle school, junior high school, and high school in the nation. It is highly probable that you will find both computer laboratories in your school as well as several in your own classroom. Assuming that your school's computers have an Internet connection, you and your students will be able to access a tremendous amount of information on the Web. This huge and diverse instructional resource opens up many possibilities to you as you work to develop instructional programs that are well fitted to the particular needs of individuals in your classes. For example, you might decide to include some Web-based options as you plan various kinds of learning stations or learning centers.

In addition to the Web, computers offer opportunities for you to take advantage of specialized software. Educational supply houses today sell programs that run the gamut from loosely organized general information about large topics to highly structured programs of study focusing on narrow issues. Some of the better software packages will

ENGLISH: PERIOD 3

In this unit, you will be required to do assigned reading, take two vocabulary tests, identify literary elements, and apply them in some creative writing. To accomplish these tasks, you will be assigned to work at one of the eight learning stations. The order of completion for the stations is unimportant. Go directly to the station to which you are assigned and begin work. You will find instructions at the station telling you what to do. [*Do not go to any other station until directed to do so by the teacher.*]

When you complete each assignment at each station, place it in this notebook. Raise your hand, and the teacher will come to you and check your work. If every thing is in order, place the notebook in the box provided for your period on the shelf along the west wall. Then proceed to the next station as directed by the teacher.

As you work through the stations, keep track of your progress by completing this form.

Stations	**Date Completed**	**Score**
Station 1: Test on "Sinking of PT 109"	______	______
Station 2: Vocabulary Test #1	______	______
Station 3: Short paper on imagery	______	______
Station 4: Short story I wrote	______	______
Station 5: Six examples of personification:	______	______
(1) ______ (4) ______		
(2) ______ (5) ______		
(3) ______ (6) ______		
Station 6: Vocabulary Test #2	______	______
Station 7: Completed crossword puzzles	______	______
Station 8: Six poems I wrote	______	______

Figure 7.3

allow you to alter most of the important variables associated with differentiated instruction. For example, you can modify some programs to allow students to work at their own pace. Others allow for variations in how new content is introduced. Many of them provide alternative ways for your students to review content.

Some software features *intelligent tutor programs*. These programs are designed to determine what a student already knows in relation to a particular learning outcome. Once this is determined, the program exposes the student to learning experiences that are designed to teach information he or she has not yet mastered.

The intelligent tutor program assesses what students already know by prompting them to respond to questions asked by the computer. Their responses are then compared to a database built into the computer. As a result of the comparison, the computer program develops a unique student profile and goes on to establish a special sequence of learning experiences for the student. Once this step has been completed, the student begins moving through the planned instructional sequence. As this process goes forward, the program provides correctives, as needed, and provides other kinds of feedback related to the adequacy of the learner's performance.

One advantage of intelligent tutor and other computer-based differentiated programs is that the computer has infinite patience. For example, a computer will allow students to recycle through difficult material as many times as they need to master the content. When your students use such programs, they are involved with an instructional process that truly allows them to progress at their own rate. In addition, many computer programs provide a useful record of student progress when they complete a learning session. This allows you to monitor this information at your own convenience. In addition, the information often will be stored and used when a student returns for additional work. Based on what they have done previously, the computer will provide an appropriate entry point for the students when they return to work again with the computer-based material.

Peer Tutoring

Another approach you can use to differentiate your instruction is peer tutoring. This procedure requires you to assign students who have mastered certain new material to work with others who need additional help. There are two basic types of peer tutoring: *same-age peer tutoring* and *cross-age peer tutoring*. As the name suggests, same-age peer tutoring features tutors who are about the same age and who are in the same grade as those being tutored. On the other hand, cross-age peer tutoring features older, more advanced students working with younger, less advanced students.

Researchers have found that both the person doing the tutoring and the person being tutored experience increased levels of learning. In fact, some studies indicate that the person doing the tutoring has the greatest achievement gain (Slavin, 1994). Given this information, you might occasionally choose students to serve as tutors who are not necessarily your brightest "academic stars." You will find that the responsibilities these students assume as tutors often will help them develop a better grasp of the content they are asked to teach. You might be interested to know that, in some places, high school students identified as being at risk of dropping out of school have been assigned to work as tutors in elementary schools. Their involvement gives the high school students an opportunity to revisit information they may not have learned well when they first encountered it. In addition, this arrangement often gives the older students a sense of responsibility that can lead to more positive attitudes toward school.

Peer tutoring is an especially useful method for differentiating instruction.

MORE FROM THE WEB

Differentiating Your Teaching

In this chapter, you have been introduced to a number of ways to meet needs of individual students. The following Websites contain information that you may find useful in applying the ideas of the chapter. Some of them contain lesson plans you can adapt to your classroom. Others provide rich resources that you can use in designing differentiated learning instruction. Still others will provide opportunities to learn from other teachers who have developed differentiated programs.

Educator's Tool Kit

This site has an abundance of resources that can be valuable in helping you design differentiated lessons. There are links to lessons plans, a whole section on students with special needs, and ideas on how to teach various subjects.

Website: http://www.eagle.ca/-~matink

Designing Web-Based Learning Stations

Tammy Worcester has made available at this site information that describes approaches you can use to develop learning stations that feature content from the Web. The information is introduced in the form of a 17-slide presentation and includes details that are helpful in developing a differentiated instruction program featuring learning stations and Web content.

Website: http://www.essdack.org/stations/sld001.htm

Plans for Differentiated Instruction

If you are interested in historical developments related to differentiated instruction, you will want to visit this site. Among other topics, you will find information about the Winnetka plan and the Dalton plan. Both were forerunners of some individualized approaches that teachers use today to differentiate instruction.

Website: http://www.coe.uh.edu/courses/cuin6373/idhistory/individualized_instruction.html

Socrates—Style and Methods

At this site, you will find an extensive discussion of Socrates' approaches to teaching. One section, titled "Individualized Instruction," explains how Socrates went about the business of discovering and responding to the special needs of his students.

Website: http://www.san.beck.org/SOCRATES3-How.html

Peer Tutoring

The Northwest Regional Educational laboratory has posted information at this site. It features an extensive discussion of peer tutoring. In addition to descriptions of the approach, you will find excellent references to research studies that have been conducted to determine its effectiveness.

Website: http://www.ncrel.org/sdrs/areas/issues/students/atrisk/at6lk20.htm

Example of Differentiated Instruction in a High School Class

If you are interested in seeing differentiated instruction in action in a high school classroom, check out this example. You may also want to explore differentiated instruction in more depth on the ASCD (Association for Supervision and Curriculum Development) site that provides this example.

Website: http://www.ascd.org/pdi/demo/diffinstr/l1hsex.html

Regardless of the type of tutoring program you decide to implement, your tutors need training (Slavin, 1994). They have to learn how to provide assistance without doing the work for the person they are helping. In addition, you have to monitor tutors' work carefully. If you fail to do so, tutoring sessions can easily turn into opportunities for social conversation having little if any connection to academics. Tutors also are more confident as they approach their tasks when they know you are readily available to help them if they run into any difficulties.

Differentiation Through Sheltered Instruction

In chapter 3, we discussed the changing population in today's classrooms. You may find yourself teaching a large population of English learners. These students require some special considerations as you design effective lessons. Although some English learners will be mainstreamed into regular classrooms, some will be grouped into special classes classified as *sheltered* or *SDAIE* (specially designed instruction in English). No matter which configuration you are assigned, the techniques discussed next will help you differentiate instruction for these learners.

Sheltered instruction is defined as grade-level content in English for nonnative speakers. It is a means of making content course work (e.g., social studies, math, science) more accessible for English learners (Echevarria & Graves, 2003). In sheltered classrooms, teachers teach academic skills while assisting development of the student's new language. Ideally, students assigned to sheltered classes should have developed both proficiency and literacy in their first language.

The following tips, provided by a number of experts, are helpful in assisting your English learners (Echevarria & Graves, 2003; Garcia, 2002; Krashen, 1981; Lessow-Hurley, 2002).

Use Simplified English Conversations Because these students are still learning English, it is imperative that you speak more slowly and enunciate clearly. Consider exaggerating key words and phrases to emphasize their importance. Emphasize vocabulary, preteaching words that you think will be challenging for the students.

Use Cooperative Groups The socialization process involved in cooperative group structures provides a vehicle for students to improve their academic language. The interaction between students gives English learners opportunities to practice their new language in meaningful ways.

Use a Variety of Visual Aids English learners need to see as well as hear the concepts being taught. Consider using realia, a variety of primary sources, photos, maps, globes, diagrams, technology, and audiovisual tools.

Don't Constantly Correct Students' Departure from Standard English Encourage students to talk. Once they do, you can paraphrase their responses to model Standard English.

Increase Your Wait Time Give English learners more time to respond to your questions than you would give proficient English speakers. They need the extra time to adequately process their thoughts in English.

Adapt Content to Meet Students' Language and Learning Needs You may be required to use textbooks that are too difficult for English learners. Locate additional resources that can supplement the required text. Consider rewriting some parts into text that is more comprehensible or make available easier editions of the text. In addition, assign real-life activities that are meaningful for students (e.g., letter writing, simulations).

Tape Record Some of Your Lessons Allow English learners to listen to the presentation several times to enhance understanding.

Reinforce Language Learning While Teaching Content Model the pronunciation of difficult words and the intonation of the English language used in content material. Emphasize basic grammatical structure to assist students in comprehending content.

Relate the Academic Content to the Students' Experiences Design lessons that draw on the backgrounds of the students in your classroom. Consider allowing them opportunities to share these experiences and suggest topics of interest.

Emphasize Literacy Activities Use interactive journals, silent reading followed by whole-group or small-group discussions, book circles, and mathematics logs. (See chapter 12 for additional ideas.)

You may be thinking that many of these are just good teaching strategies for any classroom. In some cases, that is true. However, these strategies are particularly important if you are teaching large groups of English learners. Your job is now twofold: you are inspiring students to learn both content and language.

Conclusion

A differentiated classroom is no longer an option; it is a necessity if you are to provide students with opportunities to learn. As you face increasingly more diverse classrooms—classrooms with gifted students, English learners, and mainstreamed special education students—we encourage you to heed the words of Howard Gardner.

He suggests that the biggest mistake in teaching has been to treat all students as if they were variants of the same individual and thus to feel warranted in teaching them the same subjects in the same way (Siegel & Shaughnessy, 1994, cited in Tomlinson, 1999). Today's students deserve teachers who are willing to abandon the one-size-fits-all delivery system in favor of a system that responds to the needs of the individual learner.

FOR YOUR PORTFOLIO

1. Standard 3 of the INTASC standards relates to understanding difference. What materials or ideas that you learned in this chapter related to differentiating for learning will you include as "evidence" that you understand difference? Select up to three items of information to be included in your portfolio. Number them 1, 2, and 3.
2. Think about why you selected these materials for your portfolio. Consider such issues as the following in your response:
   - The specific purposes to which this information can be put when you plan, deliver, and assess the impact of your instruction
   - The compatibility of the information with your own priorities and values
   - The contributions this information can make to your personal development as a teacher
   - The factors that led you to include this material as opposed to some alternatives you considered
3. Prepare a written reflection in which you analyze the decision-making process you followed. In addition, mention the INTASC standard(s) to which your selected material relates. (First complete the following chart.)

Materials You Selected and the INTASC Standards

There are other INTASC standards that you might address. Put a check under those INTASC standards numbers to which the evidence you have selected applies. (Refer to chapter 1 for more detailed information about INTASC.)

Item of Evidence Number	INTASC Standards									
	S1	S2	S3	S4	S5	S6	S7	S8	S9	S10
1										
2										
3										

KEY IDEAS IN SUMMARY

- The diversity of students in classrooms today means that teachers have learners with highly varied interests and aptitudes. This provides a context that is particularly appropriate for differentiated instructional approaches that seek to take advantage of unique characteristics of individual students.
- One approach to differentiating involves altering the rate of learning. When this is done, all students are exposed to the same basic instructional program, but the speed at which individual students progress through the program varies. Mastery learning is an example of altering the rate of learning to differentiate instruction. Mastery learning presumes that observed differences in students' levels of achievement have little to do with differences in their levels of intelligence or in their aptitudes. Rather, differences occur because individuals vary in terms of how much time they need to do the required work.
- Another approach to differentiating involves altering the context of learning. Goals pursued by all students may be the same, but the teacher seeks to identify areas in which students are particularly interested and to provide relevant instruction within the context of these enthusiasms. This approach assumes that students' levels of motivation increase when learning materials are closely matched to their interests.
- Differentiated programs that attend to the learning-style differences of learners often involve teachers in altering the method of learning. Objectives and content remain the same for all students, but individuals are allowed to pursue different paths as they seek to learn the material. For example, some students may read about it, others may work with appropriate CD-ROMs, and still others may interview people and take notes.
- A fairly unusual approach to differentiating, at least in public school settings, involves altering the goals of learning. In this approach, great latitude is given to students to select the goals of instruction and to make other important decisions about what they wish to learn. There is an assumption that, given the freedom to do so, students will make intelligent choices.
- One approach to differentiating involves the use of activity packages. These are highly structured and self-contained guides that break learning content into a series of small steps. Students must successfully complete one step before going on to another. Activity packages represent a flexible format. They can be designed to respond to a variety of individual student needs.
- A learning center is a designated place within a classroom where a student pursues learning activities related to a single topic. This self-contained environment for learning often provides general information about the topic, a selection of learning options for students, needed learning materials, and information about tests or other assessment alternatives.
- Learning station approaches subdivide large topics into important subtopics. Each station focuses on one part of the general topic. Organizationally, each learning station is set up much like a learning center, but learning stations require more teacher time to prepare than learning centers. This is true because several of them must be set up at once and complete instructions and support materials provided for each.
- Book circles are an increasingly popular approach to differentiation. Teachers select four or five books that are tied to the learning objectives in a given unit. Students then are grouped with others reading the same book. Structure is imperative if book circles are to work effectively.

- Emerging electronic technologies, particularly those based on computers, are providing more options for teachers who wish to individualize their instruction. In recent years, there have been great advances in software that can be used to generate instructional options suited to the needs of individual students. In addition, much material on the Internet can be incorporated into differentiated learning programs.
- Peer-tutoring approaches feature students who have mastered new material working with other students who need additional help. Same-age peer tutoring uses tutors who are about the same age and in the same grade as the students they are helping. Cross-age peer tutoring features tutors who usually are older and more advanced than the students they have been asked to assist.
- Sheltered classrooms require techniques especially designed to provide comprehensible content for English learners. Some of these include (a) using simplified English conversations, (b) using cooperative groups, (c) using a variety of visual aids, (d) not constantly correcting students' departure from Standard English, (e) increasing your wait time, (f) adapting content to meet students' language and learning needs, (g) tape recording some of your lessons, (h) reinforcing language learning while teaching content, (i) relating academic content to the students' experiences, and (j) emphasizing literacy activities.

REFLECTIONS

1. What is your definition of differentiated instruction? Which variables associated with differentiation do you think you should be most comfortable altering? Why?
2. What concerns do you have about altering each of the variables for differentiating instruction?
3. Some individuals see a conflict between recent state-level efforts to mandate specific tests that all students must complete and the need to meet the needs of diverse students. What is your response to this issue?
4. Which approaches to differentiated instruction do you see as most consistent with recent trends in education?
5. Which of the specific approaches to differentiated instruction do you think would fit best with your beliefs and skills? Why?
6. Several approaches to differentiating instruction were introduced in this chapter. How would you rate your interest in each? Which do you think would be most difficult for you to implement, and why?
7. Some people suggest that the Internet offers an exceptionally rich resource for the teacher who wants to individualize. However, others argue that to use this resource requires considerable teacher control in order to prevent abuses. What is your opinion?
8. Suppose you decided to use peer tutors in one of your classes to assist students having difficulty mastering some new content you have introduced. How would you specifically prepare your tutors for their responsibilities?
9. Some critics of differentiated instruction suggest that it is an impractical sham. They allege that the term "sounds good" but that, in reality, teachers simply lack sufficient time to plan programs uniquely suited to the needs of each student. What do you see as strengths and weaknesses of this argument?
10. As you reflect on your professional knowledge, what additional information do you think you need to acquire to better meet the needs of diverse students?

LEARNING EXTENSIONS

1. Observe in a secondary school. Look for ways the teachers differentiate and adapt their instruction to meet the needs of diverse students. Using what you have learned in this chapter, identify places where these teachers have altered one of the four differentiated instruction variables introduced. Share your observations with others in the class.
2. Identify a specific topic you would cover in one of the courses you would like to teach. Develop a complete set of plans for a learning center devoted to this topic. Present your plans to your instructor for review.
3. Educational professional journals include many articles that report practical ideas for differentiating instruction. Begin a differentiated instruction folder that includes reprints of at least 10 articles. You might begin by looking at entries in the Education Index. Your instructor may have other suggestions to help with this project.
4. Identify a topic you may wish your students to learn. Suppose you wanted some students to gather as much information as possible about this topic using resources only available on the Internet. Develop a master list of URLs of Websites with information that might help your students. Share this material with members of your class and describe how you might use this information to individualize your instruction.
5. Reread the material in this chapter that deals with activity packages. Choose a topic from your own field and prepare an activity package for students. Include alternate ways for students to do the work. Share your work with others in the class and be prepared to discuss any special challenges you faced in assembling this material.
6. Identify some content that you will teach. Find five or six books that you might use in a book circle approach in your classroom. Prepare material for a book talk on each book and set up the group roles in a format ready to distribute to students. Design some end-of-reading projects that will provide students with alternatives for demonstrating their understanding of the reading.
7. Work with a group of classmates who plan to teach the same subject. Use a content textbook to design a sheltered lesson using the ideas presented in this chapter.

REFERENCES

Bloom, B. S. (1976). *Human characteristics and school learning*. New York: McGraw-Hill.

Bloom, B. S. (1980). *All our children learning*. New York: McGraw-Hill.

Cuban, L. (1984). *How teachers taught: Constancy and change in American classrooms, 1890–1980*. New York: New Press.

Daniels, H. (2001). *Literature circles: Voice and choice in book clubs and reading groups*. Portland, ME: Stenhouse.

Dunn, R., & Griggs, S. (1988). *Learning styles: Quiet revolution in American secondary schools*. Reston, VA: National Association of Secondary School Principals.

Echevarria, J., & Graves, A. (2003). *Sheltered content instruction: Teaching English-language learners with diverse abilities* (2nd ed.). Boston: Allyn & Bacon.

Garcia, E. (2002). *Student cultural diversity: Understanding and meeting the challenge* (3rd ed.). Boston: Houghton Mifflin.

Gardner, H. (1999). *Intelligence reframed: Multiple intelligences for the 21st century*. New York: Basic Books.

Good, T., & Brophy, J. (2004). *Looking in classrooms* (9th ed.). New York: Longman.

Gregorc, A. (1982). *Gregorc style delineator: Development, technical and administrative manual.* Maynard, MA: Gabriel Systems.

Guild, P., & Garger, S. (1985). *Marching to different drummers*. Alexandria, VA: Association for Supervision and Curriculum Development.

Guskey, T. (1985). *Implementing mastery learning*. Belmont, CA: Wadsworth.

Krashen, S. (1981). *Second language acquisition and second language learning*. London: Pergamon Press.

Lefrancois, C. (1994). *Psychology for teaching* (8th ed.). Belmont, CA: Wadsworth.

Lessow-Hurley, J. (2002, Fall). Acquiring English: Schools seek ways to strengthen language learning. *ASCD Curriculum Update*. Alexandria, VA: Association for Supervision and Curriculum Development.

Siegel, J., & Shaughnessy, M. (1994). Educating for understanding: A conversation with Howard Gardner. *Phi Delta Kappan, 75*(7), 564.

Slavin, R. (1994). *Educational psychology* (4th ed.). Boston: Allyn & Bacon.

Tomlinson, C. (1999). *The differentiated classroom: Responding to the needs of all learners.* Alexandria, VA: Association for Supervision and Curriculum Development.

Tomlinson, C. (2000). Reconcilable differences? Standards-based teaching and differentiation. *Educational Leadership, 58*(1), 6–11.

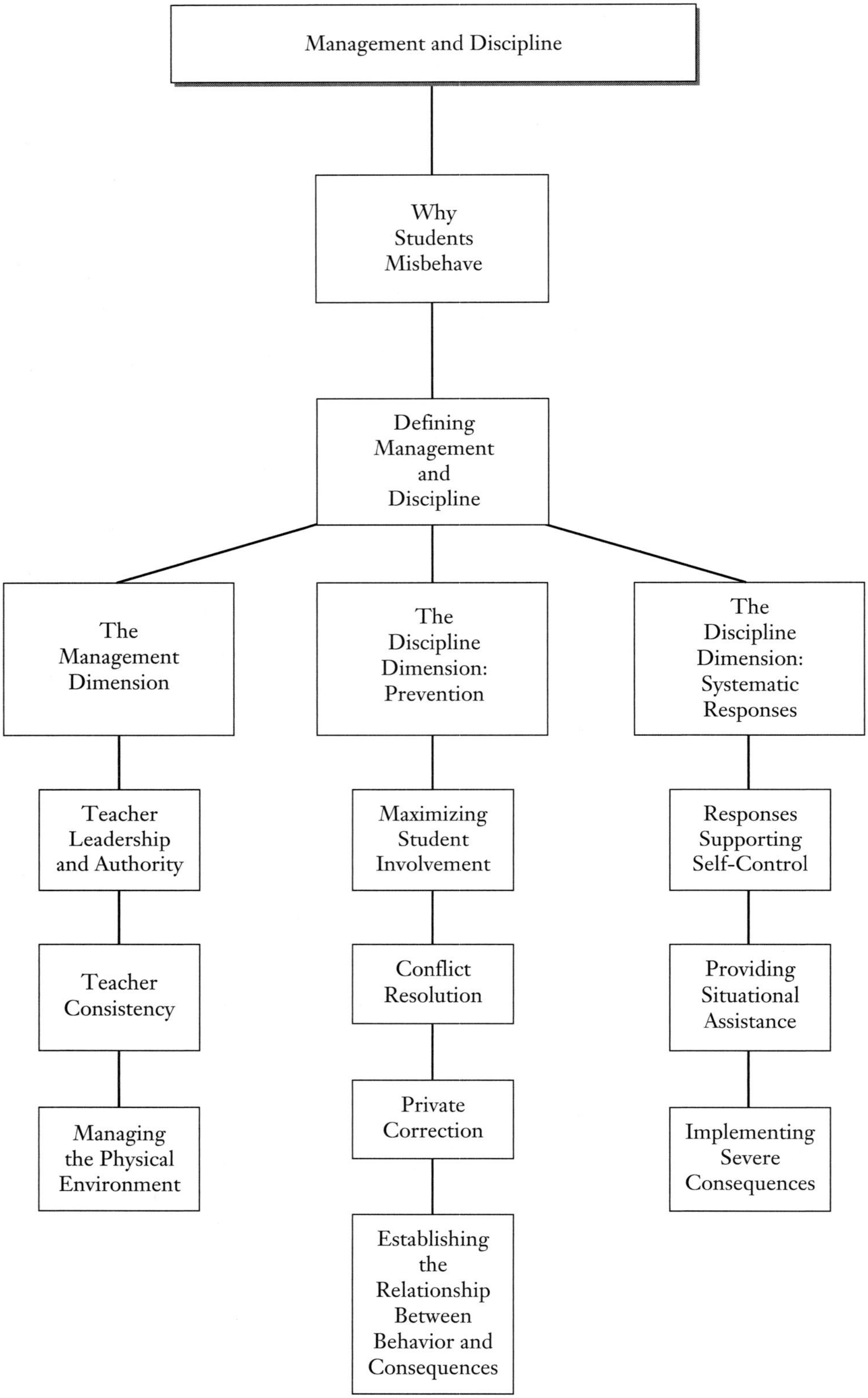

Figure 8.1
Graphic Organizer

CHAPTER **8**

Management and Discipline

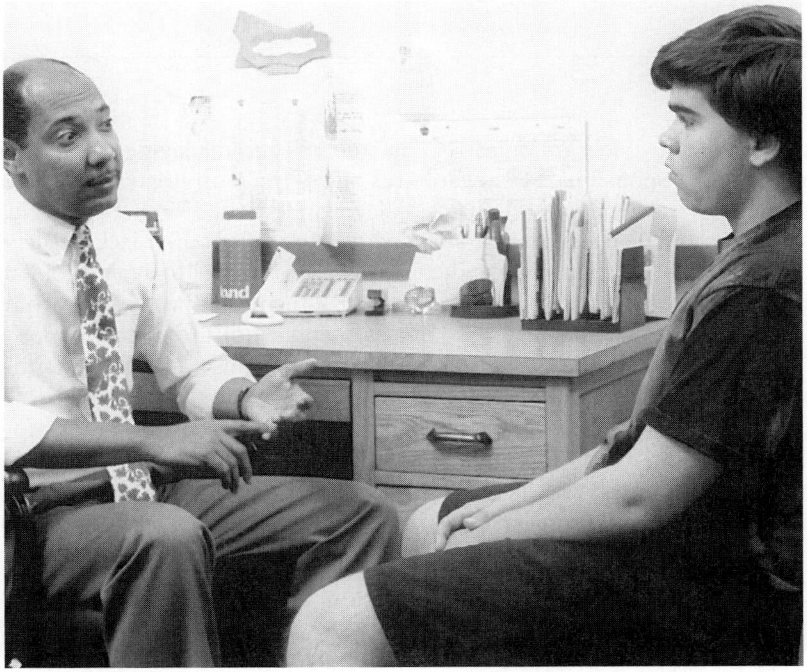

OBJECTIVES

This chapter will help you

- define the terms *management* and *discipline;*
- list the key areas that lead to success in management and discipline and explain how you can go about establishing authority in the classroom;
- describe elements of the physical environment that need to be considered when organizing the room for instruction;
- explain how to manage time in order to prevent problems;
- define principles to be followed when responding to behavior problems;
- state the importance of dialogue and negotiation in the classroom;
- describe some approaches to conflict resolution in the classroom; and
- list a range of responses that can be used when responding to misbehavior.

Introduction

As a teacher, you play two key roles: instructing students and managing the classroom. The second of these responsibilities is regarded as one of the most important challenges that new secondary teachers face (Williams, Alley, & Henson, 1999). Few beginning teachers fail because of a lack of content knowledge. Most often, their lack of success is associated with an inability to manage and control the classroom. To avoid problems of this kind, you need to work toward creating an environment that facilitates learning.

The graphic organizer at the beginning of this chapter indicates that in order to be effective in the management and discipline domain, you must first understand why students misbehave. Next, you need to define what management and discipline means. Then the domain can be divided into three basic areas: management, actions to prevent problems, and systematic responses to problems.

Marzano, Marzano, and Pickering (2003), in a review of the research on classroom management, underscore the importance of the management and discipline domain. They indicate that teachers who used effective disciplinary interventions had an average of about 980 disruptions over the course of a year, whereas those who did not had an average of about 1,800 disruptions. When the increased learning time and student engagement is translated into student achievement, those teachers with effective management techniques had student achievement scores that were about 20 percentile points higher than those who did not.

It is encouraging to note that there are some concepts and techniques that can change teacher behavior and make you a more effective classroom manager. However, if your teacher preparation program is typical of those found around the country, you will have spent a good deal of time acquiring content knowledge and learning how to transmit it effectively to students and much less time acquiring information about your management role. Although we agree that many refinements in your expertise as a classroom manager will come through direct experience in the classroom, we believe that there are concepts and skills associated with management and control that you can learn in your preparation program. That is the focus of this chapter.

However, you need to understand that there is no universally applicable set of "quick fix" remedies that you can learn that will readily resolve every potential management difficulty you may face. If there were easy solutions, classroom management would not be a topic of such serious concern among teachers, parents, and students.

The key to developing a program that results in successful and effective classroom control is in knowing something about these four areas:

- Actions you take in the classroom that are designed to prevent control problems
- Actions you take to establish your credibility and authority
- Actions you take to motivate and engage pupils
- Actions you take in response to inappropriate student behaviors

Why Do Students Misbehave?

Recent acts of violence in secondary schools across America have prompted a search for causes. Secondary schools, regardless of their location, enroll some students who are frustrated, angry, alienated, and disengaged. Eleven percent of all crimes occurs in schools, and approximately 160,000 students report staying home each day for fear of being hurt or killed (Charles, 2005). Although less publicized than violent acts involving weapons, one of the most serious school problems is that of bullying. Bullying has been identified as the unacknowledged crime of violence in schools because adults are generally unaware of its prevalence. It is estimated that one in six students is bullied each week in school (Charles, 2005).

Charles (2005) states that TV violence, dysfunctional families, poverty, unequal educational opportunities, child abuse, domestic violence, drugs, gangs, and poor emotional and cognitive development are all factors that contribute to school violence and behavior problems. It is clear that many of the causes of discipline problems are outside the control of the teacher.

Many students also experience frequent change in their lives. Such changes, particularly in family circumstances, mean that some of your students will come to school without the benefit of ongoing family support and encouragement. Many of these young people lack a strong sense of self-identity and an accompanying sense that they have the ability to succeed at school-related tasks.

In addition, your students do not leave their personal histories at the classroom door. Their diverse backgrounds provide you with an opportunity to learn more about each of the individuals in your classes and to adapt your teaching methods in response to their personal circumstances. For example, students who have a history of responding to frustrations and conflicts in unproductive ways can acquire patterns of behavior that will allow them to meet these challenges in more acceptable ways.

Finally, secondary students are at an age when they are searching for meaning and purpose in life. They are drawn to people and places that offer opportunities for meeting these needs. If you implement fair and consistent management and discipline practices, your students will see you as someone who cares about them and who can provide reliable guidance when they face difficult situations. Your goal should be to establish a learning environment based on mutual respect where your students feel safe from emotional and physical threat and where your rules are logically and consistently applied.

However, we want to emphasize that although even one act of violence in schools is too many, most of the problems you experience in the classroom will be those that are best classified as "minor." About 95% of your problems will be related to such behaviors as talking, out-of-seat, tardiness, and inattention. Often, these behaviors are related to issues such as boredom, lack of involvement, lack of success, fear of failure, seeking to belong, and lack of attention. Fortunately, you can address these issues by taking actions to reduce the incidents of misbehavior related to them. The payoff will be a decrease in misbehavior.

Initially, your focus should be on those factors you can control and what you can do to create an environment that will lead to the prevention of many of the less serious types of misbehavior. In doing this, you can begin by asking yourself these questions:

- Are you creating educational environments that respect students and value their input?
- Do your students feel a sense of power and control?
- Is the curriculum culturally relevant and worthwhile?
- Does your school provide opportunities for success rather than posing threats of failure?
- Do your students feel they really belong in your classroom?
- Does the educational experience offered to students by your school offer them opportunities to simply have fun?

Defining Management and Discipline

Before proceeding any further, you need to have clear definitions in mind of the terms *management* and *discipline*. How people define terms influences how they react in situations where these terms have relevance (Slee, 1995). Both management and discipline are examples of concepts that have often been misunderstood. These misunderstandings sometimes have led to inappropriate reactions when problems have arisen in school settings.

Management

Management includes the part of your role as a teacher that focuses on creating an environment and establishing conditions that facilitate student academic and social success. It involves your exercise of classroom leadership, facilitation of student motivation, arrangement of the physical environment, and management of time and lessons.

There are those who react negatively to the idea of management, viewing it to be characterized by autocratic teacher behaviors. We do not endorse this view. Indeed, this conception of management is rejected by many contemporary business leaders who have embraced an understanding of management that focuses on development of collaborative, democratic, and humane patterns of interaction (Kouzes & Posner, 2003). As you consider contemporary management in schools, you need to think about it in terms of your responsibilities for organizing and running the classroom and for nurturing student behaviors that will allow students to have productive interpersonal relationships with a wide variety of people.

Your responsibilities as a classroom manager require you to establish priorities as well as an environment that will allow students to achieve worthwhile and important goals. William Glasser, in his book *The Quality School* (1990), defines this type of management in detail. He points out that it is the role of the manager to behave in ways that encourage students to see the connection between what they are being asked to do and the satisfaction of basic needs. Glasser describes teachers who exercise management in this way as "lead managers." This carries the connotation of management by leadership. If you function as a lead manager, you will do the following:

- Involve students and get their input in discussions of the work to be done and the conditions under which it is to be completed
- Communicate expectations clearly, model tasks you assign, and continually solicit input from students
- Ask students to inspect and evaluate their own work for quality and willingly listen to students and accept that they know a good deal about how to produce high-quality work
- Function as a facilitator who provides students with the tools they need to learn in an environment that is noncoercive and nonadversarial

Your definition of management directly relates to the issue of discipline. If your students do not feel a sense of ownership in the classroom, do not feel respected, and do not believe you are addressing their needs, then they may feel they have no choice but to engage you in a power struggle in an attempt to meet their needs. They may end up seeking attention and recognition in ways you find unacceptable. If, on the other hand, your students believe you are meeting their needs, behaving in ways that imply respect for members of the class, and helping them reach important goals, there is little incentive for your students to adopt disruptive behavior patterns.

MORE FROM THE WEB

There are a number of sites on the Web that provide information about classroom management and discipline. The following Website provides excellent links to a number of topics related to the general theme of classroom management. It provides ideas on topics such as dealing with late-arriving students and getting the period started:

Website: http://www.teachnet.com/how-to/manage/index.html

Another site that can be useful is one complied by the Northwest Regional Educational Laboratory's School Improvement Research Series. Author Kathleen Cotton provides excellent information on topics such as defining discipline, research findings related to discipline, discipline practices that have been found to be successful for different types of students, and formal discipline programs that have been adopted around the country:

Website: http://www.nwrel.org/scpd/sirs/5/cu9.html

Discipline

Some people view the terms *discipline* and *control* as synonymous. According to this view, the teacher's disciplinary role should center on enforcing conformity and obedience to a set of rules that, if followed, will minimize disruptions and allow academic content to be covered (Hoover & Kinsvatter, 1997). We reject this conception of discipline as inconsistent with an educational system designed to prepare students to become citizens in a democratic society. It unacceptably places teachers and students in unproductive adversarial roles.

We define discipline as the process of helping students develop self-control, character, orderliness, and responsibility. These are among the most important purposes of education. Bear (1998) cited recent Gallup studies as evidence that the role of the school in teaching self-discipline is more important than it has ever been. However, Shapiro and Cole (1994) contend that teaching responsibility and self-discipline is rarely addressed and that teachers tend to resort to teacher-control types of responses.

When you act on the conception of discipline as the development of self-control, your interactions with students are based on the intention of promoting the acceptance of responsibility required of individuals living in a democratic society (McLaughlin, 1994).

WHAT DO YOU THINK?

Reflecting on Personal Experience

Your experiences as a secondary school student can serve as a valuable source of information for teaching. However, you need to think seriously about specific experiences you remember. For example, consider how your own teachers handled discipline problems. Think about things they did that worked well and those that did not. What do you remember about teachers who seemed to have few discipline problems? What do you remember about those who had difficulty in this area of professional responsibility?

Prepare a list of characteristics of both effective and ineffective managers of student behavior. How were students regarded and generally treated by teachers in each category? What are some things teachers in each category did when they had to respond to student behavior problems?

Questions

1. What differences do you remember about teachers in each category?
2. What do you think are the most important differences?
3. What are some principles that you might formulate based on your reflections about teachers in each category?
4. Share your principles with others in your class. How are yours similar and different from those developed by other class members?
5. Develop a master list of principles and compare them to ones outlined later in this chapter.

This view of discipline also provides you with criteria for determining how to respond to classroom incidents. It encourages you to consider responses that will help your students move toward increased self-control. This perspective will also allow you to see incidents of misbehavior as opportunities to teach students important lessons that will yield personal benefits to them throughout their lives. Your responses will be designed to promote students' development of patterns of self-control that are a key to productive and satisfying adult interpersonal relationships.

In summary, as a teacher, you have responsibility for both management and discipline. Your responsibilities for management should focus on organization and planning practices that can prevent problems. Your role in the area of discipline should focus on helping students develop responsible patterns of self-control. These patterns, once mastered, will serve students well throughout their adult lives.

The Management Dimension: Preventing Problems

Your management responsibilities require you to organize and manage time, materials, and space for the purpose of facilitating a smooth and productive operation of your classroom. They also require you to take actions that will establish your leadership and motivate students.

Visitors to classrooms where teachers are good managers often are unaware of specific decisions these teachers have made. These classrooms sometimes seem to run themselves. As skilled professionals, expert teachers make management look easy. In fact, these apparently problem-free classrooms are the result of hard work. They certainly are not chance occurrences that have come about because these teachers have been lucky enough to draw groups of unusually well-behaved students (Evertson, Emmer, & Worsham, 2003).

Teacher Leadership and Authority

Effective classroom management begins with you. Your philosophy, values, understanding of individual students, beliefs about learning, and leadership style all affect the social environment of the classroom. If you are to be effective, your students have to willingly accept you as a leader. In general, teachers who are viewed as leaders are secure, confident, and optimistic. This means that you should not be intimidated or fearful when you encounter challenging situations, and you should not be easily discouraged when you find your students initially unmotivated to learn what you want to teach them. One of the roots of serious discipline problems at the secondary level is a sense of hopelessness. As a teacher, you must maintain a sense of optimism and hopefulness even in difficult times. You must maintain a sense of hope for all students if you are to expect them to remain hopeful.

Your beliefs about your students will affect your personal leadership style (Clark & Peterson, 1986). For example, if you are a person who believes students are lazy and untrustworthy, you will develop management and control patterns different from those who trust and respect students. Students will quickly sense any negative attitudes you may have about them. If they believe you do not respect or trust them, they become very reluctant to accept you as a leader.

In preparing to work with secondary students, you need to remember that young people in this age-group are striving to establish some sense of personal identity. As part of this effort, it is natural for them to engage in some limit testing of imposed authorities (parents, teachers, and others). Secondary students cannot be expected to defer quietly to every one of your demands, particularly if they sense an element of unfairness or if they feel you are challenging their self-respect.

Many sources will contribute to students' perceptions of your leadership authority. French and Raven (1959) identified some perspectives you might consider as you develop your own approach to leadership in the classroom. They identified five sources of power or authority that are applicable to classroom environments:

- Legitimate power
- Reward power
- Coercive power
- Expert power
- Referent or attractive power

Legitimate Power Some roles in American society, including teaching, carry with them a certain power and expectation of leadership regardless of who fills the role. This is termed legitimate power. Your position as a teacher invests you with some power and authority. However, your legitimate power will not result in your students automatically respecting and following your leadership. Indeed, if you are foolish enough to tell your students to do something simply because you, as their leader, believe they should do it, you will be disappointed. Some members of your class may even laugh. Simply put, authority-based power is not something you should put too much stock in as a way to motivate students.

Reward Power As a teacher, you will be able to provide certain benefits to students. As a result, you benefit from having some reward power. Rewards at your disposal include such things as grades, verbalized praise statements, certain privileges, and other actions in areas that individual students may see as having some personal importance.

However, there are limitations on your reward power. In some situations, all students may not value the kinds of rewards you are in a position to give. For example, if a given student attaches no importance or value to getting good grades, he or she will not be motivated to work hard or behave in order to get a high grade. A few students value the attention and praise they get from other young people more than the grades they receive. Many of them may have arrived at a point in their school careers where they have lost any confidence in their abilities to earn high grades. If you attempt to assert your leadership by making threats related to grades, these students may be quite indifferent to your approach.

Coercive Power Individuals in positions of authority also hold the capacity to punish members of groups they lead. As a teacher, you are in a position to discharge some of this coercive power. Students who respond to coercive power accept certain patterns of behavior not because of a real commitment to them but because they seek to escape punishment.

There are great limitations on coercive power as an approach to working with students. If you administer punishment of some kind, the result may be a temporary cessation of an objectionable student behavior. However, unless you provide support for an alternative, appropriate pattern of behavior, an even more unacceptable pattern may develop. In addition, if you rely too much on punishment to assert your authority, you may encourage your students to view combat as the normal character of their relationship with you. They may feel challenged to outwit you and get by with breaking rules to show you that they are not intimidated. Vandalism, truancy, and student anger frequently characterize classes taught by teachers who depend too much on punishment and coercion to maintain their authority.

Expert Power Individuals perceived by a group to have superior knowledge or skill are accorded some leadership or authority. As a teacher, you are in a position to enjoy some of this expert power. Leadership that comes to you because students appreciate your expertise can be very effective. This is true because this authority is awarded to you out of respect, not because it is demanded. Researchers have found that students consistently report admiring teachers who know their content well and who are able to explain it clearly (Tanner, 1978).

Two dimensions of expert power can enhance your relationships with students. The first relates to your grasp of the content you will be teaching. The second has to do with your commitment to plan and execute lessons that enable students to learn. You cannot fake an understanding of content you do not have; you cannot teach off-the-cuff without preparation. Attempts to do either of these things will be detected by students and will undercut your expert power. When this happens, students will lose respect for you as a teacher. Once you lose their respect, your ability to discipline students effectively is diminished.

Referent or Attractive Power Individuals who are perceived to be trustworthy and interested in the well-being of others are also accorded leadership status and authority. For example, you willingly seek advice from and even entrust prized possessions to those friends and family who you believe have your best interests at heart. These are individuals who have what is termed referent or attractive power.

You should seek to develop relationships with students that will lead them to defer to your referent or attractive power. William Glasser (1990) considers this kind of leadership to be particularly important. He points out the need for teachers to create warm and personal classroom atmospheres where students believe they belong and where their needs are regularly met. This can be a difficult task for you as a secondary school teacher since you may see many of your students only once a day for less than an hour. However, many of us had secondary teachers who were able to do so.

You can begin to build referent power by doing things such as learning students' names, encouraging them, and treating them respectfully. Fairness in testing and grading also plays a role. Students are particularly troubled when they believe that the tests administered are unfair and seem more designed to trick them than to honestly measure what they have learned.

The most powerful combination of authority styles involves both expert and referent power. If your students see you as an expert who is interested in their welfare, you may well find that your legitimate, reward, and coercive powers are also increased. Rewards given by highly valued and trusted individuals are especially powerful. By the same token, reprimands or punishments meted out by someone who is valued and trusted are also very powerful. In fact, a simple reprimand by a highly valued teacher is often more powerful than a physical punishment administered by someone who is not trusted or respected.

Teacher Consistency

Another category of your behavior that is a foundation to a smoothly functioning classroom is consistency. To be perceived as consistent, you do not have to engage in mindless and unthinking conformity to a set of procedures or rules. Rather, being consistent simply means that you will apply rules and enforce your expectations in ways that do not vary from situation to situation so dramatically that they are unsettling to students (Savage, 1999).

This means that student behavior you find unacceptable on one day should generally also be considered unacceptable on another. If you fail to be consistent, some of your students may come to class wondering, "What can we get away with today?" This may lead them to test you to see how far they can go. When you consistently apply your rules across time, you will eliminate students' incentives to challenge the limits you have established.

You must also apply rules and regulations consistently to all students. This means you cannot simply overlook a situation when one of your "model" students breaks a rule. Selective enforcement will undermine your referent power and credibility. Student hostility and disrespect may result. Consistency of follow-through is also important. This means that when you make a promise, you need to carry it out. If you make a threat, be prepared to implement it.

Managing the Physical Environment

Your classroom's physical environment influences how your students behave. In thinking about furniture arrangement and other items in the classroom, you might consider your answers to questions such as these:

- Do I want to encourage interactions among students?
- Do I expect students to move from place to place during the class period?
- Do I want to focus students' attention on a specific part of the room?

As you go about arranging your classroom, you will need to direct your attention to the following categories of concern:

- Classroom ambiance
- Floor space
- Time management
- Establishing routines
- Providing assistance

Classroom Ambiance The ambiance of a place refers to its general atmosphere or feel. The ambiance of the classroom affects behavior patterns of both teachers and students (Weinstein, 1979). As the quality of the physical environment declines, teachers make more control statements and are less friendly. Students in such classrooms are less involved in lessons, and feelings of conflict among students increase.

To create a positive ambiance, you need to work toward an overall orderly classroom appearance and make good decisions regarding the nature of lighting, decoration of wall space, and control of temperature.

Floor Space The arrangement of desks and other classroom furniture can cue students to your expectations. Arrangements need to vary to accommodate different kinds of learning activities. For example, different patterns may be helpful when you want students to listen to you, work individually, study together in small groups, or take part in a large-group discussion.

In determining a specific arrangement, you should begin by thinking about what your students will be required to do. When you plan to present new information, it is important that student desks be arranged in such a way that each student can see you without having to look around visual obstructions. Sometimes you may want to widen the spaces separating individual desks to discourage too much social interaction among students.

However, if your intent is for students to work individually on assignments, it makes sense to arrange classroom furniture so that you can move quickly to help any individual in the class. Ideally, you should be able to move easily to help anyone experiencing a problem. An arrangement that allows you to go immediately to any place in the classroom also promotes on-task behavior. (Students know you will arrive in a hurry if a disturbance breaks out.)

When you want students to work in small groups, you need to decrease spaces separating individuals in each group. This will allow all group members to see papers and other materials, and it will permit easy conversation among all participants. It is helpful if you can arrange chairs so that all group members can easily see one another. (This is difficult if your students are required to sit in rows.)

Managing Time You will diminish the number of classroom control problems you experience if you develop good time management practices. Researchers have found that there is much unproductive time in many classrooms (Good & Brophy, 2004). Effective teachers skillfully maximize the amount of time students spend on productive tasks. The operating principle here is that busy students don't have time to misbehave.

Two aspects of time management that can help you make productive use of classroom time are (a) establishing and using routines and (b) providing assistance to those students who need help.

Establishing Routines Many classroom events are routinely repeated. These include collecting and distributing materials, making announcements, responding to students' requests, using equipment, and taking attendance. Much time can be lost if you do not carefully plan and execute these routines.

For example, suppose you develop a practice of returning papers to students individually at the beginning of each period. This routine might be consistent from day to day, but it is a procedure that has the potential to consume a lot of class time. Students may want to ask you questions about comments you have written on their papers or about grades you have awarded. You might easily find yourself using 10 to 15 minutes of classroom time to complete this task. In addition, if you spend part of this time responding to concerns of individual students, others in the class may have little to do. They might use this time to socialize, and you might find it difficult to settle the group down when you want to start the day's lesson.

You can avoid these problems by using a better time management scheme. For example, you might establish a goal of returning all papers in no more than 2 or 3 minutes. To do this, you can select from among several approaches. For example, in advance of the class, you can organize papers by rows (if your classroom is organized by rows) and simply ask the person seated in front to pass them back. Alternatively, you may decide to pass them out to individuals during a part of the lesson when students are working quietly on tasks you have assigned. These approaches tend to reduce the number of opportunities for student comments that delay the beginning of instruction. In addition, these approaches help you get a routine task accomplished in a way that does not promote side conversations among students—something that can make it difficult for you when you want undivided attention as you begin teaching a lesson.

Providing Assistance Assisting individual students can consume tremendous quantities of classroom time. Frederic Jones (1979), a scholar who studied this issue, concluded that many teachers spend more time than necessary working one on one with each student in their classrooms.

Jones suggests that you should begin helping an individual student by commenting positively about something he or she has done. Next, provide a brief and direct suggestion regarding what the student should do next. This should be a recommendation that leads the student to act; it is important not to do the work for the student. As the student begins working in response to this suggestion, you should move quickly to assist another student (following the same process with this individual). If needed, you can check back briefly with students who have been helped to see that work is being done correctly and to provide a few additional suggestions if needed. If you follow this pattern, you will probably need to spend no more than about 20 seconds working individually with each student (Jones, 1979).

You do not always have to be the one providing the help. One junior high school teacher created consultant badges that a few students earned and wore proudly. The

Keeping students actively involved reduces discipline problems.

teacher allowed these individuals to leave their seats to help other students who requested assistance. The teacher limited the number of consultants, and members of the class worked hard to win the honor of being among the "consultants of the week."

The Discipline Dimension: Preventing Problems

There are no surefire remedies or guaranteed fixes for behavior problems. What is effective in one setting and with one individual may not be effective in another. However, there are some things you can do to increase the probability that your management plan will be effective.

Maximizing Student Involvement

Productive learning in the secondary school depends on high levels of student engagement. You want to establish conditions that will allow students to be actively involved in their learning. Your purposes are to encourage them to develop a sense of ownership in the instructional program they are experiencing and to help them acquire a

CRITICAL INCIDENT

How Do You Establish Control?

Hillary Carter remembers dreaming about becoming a teacher when she was in high school. She recalls the thrill of encountering new literature and applying the insights of the great writers to her own life. As an undergraduate student, her enthusiasm for her subject increased. She worked at perfecting the communication and planning skills she knew she would need to inspire high school students. She had great confidence in her ability to be a good teacher. She started her first teaching job this fall. Things have not worked out quite as she imagined they would.

For one thing, her students are quite different from what she expected. She had wanted to teach advanced secondary students who were capable of appreciating good literature. Instead, she finds herself teaching ninth graders. The students display little enthusiasm for academic pursuits and seem consumed by social and recreational interests. They view Hillary's classroom as a social gathering place where they can show off and challenge her authority. In addition, a number of students have limited English proficiency and consequently have difficulty reading some of the literature selections she would like to use.

To remedy the situation, Hillary has tried several things, but nothing has worked. She started the year by being friendly with all the students and hoped her enthusiasm would be contagious. She told the students that she trusted them and was sure that they didn't need a lot of rules. Instead of appreciating this expression of confidence, the students have taken this as an invitation to do whatever pleases them.

In thinking about this situation, Hillary has concluded that the students behave this way because they don't understand why it is important to know something about good literature. Yesterday, she took time to talk to the class about the importance of good literature. The students rejected her logic. One student made this comment: "Look, you may like this stuff, but we think it is really boring. We would much rather see a movie."

She has considered using some literature that ties in more clearly to students' interests. But the more she has pondered this approach, the less promising it has seemed. "How," she wonders, "can I build a responsible literature program around student interests that seem limited to film stars, sports, and sex?"

Recently, she's also been thinking about the advice experienced teachers sometimes give newcomers: "Don't smile until Christmas." She thinks she may have been demanding too little of her students. For the past several weeks, she has started lowering grades of students who misbehave or fail to do their work. This has only made matters worse. Many students laugh when they get a failing grade. Some actually seem to be competing to see who can get the most Fs.

At this point, Hillary is about to give up. She has been telling her friends that "students have really changed since we were in school." She is thinking about looking for a job where she can work with college-bound students. She commented recently "I would do anything to work with some students who care."

■ ■ ■

What do you think are the key issues in this incident? What do you think about what Hillary has tried? Do you agree that students have changed a great deal in the past few years? What supports your view? What are Hillary's key values? Where did she acquire them? How might her values be different from those of the students? How might these differences affect what Hillary thinks is important and what the students think is important? Is there any way Hillary can bridge these differences, or do you think a move to another school would be the best solution for her? What do you think she needs to change? Where might she go to get help? What should Hillary's next step be?

sense of solidarity with you and other students. Researchers have found that students become more engaged in learning subject matter content when they are involved in all aspects of classroom life and that there is merit in taking actions to give them a sense of ownership as early as the first day of class (Vars, 1997).

In recent years, there has been an increased emphasis on the uses of dialogue and negotiation in creating an environment where the important issues of commitment and engagement can be addressed. Dialogue can help individuals understand the balance between rights and responsibilities. It can help your students redefine power relationships in schools that, when not examined or discussed, may appear oppressive and threatening to them (Gillborn, Nixon, & Rudduck, 1993). There is evidence that some negotiation with your students sends a strong signal to them that you are a caring teacher (McLaughlin, 1994). When you are perceived as caring, you begin to move into a relationship characterized by power *with* students as opposed to power *over* students. This type of relationship contributes to students' sense of self-worth and helps them value their status as "belonging" members of your class (Glasser, 1990).

Including dialogue and negotiation in the classroom does not mean you turn every thing over to students. Many things about school are not negotiable. For example, you have no authority to negotiate about such items as mandatory attendance, the length of the class period, and other aspects of school life governed by district and state regulations. When you set out to negotiate certain aspects of classroom life with students, you should explain these limitations up front so that students understand the context within which negotiation can take place. Though the list of limitations may seem long, there still are many aspects of the educational experience that you and your students can negotiate. These include setting the rules and the goals for the classroom, determining how conflicts are to be settled, identifying topics in the curriculum that center on student interests, organizing the classroom, setting class procedures and routines, and establishing and managing the physical environment.

Teaching Conflict Resolution

A valuable way of extending negotiation into the discipline arena is to teach your students conflict resolution strategies (Dear & Advisory Panel on School Violence, 1995). Don't forget, though, that conflicts are a natural part of life, and they will inevitably occur in your classroom from time to time. Actions you initiate with your students related to conflict resolution will make life in your classroom better for both you and the young people you serve (Lee, Pulvino, & Perrone, 1998).

Schools that have adopted formal conflict avoidance strategies tend to follow one of two basic approaches (Johnson & Johnson, 1995). One of these focuses on training groups of students who serve as peer mediators for the school. The other approach teaches all students in a school or a classroom how to manage conflict constructively. Johnson and Johnson (1995) point out that this involve-all-the-students model has proved the more effective of the two basic approaches in helping young people learn how to negotiate and mediate conflict.

Johnson and Johnson (1995) define the conflict resolution approach as involving six basic steps:

- Getting students to describe what each person wants
- Having students describe their feelings
- Explaining the reasons underlying their wants and feelings
- Reversing perspectives in order to view the conflict from both sides
- Inventing options that have mutual benefit
- Reaching a wise agreement

You may find it useful to address conflict resolution by developing specific lessons that focus on these steps. For example, you might develop lessons that include emphases on such issues as identifying conflicts, identifying different conflict resolution styles, identifying emotions, practicing active listening, identifying problem-solving approaches, and evaluating resolutions. The conflict resolution component of lessons can be embedded within large lessons that focus on your regular academic content. For example, if you are teaching English, you might choose to use a particular literary selection as a starting point for a discussion of an issue related to conflict resolution.

Content is best taught and learned when students have a need to know. Therefore, the best time to teach conflict resolution is when your students face a real conflict. In addition, you need to remember that a certain amount of repetition is needed for learning. You cannot expect one or two lessons taught at the beginning of the year to have much impact on your students' patterns of behavior.

Emphasizing Private Correction

Another important aspect of dialogue and negotiation in the secondary classroom involves how you respond to inappropriate behavior. When dealing with the issue of correction, you want to keep your conversation with the student involved as private as possible. By correcting misbehavior in private, you show respect for the student's dignity. Often it is helpful to work with a misbehaving student in a place where this discussion cannot be overheard by other students. This allows your conversation to take place in a setting that frees the student from trying to save face in front of others in the class. Private correction also affords opportunities for you and the student to improve your personal relationship. This arrangement gives you a chance to communicate your respect for the student while, at the same time, indicating your disapproval of a particular unacceptable behavior.

Choosing Misbehavior Means Choosing to Experience the Consequences

Focusing on dialogue and negotiation does not mean that there are no consequences for inappropriate behavior. It means that you give students some voice in negotiating the consequences. Part of this dialogue allows you to point out that when people choose to misbehave or violate the law, they also choose the consequences of their actions. Students must understand that you are not the one responsible for what happens to them when they misbehave. They need to realize that they will be held accountable for their own inappropriate actions. This connection between behavior and consequence is not understood by some secondary students. They blame others for the consequences they experience. For real progress toward self-control, individuals first must understand and accept that they choose the consequences through their own actions. However, this also implies that, as a teacher, you need to clearly spell out both acceptable and unacceptable behavior and the nature of the consequences for each choice.

To help students grasp the tie between unacceptable behavior and consequences, William Glasser (1965) suggests that you use a series of questions when speaking to students about their behavior. The first question is, "What are you doing?" The intent is to get the student to focus on and describe their behavior. If a student is unable to do this, you should explain carefully what the problem behavior is. The second question is, "What happens when people behave this way?" This focuses attention on the relationship between the behavior and its consequences. The final question is, "Is this what you want to happen to you?" This helps students reflect on what they have done and to begin thinking about whether they really want to face the consequences likely to befall them when they behave inappropriately.

In some instances, students will respond with, "No." When they do, the door is now open to discuss, "What can you do to make sure it doesn't happen again?" If they respond with an "I don't care," don't be dismayed but just go ahead and apply the consequences in a matter-of-fact manner and go on with the business at hand.

It is best to discuss the consequences in an individual conference with the student. If this is done privately, students are more likely to be honest with you in discussing the issue of consequences. During such a conference, you may discover that underlying emotions and feelings need to be addressed to help the student accept the consequences and a sense of responsibility for his or her own behavior.

The Discipline Dimension: Responding Systematically to Problems

Effective teachers anticipate typical problems that may occur and plan possible responses. You will find it useful to develop a range of responses that can be organized into two categories: (a) responses that are less intrusive to those that are more intrusive and (b) responses that allow students to exercise self-control to those where the teacher takes a more direct role.

Choice of a particular response in a specific situation depends on the severity of the problem and the probability that the student will be able to exercise self-control. In general, serious problems will require you to use more intrusive teacher responses than those that are less serious. In situations where an individual student persists in misbehaving over a period of time, you will want to begin with a less intrusive response and gradually escalate both the severity and the intrusiveness of your reaction.

Responses Supporting Self-Control

Responses in this category are designed to be nonintrusive. The hope is that your actions will not interfere with the flow of instruction and that students will self-correct their behavior when you give them an opportunity to do so. There are several specific actions you can do in this category.

Reinforce Productive Behavior A commitment to reinforce desirable behavior is essential to any discipline plan. Students need to know that there are rewards for productive, acceptable patterns of behavior. Positive reinforcement helps them become more self-controlled. It is important, too, that students recognize they will receive some attention when they behave properly.

Students sometimes feel that the only way to be recognized is by misbehaving. A student in such a classroom once made this comment to one of the authors: "In this school everybody knows me because I'm not afraid of the teachers. What do you get for being good?" In the minds of some students, "being good" earns contempt from other students or an expectation that they will be asked to do more work than others in the class. In other words, the consequences for being good are much less powerful than the consequences for misbehaving. In fact, the consequences for being good are often either nonexistent or negative.

One positive consequence that is usually suggested is to make sure that there is plenty of praise. Indeed, all of us like to be recognized and given some attention. However, there are some conditions for effective praise. It must be given genuinely, it must be related to a specific behavior, and it is most effective if it is not overdone.

Some secondary students will react negatively if you praise them excessively in front of other class members because they do not want to be seen as a teacher's pet. You will find that private comments, brief notes, and awards of special privileges are more effective.

Providing positive reinforcement, which includes praise, is important in helping students understand that when you do good things, good things happen to you. For example, when the entire class has been working and behaving well, it makes sense to provide the whole group with some positive reinforcement. Giving class members a few minutes to chat freely or allowing them to choose a high-value activity are examples of positive reinforcement. When students know that this is an option, they often exert peer pressure to make sure all students engage in productive behavior.

Nonverbal Signals Minor misbehaviors are much more common than serious ones. Often you can stop them through use of nonverbal signals. These include eye contact (the famous "cold, hard stare"), nodding the head in the direction of the offending student, or using an appropriate gesture. All these actions send a message to a student that you have noted a particular behavior and found it to be unacceptable. This kind of nonverbal notification often is sufficient to prompt the student to stop doing whatever has attracted your negative attention.

Proximity Control Proximity control is another technique teachers can use that sends a message to a misbehaving student without interfering with the flow of a lesson. It involves nothing more than your moving closer to the student while continuing the lesson. Many students find it difficult to continue misbehaving when they know you are nearby.

Using the Student's Name in the Context of the Lesson When efforts to gain student attention through nonverbal techniques fail, a technique that often works is to use a student's name in the context of a lesson. The technique requires that you simply insert the name of the student as part of the general flow of information that is being presented. ("If John were a member of a scientific team, he would need to know . . ."). Typically, a student will perk up when you say his or her name. You can then make eye contact and communicate to the student that you have been watching, have found something unacceptable, and expect the behavior to change.

Self-Monitoring Students who have difficulty in the area of self-control often benefit from direct instruction on how to monitor their own behavior. One way of doing this involves having the student make a list of his or her own desirable and undesirable behaviors. Together, you and the student can identify the kinds of reinforcers that might be employed to encourage the desirable patterns.

You may also find it useful to teach students to ask themselves a series of questions when they sense they may be about to lose control. Questions might include the following: "What will happen to me if I do this?" "Is it worth the risk?" and "What should I be doing instead?" You can teach those students who frequently experience self-control problems to take other kinds of actions when they find themselves becoming upset, anxious, or angry. For example, you might encourage them to close their eyes, think of a favorite place or activity, and then refocus on their work.

Providing Situational Assistance

When responses designed to support student efforts at self-control are not effective, you need to become more involved and more intrusive. You have given students an opportunity to self-correct, and they have chosen not to do so. You now need to deal directly with the student or restructure the learning environment. Again, there are a variety of actions that you can take. These start with the least intrusive and move in the direction of more intrusive and direct action.

A Quiet Word This response requires you to move directly to the student who is misbehaving and to provide a quiet reminder of what you expect his or her behavior to be. You want to do this as unobtrusively as possible. Ideally, you want to communicate firmly your expectations to the student without drawing too much attention to the offending student and the inappropriate behavior.

Implementing Logical or Natural Consequences Sometimes nonverbal signals are not effective, a quiet word fails to get the job done, and a student contends that following rules is unimportant. When this happens, the student needs to experience negative consequences resulting from his or her failure to correct an inappropriate behavior. When possible, the consequences should have a logical relationship to the nature of the inappropriate behavior. For example, if a student destroys something, he or she should be required to make restitution. If a person cannot work productively in a group, he or she should be removed and required to work alone. If an entire class is failing to stay at task during a lesson, you may require that wasted time be made up later when the group would be engaging in an enjoyable activity.

Responding with Clarity and Firmness When other techniques fail or when a given behavior is seriously disrupting an entire class, you need to take quick action. This action should be characterized by clarity and firmness. Clarity means that you make a specific reference to the student who is misbehaving, what he or she is doing that is unacceptable, and an appropriate alternative behavior. You might say something like this: "Susan and Jose, your whispering and note passing are disruptive. Take out your lab manuals and begin the assigned work now." The opposite of clarity might be, "Please behave." These unclear messages are seldom effective.

In addition to being clear, your messages need to be firm. This means they should be sent in an "I mean business" manner. You can accomplish this by using a steady, serious tone of voice; direct eye contact; an erect body posture; and proximity control. Lack of firmness communicates to the student that you are really not serious and don't mean business. Surprise and anger often result when you move to more serious action.

Removing the Student from the Situation Students who continue to misbehave sometimes need assistance to exercise self-control. The environment might simply be too inviting for inappropriate behavior. They may need to be shifted to another place in the classroom. This is particularly true if the problem involves a student talking to someone else in the class while you are trying to teach.

One solution is moving the student closer to your desk, thus permitting you to easily monitor the individual's behavior. In addition, physical proximity to your location in the classroom will prompt a misbehaving student to do a better job of managing his or her behavior.

Student Conferences A personal conference with a student who continues to misbehave often yields productive results. During such a conference, you need to encourage a misbehaving student to do most of the talking and to make decisions regarding how the offending behavior might be changed for the better. You might also consider using conferences as opportunities to develop informal behavior contracts with students who exhibit unsatisfactory patterns of behavior. These contracts specify what students need to do to improve their behavior, and they might reference some good things that will come to them as a result of positive changes in their behaviors.

Conferences need to be conducted in a firm, businesslike manner. Often students will be upset when a conference begins. If you fail to keep your own emotions under control, an unproductive exchange featuring angry accusations and unproductive debates is likely to be the result. One of your tasks is to cool the situation, explain exactly what is amiss with the student's behavior, and work calmly to lay out some possible solutions.

Implementing Severe Consequences

If unobtrusive measures such as supporting self-control and situational assistance do not work, you must move to more serious and severe consequences. Severe consequences are the most intrusive responses. For these actions to be effective, they need to be implemented sparingly and only when there is a serious problem of persistent misbehavior. When these actions are implemented too frequently or in response to minor problems, they lose their effectiveness.

Removing the Student from the Classroom When a student's misbehavior has not improved as a result of other actions, you may find it necessary to remove the individual from the classroom. This can accomplish several things. First, it tells the student that you are serious about maintaining order. Second, because most students like to be with their friends and peers in the classroom, removing someone takes him or her away from a rewarding social situation. Among other things, your action eliminates the possibility that the student will gain status in the eyes of others in the class by challenging you. Finally, removing a student from the class gives you and the student some time to cool off.

When you remove students from the classroom, you need to send them to a supervised area. Never tell them simply to go out into the hall or into an unsupervised situation. If anything should happen to them or if they should act in ways that hurt people or damage property, you could face serious legal complications. What you want to do is send students to a counselor's office, the principal's office, or to a special designated area set aside by the school (staffed by adult supervisors) for students who have been asked to leave class for disciplinary reasons.

Once you have sent a student out of your classroom, you need to notify personnel in the school's central administrative office. They will alert individuals in the appropriate office that the student is expected. If a student fails to arrive in a timely manner, many schools have guidelines calling for someone to look for the student and to accompany him or her to the designated area.

Conference with Parents or Guardians When students seriously misbehave, their parents or guardians must be notified. Often a telephone call or a note will initiate actions at home that will encourage the student to change an unacceptable pattern. If serious misbehavior persists, you should try to schedule a face-to-face conference with the student's parent(s) or guardian. In preparing for such a meeting, you should gather anecdotal records (brief summary accounts) of misbehavior. These should include dates and times of episodes of misbehavior and summaries of what you have already done to try to change this unacceptable pattern.

During the conference, remember that many parents are uncomfortable meeting with a teacher. They already know that there is a serious problem, and they may be defensive. It is important that during the conference, you avoid an adversarial relationship. You want to communicate to the parents that you are interested in the welfare of their youngster and want to work together in order to solve the problem. It is important for the parent(s) or guardian to share their perspectives on issues that are raised. Therefore, allow them an opportunity to talk and do not become angry or defensive if they share some things about which you do not agree. For example, if parents state that the problem is that teachers are unfairly picking on their child, you might state that you are sorry that they feel that way and ask for them to give you some specific examples. You might then ask for suggestions on how the situation can be changed.

On some occasions, the parents will express a sense of hopelessness and frustration. Be prepared to share addresses and phone numbers of various social service agencies that the parent can contact for help. You are not a professional psychologist or counselor, and you should not try to be one. If parents are reluctant to follow through, you need to point out that it is really for the welfare of the student.

If possible, the conference should conclude with a plan of action to which all agree. You may wish to prepare a written summary of the meeting, share it with the appropriate administrator in your school, and mail a copy to the parent(s) or guardian.

After several days have passed, initiate a follow-up communication with the parent(s) or guardian to bring them up to date on how the student is doing and solicit any further comments or reactions. The idea is to build a common team approach to helping the student. Often, if the student perceives that the teacher and the parent(s) or guardian are working together in support of a common plan of action, behaviors begin to change into more productive patterns. However, this will not happen overnight. Unacceptable patterns often take a long time to develop. Logically, it also takes time for more acceptable patterns to displace them.

Involving Other Professionals Because management of the classroom is seen as such an important aspect of being a successful educator, you may feel hesitant about seeking the advice of others. Seeking advice is not a sign of incompetence; rather, it is a hallmark of a true professional. The fact is that there is a percentage of students in every school who have serious problems and are in need of professional help. Your unwillingness to seek help from other professionals could be harmful to the student.

Several alternatives can provide assistance from other professionals. One of these is through what might be called a buddy system, a system where teachers are teamed together to help each other in a time of crisis or need. If your school has such an arrangement, your assigned buddy probably will be a teacher assigned in a classroom located close to yours. If either of you experiences a serious problem (perhaps an out-of-control student or a fight), the other person can be there in a matter of seconds to provide extra help. Pairs of buddy teachers frequently spend some time at the beginning of the school year laying out general plans for how they will react to crisis situations. If your school lacks a formal buddy system, you might want to work out your own arrangement with an experienced teacher you trust.

Some secondary school principals, in recognizing the serious consequences of frequent misbehavior and its relation to school violence, have instituted a formal on-call support system. This system designates a member of the staff for each period of the day who will be available to render quick assistance to a teacher who needs it. This person can be an administrator or an experienced faculty member trained in conflict management and mediation.

In extremely serious situations, a group of professionals may need to be consulted to develop a plan of action for a student with a particularly difficult and persistent misbehavior problem. These professionals might include school administrators, counselors, psychologists, other teachers, and even representatives from youth and community services agencies outside the school. When this is done, you need to present a well-documented case to the group so that members will have a clear picture of the situation. This team can then recommend specific courses of action that might even include removing the student from the classroom or the school.

Conclusion

Keeping issues associated with classroom management and discipline in a proper perspective is a challenge for those who are new to the teaching profession. On the one hand, it is important to recognize that the problems of discipline and violence in the school are important ones that cannot be ignored. On the other hand, you also need to understand that more than 90% of the problems that occur in classrooms are minor ones. We do not want to needlessly raise your level of anxiety about the problem of discipline in the schools or give the impression that students in secondary schools are out of control. That simply is not the case.

In every secondary school across America, regardless of the community context, there are teachers who experience few problems. You, too, can be a part of this group. However, this will not happen automatically. It requires considerable thought and hard work. Some of the ideas introduced in this chapter will help you as you strive to develop effective management and discipline procedures.

FOR YOUR PORTFOLIO

As might be expected, classroom management is a major concern of those who will be supervising and hiring you. You can certainly expect questions in your interview focusing on your management abilities. This is also recognized in the INTASC Standards. Standard 5 combines motivation and management and focuses on creating a learning environment that encourages positive social interactions. Therefore, this dimension of your teaching should be clearly represented in your portfolio.

1. Select at least three items related to the content of this chapter that you will include in your portfolio. One suggestion is to include a discipline plan that clearly spells out how you plan to organize the environment and how you plan to respond to incidents of misbehavior.
2. Think about why you selected these materials and consider the following:
   - Does the information communicate your values and priorities?
   - Does this material give the person reviewing them a clear picture of your abilities and understanding in this important dimension of teaching?
   - How does this material relate to your professional growth?

3. Prepare a written reflection on the material you have chosen. Indicate why you chose it and what you think it communicates about your ability to manage a classroom.

KEY IDEAS IN SUMMARY

- Establishing and maintaining discipline in the classroom is one of the key elements of achieving success in teaching. Changing societal attitudes have made this a more difficult task for teachers. There are four key areas that teachers need to attend to in meeting this challenge: (a) managing the classroom environment, (b) establishing teacher authority and credibility, (c) motivating and engaging the students in learning, and (d) responding appropriately to incidents of misbehavior.
- The major purpose of classroom management and discipline is to help individuals learn self-control and the acceptance of responsibility. Therefore, discipline is connected to one of the central values of education and is critical to the development of effective citizenship.
- You, as a teacher, are the key player in establishing good classroom control. A vital part of the process is how you establish your authority in the classroom. Authority based on students perceiving you to be an expert and a trustworthy, dependable individual is the best type of authority. Your consistency will contribute importantly to your effort to establish credible authority with students.
- The physical environment of the classroom has an impact on students. You need to attend to how you organize the floor space and where your desk is located. Having an attractive and inviting classroom also contributes to positive behavior patterns.
- Establishing routines for recurring events and handling student requests for assistance are two ways of using time efficiently.
- Involving students in classroom dialogues and in negotiation gives them a sense of shared power in the classroom and communicates that they are respected. Dialogue and negotiation not only help prevent problems but also are desirable steps to follow when problems do occur.
- Teaching students that conflict is a naturally occurring part of life and helping them learn how to manage and respond to conflict are important tools in helping to defuse potentially disruptive situations in the classroom. This also involves teaching students verbal and nonverbal communication skills as well as specific steps in mediation and conflict resolution.
- When students choose to misbehave, they need to realize that they are also choosing to experience the consequences of their actions.
- Developing a range of responses to potential problems allows you to choose a response that will best help students learn how to exercise self-control. Responses can be organized on a continuum moving from those that are relatively nonintrusive to those that are more intrusive.
- When serious problems occur, it is important to involve other professionals. Involving others is not a sign of poor teaching but rather a signal of a good professional attitude. The seriousness of many problems may well go beyond your capacity to solve; hence, it makes sense to involve others.

REFLECTIONS

1. What perceptions do you have about the problem of discipline in the classroom? Did they change as a result of reading this chapter? How can you check the accuracy of these perceptions?
2. Why do you think students misbehave?
3. What do you define as the purpose of discipline in the secondary school? What are the implications of this purpose for the way you will respond to classroom incidents?
4. How can a teacher demonstrate respect for the dignity of all students and at the same time communicate that certain behaviors are unacceptable in the classroom?
5. How do you think teachers go about establishing credibility and authority in the classroom? What is your plan for doing this?
6. What do you think are some advantages and disadvantages of a formal buddy system as an approach to dealing with misbehaving students?

LEARNING EXTENSIONS

1. Take a few moments to list some of the concerns you have about classroom management and discipline. What worries you most? Brainstorm possible actions that you could take to address these concerns. Share your concerns and responses with others.
2. Research the seriousness of violence in the secondary classroom. Do this by reading articles in professional journals and then check that information by interviewing several secondary teachers. How serious is the problem for them? Are their perceptions similar to those found in the literature? What might account for any differences you find?
3. Visit a secondary school and pay attention to the physical arrangement of the classroom. What aspects of the physical environment might contribute to problems? How might they be altered?
4. Discuss with experienced teachers the routines they have established for recurring classroom events. Begin making your own list of routines and procedures you will implement. Follow this by developing your own range of possible responses to misbehavior. Develop them into a range of responses similar to the example presented in this chapter.
5. Do some research to see if any secondary schools in your area have implemented conflict resolution. Visit the schools and talk with students and teachers about the process. What are the steps that are used, and how are they implemented?

REFERENCES

Bear, G. (1998). School discipline in the United States: Prevention, control and long-term social development. *School Psychology Review, 27*(1), 14–32.

Charles, C. (2005). *Teaching and learning in middle schools and secondary schools: Student empowerment through learning communities*. Upper Saddle River, NJ: Merrill/Prentice Hall.

Clark, C., & Peterson, P. (1986). Teachers' thought processes. In M. Wittrock (Ed.), *Handbook of research on teaching* (pp. 256–296). New York: Macmillan.

Dear, J., & Advisory Panel on School Violence. (1995). *Creating caring relationships to foster academic excellence: Recommendation for reducing violence in California schools*. Sacramento, CA: Commission on Teacher Credentialing.

Evertson, C., Emmer, E., & Worsham, M. (2003). *Classroom management for elementary teachers* (6th ed.). Boston: Allyn & Bacon.

French, J., & Raven, B. (1959). The bases of social power. In D. Cartwright (Ed.), *Studies in social power* (pp. 118–149). Ann Arbor: University of Michigan Press.

Gillborn, D., Nixon, J., & Rudduck, J. (1993). *Dimensions of discipline: Rethinking practice in secondary schools*. London: Department of Education, Her Majesty's Stationery Office.

Glasser, W. (1965). *Reality therapy: A new approach to psychiatry*. New York: Harper & Row.

Glasser, W. (1990). *The quality school: Managing students without coercion*. New York: Harper & Row.

Good, T., & Brophy, J. (2004). *Looking in classrooms* (9th ed.). Boston: Allyn & Bacon.

Hoover, R., & Kinsvatter, R. (1997). *Democratic discipline: Foundation and practice*. Upper Saddle River, NJ: Merrill.

Johnson, D., & Johnson, R. (1995). *Reducing school violence through conflict resolution*. Alexandria, VA: Association for Supervision and Curriculum Development.

Jones, F. (1979). The gentle art of classroom discipline. *National Elementary Principal, 58*(4), 26–32.

Kouzes, J. M., & Posner, B. Z. (2003). *The leadership challenge: How to get extraordinary things done in organizations* (3rd ed.). San Francisco: Jossey-Bass.

Lee, J., Pulvino, C., & Perrone, P. (1998). *Restoring harmony: A guide for managing conflicts in schools*. Upper Saddle River, NJ: Merrill.

Marzano, R., Marzano, J., & Pickering, D. (2003) *Classroom management that works*. Alexandria, VA: Association for Supervision and Curriculum Development.

McLaughlin, H. J. (1994). From negation to negotiations: Moving away from the management metaphor. *Action in Teacher Education, 16*(1), 75–84.

Savage, T. (1999). *Developing self-control through classroom management and discipline* (2nd ed.). Boston: Allyn & Bacon.

Shapiro, E., & Cole, C. (1994). *Behavior change in the classroom: Self-management interventions*. New York: Guilford.

Slee, R. (1995). *Changing theories and practices of discipline*. Washington, DC: Falmer Press.

Tanner, L. (1978). *Classroom teaching for effective teaching and learning*. New York: Holt, Rinehart and Winston.

Vars, G. F. (1997). Student concerns and standards, too. *Middle School Journal, 28*(4), 44–49.

Weinstein, C. (1979). The physical environment of the school: A review of the research. *Review of Educational Research, 49*(4), 577–610.

Williams, P., Alley, R., & Henson, K. T. (1999). *Managing secondary classrooms: Principles and strategies for effective discipline and instruction*. Boston: Allyn & Bacon.

PART 3 The Instructional Act

9 Models of Direct Instruction

10 Teaching for Higher-Level Outcomes

11 Small-Group and Cooperative Learning

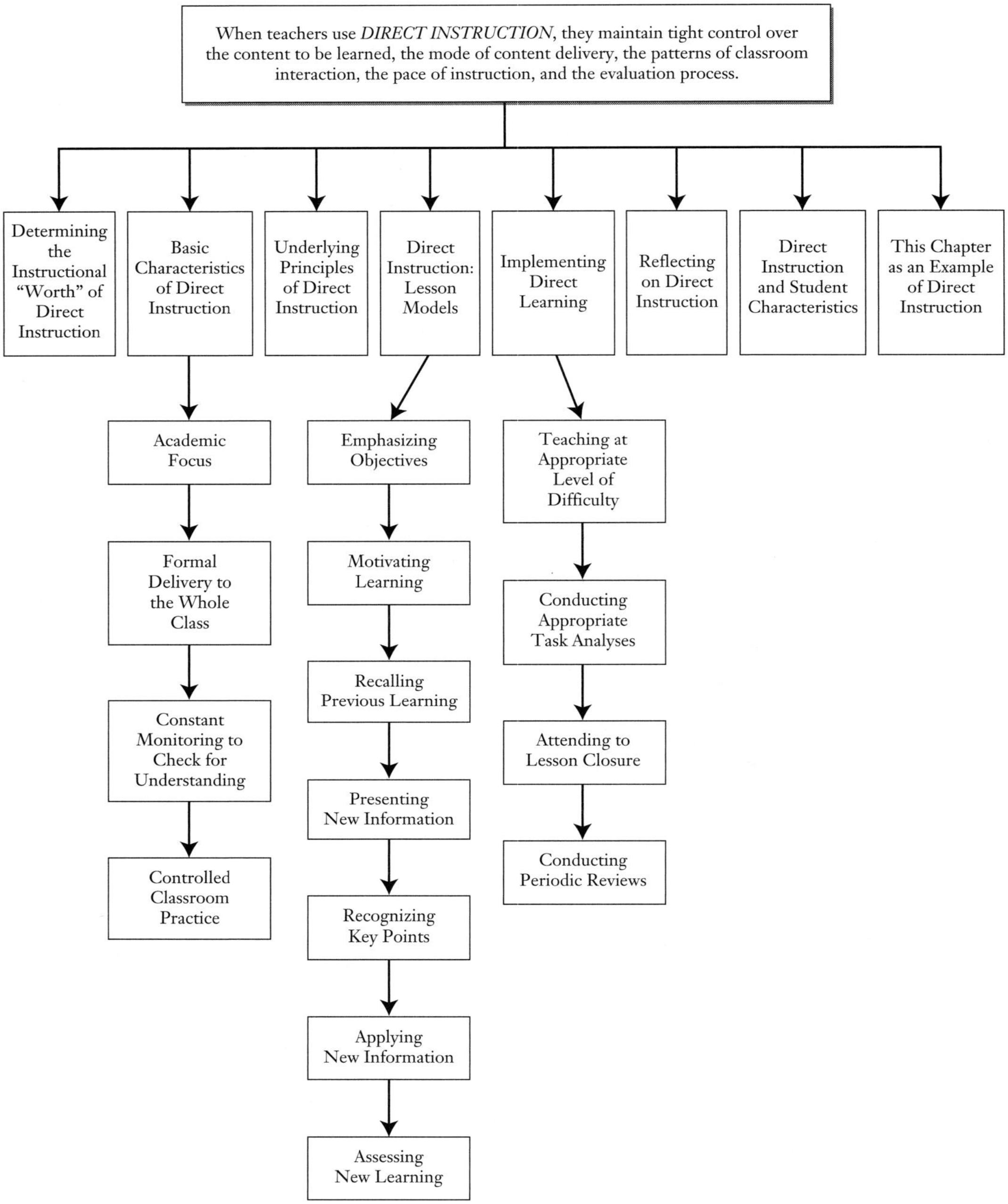

Figure 9.1
Graphic Organizer

CHAPTER 9

Models of Direct Instruction

OBJECTIVES

This chapter will help you

- describe components of several direct instruction models;
- point out features of direct instruction that explain the popularity of this approach among teachers, school leaders, and parents;
- identify learning intentions for which direct instruction is appropriate;
- describe situations for which direct instruction has been found to be a useful instructional approach; and
- apply the direct instruction model to specific instructional situations.

Introduction

What types of teaching do you remember as most common when you were a student? Chances are that what you recall as typical teaching falls into a category called direct instruction, one of the least understood and most misused instructional models (Lasley, Matczynski, & Rowley, 2002). Too many teachers talk for 50 minutes each class period and assume that because they have talked, they have taught. These teachers violate the basic principles of direct instruction: that teachers must make explicit instructional decisions and assess thoughtfully whether students have learned (Lasley et al., 2002). When you use direct instruction in the classroom, you act as the major provider of information. You maintain direct control over the content to be learned, the delivery of the content, the patterns of classroom interaction, the pace of instruction, and the evaluation of what is learned. You deliver content in a systematic, step-by-step fashion and work with students until they master one idea before you introduce another. The approach typically features whole-class or large-group instruction rather than individualized or small-group learning.

Several different names have been applied to this approach, including explicit teaching, systematic teaching, target teaching, active teaching, clinical teaching, and mastery teaching. Some variants of this approach have been used in classrooms for many years. Although Madeline Hunter's name is most often associated with this model, she did not create it. Her persuasive speaking style allowed her to popularize the model (Lasley et al., 2002). Other educators, such as Bereiter and Engelmann (1966), Gagne (1977), and Rosenshine (1983), deserve mention for their part in creating and/or popularizing different variants of the model.

This approach has achieved popularity for a variety of reasons. First, it does not ask you to do anything in the classroom that radically departs from what you observed many of your own teachers doing. In addition, procedures for implementing direct instruction are easy to learn, and the approach has been found to be especially effective in teaching students the kinds of basic information often evaluated on standardized tests. The current emphasis on accountability and the use of test scores for evaluating school districts, schools, and even teachers has made any approach that promises to help students score well on standardized tests attractive to school leaders. Finally, parents remember this kind of teaching from their own school days. Because they have experienced direct instruction, many of them presume that this approach is both logical and legitimate.

In this chapter, we make suggestions about appropriate and inappropriate uses of direct instruction. We also introduce basic components of a direct instruction model in our presentation of this chapter's contents. After you finish reading this material, you may wish to revisit various sections to see how parts of our direct instruction model have been incorporated.

Determining the Instructional "Worth" of Direct Instruction

If you visit some Websites with information about direct instruction, you probably will encounter a pattern that we have always found troubling. That is, much material written about specific approaches to delivering instruction lacks balance. Particularly on the Web, you will find materials about "approach A" that fall into two major categories. Some of them will suggest that the approach is the answer to every teacher's dream and that its use in the classroom will excite, motivate, and thrill all students. Others will attack the approach as being totally beyond redemption and hint that true professional teachers would rather perish than be caught using it in their own classrooms. Perhaps our examples are a bit overdrawn, but you definitely will find yourself occasionally longing for a discussion of an instructional approach that features a dispassionate consideration of pluses and minuses rather than heavy-handed assertions of its "absolute excellence" or its "complete lack of redeeming qualities."

Why is there so much strident opinion-mongering in discussions of instructional methodologies? Doubtless many variables contribute to this pattern. One key point is that teachers work within large bureaucracies. It is difficult to win support for a dramatic expansion in the use of a proposed new instructional approach unless it generates enough strong feelings to overcome the inertia of established tradition. Hence, proponents more often feel pressed to "oversell" its benefits. Similarly, they also often feel compelled to engage in open attacks on alternative approaches as a way of attracting support for what they are espousing. You need to consider these realities of the public school setting when you read information about alleged benefits and shortcomings of a given instructional approach.

Fortunately, there are some research-based findings related to the effectiveness of direct instruction. The largest study was Project Follow Through. This study, completed in the 1970s, involved 79,000 students in 80 communities. The results indicate that "direct instruction dramatically improved cognitive skills" (http://www.jefflindsay.com/EducData.shtml). Unfortunately, most of the research on direct instruction has been conducted at the elementary level. This does not suggest that direct instruction is inappropriate at the secondary level; it does, however, "indicate the limited scope of research to determine the power of the technique with different populations" (Lasley et al., 2002, p. 273).

In general, studies have found this approach to be particularly good for such purposes as teaching basic facts, concepts, procedures, and skills (Borich, 1992). Research on direct instruction and other instructional approaches typically points out that individual approaches have varying degrees of value for achieving particular purposes with certain kinds of students. The most important thread that runs through research on instructional techniques can be summed up as follows: No single approach is most appropriate for all situations. Your obligation as a professional is to vary what you do depending on the content to be taught, the nature of your students, the specific learning intentions you have established, your personal comfort and familiarity with a particular instructional approach, and the availability of needed instructional support materials.

Basic Characteristics of Direct Instruction

When some people hear the phrase "direct instruction," they immediately think of the lecture method. It is true that lecturing features many elements of direct instruction, but there is much more to this approach than simply telling. In a typical lecture, teachers stand in front of the class and deliver information the students are supposed to remember. The communication is generally one way, from the teacher to the students, with occasional interjections of student questions. A fully developed direct instruction approach involves more. It is faster paced, includes more student involvement, contains a highly organized set of interactions under the control of the teacher, and focuses more on student learning than on teacher performance.

An elaboration of some of the basic characteristics of direct instruction will indicate how direct instruction goes beyond what you might do in a typical lecture. In fact, in some direct instruction lessons, you will not be involved in anything resembling a lecture at all. For example, you may choose to do demonstrations, show slides and provide comments, or present new content in other ways. The key to direct instruction is not lecture; rather, it is the presence of your control, as the teacher, over the flow of new information. In general, a complete direct instruction lesson includes these basic characteristics:

- Academic focus
- Formal delivery to the whole class
- Constant monitoring to check for understanding
- Controlled classroom practice

Academic Focus

Academic focus means that the lesson concentrates on teaching academic content or skills. This focus is maintained throughout the lesson. Explicit instructional objectives guide your planning and teaching. Your decision making as the lesson is taught centers on keeping the lesson on target so that students master the objectives. You should seek to avoid digressions from the content focus and, when these occur, act quickly to get students to refocus on content associated with the lesson purpose. Independent seat work activities should follow your presentation of information, and these activities should relate clearly to content you have introduced.

Formal Delivery to the Whole Class

Direct instruction features systematic and formal presentation of information to the whole class. You instruct in a logical, step-by-step fashion. Typically, you ask students to demonstrate their understanding of each step before they go on to the next. You control classroom interactions and the rate at which content is introduced. Under

MORE FROM THE WEB

Direct Instruction

Direct instruction has advocates as well as critics. Widespread interest in the topic has prompted development of much related information on the Web. The following sites are ones you might want to visit.

Association for Direct Instruction

This is the home page of a national group dedicated to promoting the use of direct instruction in schools. You will find many links to useful information. For example, if you follow the Who We Are link, you will learn of the existence of a journal produced quarterly by the Association for Direct Instruction titled *Effective School Practices*, which prints articles on direct instruction research and practice.

Website: www.adihome.org

Slavin's QAIT Model

At this site, you will find information related to work that instructional design specialist Robert Slavin has done to update an earlier mastery learning model. Slavin argues that a successful mastery learning program depends on (a) the quality of instruction, (b) delivering instruction at a level students can understand, (c) the nature of incentives that are provided, and (d) the time allotted for students to learn the material being taught.

Website: http://www.valdosta.edu/~whuitt/psy310/QAIT.html

optimal conditions, you maintain as brisk a pace as possible consistent with students' ability to grasp what is presented. It is important to note that your control of the classroom does not mean an absence of active student participation. On the contrary, when direct instruction is effectively implemented, there is a high degree of student involvement associated with actions you take to ensure that students understand the new material.

Direct instruction lessons feature many teacher-to-student questions. A large number of these tend to be recall questions. When your instruction is effective, students are able to respond to a high percentage of them (Rosenshine & Stevens, 1986). Questions often focus on either a request for specific answers or a request for an explanation of how a student arrived at an answer (Rosenshine, 1987). The general pattern that is followed has been described as factual question–student response–teacher feedback (Stallings & Kaskowitz, 1974).

The large number of questions asked during a direct instruction lesson gives you many opportunities to interact with your students. This tends to keep all students in the class alert and actively involved. Your questions give them opportunities to repeat and practice what they have learned, thus facilitating student learning of the new content.

Constant Monitoring to Check for Understanding

During a direct instruction lesson, you regularly ask questions and take other actions to ensure that students understand the material. Students' responses provide cues you can use to adjust the pace of the lesson and to spend more time dealing with content aspects that students find difficult. You want to make sure that the students have mastered each subsection of the lesson before moving on to the next subsection. Sometimes it is necessary to reteach some material in order to ensure mastery.

Controlled Classroom Practice

Effective direct instruction lessons feature substantial opportunities for students to engage in controlled practice. The key word here is *controlled*. Before students are allowed to engage in application activities requiring the use of presented information, you need to ensure that they have the necessary understanding to successfully complete the application exercises.

■ ■ ■

Take a minute to review what you have just read to this point. What accounts for the popularity of direct instruction? How is direct instruction similar to and different from a lecture? What would you need to do to change a traditional lecture format to make it more consistent with characteristics of effective direct instruction? What questions do you have about direct instruction? Summarize the basic characteristics of direct instruction.

■ ■ ■

Direct instruction requires continuous monitoring of student progress.

Underlying Principles of Direct Instruction

Rosenshine and Stevens (1986) identify the basic principles underlying the direct instruction model. These principles are taken from research and theory related to how individuals process information. The first principle states that individuals can process only a limited amount of new information at one time. If too much information is presented at once, students' abilities to process it are hindered. When this happens, they become confused, make faulty associations, and fail to attend to some key points of information. In frustration, students may turn off the processing altogether.

To prevent these kinds of problems, you have to avoid overwhelming students with too much information at once. New material should be presented in the form of small steps. As you introduce material, you need to check frequently to ensure that your students are adequately grasping key points.

Another principle underlying direct instruction concerns the importance of prior knowledge. What people already know establishes a framework for helping them process new information. This means that you need to take time to find out what your learners already understand about a topic that you want to introduce. When you are armed with this kind of information, you can take appropriate action to help your students establish a learning set, or framework, that will help them correctly process the new information. To ensure that students have a good understanding of important prerequisite information, it makes sense for you to review with them what they have already learned and to point out how it connects to the material you are about to introduce.

A third principle of direct instruction relates to the transfer of sensory perceptions from short-term memory to long-term memory. Short-term memory is the memory storage system where bits of information received by our sensory perceptors are stored for a brief time—a period up to about 30 seconds (Slavin, 1994). Unless something is done with the information, it will be lost and cannot be recalled. You need to find ways to help students retain important information for longer periods of time. To do this, you have to facilitate a shift of information from short-term to long-term memory.

A movement of information into long-term memory requires the brain to review, practice, summarize, and elaborate on the information received. You have to give your students opportunities to engage in active practice of what they have learned. They need to respond to questions, summarize information in their own words, and, in general, do something with the new information. There are considerable benefits when these actions result in a shift of information into long-term memory. Some experts believe that nothing is ever permanently lost from long-term memory. There are times when the information cannot be readily retrieved, but when conditions are right, details stored in long-term memory can be recalled and used.

The interest in moving information into long-term memory provides a rationale for another basic principle of direct instruction: the emphasis on practice. Information is most readily recalled when it has been acquired through processes involving what sometimes is referred to as overlearning. Overlearning occurs when students practice using the new information to the point that little effort is required to give a correct response. When students can readily recall overlearned prior information, their information processing systems are free to devote full attention to the task of comprehending new information you are presenting to them. Because new learning builds on old, it makes sense for you to give students opportunities to overlearn by providing them with numerous opportunities to rehearse and repeat what they have learned. Overlearning experiences that provide students with opportunities to rehearse and review material in a variety of settings are particularly effective.

■ ■ ■

This section has reviewed the basic principles that form a foundation for direct instruction. Stop your reading at this point. How do these principles fit with the way you think people learn and remember? Briefly write each principle in your own words. Give an example of short-term memory and long-term memory. Compare your responses with those of another person who is reading this chapter.

■ ■ ■

Direct Instruction: Lesson Models

Several variations of direct instruction have been developed based on these basic principles (Denton, Armstrong, & Savage, 1980; Hunter & Russell, 1977; Slavin, 1999). As indicated in Figure 9.2, there are great similarities among components of these models. (Though each of the three models illustrated in Figure 9.2 features seven phases, this is simply a coincidence. It is quite possible for direct instruction models to have either smaller or larger numbers of components.)

Note that the reference to parts of the model has been to components, not to steps. The term "steps" would suggest that users of direct instruction should follow a rigid, mechanistic sequence while delivering lessons to students. This kind of

Hunter and Russell Model (1977)	**Denton, Armstrong, and Savage Model** (1980)	**Slavin Model** (1994)
1. Anticipatory set 2. Teaching to an objective 3. Presentation of new material or academic input 4. Modeling 5. Checking for understanding 6. Guided practice 7. Independent practice	1. Emphasizing objectives 2. Motivating learning 3. Recalling previous learning 4. Presenting new information 5. Recognizing key points 6. Applying new information 7. Assessing new learning	1. Stating learning objectives and orienting students to lesson 2. Reviewing prerequisites 3. Presenting new material 4. Conducting learning probes 5. Providing independent practice 6. Assessing performance and providing feedback 7. Providing distributed practice and review

Figure 9.2

by-the-numbers teaching is not what proponents of direct instruction espouse. Rather, the models seek to provide you with information about instructional responsibilities that you need to discharge as you engage students in new material. The way you decide to accommodate each of the responsibilities should be based on the following:

- The type of content you are teaching
- What you expect your students to be able to do
- Specific modifications you decide to make based on your professional reactions to how students are performing as you engage them with the new content

Suppose you reviewed various models and decided to work with the one developed by Denton et al. (1980). In using the model, you need to make decisions about what you would do in these seven areas:

1. **Emphasizing Objectives.** Students need to have a clear answer to the "what-am-I-supposed-to-be-learning?" question. This component of the model requires you to decide how you will provide students with information they need to answer this question.
2. **Motivating Learning.** This component of the model highlights your response to "build interest" in what you will be teaching. Actions you take to motivate students need to occur throughout an instructional sequence, not only at the beginning.
3. **Recalling Previous Learning.** Decisions you make that relate to this component seek to help students recall previous information they have learned, particularly information that ties in closely to new content you are planning to introduce.
4. **Presenting New Information.** Your responsibility in this area is to decide how best to present new information to your students in a comprehensible and interesting manner.
5. **Recognizing Key Points.** When students are presented with new information, the volume of what has been presented may overwhelm them. Decisions you make that relate to this component of the model seek to reduce confusion and promote a focus on the most important parts of the newly introduced material.
6. **Applying New Information.** If students are to master new information, you must do more than simply expose them to it. They must have opportunities to use it. Decisions you make in this category identify ways in which students will be asked to put new learning into practice.
7. **Assessing New Learning.** To improve your instructional practices, you need to develop procedures that will provide you with a flow of information about (a) how each individual student is doing and (b) how the class, in general, is responding to your instruction. Decisions you make related to assessing new learning identify procedures you will follow to obtain this information.

Jot down the seven components of direct instruction as outlined in the Denton et al. (1980) model. See if you can give an example of each component. Share your example with someone else who is reading this chapter.

■ ■ ■

Emphasizing Objectives

Instructional purposes expressed as objectives establish an academic focus for direct instruction lessons. They provide you with targets you can use in planning instruction and adjusting what you do as you teach. They also can help you keep on track and avoid temptations to dwell too long on unimportant or minor details.

CRITICAL INCIDENT

This Is the Way We Teach

Rosa Garcia has just finished her teacher preparation program. She had an extremely positive student teaching experience with a very creative master teacher. Overall, she feels pleased with her preparation and is anxious to begin her teaching career. She has been hired to teach in a school district near her hometown. She knows little about the district other than that students there typically score below state averages on standardized achievement tests.

Rosa was somewhat surprised by what she learned at the district's 3-day orientation session for new teachers. During the first morning of the orientation session, the superintendent mentioned the lower-than-average scores of the students in the district. She noted that the scores are published in the newspapers across the state, tarnishing the reputation of the school district and leading to enormous pressure by the local community to correct this situation. Therefore, the school district has implemented a series of workshops covering a teaching approach that all teachers are expected to use. The superintendent went on to point out that this approach has been found to be the most effective approach to teaching. It includes seven steps that must be included in every lesson that is taught regardless of the subject or the grade level.

A districtwide lesson plan format including these seven steps has been developed, and all teachers are expected to use this lesson plan model and to turn in lesson plans on Friday for the following week. Furthermore, the school district has revised the teacher evaluation forms for the district. The evaluation form focuses on these seven steps and includes a rating for how well a teacher performs each of them. Continued employment in the district will be based on teacher performance on this evaluation form.

Finally, the superintendent stated that because many new teachers were prepared in teacher education programs that did not stress this model, the remainder of the 3-day new-teacher orientation would be spent teaching them how to implement the seven-step lesson model. This training would prepare them for success in the district.

Rosa was shocked to hear these words. It was as if the superintendent was telling everyone that their preparation was worthless. She began to wonder how the interesting approaches she had learned in her student teaching could be applied. She sensed that the superintendent's final comments seemed to be an uncanny answer to what she was thinking.

"I know that there are some teachers who believe that this approach limits their creativity," the superintendent said. "Well, we believe there is plenty of room for teacher creativity within this approach. If your lesson is so creative that it doesn't fit within this model, then it is probably inappropriate for our students. Education is a serious business here. We expect to see student learning take place, and we won't tolerate cute lessons that don't result in observable student learning."

■ ■ ■

How would you react to this superintendent's approach to teaching? What are some positive aspects of this approach to improving education? What do you see as problems with this approach to school improvement? When you hear that an approach has been found to be the most effective method of teaching, what should you ask?

What are the superintendent's priorities? How are these priorities reflected in the policy requiring all teachers to adopt a common approach to planning and delivering instruction? How might Rosa's views (or those of other teachers) differ? What might their priorities suggest about their values? What do you think you would do if you were Rosa? Would you feel comfortable in this situation? Because this is an approach that is mandated by the school district and is the focus for evaluation, what course of action should Rosa pursue? From what you know about this approach, do you think that there is room for her to use some of the other approaches she has learned?

What could Rosa have done to avoid finding herself in this situation? What implications does this have concerning your future job search?

Giving the objective to the students helps establish a framework for what they are learning. You do not have to do this using the somewhat stilted language you might employ in a formal lesson plan. It is perfectly acceptable to provide students with a simple statement that lets them know what you want them to learn. More information on establishing learning intentions and providing worthwhile objectives is found in chapter 7.

Motivating Learning

Secondary students enter your classroom with a number of agendas. They have recently left another classroom, have been engaging in social conversation with peers, and may be anticipating future events. In short, they do not usually come into class thinking seriously about the forthcoming content of the class. In addition, they have been away from the class for a day (sometimes more) and have had many other events intervene since you last taught them. Finally, the topics you wish to introduce may not initially be of great personal interest to members of your class. To respond to these circumstances, you need to think through ways of capturing and maintaining student interest in what you want them to learn.

Ideally, you should do something that communicates information to students about the importance of what is to be learned and why it may be of special interest to them. Ideas for motivating students need to be planned not just at the beginning of a lesson but also for use at various times throughout the entire time you are teaching the material. You need to develop a sense for when students' attentiveness begins to decline and then do something to rekindle their interest in what you are presenting.

In planning your motivational strategies, you might find it useful to consider how to respond to questions students might ask themselves. Here are some examples:

- What personal use will I make of information in this lesson?
- Do people I respect other than the teacher have any interest in this material?
- Can this new information help me in my other classes?
- Will I have the necessary background to master this new content?

Recalling Previous Learning

Daily reviews are a common feature of direct instruction lessons. The idea is for you to provide students with opportunities to practice information they have learned previously. A daily review can help students understand that they have the background needed to master the new content you are about to introduce. Information you gather from students when you engage them in recall of previous learning can provide you with insights regarding some mistaken information or ideas that need to be corrected before you introduce the new material.

Rosenshine and Stevens (1986) recommend some of the following ideas for making the recall of previous learning experiences effective:

- Administer a short quiz on previously introduced material
- Have students correct one another's homework
- Ask students to summarize the main points of content introduced during the previous lesson
- Assign students to prepare questions for each other based on previously introduced content
- Require students to review content of the previous lesson in small groups

Presenting New Information

Presenting new information (sometimes called input) is central to all teaching. Your aim is to present new material to students so they will understand it. No single way to do this has proved to be universally effective. To accomplish this task successfully, you have to know your students, your subject, and other characteristics of your instructional setting. Both artistry and technical skills are required as you develop presentation techniques that are well fitted to your unique instructional circumstances. Do not rely strictly on lecture to complete this part of the lesson. Consider using demonstrations, computer-enhanced instruction, or other media.

Planning for presentation begins with a careful analysis of the content you want to teach. You have to make decisions about sequencing the new information and about breaking it into logical chunks. For example, if your students are easily distracted and are not especially task oriented, then you should present content in small steps and allow time for yourself to make frequent checks on student progress. If, however, they are interested in the topic and more mature, then it makes better sense for you to give them larger chunks of content at a time so that they don't become impatient and frustrated.

If good instructional resources are available, you want to use them to support your introduction. For example, you might choose to present some information using a computer or a DVD player. However, you have to keep in mind that even when you use alternative means to transmit information, you still need to incorporate the basic components of a direct instruction lesson. You cannot expect success if you show a film without taking time to adequately prepare students to profit from this experience. You also have to engage in some serious checking-for-understanding instruction at the conclusion of the film. In other words, alternative presentation modes do not excuse you from exercising your professional responsibilities.

In deciding how to introduce material clearly and logically, you need to ask yourself questions such as these:

- How should the material be sequenced?
- How rapidly should information be presented?

Answers to these questions will vary, depending on the nature of students in your class, the kind of content to be introduced, and the nature of the lesson's instructional objectives.

As you introduce new information, you need to think about what you will do in four important areas:

- Providing an overview or structure
- Establishing a step-by-step progression
- Highlighting main points
- Modeling what students should do

Providing an Overview or Structure A lesson structure or overview helps students see relationships among various parts of a lesson. You can present this kind of information in several ways. For example, you might project an outline on an overhead transparency, list main topic headings of the lesson on the chalkboard, or provide students with an incomplete lesson outline to fill out as new information is provided to them.

The outline or structure of the lesson can be presented as the lesson develops. You might write key words on the board or use simple diagrams that show interrelationships among isolated pieces of information. This can be an especially important aspect of direct instruction because of the focus on step-by-step progression. When you emphasize the importance of students' mastering each part of the lesson before moving forward, some individuals in your class may focus on the parts and miss the big picture. Diagrams and outlines can help them see how the pieces go together.

Establishing a Step-by-Step Progression Good direct instruction lessons proceed one step at a time. These steps should be presented at a pace sufficiently rapid to maintain student interest but not so rapidly that they fail to keep up. You must watch individual students carefully and alter your pace as needed to maintain levels of motivation and maximize learning.

You can start this process by identifying individual steps of your lesson before instruction begins. This requires you to think about all the things the students must be able to do to master the new material. Once you have identified this information, arrange content into a sequence that is logically consistent and compatible with students' characteristics. The process of doing this is sometimes referred to as task analysis.

Highlighting Main Points Students retain critical information better when it is highlighted for them during presentations. Students' attention can be drawn to key points in a variety of ways, including writing main points on the chalkboard, repeating important information several times, and using marker phrases such as "now pay attention to this—you will need to use this material."

Modeling What Students Should Do Many students fail not because of lack of effort but because they fail to understand what is expected of them. Similarly, if students see examples of what you want them to produce or do, the probability of their mastering the material you want them to know increases. Good modeling features frequent use of concrete examples, illustrations, or demonstrations.

Providing models or examples can take several forms. For example, you might simply show an example of a finished product. Sometimes you may be interested in helping students master a process of some kind. To help students better understand what you want them to do, you can talk them through the process as they engage in it themselves. This kind of demonstration reassures students that they will be approaching your assignment in a manner that is consistent with your expectations.

■ ■ ■

What should you consider when you are planning to present new information to a group of students? How would you apply the direct instruction approach when using media to present new material to a class? How does teacher creativity enter into planning?

■ ■ ■

Recognizing Key Points

When you introduce new material, students may experience problems that run counter to your expectations. If you find that they have trouble responding to questions you ask during the lesson, it is easy to conclude that they have not been exposed to sufficient new information. This doesn't happen often. Students are more likely to suffer from what we call temporary information overload. The new information may have come at them faster than they have been able to absorb it. Actions you take to help them recognize key points can help them overcome this problem.

Use of internal summaries and marker expressions can help students identify aspects of new content that are important. When you use internal summaries, you break the flow of presentation of new content to briefly recapitulate what you have introduced so far. This allows you an opportunity to underscore for students the key ideas you have introduced that you particularly want them to master. You can also use marker expressions. These are phrases you use to draw the attention of your students to key points. Some examples of marker expressions include the following:

- "Write this down."
- "Pay attention to this point. It's important."
- "I want you to remember this."

Applying New Information

Practice promotes permanence of learning. You need to give your students sufficient experience in working with new content so their responses will become quick and automatic. For example, you can provide opportunities for them to "do something" with newly introduced content during the latter part of a lesson.

To gain the maximum benefit from providing students with opportunities to work with new information, you have to actively monitor them during this phase of instruction. It is important to move through the room to ensure that your students are engaging lesson content. You need to be easily accessible. You want students to feel free to ask you any questions they have about the new information with which they are working. Applying new information facilitates learning only when your students have a good grasp of the information they will be asked to use. If they do not, the practice activity can reinforce mistaken impressions and can be a barrier to appropriate learning.

Your students need to experience a high degree of success as they apply new information. To optimize their learning, researchers have found that students should respond to questions and perform other guided practice activities with about 80% accuracy before teachers introduce additional new information (Rosenshine & Stevens, 1986).

■ ■ ■

What are the purposes of actions you might take during the "applying new information" phase of a lesson? Why is a high rate of student success during this part of a lesson considered important? What are some things you might do to maximize students' learning when they are applying content you have just introduced?

■ ■ ■

Assessing New Learning

Actions you take during this phase of the instructional process give you information you can use in deciding whether to move forward with new content or to reteach and reinforce what you have already introduced. Assessing new learning may initially sound like nothing more than a recommendation to give students a test at the end of a lesson. While such assessments are important, your obligation to assess new learning requires you to check for student understanding after each part of your introduction of new information. Actions you take to ensure that students are grasping what you are teaching give you confidence that students do understand what you think they understand before you go on to introduce additional material. You have several options when you consider actions to take to assess new learning.

One approach you can take is to ask students questions about what has been covered and to think carefully about the nature of their responses. When you do this, it is important to sample answers from a broad range of students. This practice will give you good ideas regarding (a) how individual students are grasping the material and (b) how the class, as a group, seems to be mastering the material.

One of your obligations during this phase of a lesson is to provide feedback to students and correct their mistakes. This is what is termed inferential diagnosis, which means that you make diagnostic inferences based on your students' responses. As you work with individual members of your class, you need to ask yourself, "What does this response tell me this student is understanding and thinking?" The inferences you make in response to this question inform instructional decisions you will make about what kind of feedback you should provide or what actions you need to take to correct a student's mistakes.

Your feedback and corrective options are varied, so what you do should be in reaction to the kinds of responses you are getting from your students. Rosenshine and Stevens (1986) have identified these categories of student responses:

- A correct and quick student response
- A correct but hesitant student response
- An incorrect student response due to carelessness
- An incorrect student response due to lack of knowledge or skill

A Correct and Quick Student Response If you get this kind of a student response, you should take it as a signal that students have properly understood the material. Your reaction should be aimed at keeping the lesson moving along at a brisk pace. Ordinarily, a brief comment to students affirming the appropriateness of their answers will suffice. What you do should take place quickly so that your actions do not interrupt the momentum of the lesson.

A Correct but Hesitant Student Response In some situations, you will get a student response that is correct but that comes so slowly and hesitantly that you will suspect the person has doubts about the accuracy of what he or she is saying. Your response should be directed at removing the student's uncertainty. For example, you might affirm the accuracy of the student's answer and briefly review reasons the response is correct. All this must be accomplished relatively quickly so that you can maintain the basic flow and pace of the lesson.

An Incorrect Student Response Due to Carelessness Over time, you will develop a feel for when a student's mistake is simply a careless slip and not evidence of misunderstanding. Asking a student to explain his or her answer often will reveal whether the mistake resulted from a lack of understanding or from carelessness. A quick comment or two from you before formal instruction resumes ordinarily will be enough to help the student who has made this kind of error.

An Incorrect Student Response Due to Lack of Knowledge or Skill When a student mistake clearly reflects a lack of understanding, you need to do some reteaching. If only a few students are having difficulty, you may be able to continue with the rest of the lesson content, make assignments to the entire group, and call together students having difficulty and reteach them the aspects of content they are finding difficult to understand. Sometimes you may want to put students who have mastered the content to work as peer tutors to work with those individuals who are having difficulty grasping it. Peer tutoring works well as long as you and members of the class have confidence in the abilities of the students selected to work as tutors. Use of student tutors allows you to monitor the work of others in the class while the tutors provide assistance to students who need some additional help mastering basic information that most class members have already learned.

What purposes are served by actions you take during the "assessing new learning" phase of the instructional process? What is the relationship between the assessment process and instructional actions you take once you have gathered and thought about information related to students' understanding of material you have introduced? What are some approaches to assessing new learning that you might use in teaching your own subject?

■ ■ ■

Implementing Direct Learning

The individual components of direct instruction models can help you when you plan for instruction. However, there are other dimensions of teaching that need to be applied that can make your use of direct instruction more efficient. Some additional variables you should consider include the following:

- Teaching at the appropriate level of difficulty
- Conducting appropriate task analyses
- Attending to lesson closure
- Conducting periodic reviews

Teaching at the Appropriate Level of Difficulty

Obviously, for your teaching to be effective, it must be at a level that is neither too easy nor too difficult for the students. Something that is too difficult for them will go over their heads. Material that is too easy will bore them.

The issue of teaching at an appropriate level of difficulty has grown in importance in recent years with the increased diversity of students in classrooms. Many students in secondary schools come from homes where the primary language is not English. In addition, many students reach secondary schools without the necessary prerequisites for success. It is no longer reasonable to assume that students at a given grade level come to school with the prerequisites they will need to complete instructional tasks successfully. The movement toward full inclusion of students in regular classrooms who, in the past, would have spent their school years in special education classrooms further emphasizes the importance of teaching at the appropriate level of difficulty

Teaching at the appropriate level of difficulty is not easy. It requires that you constantly diagnose the ability levels of your students. This means that careful analysis of students' present levels of knowledge and general interests should be an integral part of your instructional planning. As you consider what you want students to learn, you need information about what individuals in your class may already know or be able to do. This information enables you to begin the instructional sequence at an appropriate entry point. It also helps you decide what approaches to take in introducing material and in involving students in meaningful applications of the new content.

Analyses you perform as part of your planning process may be formal, informal, or both. Sometimes you may wish to administer formal pretests to determine students' entry-level understanding. On other occasions, you may find that a review of students' previous work is sufficient. Of course, after you have worked with a class for a while, you will be able to make inferences about what individuals know and do not know simply by observing their daily performance in class.

Teaching at the appropriate level of difficulty requires you to look at student work not just as a means of assigning a grade but also as a source of useful diagnostic data. This information can help you decide what to teach next and how you might introduce new material. A diagnostic mind-set will lead you to regard performance of students that is below your level of expectations as an opportunity for analysis and reflection. The result of this kind of thinking can help you design new instructional approaches with the potential to respond more effectively to students' needs.

Conducting Appropriate Task Analyses

Teaching to the correct level of difficulty and performing sound diagnosis is facilitated by task analysis. Task analysis is the breaking down of complex learning into smaller components and then sequencing those components in a logical manner. Hunter (1994) identifies task analysis as an essential component of all instructional planning. Task analysis can help you deal with the special needs of diverse learners. For example, when you are teaching students with a primary language other than English, you may have to begin at a different place than when you work with students who are native speakers of English.

To illustrate how you might use task analysis, consider this example. Suppose you were teaching English and wanted your students to learn how to write a three-paragraph essay. The purpose of your task analysis would be to find out what basic information students already have that will enable them to complete this assignment successfully. You might decide that the proposed activity assumes that (a) students understand what a paragraph is, (b) they understand how to punctuate sentences correctly, and (c) they will be able to deal adequately with the proposed subject you want them to write about in an essay that is just three paragraphs long.

If you determined that students were deficient in any of these areas, you would want to spend time teaching whatever might be needed to fill in any identified knowledge gaps. Additional thought about students' levels of understanding might also lead you to identify places where it would be wise to pause and check for understanding once you began teaching the new material.

Attending to Lesson Closure

Another important support for the direct instruction model is something called lesson closure. Lesson closures refers to a lesson's culminating activity or conclusion. It requires you to do more than simply inform your students that it is time to stop or that the lesson is over.

During lesson closure, you help students draw together the pieces of what they have learned so that they can make sense out of what they have been doing. Actions you take at this time help students organize what they have learned. They also allow you to reemphasize the major points of the lesson. The thinking students do during lesson closure enhances their levels of comprehension and helps ensure that they process new information so that it can be moved into long-term memory (Shostak, 1994).

Conducting Periodic Reviews

It is important for you to provide periodic reviews when you teach direct instruction lessons. These allow you to help students recall critical aspects of new content that you have introduced. You should schedule regular times for periodic review activities. For example, you might choose to set aside the first few minutes of class periods on Mondays to review what was learned the previous week. Such periodic reviews reinforce learning and help students maintain levels of expertise. They also help your students see that they are making progress. This kind of evidence enhances their self-images by allowing them time to reflect on their academic accomplishments.

■ ■ ■

Review what you have read about some important instructional actions that you can take to make your direct instruction lessons more effective. What are the purposes of these actions? Think about a particular lesson you might teach. Specifically, what might you do to make sure that you will be teaching the appropriate level of difficulty? What kinds of task analyses might you perform? How would you attend to the need to provide for lesson closure? How would you accommodate the need to provide periodic reviews?

■ ■ ■

Reflecting on Direct Instruction

Direct instruction has several advantages. Because lessons are presented to the class as a whole, planning is simplified. One lesson plan suffices for the entire group; hence, planning time is less than when you must develop alternative plans for individuals or small groups. (Of course, this single-lesson plan may have several tracks or options that allow you to differentiate what you do to meet the needs of inclusion students, students who are nonnative speakers of English, and other students with special learning requirements.) Direct instruction puts you in a controlling position.

Direct instruction's focus on transmitting important elements of teacher-selected content allows you to prepare students well for tests. This is viewed as a particular advantage in schools and districts where there are pressures for students to achieve high scores on standardized achievement tests. (For more information about standardized tests in the schools, see chapter 13.) Researchers have found that students score well on achievement tests when they have been exposed to direct instruction in their classrooms. Direct instruction seems to increase the amount of student engagement with the kind of content that is featured on tests (Good & Brophy, 2004; Rosenshine & Stevens, 1986).

In a more general sense, direct instruction has been found to be effective when students are asked to master a well-defined body of content or a skill that can be broken down into parts and taught one step at a time (Rosenshine & Stevens, 1986). Basic skills instruction of all kinds is facilitated by direct instruction (Savage, 1989). These studies suggest that direct instruction makes sense when teachers are interested in providing students with basic information they will need as a prerequisite to engaging in complex higher-level thinking and problem-solving activities.

There are also negatives associated with direct instruction. For example, since it tends to work best when your intent is to transmit specific content items to students, direct instruction may be less effective when you seek to develop students' abilities to reflect on complex problems and develop solutions of their own. Successful direct instruction also requires you to have excellent presentation skills. You must be well organized, able to identify an appropriate pace, and quick to gauge levels of student interest and adapt instruction, as needed, to maintain students' attention.

Because so much content can be disseminated in a relatively short period of time during a direct instruction lesson, if you fail to pay attention to students' reactions, you may overwhelm them with too much information. This can lead to high levels of frustration and undermine students' confidence. When this happens, both their motivation and achievement levels may decline.

■ ■ ■

At this point, stop and take a minute to write your own brief definition of direct instruction. Compare your version with that of another person in your class who is also reading this chapter. How are they alike? How are they different? What questions do you have about implementing direct instruction?

■ ■ ■

WHAT DO YOU THINK?

Appropriate Uses of Direct Instruction

No single instructional approach is best for promoting the wide range of learning outcomes expected in the schools. The direct instruction model is more appropriate for some than for others.

It is more appropriate for the content that can readily be divided into parts, teaching basic skills, teaching students with an external locus of control, introductory material, and a prescribed body of content. It is less appropriate for content for which constituent parts are difficult to define, teaching higher-level thinking, teaching students with an internal locus of control, affective outcomes, and learning that requires creative thinking.

Questions

1. Why do you think direct instruction is less appropriate for some students and some outcomes?
2. What are some specific outcomes in your teaching areas for which direct instruction would be most appropriate?
3. What parts of the direct instruction model (and supplements to it introduced in this chapter) do you think will be easiest for you to master? Most difficult? What might you do to prepare yourself better to do a good job with those components that, at this point, seem most troublesome to you?

Direct Instruction and Student Characteristics

Direct instruction has been found to be particularly effective with younger students, students who are having academic difficulty, and students who are in the introductory phases of learning a specific body of content (Rosenshine & Stevens, 1986). Direct instruction works well with students from lower socioeconomic backgrounds and with those who have an external locus of control (Savage, 1989). (Students with an external locus of control tend to attribute their successes and failures in school to chance factors or to factors they perceive as being beyond their personal ability to control.)

Approaches other than direct instruction seem to be more effective with high-achieving, task-oriented students who have an internal locus of control. (Students with an internal locus of control perceive school failures and successes to be directly connected to their own controllable behaviors.) These students seem to benefit from instructional approaches that give them more choices in the classroom and that feature an instructional pace that is less subject to direct teacher control.

■ ■ ■

In summary, what questions do you have about general characteristics of direct instruction? Write down your questions and share them with several others. Present a master list of questions from your group to your instructor and ask your instructor to react to them.

■ ■ ■

This Chapter as an Example of Direct Instruction

We attempted to use some elements of direct instruction in organizing content in this chapter. The direct instruction approach calls on instructors to provide students with information about learning intentions or objectives as well as with an overview and structure for the new learning. We began this chapter with a list of chapter purposes, followed by a formal introduction to the content. (This same approach is followed throughout the text.)

Direct instruction lessons break content into small pieces or steps. Content in this chapter is broken down into major sections as well as subordinate subsections. At the end of many of these chapter divisions, we checked for understanding by asking you to reflect on what you had read by responding to questions, summarizing the content, checking your reactions with someone else, or generating questions of your own.

Direct instruction lessons often feature examples, illustrations, or models. Illustrations are provided at various points throughout this chapter, and the general layout of the chapter is consistent with a direct instruction format.

Authors of a text are not really in a position to see that guided practice takes place (because we are not with you in the classroom, we cannot listen to you, watch what you do, and react to your comments in person). However, we hope that some of the practice activities scattered throughout this chapter as well as those at the end will allow your instructor to monitor your progress as you engage in various guided practice activities.

FOR YOUR PORTFOLIO

1. What ideas have you learned in this chapter related to direct instruction that you will include as "evidence" in your portfolio? Select up to three items to be included. Number them 1, 2, and 3.
2. Think about why you selected these materials for your portfolio. Consider such issues as the following in your response:
   - The specific purposes to which this information can be put when you plan, deliver, and assess the impact of your instruction
   - The compatibility of the information with your own priorities and values
   - The contributions this information can make to your personal development as a teacher
   - The factors that led you to include this material as opposed to some alternatives you considered
3. Prepare a written reflection in which you analyze the decision-making process you followed. In addition, mention the INTASC standard(s) to which your selected material relates. (First complete the following chart.)

Materials You Selected and the INTASC Standards

Put a check under those INTASC standards numbers to which the evidence you have selected applies. (Refer to chapter 1 for more detailed information about INTASC.)

Item of Evidence Number	INTASC Standards									
	S1	S2	S3	S4	S5	S6	S7	S8	S9	S10
1										
2										
3										

Some of the end-of-the chapter activities are designed to provide you opportunities for independent practice. They call on you to apply what you have learned and to extend your understandings of the material. Ideally, an independent practice experience related to direct instruction would be for you to prepare and deliver a direct instruction lesson to a group of students. If you are currently in a classroom, perhaps you could plan a lesson to teach to one of your classes. If you are not, you might teach a lesson to a small group of your peers in your university classroom.

To summarize, we hope the way we have introduced direct instruction in this chapter has helped you grow in your understanding of this approach. Its success is something you will have to evaluate for yourself. If you feel more comfortable about your knowledge of the essentials of a direct instruction lesson and have confidence in your ability to design and deliver this kind of instruction, we will have met our own aims. We hope you think we have succeeded.

KEY IDEAS IN SUMMARY

- There is no one best method for teaching. Various approaches are appropriate for helping students master different kinds of objectives. For some purposes, direct instruction has proved to be a desirable way to organize and deliver instruction.
- Direct instruction is a teacher-centered approach in which the teacher controls selection and delivery of content, mode of presentation of content, pace of lesson development, and patterns of classroom interaction. Continuous monitoring throughout the lesson ensures student understanding. The focus is on transmission of academic content. Instruction is provided to the class as a whole, not to individual groups of students. Complex content is broken down into parts, and each part is introduced sequentially, one step at a time. The teacher takes pains to ensure that students grasp information associated with one step before going on to the next.
- The underlying principles that support the direct instruction model are taken from information processing theory and research. Among these principles are that (a) an individual can process only a limited amount of information at one time, (b) prior knowledge influences how a person processes new information, (c) information must be transferred from short-term to long-term memory for retention to occur, and (d) overlearning through rehearsal or practice is necessary to facilitate comprehension of future information.
- A number of direct instruction models are available, including those developed by Denton et al. (1980), Hunter and Russell (1977), and Slavin (1994). These models present components that should be included in complete direct instruction lessons.
- In addition to accommodating components enumerated in formal direct instruction models, there are other things teachers can do to increase the probability their students will learn. They can also take actions related to (a) teaching to an appropriate level of difficulty, (b) task analysis, (c) lesson closure, and (d) periodic reviews of newly presented information.
- There are claimed advantages of direct instruction. Because the teacher works with the whole class, planning is somewhat simplified. Planning assumes that all students will be exposed to basically the same instruction. The teacher is very much in a central, controlling position during direct instruction lessons. Direct instruction allows for a clear focus on specific academic content. Some people feel that the approach functions well as a means of preparing students for standardized tests.
- Some criticisms of direct instruction have been identified. Although the approach has merit as a way to help students recall specific information, it is less effective in helping students develop higher-level thinking skills that require them to reflect on complex issues and generate solutions of their own. Some teachers, too, lack the ability to diagnose the needs of their students and student reactions as instruction is being delivered. This is a particular problem when direct instruction is being used. Because it is so teacher centered, an unaware teacher can overwhelm students with content and undermine their interest in what is being taught.
- Direct instruction is more appropriate for meeting some kinds of instructional objectives than others. It works best when the content to be covered lends itself to being bro-

ken down into small parts that can be presented in sequential steps. Researchers have found that direct instruction works particularly well when the intent has been to teach skills. However, it has been found less appropriate when lesson objectives call on students to engage in higher-level thinking and problem-solving activities. It also is not a favored approach when instructional plans are guided by affective objectives.

- Some kinds of students seem to profit more from direct instruction than others. It has been found especially effective with younger students, students who are having academic difficulty, and students who are just beginning to work with a new content area. Studies have found that direct instruction lessons often are effective in working with students who have an external locus of control.

REFLECTIONS

1. What are some reasons for the popularity of direct instruction?
2. What are some basic characteristics of direct instruction?
3. What advantages and disadvantages have been claimed for direct instruction?
4. What is meant by the statement "direct instruction lessons feature a strong academic focus"?
5. How would you explain the phrase "*controlled classroom practice*"?
6. For what kinds of learning outcomes does direct instruction seem most appropriate?
7. What elements would you expect to see in a complete direct instruction lesson?
8. Some people argue that direct instruction is rigid, cold, and likely to create negative student attitudes. How do you react to this contention?
9. How would you feel if an administrator told you that he expected you to use a direct instruction approach every day?
10. What problems, if any, do you envision as you think about implementing direct instruction in your own teaching?

LEARNING EXTENSIONS

1. Review your content field. Identify three or four topics that might be appropriately delivered using a direct instruction approach. For each topic, identify a series of parts or steps you would use in presenting information to students. Share your ideas with your instructor and ask for a critique of your work.
2. Take time to look over parts of one of the direct instruction models introduced in this chapter. Observe a teacher in a secondary school who is using a direct instruction approach to introduce information. To what extent did you find each of the elements of a formal direct instruction model being used? Write up your findings in the form of a brief report and submit it to your instructor.
3. Organize a debate on this topic: "Resolved that too much direct instruction occurs in today's secondary schools." Hold the debate during a regular class session. When it is over, engage the entire class in a discussion of this issue.

4. With assistance from your instructor, identify some summaries of what researchers have found about the effectiveness of direct instruction. Prepare a short oral report for class members in which you summarize what researchers have found.
5. For a topic in your own subject area, prepare a complete lesson plan based on direct instruction. Share it with others in your class and ask them to suggest places your plan might be improved. You might also solicit reactions from your instructor.

REFERENCES

Bereiter, C., & Engelmann, S. (1966). *Teaching disadvantaged children in the preschool.* Englewood Cliffs, NJ: Prentice Hall.

Borich, G. (1992). *Effective teaching methods* (2nd ed.). Upper Saddle River, NJ: Merrill/Prentice Hall.

Denton, J. J., Armstrong, D. G., & Savage, T. V. (1980). Matching events of instruction to objectives. *Theory into Practice, 19*(1), 10–14.

Gagne, R. M. (1977). *The conditions of learning* (3rd ed.). New York: Holt, Rinehart and Winston.

Good, T., & Brophy, J. (2004). *Looking in Classrooms* (9th ed.). New York: Longman.

Hunter, M. (1994). *Enhancing teaching.* New York: Macmillan.

Hunter, M., & Russell, D. (1977). How can I plan more effective teaching lessons? *Instructor, 87*(2), 74–75, 88.

Lasley, T. J., II, Matczynski, T. J., & Rowley, J. B. (2002). *Instructional models: Strategies for teaching in a diverse society* (2nd ed.). Belmont, CA: Wadsworth.

Rosenshine, B. (1983). Teaching functions in instructional programs. *Elementary School Journal, 83*(4), 335–352.

Rosenshine, B. (1987). Direct instruction. In M. Dunkin (Ed.), *The international encyclopedia of teaching and teacher education* (pp. 257–262). New York: Pergamon Press.

Rosenshine, B., & Stevens, R. (1986). Teaching functions. In M. Wittrock (Ed.), *Handbook of research on teaching* (3rd ed., pp. 376–391). New York: Macmillan.

Savage, M. K. (1989). *The impact of different instructional models on teacher performance scores as measured by the Texas teacher appraisal system.* Unpublished doctoral dissertation, Texas, A&M University; College Station.

Shostak, R. (1994). Lesson presentation skills. In J. Cooper (Ed.), *Classroom teaching skills* (pp. 90–113). Lexington, MA: DC Heath.

Slavin, R. (1994). *Educational psychology: Theory and practice* (4th ed.). Boston: Allyn & Bacon.

Slavin, R. (1999). *Educational psychology: Theory and practice* (6th ed.). Boston: Allyn & Bacon.

Stallings, J., & Kaskowitz, D. (1974). *Follow-through classroom observation evaluation, 1972–1973.* Menlo Park, CA: Stanford Research Institute.

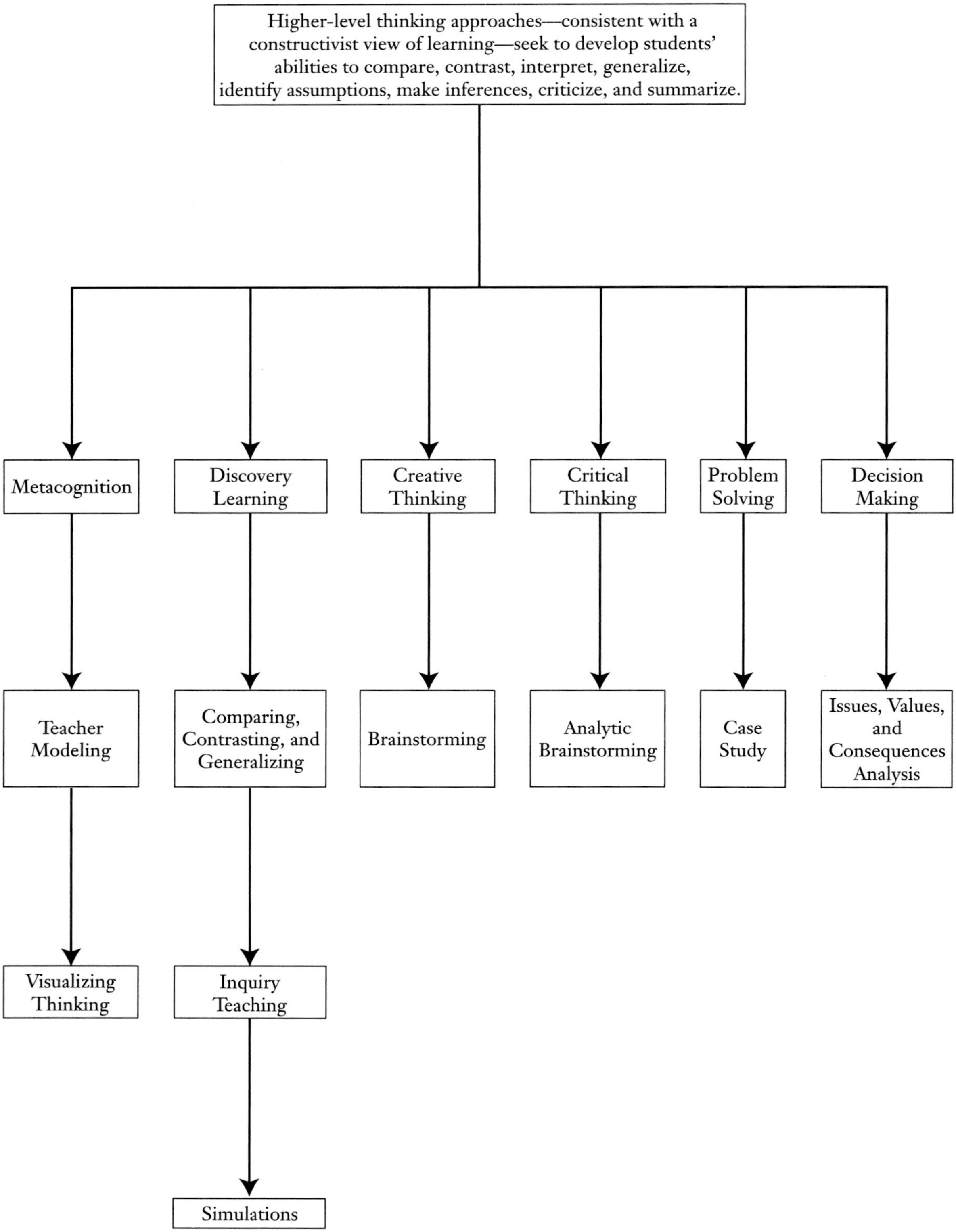

Figure 10.1
Graphic Organizer

CHAPTER 10

Teaching for Higher-Level Outcomes

OBJECTIVES

This chapter will help you

- explain how to implement metacognitive techniques that can help students learn how to direct their thought processes to higher levels;
- define discovery learning;
- describe the process of inquiry teaching;
- suggest how comparing, contrasting, and generalizing might be used in the classroom;
- explain how simulations can be used; and
- describe implementation procedures for and differentiate among purposes of creative thinking, critical thinking, problem solving, and decision making.

Introduction

What do you want education to do for your students? Do you want them to take what they learn in school and apply it to real situations? If so, you are one of the many people who see education as dedicated to preparation for life. This orientation will lead you to help students develop sophisticated thinking processes such as comparing, contrasting, interpreting, generalizing, identifying assumptions, making valid inferences, criticizing, and summarizing. Educators use the term "higher-level thinking" to describe these abilities.

Teaching higher-level thinking processes is consistent with the constructivist view of learning. This orientation assumes that you, as a teacher, cannot simply give students knowledge. They must construct knowledge and meaning in light of their past experiences and their present interactions (Gennrich & Long, 1999). Methods that facilitate learning are those that (a) encourage students to experiment, discover, and apply things on their own and (b) help students consciously monitor their own learning strategies (Slavin, 1994).

Constructivist learning assumes that instruction should begin as close to the reality that students experience as possible (Boudourides, 1998). You need to teach whatever basic skills are needed as part of lessons that emphasize resolution of complex, authentic problems. This kind of instruction focuses simultaneously on development of basic skills and higher-level thinking abilities. Some research indicates that this type of instruction is invaluable for those students who have experienced academic difficulties (Woolfolk, 1995).

A constructivist approach requires you to adopt a role that differs from what you might do in implementing instruction that is more traditional. You have to place more responsibility on students to control their own behavior and to take responsibility for their own learning. In addition, you have to be prepared for the possibility that at least some students will arrive at conclusions different from your own. You also have to accept that it is more difficult to evaluate what students have learned from lessons focusing on higher-level thinking than those that focus on more basic thinking processes. Simple paper-and-pencil tests featuring objective items are not satisfactory. You must be willing to rely on essays, oral presentations, assessments of student products, and other kinds of evidence of learning that require considerable time to develop and to evaluate.

A special atmosphere permeates classrooms that feature an emphasis on developing higher-level thinking abilities. For example, you will need a wide repertoire of instructional techniques, a tolerance for considerable ambiguity, and a general sense of personal and professional security for these kinds of lessons. You have to be comfortable with turning a great deal of responsibility for learning over to students. You must know how to model higher-level thinking processes in ways that connect with students. In essence, you must be willing to act as a learning manager. Your obligation is to present students with the task to be accomplished, provide the basic information they will need to use as they work toward a solution, nurture their thinking processes as they engage the assigned problem, and challenge them to test their conclusions.

Interest in promoting higher levels of thinking has led many educators to advocate the direct teaching of specific thinking skills to students. They point out that instruction that emphasizes how to think is at least as important as instruction that focuses on learning traditional academic content (Beyer, 1987, 1988). However, this position does not imply an either–or dichotomy; it is necessary to teach both academic content and thinking skills (Joyce &Weil, 1996). Sound thinking skills help students achieve maximum benefit from the learning of academic subjects and prepares them to cope with challenges they will face throughout their adult lives (Ruggiero, 1988). What is important for you to remember is that you must plan strategies based on your objectives. Once you have written the objectives, choose strategies that allow you to present material in a way that is most appropriate for a given objective.

This chapter introduces several strategies designed to promote higher-level thinking skills:

- Metacognition
- Discovery learning
- Creative thinking
- Critical thinking
- Problem solving
- Decision making

Metacognition

Metacognition refers to knowledge about one's own learning or knowing how to learn (Slavin, 1994). It involves bringing to a conscious level the kinds of procedures people follow as they think. Metacognitive processes serve an important monitoring function. When people are aware of the steps they are taking as they think, they make more conscious choices about whether approaches they have selected for a given task are appropriate. The basic idea is to help develop conscious control over the process of learning. This is important because the student must actively be engaged if learning is to take place.

You can provide instructional experiences that help students learn strategies for monitoring and modifying their patterns of thinking. Several approaches will help you achieve these purposes. Two that have been used by a number of teachers are teacher modeling and visualizing thinking strategies.

Teacher Modeling

Modeling has long been known to be a powerful instructional tool. As applied to metacognition, modeling seeks to help students recognize that people who successfully think about challenging topics carefully monitor their own thinking processes. They engage in a type of silent personal dialogue as they confront pertinent issues. They may speculate about alternatives, consider numerous responses, evaluate available evidence, weigh the relevance of competing views, and get deeply involved in other considerations related to the issue at hand. To help students understand how such thinking processes operate, you will find it useful to model these processes by thinking aloud as you and members of your class attack an issue together.

In doing this, the idea is to prompt your students to use thinking patterns that are appropriate for accomplishing a similar task. As students observe you, they will note general approaches to the issue that have proven to be productive. They will see the importance of thinking carefully about their own approaches to the task. If you have done a good job in thinking aloud with them, you will find that your students often perform better on an assigned task than if you simply assume that they already know how the task should be approached.

Suppose you are a teacher in an English class and are about to introduce a unit on descriptive writing. You might ask each student to write a two- to three-page paper on tourist attractions of a selected world place. Your intention might be for students to prepare an initial draft, think about it, and then prepare a revised version. If your directions to students go no further than a statement such as "prepare a draft, think about it, and then rewrite it," you will not cue students to the kinds of thought processes that should be used as they approach the task of revision. A more productive way to get them successfully started on the revision task would be for you to model what they should do.

For example, you might prepare an overhead transparency from a first draft of the same assignment prepared by a student from a previous semester. Then, you could think aloud with students in this way:

> All right, look at this draft of a paper on Easter Island. Now, if this were my paper and I were about to revise it, these are some of the changes I would want to make.
>
> First of all, people will be reading literature about many different places. They will be turned off by anything that has been written hastily without careful attention to spelling and grammar. The first thing I'll want to look for is spelling errors. Then, I'll want to be sure that verb tenses are correct and consistent throughout.
>
> I will want to hold the attention of my reader. I don't want to lose anyone with long, complicated sentences. As a quick check on this, I'll read the paper aloud. Anytime I run out of breath before I finish a sentence, I am going to mark that sentence. Later, I will go back and cut these long sentences into shorter ones. Also, as I read I will try to spot any places where I am using the same word too frequently. If I find any excessive repetition, I will make a note to correct this situation in a revision.
>
> As I read through the material, I will mark every sentence that has as its main verb some part of the verb "to be." This tends to be a very weak, dull verb for the reader. As I rewrite the material, I will try to replace these verbs with more action-oriented words.
>
> Look at this sentence: "The giant statues are visited by many tourists." There are two serious problems here. First of all, the verb is in passive voice, a weak, uninteresting construction.

> Second, the reference to the statues simply being "visited" is not particularly exciting. I would rewrite the sentence to eliminate the passive voice and to add some color. One possibility might be a sentence something like this: "The giant statues of Easter Island challenge tourists' views of so-called primitive peoples."

As students listen to you think aloud about the thought processes involved in revising the sample paper, they have a model to follow as they begin to work on their own revisions. Modeling can also plant the idea that thinking about what the task requires is an essential prerequisite to beginning to address the task. This perspective is one that you want them to adopt as a result of your thinking-aloud demonstrations.

Visualizing Thinking

Visualizing thinking encourages students to monitor their own thinking processes. This technique helps students think about the nature of an assigned task, consider the kinds of thinking they will be required to engage in, and identify the nature of the information they will need to gather. Once students decide on their responses to these issues, they are encouraged to develop diagrams. The diagrams help them take and organize notes consistent with the requirements of the assigned task.

Suppose that you decided to have class members read the following material from a text:

> *Early Spanish Explorers of the Caribbean*
> In the year 1492, the Spanish explorer Christopher Columbus landed on San Salvador Island, a rather small island in the West Indies. San Salvador is in the group of islands that we know today as the Bahamas. Columbus later explored many other Caribbean islands. He set up a fort on one of the largest islands in the region, Hispaniola. Today the countries of Haiti and the Dominican Republic occupy Hispaniola.
>
> Another well-known early Spanish explorer was Nicolas de Ovando. In the year 1502, he was sent out from Spain to become governor of Hispaniola. He brought a large number of colonists with him. These colonists sought to make their fortunes in two ways. Some of them attempted to strike it rich in gold mining. Others started large plantations. A common problem all these early Spanish colonists faced was a lack of a large supply of local workers.
>
> In response to this situation, the colonists initially tried to make slaves of the local Indians. This was not successful. The Indians did not take to slavery, and many of them died. Once the local supply of Indians on Hispaniola had been exhausted, the Spanish for a time tried bringing in Indians from other Caribbean islands. They, too, died. Later, slaves from Africa were brought to the island. Though many of these slaves survived, Hispaniola continued to have a need for more workers than could be supplied.
>
> As a result of this labor shortage, many Spanish colonists began moving from Hispaniola to other islands in the region. One of the other large islands that attracted a number of Spanish settlers was Puerto Rico. The first settlers arrived there in 1508 under the leadership of Ponce de Leon. The Spanish moved into Jamaica in 1509 when Juan de Esquivel led a group of settlers there. Spanish settlers reached Cuba, the largest island in the region, in 1514. In time, it became the most prosperous of Spain's Caribbean territories.

Because of differences in ability levels of students, you might wish some students to focus on different aspects of this material than others. For example, you might want some of your students to read with this learning task in mind:

Leaders and Islands

Leaders	Islands

Figure 10.2

Task: Who were four famous Spanish explorers who made discoveries in the Caribbean between 1492 and 1514, and what large islands did Spain occupy during this period?

To help them focus on this task as they read the material and take notes, you might prepare a visual thinking diagram something like the one in Figure 10.2.

You might want others in the class to read for the purpose of accomplishing this somewhat different task:

Task: What actions were taken by the early Spanish settlers of Hispaniola to solve the labor shortage, and what happened as a result?

To help students focus on this task as they read the material and take notes, teachers might prepare a visual thinking diagram something like the one in Figure 10.3.

Note that although the students were assigned the same material to read, the thinking task assigned to some students differed from the thinking task assigned to others. These differences are reflected in the visual thinking diagrams. Use of such diagrams can help students focus on information that is relevant to a specific assigned task.

When you try this approach for the first time, you will want to provide members of your class with the blank diagrams. Once your students get used to working with them, you can ask them to develop visual thinking diagrams of their own. The process of constructing the diagrams forces them to think about the nature of the task and about the nature of thinking that will be required in responding to it.

Use of the diagrams helps students monitor and adjust their own thinking processes as they work with assigned materials. As a result, their work is likely to be more productive and their levels of achievement and self-satisfaction higher. A variety of additional reading and thinking tools are included in chapter 12.

Why Were Laborers Needed?

What Was Tried First?	What Was Tried Second?
What Were the Results?	What Were the Results?

Final Outcome

Figure 10.3

Discovery Learning

Discovery learning refers to learning that requires students to identify key ideas and principles themselves rather than be taught directly by teachers. Discovery learning has been given considerable support by the work of Jerome Bruner (1960), who emphasized the importance of students' understanding the structure of a subject, that is, the basic concepts and principles that form its foundation.

If a student is to grasp the structure of a subject, Bruner believes that he or she must be actively engaged in the learning process. This kind of activity requires students to identify the concepts, the principles, and their relationships for themselves (Woolfolk, 1995). Good discovery learning lessons demand extremely careful teacher planning. In part, to emphasize this point, some proponents of the approach use the term "*guided discovery*" to indicate that the teacher has an important guidance function in creating conditions that help students discover meaningful concepts and principles.

One of the primary tasks in a guided discovery lesson is to identify and present activities or examples that will stimulate and facilitate students' search for information. For example, if you are teaching a social studies class, you might give students a blank map of a country and ask them to mark places where they think cities might be located. Once they have done this, you can encourage them to compare their guesses with a printed map. As they seek to explain the reasons for their correct as well as incorrect guesses, students move toward identifying some basic concepts and principles related to urban location and growth. You can go on to provide additional information and to ask good questions as you guide students through the processes of evaluating their responses and seeking deeper understanding.

Discovery teaching presents several challenges. You must have a solid academic understanding of the subject in order to identify its basic concepts and principles. You also need to have available good examples or situations that will stimulate student discovery of the basic concepts and principles. Asking good questions, providing additional information, and guiding students require you to have both excellent content knowledge and good teaching skills.

Today's electronic technologies make it easier to implement discovery approaches. A major condition for the effective use of discovery learning is the availability of information and data. The ready availability of data on the Internet makes it possible for students to access tremendous quantities of information. No longer are they limited to what is available in the school library. Once students have learned how to ask the right questions and how to connect to the available sources, discovery learning activities can be taken to levels that were unimaginable only a few years ago.

Discovery learning is based on the inductive reasoning process. This process proceeds from the specific to the general. A simple example will illustrate the general procedure. Suppose you want to teach a group of learners the concept *fish*. You might begin by providing them with photographs of different fish. Through a series of questions, you would encourage students to identify common features of the things in the individual photographs. To conclude the exercise, you would urge students to develop their own description of the concept *fish* and would ask them to describe its necessary defining characteristics.

In summary, discovery learning can take many forms. The following are some variations of discovery approaches:

- Comparing, contrasting, and generalizing
- Inquiry teaching
- Simulations

Comparing, Contrasting, and Generalizing

One effective way of helping students discover basic concepts and principles is by presenting individual pieces of information in ways that allow them to be easily compared and contrasted. By then looking at the data, students can note patterns and subsequently form generalizations or principles.

A data retrieval chart is one approach to organizing data for learning activities that require students to compare, contrast, and generalize. This chart is basically a matrix that includes concept categories under which relevant information can be listed.

A lesson using a retrieval chart might develop along these lines. Suppose you were teaching English and decided to have your students read a novel called *Mines and Dreamers*. This novel features many interactions among the five major characters: Joe Carmody, Luella McPhee, Tony Marino, Gordon Duffy, and Selma Steele. In planning lessons designed to promote students' abilities to compare, contrast, and generalize, you might develop a chart that students could use to organize basic information from the novel. The chart might call for information about each character under these major headings:

- Family background
- Education
- Occupation
- Basic motives

You could ask students to gather information individually; you might have members of the class develop the information as part of a group discussion focusing on the novel. In either case, the result would be a completed data chart. This could take the form of a large chart in the front of the room, a chart prepared on an overhead transparency and projected on a screen, or individual charts that would be printed and distributed to each student. An example of such a chart with data filled in might look something like Figure 10.4.

	Family background	**Education**	**Occupation**	**Basic motives**
Joe Carmody	Divorced parents; reared by mother	Grade 8	Union organizer; former coal miner	Improving lives of the working poor
Luella McPhee	Divorced parents; reared by mother	Grade 10	Owner of successful real estate firm	Personal social advancement; wants to hide nature of her family background
Tony Marino	Upper middle class; reared by both parents	College graduate	Attorney	Betterment of the condition of the working poor
Gordon Duffy	Upper middle class; divorced parents; reared by father	College graduate	Attorney	Promotion of his own economic self-interest; insensitive to needs of others
Selma Steele	Upper class; reared by both parents	College graduate	Business manager	Believes that what is good for business is, in the long run, good for everyone

Figure 10.4

Use the completed chart as a basis for a discussion designed to prompt students to compare, contrast, and generalize. You might begin such an exercise by asking students to look carefully at the information on the chart and to respond to this sequence of questions:

1. What similarities do you see among these characters? Possible responses:
   - Joe Carmody, Luella McPhee, and Gordon Duffy were reared in one-parent homes.
   - Joe Carmody and Luella McPhee have less than a high school education.
   - Tony Marino and Gordon Duffy are attorneys.
   - Joe Carmody and Tony Marino are both interested in improving the conditions of the working poor.

   (These are examples. Students may identify additional and different responses.)
2. What are some differences you see among these characters? Possible responses:
   - Their educational levels are different.
   - They come from a variety of home backgrounds.
   - Some of them are basically out for their own interests.
   - Some of them are interested in improving the conditions of others.

   (These are simply examples. Students may identify additional and different responses.)
3. From looking at this information, what general statements can you make about what the author may believe to be true? Possible responses:
   - There is not necessarily a connection between a person's occupation and his or her sensitivity to the needs of others.
   - The kind of home a person grows up in as a child does not necessarily predict the kinds of attitudes toward others he or she will have as an adult.

   (These are simply examples. Students may develop different and additional generalizations from the information in the chart.)

The generalizations that students develop in this exercise result from consideration of a very limited amount of information. You would need to remind them that these conclusions should be regarded as only tentatively true. As you involve your students in the study of additional material, you can have them test the accuracy of these generalizations as they acquire new information.

Inquiry Teaching

Inquiry teaching is a specific form of discovery learning that emphasizes use of the scientific method. When using an inquiry approach, you engage students in hypothesizing, gathering data, and verifying or modifying their conclusions.

Inquiry thinking involves students in the process of knowledge creation. This is true because students develop their own conclusions after considering independent pieces of evidence. Many students enjoy the process of knowledge generation. In addition to its high potential to motivate students, inquiry teaching helps young people develop the kinds of rational thinking abilities they will be called on to exercise throughout their adult lives. In short, supporters of inquiry thinking are as much interested in students mastering the scientific process as in their mastering the academic content that provides the focus for a given inquiry lesson. Lasley, Matczynski, and Rowley (2002) remind us that "inquiry requires many more intellectual skills of a student than merely knowing content; the student must also be able to understand the dynamics that ground that academic content" (p. 147).

Basic Steps in Inquiry Teaching Inquiry teaching in American schools traces back to a famous book published by the eminent American educational philosopher John Dewey. In *How We Think*, originally published in 1910, Dewey suggested basic steps for sequencing inquiry instruction. With some variation, the following steps, derived from Dewey's work, are featured in many inquiry lessons:

- Identify a focus and describe the essential dimensions of a problem or situation
- Suggest possible solutions to the problem or explanations of the problem or situation
- Gather evidence related to these solutions or explanations
- Evaluate possible solutions or explanations of the problem in light of evidence
- Develop a conclusion that is best supported by the evidence

The first step is the establishment of a focus for the inquiry. Your function at this step is to present a puzzling situation (sometimes called a *discrepant event*) to students. This should be something that challenges their present conceptions. For example, you might conduct a science demonstration where something unexpected or surprising occurs. One that social studies teachers sometimes use begins with this question: "Why do cities grow up in some places but not in others?" Often many students comment that many cities seem to grow up near a river, large lake, or ocean. When this idea surfaces, the teacher presents them with the example of Mexico City, located in the south-central highlands of Mexico, a considerable distance from large and important bodies of water. The puzzle presented by the inland location of one of the world's largest cities becomes a point of departure for further development of the lesson.

The second step in the inquiry process requires students to develop hypotheses or possible explanations for the puzzling event. This is usually accomplished in a group setting, and students are asked to generate as many explanations as possible. When you work with students during this phase of an inquiry lesson, your role is to help them clarify their hypotheses and encourage them to state these ideas clearly so that others understand the relationships they are establishing.

The third step in the process requires students to gather specific information related to the guesses or the hypotheses they made. During this part of the lesson, your task as a teacher is to challenge students to think about the type of information or evidence that they would need to help them determine whether their guesses or hypotheses are correct.

At this point, there are two ways you can proceed. One option is for you to function as a data source. If you do this, students will ask you questions, and your answers will help them arrive at conclusions. This approach requires you to take time to teach students to phrase questions clearly so that your answers will be responsive to the kinds of information they need. In general, you want them to ask questions that elicit information about facts that will help them arrive at a supportable conclusion. Formal models have been developed that feature the teacher as information source. Some of these place limitations on the kinds of questions students can ask. For example, the inquiry approach developed by Suchman (1962) in science requires that students ask only questions that can be answered with a *yes* or a *no*.

Another alternative at this point in the lesson is for you to direct your students to seek information about their tentative hypotheses elsewhere. If you decide to proceed in this manner, you will need to help students identify appropriate questions and direct them toward the type of information they need to gather. Then you'll need to make arrangements for them to access appropriate information sources. These may include such options as the Internet, documents, books, CD-ROMs, software, and films. After students have gathered data, your role is to encourage them to review and evaluate hypotheses they formulated in light of the new information. This results in their accepting, rejecting, or modifying their original hypotheses.

Finally, you need to bring the lesson to a close by summarizing the explanation and the evidence supporting it. It also is useful to review the steps that students followed to arrive at their conclusion. This step is important because helping students master rational thinking processes is one of the main purposes of inquiry instruction.

When a class is involved in an inquiry lesson, often individual students will arrive at different conclusions. If you find yourself confronted with this situation, you will have a marvelous starting point for engaging the class in a follow-up inquiry lesson. This lesson can help class members test the relative merit of each of the alternative conclusions.

An Example of an Inquiry Lesson Let's see how an inquiry lesson might develop. Suppose you wanted students in a high school humanities class to probe the relationship between urbanization and life expectancies of American women. An inquiry lesson with this focus might develop along these lines:

Step 1

Focus: You might begin by writing the statistics shown in Figure 10.5 on the board.

You: Look at this information. What trends do you see? Notice that women seem to be living longer in each of the 3 years. Notice, too, that more people seem to be living in cities. Now, I want you to think about two questions. First, what might be the connection between longer lives for women and the trend toward living in cities? Second, are there other possible explanations for women living longer in the later years?

Step 2

Students provide answers to each question.

Question 1: What might be the connection between longer lives for women and the trend toward living in cities?

A Sample of Possible Student Responses

- People in cities might have earned more. Women may have eaten better and stayed healthier in the cities.
- Women in cities may have had better access to newspapers. They may have read more about good health standards.
- There may have been better access to doctors in the cities. Thus, women may have begun to live longer because they were more likely to get treated when they were sick in cities than when they were sick in rural areas.

Percentages of Females in Three Age-Groups

Year	Under 30 (%)	30 to 50 (%)	51 or older (%)
1850	71	20	9
1910	61	25	14
1970	50	23	27

Median Age of U.S. Females in 3 Years

Year	Median age (in years)
1850	18.8
1910	23.9
1970	27.6

Percentages of U.S. Urban and Rural Population in 3 Years

Year	Rural (%)	Urban (%)
1850	84.7	15.3
1910	54.3	45.7
1970	26.5	73.5

*Data are adapted from U.S. Bureau of the Census. (1975). Historical statistics of the United States, Colonial Times to 1970, Bicentennial Edition, Part I (pp. 11–12, 16, 19). Washington, DC: U.S. Bureau of the Census.

Figure 10.5

- Cities tended to bring more medical scholars and researchers together. This resulted in an explosion of new information about health and medicine. This new information increased the life spans of all people in the later years.

Question 2: Other than the move from rural areas to the cities, what things might have led to higher percentages of women in older age-groups in the later years?

A Sample of Possible Student Responses

- Women could have started having fewer children. If this happened, fewer would have died in childbirth, and more would have lived to an older age.
- In the earlier years, a high percentage of women could have been immigrants. Immigrants tend to be younger. This would account for higher percentages of younger women in the earlier years.

- There could have been some fatal diseases that killed women in their 20s and 30s for which cures became available in later years.
- In earlier years, society may not have cared as much for older women as it did in later years. There could have been a deliberate failure to care for older women in the earlier years.

Step 3

During this phase of the lesson, you direct students to gather evidence supporting or refuting each of the possible explanations they had generated in response to the two questions. You will want to direct them to additional resource materials containing information. Students proceed to gather as much relevant information as possible.

It is important to have specific sources of information readily available for student use. Directions to students to "go to the library and find it" are a sure prescription for failure. Many will give up. Even those who do not will be frustrated. These negative attitudes can undermine the motivational potential of a good inquiry lesson. Classroom computers are especially useful for this step. Students can access numerous databases through the Internet, from CD-ROMs, or from other sources.

Step 4

During this phase, the responses to the focus questions are reexamined in light of the additional information that has been gathered. The nature and reliability of the evidence is discussed. Once all information related to a given explanation has been considered, the class decides whether to accept, reject, or revise the explanation.

You conclude this phase of the activity by writing on the board those explanations for which students found the most evidential support.

Step 5

Ask students to look at the explanations for which they have found good support. You may ask questions such as these:

- Given all the evidence you have seen supporting these explanations, what do you think is the single best explanation for more women living longer in 1910 than in 1850 and in 1970 than in 1910?
- Why do you make this choice?
- How confident are you that it is correct?

When the students make a final choice, review the supporting evidence and remind class members that this conclusion should not be regarded as final. They might revise it if additional information becomes available.

This description has been compressed for purposes of illustration. Good inquiry lessons require time, and issues addressed are often complex. It takes time for students to master skills associated with logical thinking. If time is at a premium and the primary objective is content coverage rather than teaching the inquiry process, an inquiry approach may not be the best choice. Once again, your objectives should guide your choice of strategy.

Simulations

Another powerful form of discovery learning involves the use of simulations. These are often called simulation games because they include a goal that is to be achieved by the player and some rules that must be followed in order to achieve the goal. The term "game" also captures the play-like environment that is often created when students are engaged in a simulation activity. Simulations are really complex forms of role playing that can be taken to quite sophisticated levels.

The goal of the simulation is to simplify reality and place the participant in a situation where the consequences of choices can be experienced. Thus, the consequences of different actions and hypotheses can be tested. An analysis of the actions and the results can help students discover principles and higher-level thinking processes as well as help them apply learning in ways that will facilitate transfer to real-world problems. Because of the realistic setting, students often find simulation activities motivating and interesting.

The increased availability of technology and computers in the classrooms has greatly amplified possible uses of simulations in the school classroom. Today, excellent educational simulation software is available from educational materials supply houses. Computer-based simulations utilize a technology that makes it possible for students to immediately experience the results of their actions. This feature allows them to try multiple approaches as they test the adequacy of their initial solutions to problems.

An important step in all simulations is debriefing. When you use a simulation with a group of students, some of the most important learning occurs in a discussion at the end of the exercise. This phase of the simulation lesson gives your students an opportunity to analyze their actions and begin to develop concepts and principles based on what they experienced. This also provides them with an opportunity to share their experiences with others and formulate statements that explain the cause-and-effect linkages they found.

Debriefing is an important part of simulation activities.

The basic steps in using a simulation in the classroom are the following:

- Assign roles to the students
- Explain the objective for each role
- Explain the rules and the operating procedure
- Conduct a demonstration
- Conduct the simulation activity
- Debrief the activity, discuss what happened, identify principles, and, if needed, repeat the activity

Creative Thinking

The world has a never-ending supply of serious problems. Throughout history, solutions to problems often have come from people who have responded to them in unusual, creative ways. Problems would not be problems if conventional solutions could be easily applied. It takes someone who has the curiosity, insight, and emotional security to try a novel approach to a solution.

Often, creative solutions result when people make unusual associations between different kinds of things. For example, Ruggiero (1988) points out that the inventor of the forklift truck got the idea from watching mechanical fingers lift donuts out of an oven. He goes on to note that Gutenberg's invention of the printing press resulted, in part, from his observation of a wine press.

Creative thinking is stimulated when people are able to defer final judgment and when they do not have fear of failure (Ruggiero, 1988). The ability to generate creative new information is not widespread among students (Perkins, 1981). To remedy this situation, specific instructional techniques have been developed to enhance students' creative thinking powers. One that is widely used is brainstorming, which is designed to stimulate original solutions to problems. It seeks to unleash mental power in ways that discourage students from relying on ordinary and conventional responses. It places a premium on the ability to generate large numbers of creative responses.

Brainstorming

Brainstorming developed in the world of business. Concerned leaders noticed that junior-level managers shied away from proposing novel solutions to problems. Often, they simply parroted positions of senior executives. As a result, insights of these younger executives rarely got a hearing. The brainstorming technique was developed to encourage a broad sharing of innovative ideas. The technique ensures that all ideas will be heard and considered.

Rules for conducting a brainstorming exercise are simple:

- Provide students with a problem to consider. ("Suppose all books were printed with an ink that would disappear after 6 months. What would happen if that were true?")
- Invite students to call out their ideas as rapidly as possible. A student is free to speak whenever an opening of silence occurs. The idea is to generate a rapid

outpouring of ideas. Tell students to say whatever comes to their minds as long as it is relevant to the problem.

- Caution students not to comment positively or negatively on any ideas suggested by others. All ideas are accepted. This rule helps break down students' fear of "saying something stupid."
- Write down every idea. (This can be you, the teacher, or a designated recorder.) The recorder should not be concerned about neatness. He or she needs to be someone who can write fast. Student ideas come at a very rapid rate.
- Stop the exercise when there is a noticeable decline in the rate of presentation of new ideas.
- Conclude the exercise with a general discussion of the ideas.

Brainstorming can be applied in a number of secondary curriculum areas. It is an effective technique for stimulating students to produce new ideas rather than rehash old ones or react to views of others.

Critical Thinking

Whereas the primary function of creative thinking is to generate ideas, the primary function of critical thinking is to evaluate ideas. Critical thinking always involves judgment. Critical thinking conclusions are based on more than uninformed opinion. Properly, judgments are made in terms of defensible criteria.

Sometimes you will be able to link activities that ask your students to engage in both creative thinking and critical thinking. When you do this, the creative thinking activity takes place first. During this phase of the lesson, you give your students directions that encourage them to produce ideas. During the second phase, you direct class members to use critical thinking approaches to evaluate these ideas.

Analytic Brainstorming

We introduced a basic procedure for brainstorming in the earlier section on creative thinking. Dunn (1972) developed an analytic brainstorming approach that applies critical thinking to the initial creative results of the first part of a brainstorming activity. You might develop an analytic brainstorming lesson along these lines:

- You begin by posing a problem in the form of a statement about what an ideal solution to a problem might be: "The best thing we could do to prevent pollution of Gulf coast beaches would be to . . . (Students brainstorm appropriate responses. You write down their answers so that all students can easily see them.)
- With responses developed during the preceding step in full view, you next ask students why the best things mentioned have not already taken place: "What things are getting in the way of those 'best things' we could do to prevent pollution of Gulf coast beaches?" (Students brainstorm responses.)
- The next phase features a question about what might be done to overcome obstacles noted in response to the question posed in the previous step: "How could we

overcome difficulties that keep us from doing what we have to do to prevent pollution of Gulf coast beaches?" (Students brainstorm appropriate responses.)

- Next, you ask students to point out difficulties of implementing ideas noted in the previous step: "What might stand in the way of our efforts to overcome difficulties that keep us from taking necessary action to prevent pollution of Gulf coast beaches?" (Students brainstorm appropriate responses.)
- Now you ask students to decide what should be done first to begin a realistic solution to the problem: "Considering all our thinking, what steps should we take first? Be prepared to explain your choices." (Students respond and defend their choices by reference to appropriate criteria.)

In general, critical thinking involves approaches to making evaluative judgments that are based on logical consideration of evidence and application of appropriate criteria. Beyer (1988), a leading proponent of teaching thinking skills to students in the schools, points out that critical thinking does not result from following a specific sequence of steps. Rather, it involves the use of a number of mental operations, including the following:

- Distinguishing between statements of verifiable facts and value claims
- Distinguishing relevant from irrelevant information, claims, or reasons
- Determining the factual accuracy of a statement
- Determining the credibility of a written source
- Identifying ambiguous claims or arguments
- Identifying unstated assumptions
- Detecting bias
- Identifying logical fallacies
- Recognizing logical inconsistencies in a line of reasoning
- Determining the strength of an argument or claim (Beyer, 1988)

Controversial issues often function well as stimuli for worthwhile lessons that feature critical thinking. Unfortunately, some teachers hesitate to bring such issues into the classroom. This is often due to fear of parent or community protests. Not wanting to stir up unnecessary resistance to school programs, these teachers steer the safe course and avoid discussing issues where there might be strong disagreement. We disagree. Students need to know that there are responsible ways of dealing with controversial issues. In addition, the introduction of real-life disputes often motivates them. Students appreciate the importance of these issues, and they often commit enthusiastically to lessons featuring content that is relevant to the world they live in outside the school.

Lessons that feature controversial issues need not generate negative parental and community concern. In teaching this kind of content, you have to recognize that it is not your role to force students to arrive at a given conclusion. Rather, your purpose is to help students apply critical thinking to the process so that each person in the class can arrive at an intelligent and thoughtful position.

Problem Solving

Problem-solving approaches are used when students are asked to think about problems for which there is likely to be a best or correct solution. This does not necessarily mean that these solutions may not at some future time be challenged. However, they are considered best, correct, right, or appropriate given the evidence that is available at the time the problem is considered. These are examples of issues that you might ask students to address when using a problem-solving approach:

- What is causing the leaves on my houseplants to turn yellow and fall off?
- Why is it colder in the winter months in Minneapolis than in Juneau even though Juneau is much farther north?
- Why do people in Maine and Alabama speak with different accents?
- Why don't armadillos live in California?
- What has caused 20th-century English to differ more from 17th-century English than 20th-century French differs from 17th-century French?

When you introduce students to problem solving, you teach them to follow certain steps:

- Step 1: Identify the problem
- Step 2: Consider possible approaches to its solution
- Step 3: Select and apply approaches
- Step 4: Evaluate the adequacy of the conclusion

Suppose you were teaching a high school algebra class and wished to apply this model. This is how your lesson might unfold:

Step 1

YOU: All right, class, I want each of you to solve this equation. (On the board, the teacher writes this equation: $2X - 46 = 116$.) In this problem, what are we trying to find? (Student raises a hand.) Ruby?

RUBY: You want us to solve for X, right?

YOU: Right.

Step 2

YOU: Now, before you start, I want someone to tell me how you're going to go about it. John, how about you?

JOHN: Well, we're going to have to get this thing down to a simpler form. The first thing I would do is get rid of the 2X by dividing both sides by 2.

YOU: Okay. That makes sense. What would need to be done next? Gabriella?

GABRIELLA: I think we'll need to arrange it so we'll have the X on one side and all the numbers on the other.

YOU:	Fine. Now what do we need to remember about the sign of a number when we move it from one side of an equation to the other? I mean, if I had the equation X − 3 = 4, what would happen if I moved the minus 3 to the other side? Kim?
KIM:	The minus 3 would become a plus 3. So you would end up with X = 4 + 3, or 7.
YOU:	Excellent. Remember the sign changes when we move from one side to the other. Now, once you moved all the numbers to one side, what would you have to do to solve for X? Jean?
JEAN:	You would need to add all the numbers together and then take the square root of the total.

Step 3

YOU:	We seem to have the basic procedures well in mind. Now I want each of you to solve the problem. If you get stuck, raise your hand, and I will try to help you. (Students individually begin working on the problem.)

Step 4

YOU:	I see that everybody has come up with an answer. Now let's check our work to see whether the answers are correct. Jennifer, tell me how we might do that.
JENNIFER:	I'm not sure.
YOU:	Anyone have an idea? Raoul?
RAOUL:	We could substitute our answer for X in the original equation to see if it works.
YOU:	Good idea. Let's try that. Raoul, what did you get as your answer?
RAOUL:	9.
YOU:	Fine, now let's substitute 9 for X in our original equation. (You write the following sequence of substitutions on the board.):

$$2X - 46 = 116$$
$$2\,(9 \times 9) - 46 = 116$$
$$2\,(81) - 46 = 116$$
$$162 - 46 = 116$$
$$116 = 116$$

Your answer seems to be correct. Does everybody see what I have done here? (Teacher goes on to answer questions and to emphasize the importance of checking the accuracy of answers to problems.)

You may also want to consider a case study as a vehicle for involving students in problem solving. For decades, the case study approach has been used in law schools and in many graduate schools of business. In recent years, case study instruction has been tried in many different subject areas. For example, if you were teaching a lesson involving geometry, you might try to liven up your instruction by presenting brief cases involving flight problems that pilots face. These cases can illustrate some practical applications of geometric principles.

When you use the case study method, you present the class with a fairly complete account of a situation that raises important questions. Students then identify the key issues and go about gathering information that will help them try to resolve them. Case studies are especially useful promoters of active student involvement. They help students understand that there are not always clear answers to problems.

Cases you select as a focus for this kind of instruction can be real or contrived. Actual cases bring an air of reality to the classroom but may have the disadvantage that some students will know the resolution and will, therefore, fail to take the problem-solving process seriously. Good cases focus on issues that the students see as important and for which there is not a simple right or wrong answer.

CRITICAL INCIDENT

Why Don't Ms. Levin's "Good" Students Like Decision Making?

Naomi Levin, who teaches 11th grade American history in a high school in a medium-size city in the Rocky Mountains, is midway through her fourth year of teaching. Last summer, she attended a special institute on higher-level thinking skills, and she came back determined to use some of the techniques she learned in her own classes.

She decided to emphasize decision-making skills in a unit on the Great Depression and selected these focus questions:

- What should the government have done (that it didn't do) to prevent the Depression?
- What should the government have done to end the Depression sooner?

To help students gather information about these questions and likely alternative responses, Naomi worked closely with the school librarian. A special shelf of resource materials was organized for members of Naomi's class to use. After she gave students a general orientation to the decision-making approach, students dug into the materials.

After students had had a chance to think about the questions, some possible responses, and some more or less final conclusions that made sense to them, Naomi led the class in a general discussion centered on the focus questions. She said that the intensity of student interest and the level of involvement were outstanding. She thought everything had gone very well. This view changed when some of her "A" students dropped by to talk after school.

These students reported that they had really enjoyed what was going on in class but that they had some concerns. Most of them indicated that they were going on to college and that the class had spent a lot of time just on one topic. They indicated that they were worried about not covering other topics that they might need to know about to do well in college.

In addition, they felt very uneasy about what kind of test they would be facing when "all this discussing and speculating ends." Though they didn't say so in so many words, they seemed to be indicating that they knew how to get As when content was taught in a more traditional way but that they weren't sure about how their performances would stack up when they were evaluated on "this decision-making stuff." Several students strongly hinted that they would prefer to go back to a more familiar way of dealing with course content.

Naomi had always counted on her good students for support. She was disappointed that these class leaders expressed concern about an approach that, in her mind, works well. Now she is in doubt as to what she should do.

■ ■ ■

What values were implied by the reaction of some students to Naomi's new approach? Why were they concerned about this change? Did their values conflict with Naomi's? How might values of others (the principal, parents, community leaders, and other teachers) influence their reactions to Naomi's approach? How concerned should Naomi be about this situation? Do you think it possible that any change from a familiar pattern will result in student concerns of this kind, or is there something attached specifically to the decision-making technique that brought it about in this situation? Is it acceptable to cover less content in more depth, or does such a decision irresponsibly deny students access to important information they should have? What kinds of assessment might be appropriate when the emphasis has been on developing students' decision-making proficiency?

Decision Making

Not all problems have answers that are clearly right, correct, or appropriate. There are questions for which there are no best answers. In this situation, people often must make choices from among a variety of acceptable alternatives. This process involves a thinking skill known as decision making (Beyer, 1988). Because it involves choices from among a number of competing appropriate responses, decision making involves consideration of personal values and relevant evidence.

The thinking model for decision making varies from that used in problem solving. The major reason for this difference is that value judgments play a much more important role in decision making than in problem solving. The following seven-step model is an example of an approach used in decision-making lessons:

1. Describe the basic issue or problem
2. Point out alternative responses
3. Identify evidence supporting each alternative
4. Identify values reflected in each alternative
5. Point out possible consequences of each alternative
6. Make a choice from among available alternatives
7. Identify evidence and values considered in making this choice

An Example of a Basic Decision-Making Lesson

Step 1 A local school board has taken under consideration a proposal to require every student to take four years of mathematics. The issue or problem might be framed like this: "Should students be required to take 4 years of mathematics in high school?"

Step 2 In this case, there are just two basic alternatives. Alternative 1 is to support a requirement for all students to take 4 years of mathematics in high school. Alternative 2 is to oppose such a requirement.

Step 3 Some of the following evidence might be gathered to support a 4-year mathematics requirement:

- SAT scores in mathematics have failed to reach levels achieved by students in the 1960s.
- The nation is facing an impending shortage of engineers and other technical people who must have sound backgrounds in mathematics.
- Students will begin college-level mathematics instruction at higher levels because of better high school backgrounds.
- The requirement will improve the general quality of the high school curriculum by making the whole program more rigorous.

Some of the following evidence might be gathered to oppose a 4-year mathematics requirement:

- The requirement will weaken existing math courses. This is true because all high school students do not have the talent for the math courses that, given the new requirements, they will be required to take.
- The requirement will result in an unfortunate reduction in the number of available electives.
- Not all high school graduates go to college.

Not all occupational fields, even for college graduates, demand an extensive background in mathematics.

Step 4 Individuals who support a 4-year mathematics requirement might cite these values, among others:

- Mathematics courses are difficult, and they provide a needed element of rigor to the high school program.
- Too much electivity in high school is not good.
- Society needs more technically trained people, and it is the school's job to provide them.

The following values might be among those cited by individuals who oppose a 4-year mathematics requirement:

- Individual choice is an important part of the high school experience.
- Mathematics is not necessarily more rigorous than other subjects it might displace.
- The society should not go overboard in imposing its priorities on individuals.

Step 5 A supporter of a 4-year mathematics requirement might cite the following consequences as among those that might follow implementation of such a policy:

- Quantitative SAT scores may be expected to rise.
- High school graduates will be better prepared for college.
- The nation will be better able to compete with such technologically oriented nations as Japan.

An opponent of a 4-year mathematics requirement might cite the following consequences as logically resulting from implementation of such a policy:

- The dropout rate among high school students will increase as academic frustrations become too much for some students.
- Discipline problems will increase among students who remain because those who are not talented in mathematics will sense that they have been put in a no-win situation.
- Because vocationally oriented electives will decrease in number, some employers will begin to attack the schools for failing to provide relevant instruction.

Step 6 At this point, a decision is made. In this case, because there are only two alternatives, a choice would be made either to (a) support the decision to require 4 years of mathematics or (b) oppose this decision.

Step 7 A person *supporting* the decision might identify the pieces of information and values relevant to his or her conclusion in this way:

> I was impressed by the data showing the decline in quantitative SAT scores since the early 1960s. The growing shortage of engineers and technicians also impressed me. Thinking back on my own high school experience, I concluded that high school students lack the maturity to choose electives wisely. In the long run, they would be better served by a more prescriptive curriculum. Finally, I think the schools do have a responsibility to require students to take courses in areas where we have a critical national shortage.

A person *opposing* the decision might identify the pieces of information and values relevant to his or her conclusion in this way:

> It is clear to me that requiring 4 years of mathematics will reduce the number of electives available to students. Many vocational electives in the high school program do a fine job of responding to the needs of students who will go to work once they graduate. We need to preserve these programs. Finally, I don't think we should allow needs identified by bureaucratic federal agencies to force content on students in the schools. Local control and freedom of choice are a cherished part of our educational heritage.

Issues, Values, and Consequences Analysis

Decision making applies to the affective or the values area of the curriculum as well as to the academic portion. One application of decision making to the values area is that of issues, values, and consequences analysis. The general steps that are followed are those usually used for decision making with the addition of components that require students to consider values related to the focus issue(s) as they move toward making a decision. Listed here are the steps that you typically would follow in implementing this approach (see Figure 10.6):

1. Identify the general issue
2. Describe faction A, including basic beliefs and values
3. Identify relevant alternatives open to faction A
4. Identify possible consequences for each alternative
5. Identify what would be valued in choosing each alternative
6. Repeat the previous steps for faction B (and any other remaining groups)
7. Compare the values, alternatives, and consequences of all factions
8. Make a choice as to the best alternative in terms of what you consider to be the highest values

Step 1: Identify the General Issue
During this step, you work with the entire class to ensure that all students understand the issue. You may do this by introducing the students to a problem. For example, during the 1950s, China was not a member of the United Nations. Some people thought it was strange that the world's most populous nation was not a member. Others feared

MORE FROM THE WEB

Higher-Level Thinking

Much information today is available on the Internet that relates to teaching higher-level thinking skills. The volume of information attests to the high interest that both professional educators and the general public have in approaches to teaching that will prepare students to deal intelligently with the complex challenges they will face as adults. You may wish to visit some of these sites.

Introduction to Creative Thinking

This material, produced by Robert Harris, includes an excellent overview of creative thinking. Among topics addressed are (a) creative methods, (b) negative attitudes that block creativity, (c) distinctions between creative thinking and critical thinking, and (d) mental blocks to creative thinking.
Website: http://www.virtualsalt.com/crebookl.htm

Critical Thinking: Primary and Secondary Information

You will find numerous resources here that you can use in lessons that integrate critical thinking into your instructional program. This site is maintained by a number of organizations that are interested in promoting the development of critical thinking.
Website: http://www.criticalthinking.org/K12/default.html

Problem Solving

At this site, you will find excellent links to sources where you can obtain useful sample problem-solving strategies.
Website: http://mailer.fsu.edu/~jflake/probSol.html

that admitting China would give additional voting power to nations with Communist governments. There was much debate over whether China should be admitted to the United Nations. What was the basic issue involved here? What was the basic disagreement? What are the two different groups that were involved?

Step 2: Describe Each Faction
Decision making is needed in lessons such as this because there are two or more positions that are in conflict. Different groups have different opinions as to what should be done. During this phase, your intent is to have the students, working in groups, gain as much information about each one of the supporting positions. Who are they? What are their goals? What are their beliefs? What things are most important to them?

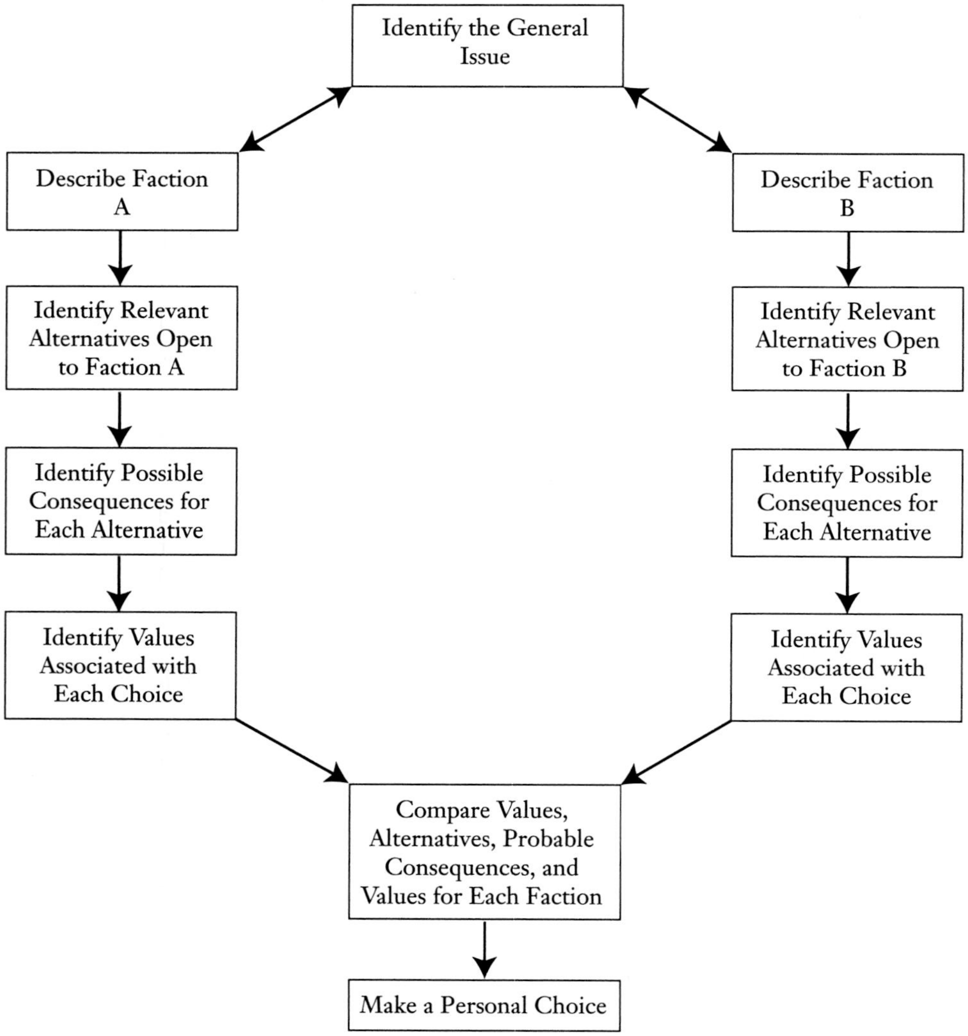

Figure 10.6

Step 3: Identify Relevant Alternatives Open to Each Faction

During this phase of the lesson, you ask students to work in groups to identify alternative courses of action open to members of the faction they are considering. Sometimes you will encourage students to brainstorm alternative answers to questions. For example, you might ask them to think about different answers to questions such as "What are some of the things those opposed to admitting China into the United Nations might have done to prevent it?" "What are some things supporters could have done to gain China's admission?" "Were there options other than full admission or full denial?"

FOR YOUR PORTFOLIO

1. Standard 4 of the INTASC standards focuses on the use of a variety of strategies that encourage higher-level thinking. What materials or ideas you learned in this chapter will you include in your portfolio as "evidence" of your learning? Select up to three items to include. Number them 1, 2, and 3.
2. Think about why you selected these materials for your portfolio. Consider such issues as the following in your response:
   - The specific purposes to which this information can be put when you plan, deliver, and assess the impact of your instruction
   - The compatibility of the information with your own priorities and values
   - The contributions this information can make to your personal development as a teacher
   - The factors that led you to include this material as opposed to some alternatives you considered
3. Prepare a written reflection in which you analyze the decision-making process you followed. In addition, mention the INTASC standard(s) to which your selected material relates. Some of your material might relate to several standards. (First complete the following chart.)

Materials You Selected and the INTASC Standards

Put a check under those INTASC standards numbers to which the evidence you have selected applies. (Refer to chapter 1 for more detailed information about INTASC.)

Item of Evidence Number	**INTASC Standards**									
	S1	S2	S3	S4	S5	S6	S7	S8	S9	S10
1										
2										
3										

Step 4: Identify Possible Consequences for Each Alternative
Alterative courses of action may produce different results or consequences. During this step, you encourage students to look at each alternative course of action and to consider the possible consequences of that action. For example, "What might have been the consequences of a massive information campaign to discredit China?" "What might have been the consequences of some sort of conditional admission?"

Step 5: Identify Values Associated with Each Choice
Once the alternatives and their possible consequences have been identified, the students should identify what would be valued by choosing each alternative. For example, "What was most important for those who opposed admission?" "What was most important for those who favored admission?" "What would those who advocated a smear campaign have valued most highly?" "What would those who advocated partial admission have valued?"

Step 6: Compare the Values, Alternatives, and Consequences of All Factions
At this point, the information gathered by the different groups investigating different factions can be brought together and compared. Your purpose here is to help students understand that many decisions involve a conflict of values and value priorities. For example, some people may have seen that their value of preserving democracy as a justification for opposing China admission to the United Nations would have been in conflict with their value of honesty, particularly if smear tactics involving the use of false information had been used by some opponents of China's admission.

Step 7: Make a Choice
At this point, you challenge students to make a personal decision about the issue that has been considered. Encourage them to think about which values they consider most important and then to reflect on which decision would be most consistent with their own values.

In summary, issues, values, and consequences analysis is designed to help students appreciate that decisions are not made just by dispassionate consideration of evidence. Individual values play a role. In addition, decisions frequently involve a conflict between two or more values. When people make decisions, they have to think about and weigh the importance of both their own values and those of others.

KEY IDEAS IN SUMMARY

- There is much less centralized teacher control in techniques designed to develop students' higher-level thinking skills than in direct instruction lessons. The teacher functions as a manager who presents students with a problem and assists them, as needed, as they work toward a conclusion.
- *Metacognition* refers to thought about the process of thinking. Metacognitive instructional approaches seek to help students become conscious of their own thought processes and to select those that are relevant for solving particular problems and tasks with which they are confronted. Examples of these metacognitive approaches include teacher modeling and visualizing thinking.
- *Discovery learning* involves getting students to learn how to identify basic concepts and principles, or the structure of a subject, rather than having them taught

directly by the teacher. Learning how to discover is at least as important as what is discovered. This develops thinking skills that will be useful in a variety of life situations. Contrary to some popular notions, effective discovery teaching requires teachers to spend more time planning than is true when some other instructional techniques are selected.

- *Inquiry teaching* is based on inductive learning, a learning process that proceeds from the specific to the general. This means that students first are presented with specific examples that they are asked to study. From this study, they derive general explanatory conclusions or principles. Inquiry teaching involves students in the creation of new knowledge. Approaches typically follow a logical, step-by-step sequence that is thought to develop students' rational thinking powers.
- *Simulation* is a powerful approach to helping students discover important processes and values as well as higher-level thinking skills. Simulations involve placing the students in situations that allow them to experience the consequences of their actions. An analysis of actions taken and the resulting consequences help students discover important principles and processes.
- *Creative thinking* frees people to develop unusual or novel solutions to problems. It involves unique insight. Creative thinking is thought to be stimulated when people are able to defer final judgment until many alternatives have been considered and when they do not fear failure. Brainstorming is an example of a classroom technique that is designed to elicit creative thinking.
- *Critical thinking* focuses on the evaluation of ideas. It aids students in making judgments based on consideration of evidence. The analytic brainstorming approach developed by Dunn and Dunn (1972) is an example of a classroom technique designed to encourage the development of critical thinking abilities.
- *Problem-solving approaches* are designed to help students consider problems for which a single best answer is thought to exist. This does not mean that this best answer will be right every time. It simply implies that it is best, given presently available evidence. These steps are included in many problem-solving approaches: (a) identifying the problem, (b) considering alternative approaches to solving it, (c) selecting and applying one or more approaches, and (d) making a final judgment regarding the best approach (or solution).
- *Decision making* refers to thinking sequences that are relevant when the problems that students confront have no generally agreed-on correct or right answers. A number of appropriate answers may be identified. The alternative selected reflects a consideration of both evidence and values.

REFLECTIONS

1. Some scholars argue that teaching students how to engage in sophisticated thinking should be the primary mission of the school. Why might they take this position? Do you agree? Explain your response.
2. Teachers today feel obligated to cover much academic content in the courses they teach. Given this reality, should they devote class time to instruction designed to help students develop appropriate metacognitive processes? Why or why not?
3. Both the Suchman (1962) inquiry approach and visualizing thinking presume that students have trouble making sense out of the enormous volume of information

that confronts them. Is this true? If so, are the Suchman technique and visualizing thinking sound approaches to helping them deal with it?

4. Why are relatively few people creative thinkers, and what might you do in the classroom to prompt more creative thinking from students?
5. What are some key features of approaches designed to elicit critical thinking?
6. How would you describe differences in the purpose of a traditional brainstorming approach and the variant called *analytical brainstorming*, developed by Dunn and Dunn (1972)?
7. Under what conditions would a problem-solving approach be an appropriate instructional choice?
8. Why do different people arrive at quite different conclusions when a decision-making approach is used to consider an issue?
9. In what ways do problem solving and decision making differ? Is it worthwhile for teachers to teach both approaches to students? Why or why not?
10. What are basic steps followed in issues, values, and consequences analysis? Is it proper for school lessons to deal with issues involving values? Why or why not?

LEARNING EXTENSIONS

1. Secondary teachers are pressed for time. Some people argue that time devoted to teaching students learning processes and thinking skills (e.g., metacognitive approaches, creative thinking skills, problem-solving skills, critical thinking skills, decision-making skills, and so forth) takes valuable time away from content instruction. Find another student in your class to work with you on a project to prepare arguments related to this question: "Is taking class time to teach thinking skills to students responsible?" Make an oral presentation to the class in which one of you presents evidence supporting a "yes" answer and one of you presents evidence supporting a "no" answer.
2. Select a topic from a subject you are preparing to teach. Describe how you might incorporate one of the following into a lesson related to this topic:
   - Inquiry teaching
   - Problem solving
   - Creative thinking
   - Decision making
   - Critical thinking

   Present this information to your instructor in a short paper.
3. Interview teachers who have incorporated inquiry teaching into their instructional programs. Ask them to describe the pluses and minuses of this approach. Share your findings with others in the class as part of a general discussion of inquiry in the secondary school classroom.
4. Prepare a collection of articles from professional journals or from Internet sources that describe practical classroom applications of inquiry and creative

thinking approaches. You may wish to use the *Education Index* to locate article titles and journals. A search engine will help you find items posted on the Internet. Try to include at least 10 articles. Present them to your instructor for review. Keep these materials as a resource to use when you begin teaching.

5. Invite several department heads from a local secondary school to visit your class. If this is not possible, try to get a director of secondary education, a director of secondary curriculum, or another central school district office administrator to come. Ask about the relative emphasis on inquiry instruction and on teaching thinking skills to students. Specifically ask whether teachers are encouraged to use these approaches and whether any effort is made to provide in-service training to help teachers become more proficient in implementing them.

REFERENCES

Beyer, B. K. (1987). Practice is not enough. In M. Heiman & J. Slomianko (Eds.), *Thinking skills: Concepts and techniques* (pp. 77–86). Washington, DC: National Education Association.

Beyer, B. K. (1988). *Developing a thinking skills program*. Boston: Allyn & Bacon.

Boudourides, M. A. (1998, July 3–6). *Constructivism and education: A shopper's guide*. Samos, Greece: International Conference on the Teaching of Mathematics. Available at http://www.duth.gr/~mboudour/mab/constr.html

Bruner, J. (1960). *The process of education*. Cambridge, MA: Harvard University Press.

Dewey, J. (1910). *How we think*. Boston: D C Heath.

Dunn, R., & Dunn, K. (1972). *Practical approaches to individualizing instruction: Contracts and other effective teaching strategies*. New York: Parker.

Gennrich, D., & Long, L. (1999, February 3–4). *How does one develop tutor-led distance materials for use in collaborative learning groups, with an emphasis on constructivist learning?* Proceedings of the 8th Annual Teaching Learning Forum, University of Western Australia. Available at http://cleo.murdoch.edu.au/asu/pubs/tlf/tlf99/dj/gennrich.html

Joyce, B., & Weil, M. (1996). *Models of teaching* (5th ed.). Boston: Allyn & Bacon.

Lasley, T. J., II, Matczynski, T. J., & Rowley, J. B. (2002). *Instructional models: Strategies for teaching in a diverse society* (2nd ed.). Belmont, CA: Wadsworth.

Perkins, D. (1981). *The mind's best work*. Cambridge, MA: Harvard University Press.

Ruggiero, V. H. (1988). *Teaching thinking across the curriculum*. New York: Harper & Row.

Slavin, R. E. (1994). *Educational psychology* (4th ed.). Boston: Allyn & Bacon.

Suchman, J. H. (1962). *The elementary school training program in scientific inquiry*. Report to the U.S. Office of Education, Project Title VII, Project 216. Urbana: University of Illinois.

Woolfolk, A. E. (1995). *Educational psychology* (6th ed.). Boston: Allyn & Bacon.

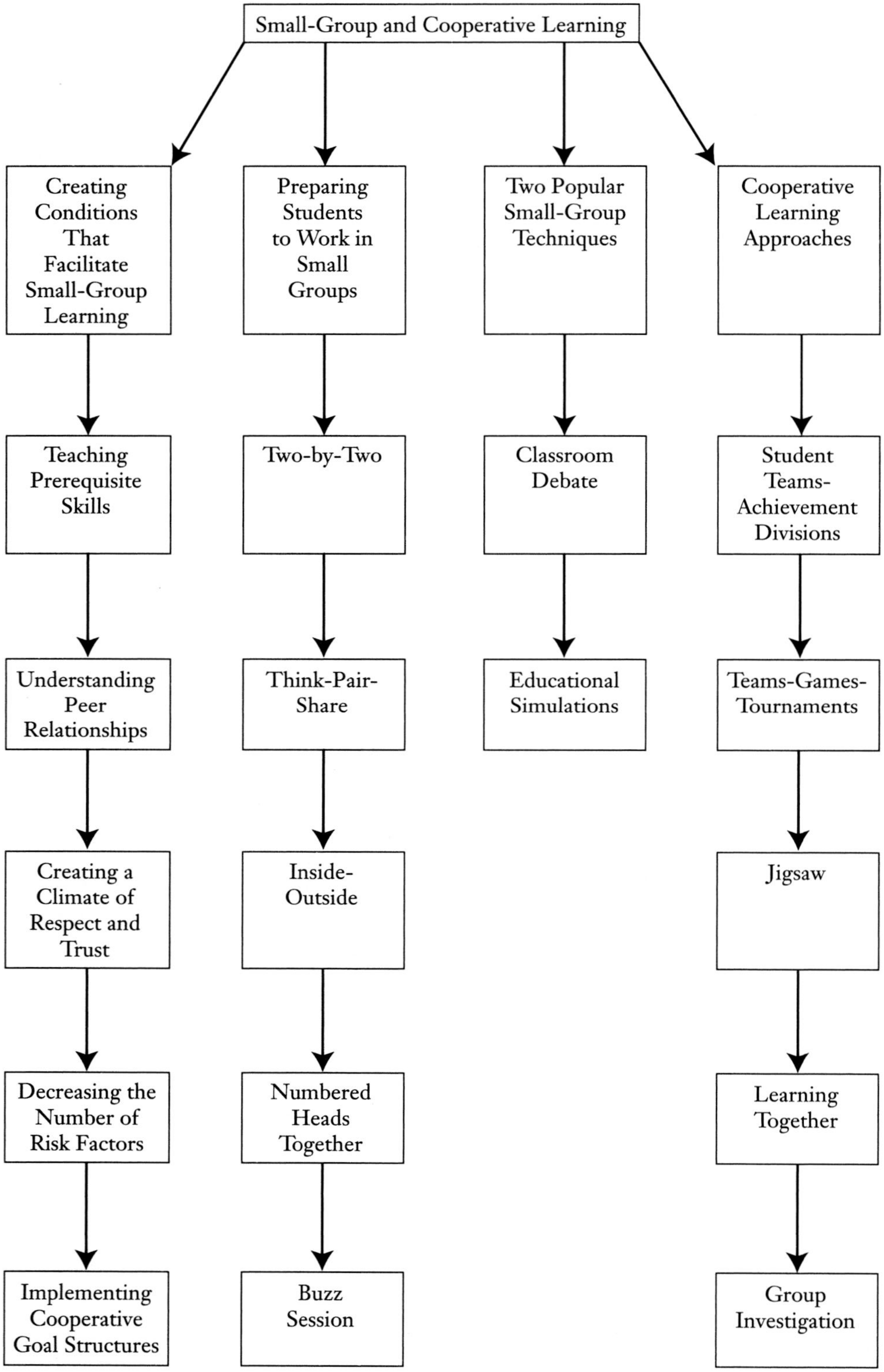

Figure 11.1
Graphic Organizer

CHAPTER **11**

Small-Group and Cooperative Learning

OBJECTIVES

This chapter will help you

- describe a rationale for using small-group learning;
- identify conditions that facilitate small-group learning;
- define competitive, individualistic, and cooperative goal structures;
- describe some techniques you can use to prepare students for small-group learning;
- point out some examples of popular small-group learning techniques;
- identify features that distinguish cooperative learning from other small-group approaches; and
- explain purposes and procedures associated with several cooperative learning techniques.

Introduction

Consider these points: (a) young people in secondary schools love to socialize, and (b) learning is primarily a social act (Putnam, 1997). In planning your instruction, you can take advantage of these two principles to organize effective lessons that require your students to work in small groups in ways that encourage mutually supportive cooperative patterns of behavior. This kind of instruction promotes learning by providing a context for students to learn as they watch, listen, talk to, and support others.

There is evidence that teaching oriented in this way facilitates student achievement (King, 1999). Why is this so? One explanation is that student motivation increases when students are allowed to work with each other and when there are group goals and rewards rather than individual goals and rewards. Another explanation is that, through interaction with others, students find they are better able to clarify, reflect, reformulate, and elaborate on material more effectively than when they work alone. This intensive engagement with new content promotes development of the kinds of cognitive changes that are necessary for learning to occur. Further, many small-group and cooperative learning techniques feature modeling.

Modeling involves actions taken by the teacher or, occasionally, someone else who seeks to provide learners with examples or demonstrations of competencies associated with a lesson. For example, when modeling approaches are used in small-group and cooperative learning lessons, students often gain tremendously in terms of their ability to apply problem-solving skills effectively as they wrestle with challenging situations and issues (King, 1999).

There is also evidence that small-group learning approaches can help you and your students develop a positive working relationship. Lessons organized in this way give you and your students opportunities to work together more personally than when you are teaching a more traditional lesson to an entire class of students. Because this kind of instruction keeps you closely involved with individuals, you ordinarily are able to spot and respond quickly to difficulties that particular students might be having. Any assistance you provide to promote students' success adds to their sense of self-confidence and tends to promote favorable feelings toward you and your teaching.

Learning occurs when students become active participants in lessons. In traditional large-group instruction, some individuals in your classes simply do not get very involved. In a group discussion, there will be some students who rarely speak up. Perhaps they are shy, perhaps they are unprepared, or perhaps that aren't feeling well. Small-group learning lessons provide contexts that encourage all students to become actively engaged in lessons. The increased student-to-student and student-to-teacher interactions that these instructional experiences provide help develop students' oral language proficiencies, increase the probability they will acquire new content, and add to their sense of personal competence.

You may face potential difficulties when you begin using small-group approaches with a new group of students. For example, they may not know how to work together productively in small groups. If this happens, you may find individuals arguing about what they should do or abandoning academically related work in favor of a spirited social chat. You also may find that a few individuals in small groups may be inclined to sit back and let others do the work. Finally, it is possible you will encounter some students who simply do not like small-group work. It may be that these students have always experienced high levels of academic success when they have been involved in classes featuring traditional large-group instruction. It could be, too, that they have had unfortunate experiences on previous occasions when they have been involved in poorly structured small-group lessons.

To remedy these problems, you need to know your students well, diagnose what obstacles may be standing in the way of their commitment to small-group learning approaches, and develop a response that seems appropriate for individual members of your class. In general, the best remedy is to plan small-group lessons carefully. If you do, you will greatly increase the probability that students will enjoy their experiences and look forward to occasions when you ask them to work in small groups. In this chapter, you will find information about some things you can do to create conditions that will facilitate small-group work and some examples of small-group learning techniques that many secondary school teachers have used successfully.

Creating Conditions That Facilitate Small-Group Learning

As is true of all instructional techniques, small-group learning operates within the context of the individual classroom. Some classroom characteristics are more compatible with certain instructional techniques than others. For example, you are likely to have more initial success with small-group learning if your students have some knowledge about how to work productively in this type of instructional setting.

One of the most important requisite conditions is that your students understand the purposes of the activity and what they are going to learn from it. You want to point out the specific personal benefits that they can derive from their participation in small-group lessons. For example, you might explain that a major reason people are dismissed from jobs is because they cannot work productively with others. You can let students know that, in addition to learning new content in a pleasing way, their involvement in small-group learning will add to their level of comfort in working in close proximity with others who may have personalities and perspectives quite different from their own.

Many teachers who have not used small-group learning techniques express concerns that some students they put into groups will not work productively in this type of instructional setting (Joyce & Weil, 1996). To be sure, if a group task is poorly structured, the purposes of the activity are unclear, and there is little individual or group accountability, then group learning approaches are likely to be ineffective. However, the reality is that most of your students will have no problem working well together if you provide them with an appropriate orientation. This implies a need to give them clear guidelines regarding what they are to do and what the expected outcome of the lesson should be (Joyce & Weil, 1996). You will find it particularly helpful to require group members to produce some kind of tangible "product of learning" at the end of the lesson. This will provide both you and your students with tangible evidence that something worthwhile has been accomplished.

Teaching Prerequisite Skills

It makes sense for you to provide students with some initial instruction that focuses on specific skills that will help them work together. These skills involve such things as active listening, giving clear explanations, resolving conflicts, avoiding put-downs, and asking for clarification (Slavin, 1994). Your students should have little difficulty mastering these competencies. During initial small-group learning lessons, you might give students opportunities to practice them by organizing members of the class into groups of two or three students and assigning each group to perform simple tasks. As students become more comfortable with these skills, you can start assigning them to larger groups of up to about six people (Joyce & Weil, 1996).

Understanding Peer Relationships

How well your students know one another, the norms of their peer group, the feelings individuals have about how well others in the group accept them, their general levels of interest in your subject, and how students in the group assess their relative chances of succeeding in your class help shape the general character of every student you will teach. As you prepare for a career in secondary education, you might want to see these variables in action. To do so, make arrangements to visit a secondary school classroom and follow a few students as they pass from class to class throughout the school day. Don't be surprised if you observe that students who are uncooperative in one class demonstrate completely different behaviors in another. The special dynamics of the group and the psychological climate created by the teacher often account for these differences.

All this underscores the importance of taking time to learn something about your students every time you get a new group. What you find will vary somewhat, depending on the particular setting of your school. For example, in small, rural secondary schools in areas where there is not much moving in and out of the area, students may know each other very well. However, this does not necessarily guarantee that all of them will get along well in your classes. If past relationships have not been positive, this interpersonal relationship history may carry forward year after year. Over the years, some of your students may have been labeled in ways that diminish their expectations of success and otherwise introduce tensions into the overall classroom learning environment.

If you find yourself teaching in a large urban school, you may find that only a few students in your classes know each other before the school year begins. Initially, this can inhibit their willingness to participate actively in classroom discussions. You may need to take action to make class members comfortable with one another and more willing to become active participants in classroom activities. In particular, you will want to identify and help students who seem to be generally isolated from others in the class and who are particularly reluctant to become fully engaged in assigned activities that require students to work together.

Creating a Climate of Respect and Trust

Productive group work demands mutual respect and trust. If your students do not respect one another, they will have difficulty accepting the contributions of all members of the class. Under such conditions, your efforts to promote cooperative learning may well fall short of their goal, and students may develop antagonistic attitudes. This is especially likely to happen if some of them feel they are being asked to do more than their share of the work. If you suspect that some students are concerned about this issue, you need to take action to ensure that each student is carrying part of the load.

In addition to working to distribute the workload equitably, you also need to help students involved in small-group work develop attitudes of mutual respect. This will not happen simply by telling students that this is your expectation. Respect must be earned. What you can do is assign individuals to complete tasks for which they have a particular aptitude. When they complete these tasks successfully, others in the group see clear evidence of their contributions. This, in turn, leads others to respect and appreciate their value as group members.

Decreasing the Number of Risk Factors

One of the greatest risk factors for students is their fear of failure. In order for individuals to cooperate, they must feel that they are in a safe environment. This requires you to take action to lower the risks of participation and active involvement. For small-group learning lessons to be effective, your students must first believe that working together will enhance their opportunities for success. Sometimes, academically talented students fear that working in small groups puts them at risk. They may be convinced that they can do better work working alone rather than as members of a small group that has collective responsibility for a task. If you are confronted with this situation, you must assure these students that there will be real benefits for them as a result of their participation in small-group lessons.

Many of your students are also likely to be concerned about the issue of grading. Some students fear any approach that alters the way grades are given. They often feel that a change will put them at a competitive disadvantage. When you introduce small-group learning, you have to take care to explain how students will be assessed and to

WHAT DO YOU THINK?

"I Don't Need Their Help"

Suppose you are teaching a group of high school sophomores and receive this reaction from a student after you announce plans to involve class members in a small-group learning exercise that will require them to work closely together and to assist one another to master the new content.

"Why do we have to do this? I don't need help from these people. I work hard, and I get good grades. I know that when we start this small-group thing that I'll end up carrying the load for everybody. It just isn't fair."

Questions

1. How legitimate are the concerns of this student?
2. Is the student really distressed about the issue of fairness, or is something else a likely cause of the student's concern?
3. What would you say to this student in response to this statement?
4. Given the concerns raised by this student, what special directions might you give to members of the groups about their individual responsibilities?

make a case in support of the idea that the evaluation scheme will not increase the risk that they will receive bad grades.

Implementing Cooperative Goal Structures

The way you structure goals of small-group work can affect students' learning. The term "goal structure" refers to the way individuals relate to each other in accomplishing a particular goal (Woolfolk, 1995). Each of the following basic types of goal structure requires a different relationship between an individual and the group:

- Competitive goal structure
- Individualistic goal structure
- Cooperative goal structure

Competitive Goal Structure In a competitive goal structure, students are placed in competition with each other. This means that the only way an individual student can succeed is by beating or finishing ahead of others. Ranking students according to their scores on tests and grading on the curve are two examples of how competitive goal structures have often been implemented in the classroom. Goals of this variety traditionally have been more common in secondary school learning programs than either of the other two basic types.

One of the reasons that competitive goal structures have been dominant is the belief that competition has motivational value and leads to higher achievement. Today, critics of this approach reject this claim. They point out that grades in a competitive goal structure environment tend to be based on tests that measure a narrow range of abilities. These tests tend to favor students with specific abilities over students who may have strengths in other areas. By the time many students who have been in classes featuring competitive goal structures reach the secondary level, they have given up. They do not believe that they have a real chance to surpass other students. For these students, competition is not motivating; rather, it is discouraging.

To illustrate this point, suppose that grades were based on a narrow range of ability, such as being able to run a mile in under 5 minutes. Some students would see this as possible, and they would be motivated to accomplish this goal. However, many others would despair of their ability to reach this goal. They would simply drop out. An inappropriate application of competitive goal structures leads some students to commit to the idea that the "cards are stacked" against them. They may refuse to play the game entirely. When this happens, there is an increased probability that their attitudes will take a turn for the worse and that they will develop unproductive patterns of classroom behavior.

Competitive goal structures can have a negative influence on several other conditions necessary for cooperation in the classroom. For example, if class leaders are not in the academically talented group (e.g., the group of students who have traditionally done well on tests), other students in your class may conclude that academic success is not important. They may choose to identify instead with the class leaders whose interests and abilities are not connected to what you are trying to accomplish at school. This situation does not comport well with your objective of establishing congruence between the enthusiasm of class leaders and the objectives of your academic program.

Individualistic Goal Structure Individualistic goals structures do not require students to perform at better levels than others. In this arrangement, attaining success is purely an individual endeavor that is unrelated to the efforts of others. An individual performance standard for each student is set. You judge an individual student based on how well he or she does relative to this standard, not relative to the performance of someone else.

Although individualistic goal structures can lead to programs that build students' self-esteem, there are also negatives associated with this approach. Though they decrease risk factors associated with competition, they do little to increase group cohesion or acceptance of others. They also overlook the fact that your students will not live their lives as isolated individuals; instead, they will be part of an interdependent culture. Individualized goal structures ignore the human need for belonging and socialization.

Cooperative Goal Structure To achieve success in classes featuring cooperative goal structures, your students have to know how to work productively together. The cooperative goal structure recognizes that different individuals have unique skills and abilities. When these are joined together, greater accomplishments are possible. For example, the success of an orchestra, a choir, or an athletic team requires individuals with different abilities to work together to achieve a goal. In fact, the goals of these groups cannot be achieved by any one person. In a cooperative setting, risk factors often are reduced. This is true because others involved in the common effort become resources who share in the risks associated with the task of accomplishing a prescribed goal.

Cooperative goal structures in the classroom respond well to the interpersonal dimension of learning. They help your students recognize that they can learn from each other. They also capitalize on peer influences and the interests of students in working together. Many students find cooperative goal structures to be motivating.

Preparing Students to Work in Small Groups

Several simple techniques are available to help in assisting students develop their abilities to function well in small-group learning situations. Committing some class time to this kind of preparation will enhance the likelihood your students will derive important benefits from lessons featuring this organizational pattern.

Two-by-Two

You can use an approach called two-by-two to break the ice with a new group of students. You begin by asking each student to find out something specific about one other person in the class. Once this has been done, ask students to join together to form groups of four. Tell students in each group that their task is to remember information about all four group members. Give them a little time to do this and then ask individuals in each group to stop and tell what they can remember about each person. Follow the same general procedure as you go on to organize the groups of four into groups of eight and then the groups of eight into groups of 16.

You will be amazed at how many students will be able to remember information about nearly every group member, even at the stage where groups feature 16 students each. This activity helps students become more comfortable with each other. When you later organize them into small groups for academic work, they will be comfortable in engaging in the intense person-to-person interaction that small-group lessons feature.

Think-Pair-Share

Think-pair-share is a technique that you can use to introduce small-group learning by beginning with a focus on dialogue between two students. You begin this approach by giving members of your class a question or problem to consider. In the first phase, each student thinks individually about the focus issue you have selected. Next, you ask students to work in pairs for the purpose of sharing their responses to the question or the problem. You follow this step by asking each pair of students to share their responses with the entire class.

Think-pair-share helps students learn how to discuss and share their ideas with others and to understand that "two heads are better than one." To enhance the probability that this approach will be effective, you want to select a focus question or problem that will be of interest to a large number of your students. To ensure that no student will feel in any way diminished at the end of the exercise because of a position he or she has taken, the question or problem you select should be one where there is no single "correct" or "right" response. Your intent is to encourage a diversity of answers and respect for a diversity of opinions. Think-pair-share can help students recognize that (a) it is possible to develop many reasonable responses to complex problems, (b) individuals of integrity may take different positions on these issues, and

(c) a willingness to think, consider, and sometimes compromise are characteristics that contribute to the successful functioning of small groups.

Inside-Outside

Inside-outside helps students develop skills that help them be more productive as members of small groups. In this approach, you organize members into two circles. People in one circle are located inside a larger, surrounding outside circle. You assign the "outsiders" (members of the outside circle) to observe behaviors of "insiders" (members of the inside circle). Each outsider is given one insider to watch. At this point, you give the insiders a problem to discuss or a task to complete. Members of the outsiders observe how the insiders go about their assigned work. You allow this phase of the lesson to continue for 10 or 15 minutes.

Next, you ask students to reverse their positions. Members of the former insider group now become members of the outsider group, and members of the former outsider group become members of the insider group. Following the same procedure as before, you assign each person in the outside group to observe one person in the inside group. Next, you give the new group of insiders a task to complete. The outsiders observe the insiders as members of this group begin doing what you asked them to do.

After 10 or 15 minutes have passed, you bring the entire class together again as a group. You ask individuals to share what they observed their insider doing. Ask them to comment especially on those contributions that helped the whole group complete the assigned task. You might also conduct a general discussion of some kinds of behaviors of individuals that were not especially helpful to the entire group. The purpose of the exercise is to help students recognize and commit to kinds of behaviors that facilitate completion of small-group tasks.

Numbered Heads Together

You can use the numbered-heads-together approach to introduce students to the idea of group scoring and individual accountability. You begin by organizing members of the class into groups of about four students each. (You can vary this number slightly if you wish to do so.) You give every student in each group a number ranging from 1 to 4. Next, you provide each group with a question or a problem. You explain that the group must develop an answer and share it among group members in ways that will ensure that every member of the group knows it. You give groups sufficient time to develop answers. At this point, you ask groups to stop. You announce one of the numbers you have assigned ("1," "2," "3," or "4"). Students in each group with the number you have called out raise their hands. If the person you identify to respond knows the answer, all members in his or her group get a point (Kagan, 1989). (If the answer is incorrect, you can go on and call on another volunteer.) You repeat this process several times. Members of the group with the most points are declared the winners.

Numbered heads together allows you to set up conditions that ensure that each student in every group will be involved. Further, there is an incentive for every person in the group who has information relevant to solving the problem or answering the question to share what he or she knows with all group members. In addition, the expectation that every group member will be able to respond correctly when called on encourages students to listen carefully to what others in the group are saying. In summary, the technique promotes the development of student behaviors that characterize effective, contributing members of small groups.

Buzz Session

Another technique you can use to build effective small-group participation skills is the buzz session. You begin a buzz session by organizing members of your class into small groups. Each group is given a focus topic. You choose one student to be a recorder. You provide this person with a piece of chart paper with three columns. This heading is written at the top of the first column: "What we already know about the topic." This heading is written at the top of the second column: "What we would like to know about the topic." This heading is written at the top of the third column: "How we might go about finding out what we would like to know." (Note: This technique is similar to the K-W-L discussed in chapter 12.)

The buzz session begins by group members generating as much information as they can related to what they already know about the topic. (The recorder writes information under the appropriate column heading.) Next, the group goes on to develop some ideas related to what group members would like to know. (The recorder writes ideas that are generated in the second column.) The group goes on to consider how they might find out what they would like to know. (The recorder adds this information in the third column.)

The buzz session technique helps students think about how they might get started on a group task. It also tends to make new tasks somewhat less intimidating as group members learn that some students may already know quite a bit about the assigned topic. Finally, this approach provides opportunities for students to think carefully about how they might proceed to get needed information. This kind of preplanning can add an important dimension of efficiency to students' work once they actually go about the business of responding to the assigned task.

Two Popular Small-Group Techniques

Secondary teachers use many kinds of small-group techniques. In the sections that follow, you will find two examples. *Classroom debates* and *educational simulations* can be used in a variety of subjects and at varying levels of sophistication, depending on the subject taught and the interests and abilities of individual students.

Classroom Debate

Classroom debates are organized differently than the familiar high school debating tournament. You can use them when teaching a variety of subjects, and you can adapt them to fit different time periods. Classroom debates feature two teams of students who prepare positions on different sides of an issue. You can structure these in various ways. Here is one format that many secondary teachers have found useful.

You take action to assign the following:

- Three students to the pro position
- Three students to the con position
- One student to the role of critic

You ask the three students on the pro side to gather as much information as possible that supports a proposal. You direct the students on the con side to gather as much evidence as possible to attack the position. You ask the critic to learn as much as possible about both sides of the issue and to ask questions toward the end of the debate that will highlight weaknesses of both positions. Each member of the team is expected to participate actively.

In preparation for the activity, select an issue that clearly has two sides. For example, if you are teaching English, you might choose an issue related to a selection of literature, such as the consistency of actions taken by one or more of the main characters. If you are teaching a social studies class, your focus issue might center on a historic event or on actions of some historic figure. If you are teaching science, you might choose a topic related to a threat to the environment.

Once you have identified a topic, you need to gather as much support material as possible for the students to use as they prepare for the debate. You may need to allow several class periods for them to develop an adequate background on aspects of the topic that will be considered during the actual debate. You will need to do considerable monitoring during the preparation phase to ensure that students are doing the necessary work to build the knowledge backgrounds they will need to make a credible case as they participate in the debate.

When the teams are ready, you can use a sequence such as the following. This example presumes that the debate will be completed during a single 50-minute class period:

1. Each member of each team speaks for 2 minutes. Pro and con speakers alternate. Approximate time: 12 minutes
2. Members of the pro team cross-examine members of the con team for a team total not to exceed 6 minutes. The members of the con team cross-examine the pro team for a team total of no more than 6 minutes. Approximate time: 12 minutes
3. Members of each team make a final statement. The total time for each team is not to exceed 3 minutes. Approximate time: 6 minutes
4. The critic questions members of both teams. His or her questions are directed to the team as a whole or to individual team members. The critic's purpose is to ask probing questions that point out the weak spots of the arguments. Approximate time: 8 minutes
5. The whole class votes to determine a winner. Approximate time: 2 minutes
6. You debrief the whole class. Your comments should be as supportive as possible and should highlight the important issues. During the debriefing stage, you might ask questions such as the following:
   - What were the best arguments you heard?
   - What made these arguments effective?
   - What other points would you have brought up?
   - What are some other questions the critic might have asked?

Classroom debates often generate high levels of student interest. They can help you teach students such important skills as cooperating, speaking in front of a group, mustering evidence to support a position, listening, and learning how to analyze and synthesize information.

Educational Simulations

The terms "games" and "simulations" are often used interchangeably. However, they do have somewhat different meanings. Games usually involve some sort of competition within a set of rules and where there is an element of chance. Simulations, on the other hand, are designed to place participants in situations that parallel reality. Simulations simplify reality in order to highlight important skills and ideas. They do not necessarily involve winners and losers. In some simulations, it is possible for everyone to accomplish their objectives. When you use a simulation, what you are trying to do is place your students in circumstances that give them experience in making decisions and then experiencing the consequences of these actions.

There are many educational simulations designed for use in secondary school class rooms. These range in sophistication from relatively simple board games that have an element of chance and involve game-like situations to complex computer-based activities that focus on such complex activities as building a city or simulating complex science experiments. Simulations featuring complicated designs and focusing on multiple variables often require several class periods to complete.

If you decide to use a simulation with your students, you must plan thoroughly, focusing on the following four phases:

- Overview
- Training
- Activity
- Debriefing

Overview During this phase, you introduce students to the simulation. You will explain the purpose of the simulation, and you will explain and assign students to specific roles. You will also point out rules associated with the simulation as well as any classroom rules that will be in force during the time the simulation activity is taking place.

Training During the training phase, you essentially will involve your students in a "walk-through" of the processes they will follow when the simulation begins. It often works best to select a few class members, assign them a role, and then illustrate how they will be involved once the simulation begins. You should invite students to ask questions that will help them better understand what they are to do.

Following your introduction, you will want to give students time to review their roles. If the simulation involves different groups of students, you need to make arrangements for groups of students to meet and discuss their roles and plot their strategy.

Activity The action component of a simulation takes place during this phase. During this time, you play the role of coach, referee, and discussant. At times, your students may lose sight of the purpose of the simulation, and you may need to stop the action and help students think about their decisions and refocus their attention on the purposes of the activity. Some students may not know how to respond to some developments. You can coach them as to their options and choices. As your students gain confidence in their roles, they will require much less of your help.

You will find that new and unexpected circumstances arise during simulations. For example, it is common for disputes to arise over situations that are not directly covered in the rules. You have to be ready to make some interpretations and decisions when problems of this kind develop. In general, you want to make rulings that are generally consistent with the overall purpose of the simulation activity.

Debriefing A well-planned debriefing is essential to the overall success of a simulation. This is the phase of the activity where you can bring closure to some important new learning that has emerged as a result of students' involvement. During the debriefing, you will review what happened and engage students in discussions related to why different things occurred. As you involve students in the debriefing, you provide them with opportunities to think about their decisions, why they took them, their consequences, and their conclusions from having been involved in the exercise. A good debriefing discussion helps students grasp the key ideas and skills that the simulation was designed to teach.

Cooperative Learning Approaches

In recent years, there has been a growing interest in cooperative learning approaches. It is a technique that features "students working together in groups, with group goals but individual accountability" (Willis, 1992, p. 1). Each student's evaluation depends, in part, on the collective success of the entire group in completing an assigned task. This feature helps students develop a prosocial commitment to helping others (Slavin, 1990), and it replicates the kind of productive group work featured in the adult workplace (Willis, 1992). Though some cooperative learning approaches involve sophisticated planning, this is by no means the case with all of them. Many ordinary class assignments can be enhanced through the use of cooperative learning (Woolfolk, 1995).

Cooperative learning can help all students achieve success.

Johnson, Johnson, Holubec, and Roy (1984) identified four characteristics that distinguish cooperative learning from other small-group approaches. The first characteristic is *positive interdependence*. This means that your students must depend on each other in order to accomplish a given task. This interdependence might be accomplished through a division of labor, a division of resources, the assignment of different roles to each individual within the group, or the establishment of goals that cannot be reached unless everyone works together.

CRITICAL INCIDENT

Cooperative Learning Blues

> I went to this cooperative learning workshop last summer. It was great. There were teachers there who were using cooperative learning in their own classrooms, and they talked us through some of the pitfalls. I left pumped up and ready to try some of the ideas myself.

The speaker was Nora Bennington, a second-year English teacher at J. V. Ortonsen High School. Rene Wu, Nora's former college roommate and herself now also a high school teacher, listened attentively.

"So how has it gone?" Rene asked.

"I got off to a smoother start than I really had expected," Nora responded. "Having those teachers work with us helped a lot. I picked up good tips, and I managed to avoid stupid mistakes I probably would have made otherwise. Also, I decided to start with Learning Together, one of the techniques that isn't a killer when it comes to planning."

Nora continued, "The students were a bit reluctant at first, but now they're really into it. I tend to mix it up a bit. We do Learning Together a while, and then we do a day or two of large-group work. By and large, I think I'd have a revolution on my hands if I went back to using large-group work all the time."

"No real problems, then?" Rene asked.

"Well," replied Nora, "there has been a glitch. I've had one parent on my back constantly since I started using Learning Together. She's come to see me, and she's complained to the principal."

"What's her problem—an unhappy son or daughter, or what?" Rene inquired.

"No, that's not it at all. Her son, Eric, is really bright. He has gotten into the swing of things, and he tells me he likes the small-group work. His mother has a real problem with the grading thing. You know, each student in the group gets the same grade."

"And, I suppose," put in Rene, "that she's convinced that her Eric is doing everybody else's work."

"Yes, that's part of it. But there's a bit more. Every time she calls me, I get this lecture about how competitive the world is and that this kind of learning just isn't preparing students for reality. She also makes pointed remarks about how each student has to take the Scholastic Achievement Test alone and that his or her personal score is what will be evaluated. She says this small-group work will make our students too dependent on others. She thinks the lazier ones will find somebody bright to carry the load and never really develop their own talents."

"Did they give you any information from the research this summer that you might use as ammunition?" asked Rene.

"As a matter of fact, they did," Nora replied. "And I've shared some of this information with her, but she's not impressed. I think she feels the researchers were people with a vested interest in cooperative learning. Since the results don't square with her biases, she questions the researchers' real motives."

"Rene, I don't mean to ramble on so long about this, but I'm in a quandary. I just don't know how to respond to this person. I hate to abandon a program I believe in and the students like. But I am afraid Eric's mother is going to make my professional life very uncomfortable unless I give up on Learning Together."

■ ■ ■

What does Nora Bennington's commitment to Learning Together tell us about what she thinks is important in teaching and learning? How do her values differ from those of Eric's mother? What should Nora do next? Can you think of some other arguments that might make sense to Eric's mother? To what extent should other professionals be brought into the picture? What might these people do? Is it fair that one parent's concern might lead Nora to change her instructional program? Or should she change only if a number of parents complain? Do you think the complaints of all parents would be equally weighed by school administrators? If not, which parents would be listened to most? What would you do if you were faced with this situation?

A second characteristic of cooperative learning is its requirement of *face-to-face interactions*. In other words, your lesson cannot be properly labeled as an example of cooperative learning if (a) it requires students to be physically separated, (b) each student works completely independently, and (c) you simply combine results of this totally independent work at the end into something called a "group product." There must be some interconnectedness among your students throughout the activity, even though specific individuals may have some specialized responsibilities.

The third characteristic is *individual accountability*. This means that each member of the group is held accountable for a particular contribution to the overall effort. The purpose of cooperative learning is to enhance the learning of all your students, not just a few. Therefore, the term does not apply appropriately to situations when one or two of your students do all the work and the rest sit and watch. All class members must be actively involved and appreciate that their contributions are vital to the success of the work of the entire group and that they will be held accountable for them.

The fourth characteristic of cooperative learning is that it requires students to use *interpersonal and small-group skills*. Indeed, one of the basic purposes of the approach is teaching students how to cooperate and work with others.

Researchers have found that cooperative learning lessons result in higher levels of student achievement than more traditional approaches from grades 2 through 12 (Slavin, 1994). The approach has been found to be effective when the learning task involves complex learning and problem solving, especially for lower-ability students (Woolfolk, 1995). In addition to its value in promoting desirable academic achievement, cooperative learning also has been determined to have a positive impact on other outcomes, such as race relations, self-esteem, attitudes toward school, and acceptance of students with disabilities (Slavin, 1994).

The following are some examples of widely used cooperative learning strategies:

- Student Teams-Achievement Divisions
- Teams-Games-Tournaments
- Jigsaw
- Learning Together
- Group Investigation

Student Teams-Achievement Divisions

The Johns Hopkins Team Learning Project developed Student Teams-Achievement Divisions (Slavin, 1980). If you are interested in trying a cooperative learning approach, yon will find Student Teams-Achievement Divisions to be one of the easiest to implement. It can be used in many different kinds of secondary school classrooms.

General Background This approach involves students in a learning format designed to promote cooperation and active participation by all. The scoring system used gives students a vested personal interest not only in their own learning but in the learning of all group members as well.

Implementing You begin by assigning students to learning teams consisting of four or five members. Each team has a mix of high, average, and low achievers. If your class has a diverse ethnic makeup, you want to make an effort to achieve a reasonable ethnic balance among members of each team. You should also try to have a gender mix on each team that closely approximates the percentages of males and females in the whole class.

Ordinarily, you will begin by introducing some new content using traditional whole-group instruction. Then the Student Teams-Achievement Division teams go to work using task sheets. The task sheets provide students with directions regarding what they are to do. You design the tasks so that they relate to the content you introduced during the whole-group instruction phase of the lesson. Students will work on the tasks as a team. You give students directions that specify responsibilities of team members, ensuring that each student understands the content. Students on the team continue to work until they are convinced that every member has a good grasp of the material. Then you test them on the material. During testing, team members may not help one another.

You use a special system of scoring that is designed to emphasize the importance of cooperation and active participation of all group members. This system yields test scores for each student; in addition, each student's score also plays a role in the process used to develop a score for the entire team.

An individual team member, depending on how well he or she does on the test, may add from 0 to 10 points to the total team score. To determine how much an individual student's score will add to the team score, you look to see how well this person did on the previous test. For example, suppose one of your students scored 15 points (out of 30 possible) on the previous test and 20 points (out of 30 possible) on this test. The difference between 20 and 15 (new test score minus old test score, or base score) is 5. Five points would be added to the team score as a result of this student's performance.

Example of a Group's Score in Student Teams-Achievement Divisions

Student	Base Score	Quiz Score	Team Points
Raoul A.	57	64	7
LaShandra C.	63	60	0
Joyce R.	40	55	10
LaRue T.	83	88	5
Samuel W.	75	95	10
		Team Total = 32	

Figure 11.2

Each student may provide a maximum of 10 points to the overall team score. There are two ways this 10-point maximum can be earned. Ten points are awarded if the student scores 10 or more points higher on the present test compared with the last test. Ten points are awarded for any perfect paper regardless of what the student received on the last test. This is an incentive to maintain the active participation of brighter students.

Figure 11.2 illustrates an array of scores for one group of students in a biology class where a Student Teams-Achievement Divisions approach was used. Notice that Joyce R., who received the lowest grade on the quiz, still contributed the maximum of 10 points to the total group score. This occurred because her quiz score of 55 was significantly higher than her base score of 40.

Student Teams-Achievement Divisions encourages less able students. These students have an incentive to do as well as they can. Even though their individual scores may not be high, they can make important contributions to the total score of their team. Brighter students are encouraged to help less able members of their group because all group members benefit when they exceed the expectations reflected in their base scores. Each member of a group has a stake in the learning of every other member. Thus, every student has a reason to want to help all group members to learn, and improvement of all team members becomes the goal as team members strive to increase overall team scores. You might want to arrange for some special recognition for high-scoring teams at the end of a regular grading period.

Debriefing During your debriefing, you will want to focus on the quality of interactions you observed among individual team members. You can share team scores with the group, making a special point of emphasizing how the contribution of every group member contributed to the group's overall score. The debriefing phase will also give you an opportunity to single out for special recognition those students who did very well themselves and who you observed to be especially helpful in assisting others to master the content.

Teams-Games-Tournaments

The Johns Hopkins Group also developed Teams-Games-Tournaments (Slavin, 1980). It requires somewhat more time to plan and implement than Student Teams-Achievement Divisions. Teams-Games-Tournaments can be used in a wide variety of secondary school classes.

General Background Teams-Games-Tournaments is basically an extension of Student Teams-Achievement Divisions. When you use this technique, you organize students into groups that participate in academic tournaments.

Implementing Your first task is to assign each student to become a member of a four- to six-member team. To the extent possible, you will want each team to include students representing both males and females and students who vary in their ethnicity and ability levels. Once you have your teams organized, you assign members to spend time studying some assigned material together. You will instruct students to help one another to master the content. Members of individual teams will compete for "team points" by participating in weekly academic tournaments.

The format for the tournaments requires you to reorganize students from the individual teams into "tournament groups." Three students of approximately the same ability level, each from a different team, constitute a complete tournament group. Once you have made student assignments to tournament groups, your next step is to direct each group to sit at its own table. For example, if you have 27 students in your class, you will need nine tables to accommodate each of the groups of three. Because students have been organized into tournament groups according to ability level, this means you will have nine different gradations of ability levels represented in your nine groups, ranging from a group that includes the three highest-ability students to the group including the three lowest-ability students.

Next, you draw out questions related to the content students have studied as members of their original teams. You ask these questions to the whole class. Points are awarded to a student's original team based on how many questions his or her team member answers correctly as compared to other people who are seated at this person's tournament group table. The same questions are drawn and directed to the entire class. A high-achieving student sitting at a table with two other high-achieving students will probably have to answer a large number of questions correctly to be the top person at the table and, hence, earn points for his or her team. On the other hand, a low-achieving student seated with other low-achieving students may be the table winner by answering correctly a smaller number of the questions you ask.

After several tournament rounds, you may wish to reassign students to different tournament groups based on how they have performed. Suppose you wished to do this. If you had a class of 27 students, you might begin in the usual way by assigning your three highest-achieving students to table 1, your next three high-achieving students to table 2, continuing this pattern until reaching table 9, the table where the three lowest-achieving students would constitute a group. For subsequent tournament rounds, you might decide to assign students to tournament groups based on how well they performed during the previous round. If you followed this scheme, in preparation for your second tournament, you would assign the three students who had the highest scores in round 1 to table 1, the three students with the next highest scores to table 2, and you would follow this pattern in such a way that the students you would assign to table 9 would be the three students with the lowest round 1 scores.

The Teams-Games-Tournament approach combines cooperative and competitive activities. You will find that this activity will develop your students' abilities to work actively in groups. This is true because the design of the approach makes it personally advantageous for individual group members to help others master the assigned content. In addition, the format tends to keep competition among students at approximately the same level, and your students will tend to feel the reward system is fair.

Teachers who have used Teams-Games-Tournaments report that even reluctant learners become interested in school when the approach is used (Slavin, 1990).

Debriefing During the debriefing phase, you will want to focus on the processes the students have followed in their groups to learn content. You need to emphasize the importance of mutually supportive, collaborative behavior. Finally, the debriefing phase gives you an opportunity to respond to students' questions.

Jigsaw

Jigsaw is a cooperative learning method that can be used in many different kinds of secondary school subjects. This approach is appropriate when you want to teach a topic that can be conveniently divided into several major components. It is also helpful if information related to each component can be organized under a common set of headings. For example, if you were teaching the Latin America unit in a geography course, the components might be the individual countries. Information about each might be organized under the common headings of (a) physical features, (b) population size and ethnic makeup of the population, (c) major languages, (d) major economic activities, and (e) education and literacy.

General Background You prepare for a jigsaw lesson by identifying a topic and preparing a list of major headings under which students can organize information gathered about each subtopic. The technique can be used to help your students work productively with others to master a complex set of content elements.

Implementing Suppose you are teaching English to a class of 30 students and have decided your focus topic will be "A Comparison of the Literary Work of Selected 20th-Century American Writers." You may decide to have students gather information related to these major writers: (a) Theodore Dreiser, (b) Eudora Welty, (c) F. Scott Fitzgerald, (d) Ernest Hemingway, (e) Willa Cather, and (f) Joyce Carol Oates. Your next step is to divide students into five *home teams*, each of which will have six members. You will assign one student from each home team to become an "expert" in information related to one writer. In this situation, each six-person team would include one Theodore Dreiser expert, one Eudora Welty expert, one F. Scott Fitzgerald expert, one Ernest Hemingway expert, one Willa Cather expert, and one Joyce Carol Oates expert.

Once you have individual experts for each of these home teams, these teams break up. Members from each home team who have been assigned to become experts on a particular writer meet together as members of *expert teams*. For example, all the Theodore Dreiser experts meet together. (There will be five of these people, one from each home team of six.) You will give members of the expert teams directions about learning resources to use. For example, you might suggest they use their own notes and recollections from previous class sessions as well as books and other materials you may be able to furnish. Members of each expert group will organize information under common headings you provide, such as (a) novels written and major themes treated, (b) short stories written and major themes treated, (c) poetry and other writings and major themes treated, and (d) general reactions of critics to this person's work. Figure 11.3 provides an example of how home groups and expert groups can be organized.

FOCUS: A COMPARISON OF THE LITERARY WORK OF SELECTED AMERICAN WRITERS

Home Groups

Group 1
Anna (Dreiser)
Rodney (Welty)
Juan (Fitzgerald)
LaRue (Hemingway)
Spencer (Cather)
Agnes (Oates)

Group 2
Paul (Dreiser)
Sondra (Welty)
Norman (Fitzgerald)
Sally (Hemingway)
Nora (Cather)
Raoul (Oates)

Group 3
Yu (Dreiser)
Monica (Welty)
Lee (Fitzgerald)
Helmut (Hemingway)
Rene (Cather)
Roy (Oates)

Group 4
Sarana (Dreiser)
Ming (Welty)
Kara (Fitzgerald)
Renaldo (Hemingway)
Price (Cather)
Travis (Oates)

Group 5
Tasha (Dreiser)
Karl (Welty)
Courtney (Fitzgerald)
Toshi (Hemingway)
Rocky (Cather)
Cole (Oates)

Expert Groups

Dreiser Group
Anna
Paul
Yu
Sarana
Tasha

Welty Group
Rodney
Sondra
Monica
Ming
Karl

Fitzgerald Group
Juan
Norman
Lee
Kara
Courtney

Hemingway Group
LaRue
Sally
Helmut
Renaldo
Toshi

Cather Group
Spencer
Nora
Rene
Price
Rocky

Oates Group
Agnes
Raoul
Roy
Travis
Cole

Figure 11.3

When the expert teams have finished their cooperative study, you direct students to regroup in their original home group. You ask experts on each writer to teach what they have learned to all members of the home group. In this way, members of each home group receive information about all six authors. Because students know you will be giving everyone a criterion test at the end of the lesson, there is an incentive for all students in the home groups to listen carefully to presentations by experts related to each writer and to insist that the experts share all of their information.

Jigsaw requires you to monitor the work of expert teams carefully. Members of each expert group must understand all the necessary information. Each expert group student must know the information well enough to pass it along successfully to members of his or her home group. You may encounter difficulties in using Jigsaw if a student is absent and misses important information being studied and shared in this individual's expert group. When this happens, you must step in to provide the missing information to the home group. This problem can be avoided if you design the entire jigsaw lesson in a way that will allow it to be completed during a single class period.

Debriefing You will typically debrief students following their participation in a jigsaw lesson by organizing them into a single, whole-class group. In your discussion, you will review all information that has been introduced. You will want to encourage your students to take notes during the discussion to record any new information that did not come out during their own group meetings. The debriefing session gives your students an opportunity to fill in any remaining information gaps. In addition, the session allows you to engage them in analytical thinking that will help them make interpretations beyond a simple knowledge-level understanding of the new content.

Learning Together

Some cooperative learning approaches include strong incentives for each student to help all others assigned to the same small group. Learning Together places an especially high premium on students helping students (Johnson et al., 1984).

General Background Learning Together can be used in many secondary school subject areas. Unlike Jigsaw, Learning Together does not require content that can be easily broken down into a set of parts or subtopics.

Implementing Your first step in implementing a Learning Together lesson is to organize students into teams that include a cross section of ability levels and talents. You give each team a task or project to complete. Individuals on each team assume responsibility for completing a part of the overall project that is compatible with their own interests and abilities. The idea is to maximize strengths of individual students to get a better overall group effort.

Roles of individuals in Learning Together teams can vary. For example, if the final product is to be a short play, one or more students might assume roles such as (a) head writer, (b) manuscript editor, (c) manuscript production chief, (d) set designer, and (e) sound and light planner.

Each team is responsible for gathering the information and materials needed to complete its assigned task or project. Your final assessment is based on the quality of the team's performance. Each student on a team receives the same grade. This encourages individuals to pool their talents in such a way that each student's work adds the greatest possible contribution to the effort.

Is it appropriate to give each team member the same grade? This issue has been researched. Johnson and Johnson (1985) report that, though students tend to favor competitive grading before they engage in cooperative tasks, after they have completed a cooperative learning project, they commit to the idea that awarding every group member the same grade is a fair approach.

Debriefing During this stage, you work with students to help them focus on the processes they used in their groups to respond to their assigned task. You want to ask questions that will encourage your students to think about what they learned from their experience and what they might do differently another time to improve levels of understanding of all group members.

Group Investigation

You can use Group Investigation when you want to give your students considerable freedom in deciding what they are going to do and how they are going to do it. You do not assign students to specific groups as you do when you are getting ready to involve students in Jigsaw or Learning Together lessons. You encourage them to form into groups that include members of their own choosing. You want to ensure that each group represents the diversity present in the class (Leighton, 1994).

General Background The basic ideas incorporated in the Group Investigation technique derive from the work of the eminent American educational philosopher John Dewey (Joyce & Weil, 1996). In this approach, you establish conditions that allow students to organize themselves into democratic problem-solving groups. Members of each small group follow the methods of inquiry as they investigate a significant topic of interest. (For more information about inquiry instruction, see chapter 10.) This approach is designed to help your students learn how to define a task, search for and synthesize information, and present it in an interesting and coherent way to others.

Each group ordinarily investigates a different topic or question. However, all these topics are usually subsumed under the umbrella of a broad issue or question. Because interaction and trust among group members are critical to the success of Group Investigation and because each member will have to assume considerable responsibility, you will want to use this approach with students who have already demonstrated some skill in small-group work and who trust one another (Leighton, 1994).

Implementing You will begin by presenting your students with a broad topic, question, or puzzling event (Joyce & Weil, 1996). For example, if you are teaching science, you might pose questions to your students related to how pollution in the local region might be reduced. If you are teaching world history, you might ask students to consider what happened to the Maya civilization of Central America. If you are teaching English, you might decide to ask students a question involving common literary themes. Sometimes, you may decide to leave choice of a focus topic up to members of your class (Leighton, 1994).

Once a focus has been established, you ask students to think about the topic individually, to list any questions they have, and to develop speculative hypotheses that might provide useful explanatory information. For example, if you are teaching science, you

MORE FROM THE WEB

Cooperative Learning in the Secondary School

As the title suggests, material at this site provides specific information about implementing cooperative learning at the secondary school level. Authors Daniel Holt, Barbara Chips, and Diane Wallace provide excellent guidelines related to such issues as (a) working with culturally and linguistically diverse students, (b) promoting students' social development, (c) maximizing content learning, and (d) implementing successful cooperative learning lessons.

Website: http://www.ncela.gwu.edu/pubs/pigs/pig12.htm

Jigsaw

This site features basic descriptive information about the Jigsaw method. There are useful links to additional details regarding how this approach can promote "positive interdependence" (the idea that group members need one another to succeed) among students while, at the same time, supporting the principle of "individual accountability."

Website: http://www.wcer.wisc.edu/nise/cl1/CL/doingcl/jigsaw/htm

General Information

Two Websites feature information organized by individuals long associated with cooperative learning:

Website: http://www.co-operation.org—This site was created by Johnson and Johnson and is maintained by the Cooperative Learning Center of the University of Minnesota.

Website: http://www.cooperativelearning.com—This site is sponsored by Spencer Kagan and his associates. It provides helpful free information as well as products that you might purchase.

might ask, "What can be done to reduce pollution in our region?" If you are teaching social studies, you might inquire, "Why did the Mayans seem to just lay down their tools and walk away from the great cities they had created?" If you are teaching English, you might say, "Why do you think these themes have been written about by many writers at different times? Are there other themes that you would expect to find in literature?"

You organize students into small groups to develop responses to your questions. After they have had adequate time to generate some responses, you instruct members to reassemble as a whole group. You ask students in each small group the group's conclusions. You list important questions, hypotheses, perspectives, or issues that arise out of this phase of the lesson on the board or on an overhead transparency. Next, you will work with the class to organize responses into categories. These categories become the topics for the group investigations that make up the next phase of the lesson.

At this point, you will organize learning teams based on students' interests. To do this, you will ask your students to look at the focus questions and decide which one they want to explore. People with similar interests will join together and form a group. If more than one group want to pursue a single question or topic, you can divide it into several parts, with one group assigned to work on each. Each group meets, and members begin working on the topic they have selected. As they begin, you need to help them understand the focus of their work, list important questions, and identify some resources they will need to complete their investigation. As they begin, members of groups have to decide what each person is going to do and how group findings will be presented to the rest of the class. In practice, different students end up doing different tasks. Some may seek the data, others may organize the data, and still others may organize findings for the group's presentation to the whole class.

Cooperative Learning in Diverse Classrooms

In an age of reform such as we are experiencing, the emphasis on standardized testing has stimulated much debate about the applicability of cooperative learning in today's classrooms. Although some conservative educators (e.g., E. D. Hirsch) have questioned the effectiveness of this model, Izumi and Coburn (2001) believe that it enhances student motivation and learning. Lasley, Matczynski, and Rowley (2002) assert that "cooperative learning is not a fad or a fashionable idea that suits the fancy of an intellectual elite. Cooperative learning is effective because the undergirding tenets of the strategy are good for all students" (p. 323).

The challenge for you is to implement cooperative learning in a thoughtful manner and to differentiate tasks in an effort to personalize learning for all students. By grouping heterogeneously, differentiating tasks by complexity and quantity, and varying criteria for success, all students can learn something new and contribute to the identified learning goals (Schniedewind & Davidson, 2000).

The key to success in your classroom is to use a variety of teaching strategies. Select the appropriate cooperative learning approach for the students you teach and combine cooperative learning with other strategies discussed elsewhere in this text. All students will then have a chance to succeed.

FOR YOUR PORTFOLIO

1. What materials or ideas you learned in this chapter related to small-group and cooperative learning will you include as "evidence" in your portfolio? Select up to three items of information to be included in your portfolio. Number them 1, 2, and 3.
2. Think about why you selected these materials for your portfolio. Consider such issues as the following in your response:
   - The specific purposes to which this information can be put when you plan, deliver, and assess the impact of your instruction
   - The compatibility of the information with your own priorities and values
   - The contributions this information can make to your personal development as a teacher
   - The factors that led you to include this material as opposed to some alternatives you considered
3. Prepare a written reflection in which you analyze the decision-making process you followed. In addition, mention the INTASC Standard(s) to which your selected material relates. (First complete the following chart.)

Materials You Selected and the INTASC Standards

Put a check under those INTASC standards numbers to which the evidence you have selected applies. (Refer to chapter 1 for more detailed information about INTASC.)

Item of Evidence Number	INTASC Standards									
	S1	S2	S3	S4	S5	S6	S7	S8	S9	S10
1										
2										
3										

KEY IDEAS IN SUMMARY

- Small-group learning capitalizes on students' interests in working together. It promotes supportive student-to-student interaction and encourages students to learn from one another.
- Success in small-group work is not automatic. To profit from this kind of instruction, students must be prepared. Conditions that facilitate group work include teaching students necessary skills for group work, understanding the peer group dynamics at work in a particular group, creating a climate so that students respect and trust one another, decreasing the fear of failure, and implementing cooperative goal structures.
- It is useful to introduce small-group work gradually by first involving students in some introductory activities that will teach them prerequisite skills and the necessary attitudes of respect and trust.
- Among small-group approaches that have been successfully used in secondary classrooms are classroom debates, educational simulations, and cooperative learning.
- Cooperative learning is a general term used to describe small-group learning techniques that base each student's evaluation, in part, on the overall level of performance of his or her group. Researchers have found cooperative learning approaches to (a) have positive effects on students' self-esteem, (b) generate peer support for academic achievement, (c) increase the amount of time students spend on academic tasks, (d) improve students' attitudes toward the class where cooperative learning has been used, and (e) help students develop more positive attitudes toward others in their class.
- There are many cooperative learning techniques. Among those that are widely used are (a) Student Teams-Achievement Divisions, (b) Teams-Games-Tournaments, (c) Jigsaw, (d) Learning Together, and (e) Group Investigation.
- Student Teams-Achievement Divisions and Teams-Games-Tournaments are similar in that they feature some competitive elements. However, the competition is between and among teams. There is an attempt to make competitive aspects fair by ensuring that they take place between and among individuals of similar ability levels.
- Jigsaw is best used for content that can be broken into separate but related components. Jigsaw involves expert groups where students learn about one aspect of the topic, and home groups where those from the expert groups teach the rest of their group about their specialty topic.

- Learning Together is best used when the task requires a diversity of skills. Students are grouped together, and each is given a specific role in the group that best matches his or her talents. The group then produces a product that is generated through the collective work of all group members.
- In Group Investigation, students are presented with an opportunity to select a general focus issue, problem, or topic. Individual students join with others to pursue an investigation of a topic of common interest. Findings ultimately are shared with members of the entire class. Two of the purposes of Group Investigation are (a) developing higher-level thinking skills such as how to learn and (b) synthesizing large quantities of information. Supporters of this approach argue that what students learn about the processes of productive inquiry is just as important as what they learn about the content they study.

REFLECTIONS

1. What are some variables that you would consider in deciding whether to use small-group learning in your classroom?
2. What are some conditions you need to create before you can expect small-group or cooperative learning approaches to function well in your classroom?
3. What do you think you need to learn in order to successfully implement small-group techniques in your classroom?
4. What distinguishes an educational simulation from a game?
5. What is the difference between a competitive goal structure and an individualistic goal structure, and why is this distinction important when you are considering using a cooperative learning approach?
6. Some cooperative learning approaches award the same grade to each member of a group. How do you feel about this practice?
7. Can you think of examples from your own experience when a group activity was tried and failed because characteristics of the classroom environment did not support this approach? What could have been done to change these circumstances?
8. What do you see as the strengths of the various cooperative learning approaches?
9. Can you think of a topic in your subject area that you would like to teach using the Jigsaw technique? If so, what would be the focus of students' work in both the home groups and the expert groups?
10. Proponents of some cooperative learning approaches argue that insights students develop about the processes of learning are as important as the content they master. Is this a defensible position? Why or why not?

LEARNING EXTENSIONS

1. Observe a secondary school classroom. What opportunities do you see for implementing small-group or cooperative learning approaches? What might be some challenges that teachers you observed would face in implementing these kinds of lessons?

2. Robert Slavin, David Johnson, Roger Johnson, and Edyth Johnson Holubec have written extensively about cooperative learning. Use a Learning Together format to involve members of your class in gathering information about articles or parts of books that each of these authors has written about cooperative learning. Working together, prepare a large chart summarizing perspectives of each of these cooperative learning experts.
3. Are educational simulations a good way to transmit academic content to secondary school students? Do some research on this topic and prepare a paper in which you discuss your findings.
4. Using content in this chapter as a focus, organize a Jigsaw scheme that members of your class can use to review chapter content. Share your design with your course instructor and, if he or she agrees, implement the technique during one of your class sessions.
5. Identify a topic in your subject area that could be the focus for a Group Investigation. Break the broad topic into some specific questions or subtopics that might be used as a research focus for different groups.

REFERENCES

Izumi, L. T., & Coburn, K. G. (2001). *Facing the classroom challenge*. San Francisco: Pacific Research Institute for Public Policy.

Johnson, D. W., Johnson, H. T., Holubec, F., & Roy, P. (1984). *Circles of learning: Cooperation in the classroom*. Alexandria, VA: Association for Supervision and Curriculum Development.

Johnson, R. T., & Johnson, D. W. (1985, April). *Structuring conflict in science classrooms*. Paper presented at the annual meeting of the National Association of Research in Science Teaching, French Lick, IN.

Joyce, B., & Weil, M. (1996). *Models of teaching* (5th ed.). Boston: Allyn & Bacon.

Kagan, S. (1989). The structural approach to cooperative learning. *Educational Leadership, 47* (4), 13.

King, A. (1999). Teaching effective discourse patterns for small group learning. In R. Stevens (Ed.), *Teaching in American schools*. Upper Saddle River, NJ: Merrill.

Lasley, T. J., II, Matczynski, T. J., & Rowley, J. B. (2002). *Instructional models: Strategies for teaching in a diverse society*. Belmont, CA: Wadsworth.

Leighton, M. (1994). Cooperative learning. In J. Cooper (Ed.), *Classroom teaching skills* (5th ed., pp. 282–325). Lexington, MA: D C Heath.

Putnam, J. (1997). *Cooperative learning in diverse classrooms*. Upper Saddle River, NJ: Merrill/Prentice Hall.

Schniedewind, N., & Davidson, E. (2000). Differentiating cooperative learning. *Educational Leadership, 58*(1), 24–27.

Slavin, R. E. (1980). *Using student team learning*. Baltimore: Johns Hopkins University, Center for Social Organization of the Schools, Johns Hopkins Team Learning Project.

Slavin, R. E. (1990). *Cooperative learning: Theory, research, and practice*. Upper Saddle River, NJ: Prentice Hall.

Slavin, R. (1994). *Educational psychology* (4th ed.). Boston: Allyn & Bacon.

Willis, S. (1992). Cooperative learning shows staying power. *Association for Supervision and Curriculum Development Update, 34*, 1–2.

Woolfolk, A. (1995). *Educational psychology* (6th ed.). Boston: Allyn & Bacon.

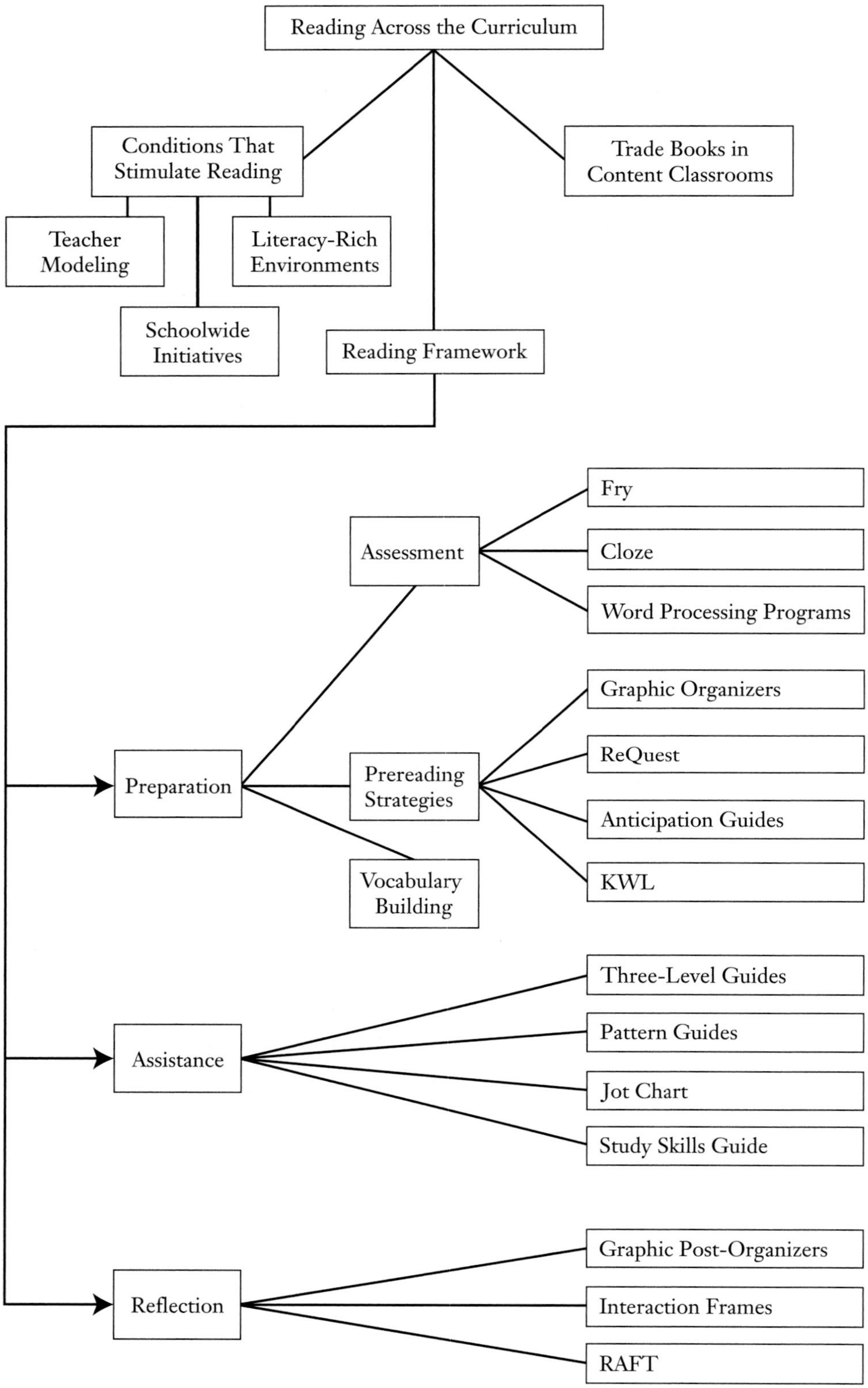

Figure 12.1
Graphic Organizer

CHAPTER 12

Reading Across the Curriculum

OBJECTIVES

This chapter will help you

- identify procedures that enhance reading development in content classrooms;
- identify different reading levels present among students in content classrooms;
- define readability;
- provide procedures to assess the readability of text material;
- identify a framework for content reading instruction;
- identify strategies appropriate for the preparation phase, the assistance phase, and the reflection phase of the reading framework;
- discuss the importance of vocabulary development in enhancing reading improvement;
- discuss the importance of the reading–writing connection; and
- implement ideas for supplementing textbooks with trade books.

Introduction

Most secondary school teachers view themselves as experts in the subjects they teach. Their enthusiasm for their subjects may lead them to overlook one of the essentials for success in the classroom: students' ability to read and understand the material. If teachers expect students to develop desired levels of competence, they must consider how they learn through reading. Postman (1979) pointed out the important linkage between reading and competence in school content areas in his statement, "Biology is not plants and animals. It is language about plants and animals. History is not events, it is language describing and interpreting events" (p. 165).

Middle and high school teachers charged with teaching content material often take the reading abilities of their students for granted. They assume that the students have learned the requisite reading skills in the elementary grades. However, this often is not the case. Even the most talented students occasionally have difficulty with some of the text material. Some students find reading so difficult that they do not succeed on many of their school tasks. Although most of them can decode, they need explicit instruction in how to use specific strategies that help them comprehend text in the content classroom (Donahue, 2003).

This chapter will acquaint you with some of the key concepts associated with teaching reading in the content areas. It cannot, however, take the place of a class that concentrates strictly on teaching this content. The reference section provides information about additional reading to enhance your knowledge about this subject.

Creating Conditions to Stimulate Reading

As a teacher in a content classroom, you have an obligation to help students learn to read and comprehend the material presented in class. Part of this obligation requires that you create conditions that support reading. You must first of all model reading. Students should see you reading books, newspapers, and magazines and deriving personal enjoyment from this activity. They should also hear you read aloud on occasion. Literacy expert Janet Allen (2002) recounts sitting in a 10th-grade classroom listening to the teacher reading aloud to her students: "No one was sleeping, no one was whispering or writing notes, no one was applying makeup, and no one interrupted the reading for a bathroom pass" (p. 1). The power of language—and a book that students enjoyed—had them mesmerized.

Second, you must create a literacy-rich environment by providing high-interest reading material in your classroom. A corner of the classroom or a special table can be set aside for reading material. Consider including all genres of young adult literature as well as state department of motor vehicles booklets and sports stories. When students have completed assignments or otherwise have some available time (perhaps before or after school), invite them to read these books. One football coach, for example, stimulated an interest in reading by making copies of the sports section of several major newspapers available on a daily basis. Students, both athletes and nonathletes, were invited to stop by his office in the morning to read the newspapers. This provided a lively forum for discussion for many students who did not normally spend much time reading.

In many communities, newspaper publishers will make newspapers available for a class of students. They might also have materials around which you can build content lessons using newspapers. Many teachers have found these "Newspaper in the Classroom" materials beneficial in developing students' interest in reading.

Finally, consider a schoolwide initiative that promotes reading and writing across the curriculum. Many schools have adopted the Sustained Silent Reading (SSR) model that sets aside time each day (or sometimes once a week) for everyone to read. Everyone, including the teacher, the principal, the janitor, and the students, stops whatever they are doing and reads something of interest to them. Although this has been most common in middle schools, high schools are beginning to adopt the model in an effort to increase literacy rates for their students.

In addition to establishing basic conditions that emphasize reading, you can also use a variety of reading strategies to increase the probability of students' learning through reading. The following sections will introduce some of the approaches that secondary teachers have found useful.

A Reading Framework

Many literacy experts (e.g., Herber, 1978; Richardson & Morgan, 2003; Singer & Donlan, 1985; Vacca & Vacca, 2002; Vaughan & Estes, 1986) have identified frameworks that can assist in planning content reading instruction. You may see these identified as prereading, during-reading, and after-reading phases or as preparation, assistance, and reflection phases. No matter what the label, the framework provides the components of an active and successful reading process in your content classroom. These frameworks are based on three assumptions:

1. The student must be ready to learn. You must, therefore, prepare the students before they read.
2. The student must be guided through the reading process in order to enhance comprehension. As a teacher, you must provide activities that assist them as they read.
3. The student must have an opportunity to review and reflect on what has been read. As a teacher, you must design opportunities for students to help them retain important ideas and concepts (Richardson & Morgan, 2003).

For our purposes in this text, we will use the framework suggested by Richardson and Morgan (2003), preparation, assistance, and reflection.

Preparation Phase

The most important yet often most overlooked phase of the reading framework is the preparation phase: the time you spend preparing students for reading text material. This phase actually begins when you assess text material and subsequently the students themselves.

One of the major problems teachers face in all subjects is the match between the material and the skill level of the students. Even when you have a variety of resources available, you usually have one major text that plays a dominant role. The inability of some students to read the text may create serious difficulties for you as you attempt to provide appropriate text material. To address this issue, you must begin by diagnosing the reading proficiency levels of your students and comparing these to the difficulty levels of available course reading materials.

Identifying Reading Levels A variety of activities can assist you in determining the reading levels of your students. One such activity is the "cloze." In the cloze, a passage is "cut up" (words omitted) so that students can fill it in. Cloze as we use it today was designed by William Taylor (1953) to determine readability of material for diverse readers. The procedure is based on the assumption that, as readers, we rely on our prior knowledge to make sense out of the whole when only parts are available. The following steps will help you construct a cloze test for your classroom.

1. Select a text passage of 250 to 3300 words from material that you plan to assign for reading.
2. Leave the first sentence intact, then consistently delete every fifth word throughout the passage until you reach 50 deletions. Make all blanks uniform length.
3. Leave the last sentence intact.
4. Write precise directions for the students. Inform them that they should work alone. Make sure they understand that this test does not affect their grade. It is important to discuss these directions with the students.
5. Count the number of correct responses for each student and multiply by 2 (unless you have chosen more or less than 50 omissions). Count as correct only exact words. Do not count synonyms. Scoring criteria have already taken this into account.
6. Use the scores to determine whether students are reading at an independent level (above 60%), an instructional level (40% to 60%), or a frustration level (below 40%).

Independent Reading Level Students are functioning at the independent reading level when there is a good match between their reading skill and the difficulty of the material being read. They understand what the author is trying to communicate, they are familiar with vocabulary, and they easily understand concepts without outside assistance. This level is best suited for independent study or homework assignments. If students are unable to read the material at the independent level, the time they spend reading the material will be unproductive. Students with a history of academic difficulty may give up if presented with an assignment that is beyond the independent reading level.

Instructional Reading Level Students functioning at the instructional reading level do not have the necessary prior knowledge or reading skill to completely understand the material and concepts contained in the material. However, these individuals are able to comprehend the material when provided with some assistance. Material at this level is appropriate for classroom use when some assistance is available. For example, in-class reading assignments may feature instructional-level materials.

Frustration Reading Level Students functioning at the frustration reading level are unable to handle the material unless given considerable assistance. The gap between the reading ability and the prior knowledge of the student is simply too great and cannot be spanned without considerable individual attention. Because the difficulty of the material clearly exceeds the skill of the student, his or her attempts to read this material may well lead to frustration and anger. These negative emotions are destructive to the development of a positive attitude about both the subject being studied and reading in general. Therefore, you should avoid asking individual students to read materials that, for them, are at the frustration level.

The cloze procedure can provide important information regarding students' prior knowledge about a given subject and whether the material is appropriate for your students. Ashby-Davis (1985, cited in Richardson & Morgan, 2003) cautions, however, that it should not be the only indicator of a student's general reading skills since it is different from the usual reading activities of students.

Analyzing Reading Material The general reading difficulty of a specific piece of prose material can be determined by applying one or more readability formulas. *Readability* refers to the relative difficulty of a given prose selection. Dreyer (1984) defines it as the match between reader and text. The readability of a selection varies with the complexity and the length of the sentences, the number of many-syllabled as compared to one- or two-syllabled words, and the number of words that, for some reason or another, the students do not know.

Readability formulas are used to identify approximate grade-level readabilities. That is, a given selection might be found to have a grade-level reading difficulty of grade 8, grade 9, grade 10, or some other grade level, depending on the results of the application of the readability formula. When you use readability formulas, it is important to recognize that grade levels are described in terms of averages. That is, simply because we find a given book to have a readability level of grade 11 does not mean that every student in grade 11 can read the material without difficulty. It means that the average 11th grader should be able to read the material. The term "average" suggests that, nationally, about half the grade 11 students will be able to read material at this level and that about half will experience difficulty.

One of the most commonly used readability formulas is the Fry Readability Graph developed by Edward Fry in the 1960s and later revised in 1977. This procedure involves selecting a number of 100-word passages from the text material and performing several simple calculations. Plotting the data on the graph provides an estimate of the reading difficulty of the material. The graph and directions for use are presented in Box 12.1.

BOX 12.1 Expanded Directions for Working Readability Graph*

1. Randomly select three sample passages and count out exactly 100 words each, beginning with the first word of a sentence. Count proper nouns, initializations, and numerals.
2. Count the number of sentences in 100 words, estimating length of the fraction of the last sentence to the nearest one tenth.
3. Count the total number of syllables in the 100-word passage. If you do not have a hand counter available, simply put a mark above each syllable over one in each word; then, when you get to the end of the passage, count the number of marks and add 100. Small calculators can also be used as counters by pushing numeral 1, then push the + sign for each word or syllable when counting.
4. Enter on the graph the *average* number of sentences per 100 words and *average* number of syllables; plot a dot where the two lines intersect. The area where the dot is plotted will give you the approximate grade level.
5. If a great deal of variability is found in syllable count or sentence count, putting more samples into the average is desirable.

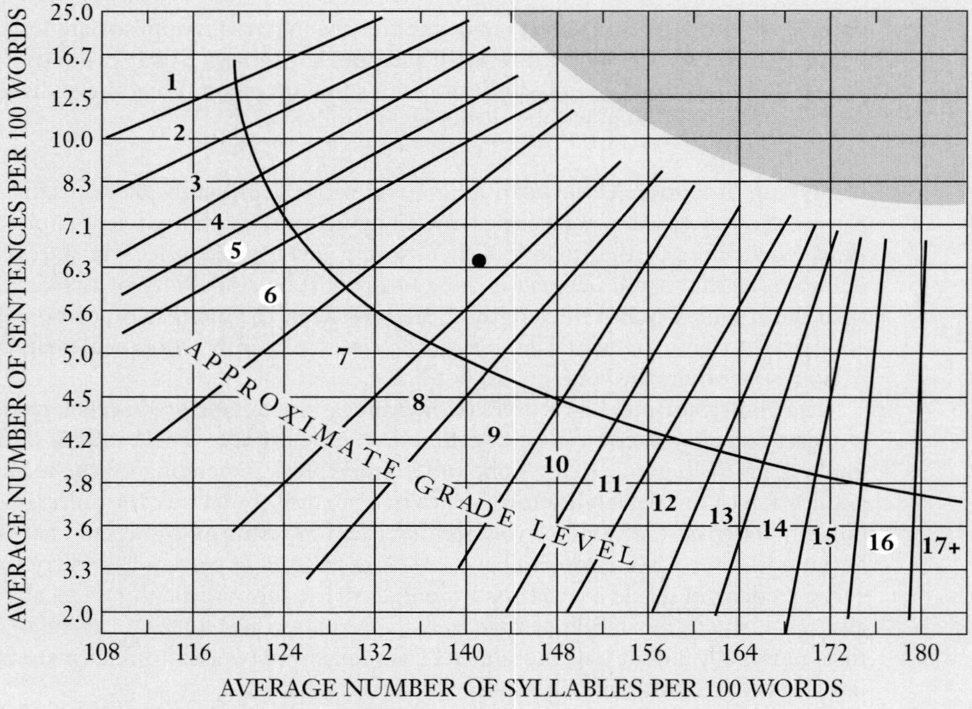

Graph for Estimating Readability—Extended.

*This extended graph does not outmode or render the earlier (1968) version inoperative or inaccurate; it is an extension.

Source: Edward Fry (1977), Fry's readability graph: Clarification, validity, and extension to level 17, *Journal of Reading, 21*(3), 249.

6. A word is defined as a group of symbols with a space on either side; thus, *Joe*, *IRA*, *1945*, and *&* are each one word.
7. A syllable is defined as a phonetic syllable. Generally, there are as many syllables as vowel sounds. For example, *stopped* is one syllable, and *wanted* is two syllables. When counting syllables for numerals and initializations, count one syllable for each symbol. For example, *1945* is four syllables, *IRA* is three syllables, and *&* is one syllable.

Using Your Word Processor Most word processing programs (WordPerfect, Microsoft Word) include statistical analysis of text material. For example, in Microsoft Word, you can perform readability statistics on text material by clicking on Tools, then Options, and finally Show Readability Statistics. Check your owner's manual to find the appropriate procedure for your word processing program. Most of these programs utilize the Flesch-Kincaid measure that reports a grade-level score similar to that reported by the Fry measure. Some programs are more sophisticated than others and provide a variety of information to assist in determining readability. Typing or scanning text rather than counting syllables, sentences, and words is a timesaver for today's busy teachers.

Even though readability formulas have provided consistent results over time, experts caution us to be aware of their limitations. Vacca and Vacca (2002), for example, describe them as a "rubber ruler" (p. 104). Many of the formulas fail to take into account student interests and motivation, the relationship between students' prior knowledge and the material, the quality and appropriateness of the visuals that accompany the text, the organizational pattern(s) of the material, and the writing style of the author. All these factors can influence the suitability of a text for a given group of learners.

Prereading Strategies Your students' prior experiences play a critical role in their ability to comprehend text material. These experiences provide the students with a frame of reference that helps them fit what is read into a meaningful pattern. To test this principle, find a technical manual in an area you know little about and try to read it. Even an excellent reader who lacks the necessary background may not be able to derive much meaning from specialized material dealing with sophisticated electrical circuits. The organization, vocabulary, and lack of a useful "mental picture" of what is being described make the reading very difficult.

This illustrates what many secondary students experience when asked to read in different subject areas. Students with little previous knowledge or background in the topic sometimes feel they are being required to make sense out of a random collection of words. The task they face is extremely difficult, so many of these students simply give up.

You will encounter two major problems as you work with students in this preparation phase of the reading framework. First, secondary students may not have sufficient previous experience in the area being studied. Second, even when they have had appropriate prior experiences, they may not recognize the relevance of these experiences for the assigned reading task. You must help them identify the connection between prior learning and present academic work. Students need a frame of reference as they attempt to derive meaning from their reading.

The famous learning theorist D. W. Ausubel (1963) emphasized the importance of this phase almost half a century ago. He suggested that the use of "advance organizers"—broad or general ideas that were provided to the student before beginning the study of material—enhanced learning and retention. These general ideas or organizing frames of reference should be drawn from the previous experience of the student.

Graphic Organizers Several techniques are available to help you build students' background knowledge and thus provide students with a frame of reference prior to the time they begin reading. One of these is the graphic organizer. These organizers include webs, structured overviews, maps, or any diagram that visually displays relationships among concepts, ideas, and/or terms.

You will find an example of a graphic organizer at the beginning of each chapter in this text. If you examine the overview at the beginning of this chapter, you will notice that this is basically a visual outline that displays relationships among the concepts in this chapter. Three major topics are highlighted in bold. Under each main topic, you find the important concepts discussed in relationship to the main topic. A content-specific example is included in Box 12.2. As with any reading strategy, you must discuss it with the students the first time you use it, model how to use it, and give students multiple opportunities to practice (Barton & Jordan, 2001).

You might be curious how the example in Box 12.2 can help build background for the westward movement. Although students studying the westward movement in American history obviously could not have had direct personal experience in this historic settlement pattern, many of them will have been involved in a permanent family move. Some of them, too, will have taken an extended trip. Use these experiences as you discuss the organizer so that when your students begin reading, they are able to connect their experiences with those of the individuals discussed in their text.

BOX 12.2 Structured Overview for Westward Movement

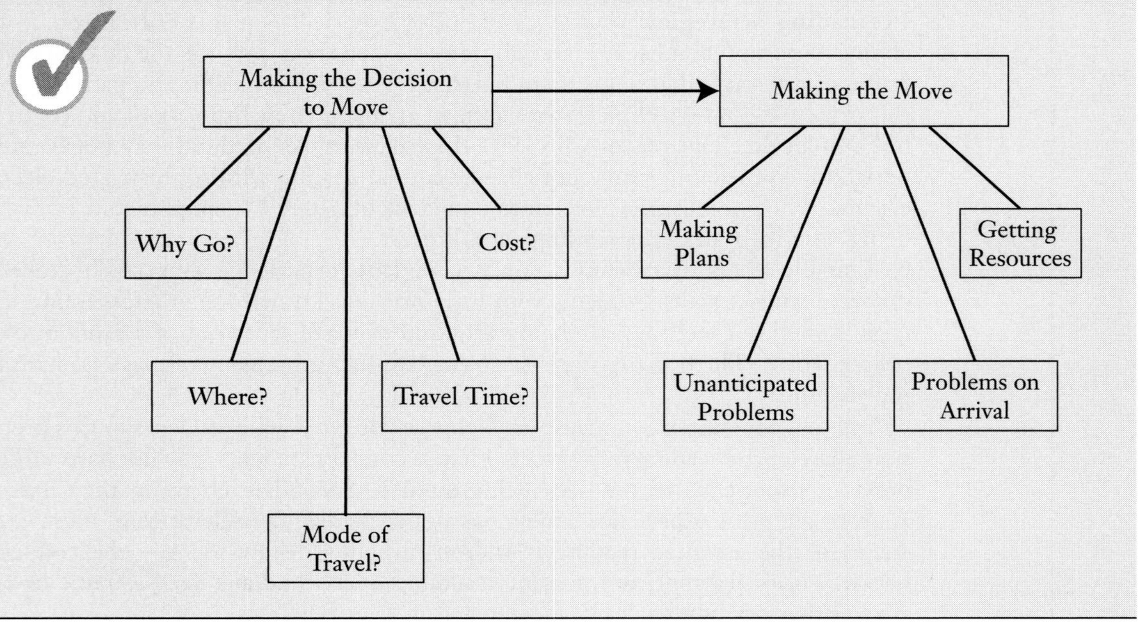

ReQuest Manzo (1969) designed a questioning procedure that is particularly appropriate for struggling readers. Those of you who are teaching classes populated with many English-language learners might find this strategy particularly helpful. It involves short text passages so that students do not become as easily frustrated.

ReQuest is an acronym for "reciprocal questioning" and involves both the students and the teacher in asking and answering questions. Student participation in the framing of the questions helps them relate their previous knowledge and their interests to the topic to be studied. A unique and important feature of the ReQuest procedure is that it provides modeling for the students in how to ask and respond to questions. The following steps provide guidance if you choose to use this procedure in your classroom:

1. The teacher and the students read the first sentence of a selection together. (If one sentence fails to provide sufficient information for meaningful questions to be asked, the teacher is free to extend the reading to include several sentences.)
2. The teacher closes his or her book while the students keep theirs open. Students may ask the teacher any question they wish that relates to the first sentence (or to whatever length of material they were asked to read). The teacher answers the questions as accurately as possible. The teacher may choose to make some comments to students about the quality of their questions, including some suggestions for improvement.
3. The students then close their books, and the teacher asks questions. The teacher should try to ask questions that will help the students recall any previous information they have about the topic or a similar topic and questions that will provide a model for student questioning during their next turn.
4. This procedure may be repeated for several paragraphs until the students can answer a predictive question, such as "What do you think you will find out in the rest of this selection?" Their answers to this question help them develop a framework for the rest of the reading as well as learning how to ask questions to guide their own reading.

You can see that this procedure provides much flexibility as you use it with different groups of students. You can extend the reading passages (especially in classrooms with proficient readers), teach students to ask questions at different levels, and help students set purposes for reading.

Anticipation Guides Some prereading techniques are designed primarily to motivate students to read text selections. These guides, also called prediction or reaction guides, require students to respond to a series of statements that are related in some way to content material (Unrau, 2004). Since a variety of possibilities exist for designing the guides, the following steps can assist you as you create and use these guides with your students. A sample guide is included in Box 12.3.

1. Read the text material and determine the important concepts you want students to learn.
2. Write four to six statements based on these concepts. The statements should reflect the students' world yet challenge in some way their prior experiences. Write some statements that will stimulate discussion and that are thought provoking enough to incite argument among your students.

BOX 12.3 Anticipation Guide for Science Lesson—Universe Unit

Prior to reading the text, place a check mark in the "Agree Now" column for each statement with which you agree. As you read, place a check mark in the "New Ideas" column if, based on new information, you change your mind about the statement. In the "Where Supported" column, make a note of the page number where this new information is discussed.

Agree Now	New Ideas	Where Supported	Statement
_____	_____	_____	1. The universe in which we live is one of many, and scientists are discovering new ones all of the time.
_____	_____	_____	2. A light-year is a unit of time.
_____	_____	_____	3. Gravity holds stars together in space.
_____	_____	_____	4. The Milky Way is the name of our solar system.
_____	_____	_____	5. About 10 billion stars exist in our universe.
_____	_____	_____	6. The Big Bang Theory and the Steady State Theory are scientific ideas that explain the origins of the universe.
_____	_____	_____	7. The stars in the constellations we see are located together in space.
_____	_____	_____	8. The brightest stars in the night sky are the closest to Earth.
_____	_____	_____	9. All planets have moons.
_____	_____	_____	10. A lunar eclipse occurs when the sun, the earth, and the moon are in a straight line.

Source: Developed by Patricia A. Nelson, Ph.D., high school science teacher.

3. Ask the students to respond to the guide. Make sure you give clear directions.
4. Discuss students' responses before they read.
5. Assign the reading.
6. Ask students to reconsider their original responses after reading the text material. Small-group discussion works well for this phase.
7. Review with students what they have learned and clarify misunderstandings.

Although many guides ask students to check either "agree" or "disagree," some, such as the one in Box 12.3, extend this learning by asking them to indicate specific pages where they find information that changes their mind about the concepts. These guides provide opportunities for you and your students to discuss the concepts across all phases of the reading process.

K-W-L Another prereading guide that many teachers find useful is the K-W-L (Ogle, 1986). This guide is designed to help teachers identify the conceptual limitations that their students are bringing to a particular piece of text. Students are given an opportunity to identify first what they already know about a given topic (the "K"). Then they list questions they want to answer as they read about the topic (the "W"). The third category (the "L") provides an opportunity for students to identify what they learned during the reading experience. Teachers enjoy these guides because they are easy to develop, they identify prior knowledge that students bring to the learning experience, and they serve as a stimulus for reflection after the students have read. To construct a K-W-L chart, simply make three columns. Title column 1 "What I Know," column 2 "What I Want to Know," and column 3 "What I Learned." Some teachers add other columns, such as one titled "What I Still Want to Know" or "How I Will Find Out What I Still Need to Know." This simple guide not only activates students' prior knowledge but also provides opportunities for exciting discussions and writing assignments once the reading is complete.

Vocabulary Instruction No discussion about the preparation phase of the reading framework is complete without some comments about vocabulary. One of the significant problems for secondary students is understanding the vocabulary they encounter in their texts. Several decades ago, reading specialist Robert C. Aukerman (1972) identified the following categories of words that frustrate many secondary school readers: obsolete words or phrases, colloquial vocabulary, unfamiliar vocabulary, and technical vocabulary:

1. Obsolete Words or Phrases. These are terms that have either undergone alterations in meaning or passed out of usage (e.g., nosegay [a small bouquet of flowers]).
2. Colloquial Vocabulary. These are words that occur frequently in prose selections that attempt to provide the reader with the flavor of regional speech. Such words may be deliberately misspelled to capture the sound of regional speech (e.g., the language in Mark Twain's *The Adventures of Huckleberry Finn*).
3. Unfamiliar Vocabulary. There are two types:
   a. Words that students know and may even use but have never seen in print
   b. Nontechnical words that are simply not known to students
4. Technical Vocabulary. These are specialized words associated with a particular discipline or area of interest.

Vocabulary Overview Guide To help students overcome vocabulary problems, consider using a vocabulary overview guide. It outlines steps that students are to follow as they work to master unfamiliar vocabulary. You begin by providing the students with a blank form and a set of directions. The directions to the students are as follows:

1. Survey the material to identify the topic.
2. Skim the material and identify unknown vocabulary words. Mark them using "sticky" notes.

3. Try to figure out the meaning of the word from the sentences around it. Then ask someone or use a dictionary to check the meaning.
4. Write the definitions on paper so that they will be available when you read the text.
5. Read the text.
6. Complete the vocabulary overview guide by including the following:
   a. The title of the passage
   b. Categories for grouping the vocabulary words according to topics the words discuss or describe (give each category a title)
   c. The vocabulary word
   d. The definition underneath the vocabulary word
   e. A clue to help you connect the word to something you already know

An example of a vocabulary overview guide is provided in Box 12.4. A collection of words learned during the semester can help students see how their vocabularies are growing. In fact, many teachers make a word wall a permanent addition to their classroom. (Word walls are simply "paper walls" attached somewhere in the classroom. Teachers record new words as students encounter them in their text material as a permanent reminder of new vocabulary learned throughout the year.) In addition, you might want to review the vocabulary overview guides to help you identify words that should be addressed the next time the material is used with a class.

BOX 12.4 Vocabulary Overview Guide

Chapter Title: The Basics of Economics

Category: Production

Word: Resources

Definition: Anything used to make a product

Clue: People, factories, natural resources

Word: Specialization

Definition: Each person doing one thing well

Clue: Plumbers, electricians

Word: ____________________

Definition: ________________

____

Clue: ____________________

Category: Consumption

Word: Market

Definition: A meeting together of people to buy and sell

Clue: Wants and demands of people

Word: Income

Definition: Money a person makes that can be spent on goods and services

Clue: Salary, wages, interest

Word: ____________________

Definition: ________________

____

____

Assistance Phase: Building Comprehension

Once you have prepared students prior to reading selected text, you will find that it is important to provide assistance as they are reading. Vacca and Vacca (2002) point out that study guides are useful to help "scaffold students' understanding of academic content and the literacy and thinking processes needed to comprehend and learn with texts" (p. 324). When used consistently, these guides can help students become independent readers.

Strategies appropriate for this phase help students gather information in a productive and efficient manner. Useful guides help students identify their purpose for reading, think about the strategy they will use, and assist them in identifying relationships in the passage they are reading. Four guides commonly used by secondary teachers are three-level guides, pattern guides, jot charts, and study skills guides.

Three-Level Guides Three-level guides are designed to develop students' higher-level thinking skills. These guides are a taxonomy similar to that identified by Gray (1960). Herber (1978) labeled the levels as literal, interpretative, and applied. In other words, students first read for literal understanding before reading between the lines and reading beyond the lines (Gray, 1960). Three-level guides are organized around three basic questions, each establishing a focus on a given level of understanding:

1. What did the material say? (This question is designed to help students grasp the literal meaning of what they are reading, e.g., to read the lines.)
2. What does the material mean? (This question encourages students to interpret and make inferences, e.g., to read between the lines.)
3. How can I apply this meaning to something else? (This question prompts students to think about how they might apply what they have learned, e.g., to read beyond the lines.)

These questions are helpful as you prepare three-level guides related to a specific reading assignment. Using question 1 as a point of departure, begin by identifying some literal information contained in the assigned reading. Next, identify inferences that might be drawn from the passage and then identify information that might suggest applications of content. This information is organized and presented for students to use as they read the material. A three-level guide is included in Box 12.5.

Pattern Guides As they write, authors usually follow a specific organizational pattern. These patterns vary in terms of their purposes. For example, historical text is often written following a chronological pattern, while scientific text is often organized into large categories. Other common patterns found in secondary school reading materials include the compare-and-contrast pattern, the cause-and-effect pattern, and the simple listing pattern. To enhance students' comprehension of text they read in your classroom, consider designing pattern guides that make them aware of the pattern of organization used in the texts.

Pattern guides can follow several formats, depending on the pattern that is followed. Some of them are simply skeleton outlines that list some main ideas with a few missing parts provided for students to fill in as they read. Somewhat more sophisticated pattern guides may list some "effects" and call on students to fill in information about their "causes." Other pattern guides appear as complex "webs" that display relationships among ideas. In these, instruct your students to fill in these missing links using information they derive from their reading.

BOX 12.5 Three-Level Guide for Math Story Problem

Problem: Tan has 145 boxes of cereal that must be placed on shelves in the supermarket. He is able to place 68 of the boxes on the biggest shelf. He must now place the same number of boxes on two remaining shelves. How many will he need to put on each shelf?

Level 1: Read the problem. Check those statements that contain important information to help you solve the problem.

_____ Tan works in a supermarket.
_____ There are 145 total boxes.
_____ The boxes contain cereal.
_____ He placed 68 boxes on one shelf.
_____ The remaining boxes are to be placed on two additional shelves with an equal number on each shelf.
_____ There are three shelves total.

Level 2: Check the following statements that contain math ideas related to this problem.

_____ Division is putting an amount into equal groups.
_____ When we take an amount away, we subtract to find the amount left.
_____ Adding groups with the same amount is multiplying.
_____ When we put an amount into groups of the same size, we divide the amount by the number of groups.

Level 3: Following are possible ways of getting an answer to the problem. Check those that apply to this problem.

_____ $145 - 68$
_____ $145 + 68$
_____ $(145 - 2) + 68$
_____ $(145 - 68) - 2$

When constructing a pattern guide, you must first read the material and identify the pattern of organization. One way of doing this is to look for key words. Words such as "first," "second," "third," "before," and "after" usually indicate a sequential or chronological pattern. Use of the conjunctions "but" and "and" often indicate comparisons and/or contrasts (Estes & Vaughan, 1985, p. 162).

After the pattern has been identified, decide on a format that will be most appropriate for the organization of the material. When you first introduce pattern guides, you might find it useful to provide students with a considerable amount of information that includes useful cues to students as they seek the information they will need to complete the guide. As students become more familiar with the procedure, more and more detail can be

BOX 12.6 Topic: Building the Transcontinental Railroad

Generalization: Improved Transportation Facilitates Growth and Trade Between Regions.

Cause	Effect
1. The first locomotive was built in 1829.	1. ____________
2. ____________	2. It was very difficult to travel between the East Coast and West Coast.
3. The government provided incentives to build the railroad by paying for each mile of track.	3. ____________
4. ____________	4. The cost of shipping goods was greatly reduced.
5. The amount of time required to go between the two coasts was reduced.	5. ____________

omitted. This makes completing the guide more difficult. An additional challenge you might try is allowing students to construct their own guides as they approach new material, especially after they have had some experience with ones you provide. This process reinforces the idea that authors' patterns vary and that, in part, a successful reading strategy involves the ability to recognize the scheme used by the writer(s) of the assigned material. A cause-and-effect pattern guide is included in Box 12.6. As you can see, this guide could be used in a variety of ways. You might choose to use it as displayed. You might, however, decide to give students all the causes and have them identify the effects. Alternatively, you could give them all the effects and have them identify all the causes.

Jot Charts A third strategy that you can use to assist comprehension is a jot chart. These charts are data retrieval charts displayed in the form of a matrix. They allow students to compare and contrast ideas as they read. Typically, teachers design the matrix, and students complete it as they read. Other variations, however, are also appropriate. Consider giving students a matrix with some cells already filled in, especially when students are first introduced to the strategy.

As you can see in the example in Box 12.7, jot charts are easy to design and have potential in any content area. This makes them a favorite of secondary teachers. The first example allows you to add as many countries and characteristics as you prefer, the second as many characters and dimensions as you prefer. Many teachers like to design these not only as handouts for the students but also as wall charts that can provide easy discussion starters.

Study Skills Guides Study skills guides are designed to help students monitor their own reading skills and think about the material they are reading. Often, students read their assignments very superficially. They may read the words but fail to think about what they have learned or about what is important. The study skills guide prompts students to stop at critical points as they read and respond to questions

BOX 12.7 Jot Charts

Jot Chart 1: Countries of the Ancient World

Country	Location	Form of Government	Religion(s)	Resources
Egypt				
Greece				
Mesopotamia				

Jot Chart 2: Character Analysis—*A Midsummer Night's Dream*

Character	Physical Traits	Personality Traits	Main Conflict	How Resolved	Quote That Is Important to Understand Character
Theseus					
Lysander					
Demetrius					
Hippolyta					
Hermia					
Helena					

or engage in an activity. The purpose is to increase their levels of motivation and to help them monitor what they have read. When they find they cannot answer the questions or perform the required activity, they can either reread the material or seek assistance from the teacher. In time, students begin to incorporate key questions of their own as they read. When this happens, their levels of comprehension increase.

Study skills guides are not difficult to construct. As a first step, you must read through the material and identify places for your students to stop reading. Questions are developed for students when they stop. Sometimes, required activities are described. If questions are used, they should prompt students to monitor their own comprehension and reading strategy. The following are examples of questions that you might include on a study skills guide:

- Summarize the section you read in one sentence.
- What do you think will happen next?
- What information from this section do you think might be on a test your teacher might prepare?

An example of a study skills guide appears in Box 12.8.

BOX 12.8 Study Skills Guide

Directions: As you read the assigned pages, follow the steps listed below. You will be asked to stop your reading at specific places and review what you have read. It is important for you to be aware of how you are thinking about and organizing the material as you read.

Step 1: Start on page 20 and read to the bottom of 21. What do you think is important for you to know about this section? ____________________

Step 2: After reading to the third paragraph on page 23, write two or three sentences about what you have learned. If you cannot do this or you do not understand what you are reading, what can you do to get help? ____________________

____

Step 3: Before reading the next section, predict what will happen. ____________________

____

Step 4: Read to the end of page 25. Was your prediction correct? What information in this section is likely to be on a test? ____________________

____

Step 5: Read to the second paragraph on page 27. List in sequence the events that happened. Are you understanding the material? Would rereading help? ____

____

Step 6: The last sentence of paragraph 3 on page 28 states the main point of this chapter. Rewrite this statement into a question. ____________________

____

Step 7: After finishing the chapter, what pictures or images of the events come to mind? ____________________

How is this like something you know about? ____________________

____

What was most difficult to understand? ____________________

Write a short summary of what you have read. ____________________

____

Reflection Phase: Questioning, Writing, and Discussing

The final phase of the reading process develops critical thinking skills, an area that is often overlooked. Research reports (Kirsch & Jungeblut, 1986; Parker, 1991; Sternberg, 1994) point out that while students are able to read, they have difficulty with reading that requires them to think critically. The Parker report suggests that the teaching of critical thinking skills is often neglected in today's classrooms. Richardson and Morgan (2003) implore us to develop strategies that teach important reflection skills: critical thinking, problem solving, decision making, and so on. These strategies will move us toward our goal of developing independent, lifelong learners.

A number of reflection strategies are available to assist you as you teach your students to become critical thinkers. Among them are graphic post-organizers, interaction frames, and a variety of writing activities such as RAFT.

Graphic Post-Organizers The graphic post-organizer technique is an extension of the structured-overview approach discussed earlier (Estes & Vaughan, 1985, p. 182). In the structured-overview approach, teachers prepare a framework for students to use while they are reading. Graphic post-organizers are developed by the students themselves. Students reflect on what they have read and construct their own structure. The process of construction helps them relate what they have read to prior levels of understanding. The technique is designed to help students refine and modify previous information by reflecting on new information and insights they have gained from their reading.

Constructing the graphic post-organizer can be done rather simply using 3 by 5 cards of two different colors. Each group of four to six individuals is given a packet of cards. The group's goal is to identify the basic concepts or main ideas that were covered in the passage read. Each group member records on the cards of one color what he or she believes were the major concepts or ideas. Each member then presents these to the rest of the group and defends his or her choice. The group then reaches a consensus on the major concepts or ideas.

Individuals then take a card of another color and identify key information or supporting ideas that fit under each of the major concepts or ideas identified on the cards completed during the first part of the exercise. Individual group members once again defend their choices of supporting information. Finally, each group arranges this information under the appropriate concept or idea.

When members of a group have arranged their cards in a manner that is satisfying to them, they design a graph or chart that visually depicts the relationship among the major ideas that have been identified and the important subordinate information associated with each. The graph can be prepared on large sheets of paper or on a blank overhead transparency. Once all groups have completed this phase, the graphs are displayed. They become a focus for a class discussion and perhaps subsequently a written assignment. The teacher as well as classmates can react to the various organizational schemes, leading students to discover that there are several ways to organize what they have read. A discussion of these issues helps students think about ways of organizing and thinking about what they read.

Interaction Frames Interaction frames are especially useful in helping students organize information from reading selections that refer to interactions between or among two or more individuals or groups. These guides are particularly appropriate for text that students read in English and social studies classes. Interaction frames are organized around these four basic questions:

1. What were the goals of the various individuals or groups?
2. What actions did they take to try to accomplish these goals?
3. How did the individuals or groups interact?
4. What were the outcomes of the interactions?

Students are asked first to respond to these questions and then provide a brief summary of their responses. Often teachers assign students to groups to complete this

BOX 12.9 Interaction Frame

Interaction Frame

Faction A	**Faction B**
Goals of Faction A	Goals of Faction B
1.	1.
2.	2.
Actions:	Actions:
1.	1.
2.	2.

How these two factions interacted

Conflicts:

1.

2.

Compromises:

1.

2.

Cooperations:

1.

2.

Results for Faction A	**Results for Faction B**
1.	1.
2.	2.

Summary

activity. However, it can also be completed individually. The group discussion does have the added benefit of providing them opportunities to consider the thinking processes of others and to reflect more carefully on what they have read. An example of an interaction frame is provided in Box 12.9.

RAFT Many writing strategies are appropriate for use during the reflection phase. RAFT (Santa, 1988) is one such strategy that many teachers have found useful in assisting students to demonstrate understanding of text material. The technique stimulates students to be much more creative as they respond to assigned text material. RAFT is an acronym that stands for

- Role of writer—What is the writer's role?
- Audience—Who will read the written product?

BOX 12.10 RAFT Technique

Role	Audience	Format	Topic
Quilt teacher	Beginning quilters	How-to demonstration	Quilting process

- Format—What is the best way to present the material?
- Topic—What (or who) is the subject of the writing?

Although you may assign the RAFT prompt, you will probably find that students prefer making some of the choices themselves. If you choose to design the prompt, the following example might work in an art classroom where students have been studying the quilting process:

> Imagine that you are giving a lecture at a local quilting show. Although most of the attendees are quite knowledgeable about quilting, many are beginners who are there to learn. Describe to these beginners the procedures and processes that they need to know in order to begin quilting.

The matrix in Box 12.10 shows the versatility of the RAFT technique. You can insert any number of RAFT components that are appropriate for the content you are teaching in your classroom. Keep in mind that although some assignments may contrive audiences and situations, others should provide opportunities for real-world writing, such as letters to newspapers, politicians, authors, and so on. (Vacca & Vacca, 2002).

In summary, the reflection phase is one of the most important phases of the comprehension process. Not only do the activities help students reflect on their own thinking, but they also help them develop more systematic and sophisticated ways of interpreting information they have read.

Using Trade Books in the Content Classroom

Considering the disconnect between the reading levels of textbooks and the levels at which many students are reading, today's teachers find that trade books offer one way of supplementing textbooks. Richardson and Morgan (2003) define trade books as "books that are considered to be in general use, such as books borrowed from a library or bought at the local bookstore, rather than textbooks bought and studied as a major course resource" (p. 65).

In today's diverse classrooms, multiple texts are almost a necessity. Trade books offer teachers the opportunity to provide reading material that appeals to a variety of cultures and student interests. Savage and Savage (1996) point out that a variety of genres are appropriate in the classrooms. Although fiction is most often recommended, nonfiction is an especially important genre to help students develop a capacity to raise critical questions. Stories about real people and real events can help students develop an understanding of the values, perspectives, and frames of reference of individuals from a variety of cultures.

McGowan and Guzzetti (1991) provide four reasons for using trade books in all content classrooms:

- Interest. Their engaging format and writing style are interesting for today's secondary student.
- Variety. Many books are available for different student reading levels and interests.
- Relevance. The books connect students' real-world experiences with the classroom.
- Comprehensibility. The books focus on relationships among concepts. For example, science trade books provide background knowledge for scientific concepts discussed in class and help students make connections with events in their everyday lives.

As you choose trade books for your classroom, choose ones for enjoyment as well as for instruction. For example, Savage and Savage (1992) remind us that we should include books that can help the reader identify with characters from other cultures. *Roll of Thunder, Hear My Cry* by Mildred Taylor is included on many required reading lists. This book provides an opportunity not only to discuss issues related to the Depression in rural Mississippi but also to discuss prejudice and racism. After reading the book, students might compare their own experiences to those of Cassie, the main character, considering issues such as what they learned that might help them confront racism and prejudice (Savage & Savage, 1992). Lois Lowrey's award-winning novel *Number the Stars*, a fictionalized account of an incident in Nazi-occupied Denmark, "offers opportunities for students to research the Holocaust and identify reasons why Nazis were attempting to annihilate the Jews" (Savage & Savage, 1993, p. 35). Many

BOX 12.11 Selection Guide for Trade Books for High School and Middle School

The Alan Review (Assembly on Literature for Adolescents, National Council of Teachers of English). Urbana, IL: National Council of Teachers of English.

Book Links: Connecting Books, Libraries, and Classrooms. Washington, DC: American Library Association

Christenbury, L. (Ed.). (1995). *Books for you: A booklist for senior high students* (11th ed.). Urbana, IL: National Council of Teachers of English.

International Reading Association. "Children's Choices." Published every October in *The Reading Teacher*.

Lesesne, T. (2003). *Making the match: The right book for the right reader at the right time*. Portland, ME: Stenhouse.

National Council for the Social Studies. *Carter Woodson Book Award Winners*. Published yearly in the spring issue of *Social Education*. Also available on their Website: http://www.ncss.org.

Norton, D. (2002). *Through the eyes of a child* (6th ed.). Upper Saddle River, NJ: Prentice Hall.

Notable children's trade books in the field of social studies. National Council for the Social Studies. Silver Springs, MD: Published yearly in the spring issue of *Social Education*.

Outstanding science trade books for children. Published yearly in the spring issue of *Science and Children*.

books provide us with similar scenarios. Make sure that you examine all alternatives available to you when including trade books in your classroom.

Finally, make sure that literacy permeates your classroom. Many students discover the pleasure of reading when they discover books related to topics that are of interest to them. Include a reading center in your room that includes not only discipline-related books but also books on topics that middle school or high school students enjoy. By doing this, you communicate that reading is important. Box 12.11 lists sources of information to help you select high-quality trade books.

KEY IDEAS IN SUMMARY

- All teachers share the responsibility for helping students learn how to comprehend reading material. Part of this responsibility involves the creation of conditions that emphasize the importance of reading. You establish these conditions by modeling good reading habits, providing a variety of reading material, and testing students over material they have been assigned to read.
- Teachers must identify the reading levels of students in their classroom. Readability, or the match between the reading level of students and the difficulty of the material, is a critical variable in creating a successful classroom environment. Material that is so difficult that it places students at the frustration level should not be used.
- Several formulas for identifying the readability of material are available. One of the most popular is the Fry Readability Formula. Using this formula or one provided on your word processing program in combination with a cloze test can help you select material that is appropriate for the reading levels of students in your classroom.
- Students' abilities to learn from a given reading assignment, in part, are related to their prior knowledge and experience. Several approaches can be used to help students relate this prior knowledge to the material that is to be read. Among useful approaches are structured overviews, ReQuest, and anticipation guides.
- Vocabulary difficulties are a prime source of confusion for students. There are several types of vocabulary that tend to cause problems for secondary students. These include obsolete words or phrases, technical vocabulary, colloquial vocabulary, and unfamiliar vocabulary. Vocabulary overview guides are useful in helping students become familiar with potentially confusing words.
- Providing guidance during the reading phase prompts students to consider whether they understand what they are reading. Classroom activities during this phase of the reading process seek to help students develop effective techniques for organizing and understanding the material they are reading. Three-level guides, pattern guides, jot charts, and study skills guides are particularly effective for accomplishing this purpose.
- Effective postreading strategies help students clarify and modify their conceptual frameworks. A good approach to the postreading phase is to have students work in small groups to reflect on and react to what they have read. In addition, working in small groups provides unsuccessful students an opportunity to observe students who are successful.
- Trade books add an extra dimension to your classroom. They not only provide one avenue for instruction but also create interest in the topic being taught.

FOR YOUR PORTFOLIO

Because most schools emphasize literacy across the curriculum, you will want to demonstrate that you have a solid understanding of how to design literacy strategies for your students. Choose two strategies that you have designed to include in your portfolio. Include a brief statement that explains why you chose each entry as well as what it indicates about your knowledge of reading across the curriculum.

Review both the material you have decided to include and the INTASC standards. State which INTASC standards these entries address or complete the following chart.

Item of Evidence Number	**INTASC Standards**									
	S1	S2	S3	S4	S5	S6	S7	S8	S9	S10
1										
2										

LEARNING EXTENSIONS

1. Examine some content reading textbooks to find specific reading activities designed for your content classroom.
2. Examine some of the research on reading across the curriculum. Use this to write your own philosophy of literacy as it applies to your content classroom.
3. Perform the Fry readability assessment on the textbook you are using in your content classroom. (Note: If you are not currently teaching, select a college text or go to your university library and select a book that might be appropriate. The process is what is important for this assignment.) In addition, design a cloze activity and administer it to your students. Based on the results of these two assessment instruments, discuss how you might need to design reading experiences that would be appropriate for your students.
4. Design a prereading activity, a during-reading activity, and an after-reading activity that would be appropriate for reading selected text material you will use in your classroom.
5. Compile a list of trade books that would be appropriate additions to your classroom.
6. One of the important components of reading text material is good note-taking skills. Visit the St. Mary's University of Texas Website (Learning Assistance Center section) to examine the appropriate procedure for using the Cornell note-taking system: http://lacweb.stmarytx.edu/?page=test/cornell. An alternate site is

http://www.bucks.edu/~specpop/Cornl-ex.htm maintained by Bucks County Community College. A Web search will identify additional sites you may want to explore.

REFERENCES

Allen, J. (2002). *On the same page: Shared reading beyond the primary grades*. Portland, ME: Stenhouse.

Ashby-Davis, C. (1985). Cloze and comprehension: A qualitative analysis and critique. *Journal of Reading, 28*, 585–593.

Aukerman, R. C. (1972). *Reading in the secondary school classroom*. New York: McGraw-Hill.

Ausubel, D. W. (1963). *The Ps of meaningful verbal learning*. New York: Grune & Stratton.

Barton, M. L., & Jordan, D. J. (2001). *Teaching reading in science*. Aurora, CO: McREL.

Donahue, D. (2003). Reading across the great divide: English and math teachers apprentice one another as readers and disciplinary insiders. *Journal of Adolescent and Adult Literacy 47*(1), 24–37.

Dreyer, L. G. (1984). Readability and responsibility. *Journal of Reading, 27*, 179–180.

Estes, T. H., & Vaughan, J. L. (1985). *Reading and learning in the content classroom: Diagnostic and instructional strategies* (2nd ed.). Boston: Allyn & Bacon.

Fry, E. (1977). Fry's readability graph: Clarifications, validity, and extensions to Level 17. *Journal of Reading, 21*, 242–252.

Gray, W. (1960). The major aspects of reading. In H. Robinson (Ed.), *Development of reading abilities* (Supplementary Educational Monographs No. 90). Chicago: University of Chicago Press.

Herber, H. L. (1978). *Teaching reading in content areas* (2nd ed.). Upper Saddle River, NJ: Prentice Hall.

Kirsch, I. S., & Jungeblut, A. (1986). *Literacy: Profiles of America's young adults*. Princeton, NJ: National Assessment of Educational Progress.

Manzo, A. V. (1969). "ReQuest Procedure." *Journal of Reading, 11*, 123–126.

McGowan, T., & Guzzetti, B. (1991, January/February). Promoting social studies understanding through literature-based instruction. *Social Studies*, pp. 16–21.

Ogle, D. M. (1986). K-W-L: A teaching model that develops active reading in expository text. *The Reading Teacher 39*(6), 564–570.

Parker, W. C. (1991). Achieving thinking and decision-making objectives in social studies. In J. P. Shaver (Ed.), *Handbook of research on social studies teaching and learning*. New York: Macmillan.

Postman, N. (1979). *Teaching as a subversive activity*. New York: Delacorte.

Richardson, J. S., & Morgan, R. F. (2003). *Reading to learn in the content areas*. Belmont, CA: Wadsworth.

Santa, C. M. (1988). *Content reading including study systems*. Dubuque, IA: Kendall/Hunt.

Savage, M. K., & Savage, T. V. (1992). Exploring ethnic diversity through children's literature. *Oregon English Journal, 14*(1), 7–11.

Savage, M. K., & Savage, T. V. (1993). Children's literature in middle school social studies. *The Social Studies, 84*(1), 32–36.

Savage, M. K., & Savage, T. V. (1996). Achieving multicultural goals through children's nonfiction. *Journal of Educational Issues of Language Minority Students, 17*, 25–37.

Singer, H., & Donlan, D. (1985). *Reading and learning from text*. Hillsdale, NJ: Lawrence Erlbaum Associates.

Sternberg, R. L. (1994). Answering questions and questioning answers. *Phi Delta Kappan, 76*, 136–138.

Taylor, W. L. (1953). Cloze procedure: A new tool for measuring readability. *Journalism Quarterly, 30*, 415–433.

Unrau, N. (2004). *Content area reading and writing: Fostering literacies in middle and high school cultures*. Upper Saddle River, NJ: Merrill/Prentice Hall.

Vacca, R. T., & Vacca, J. L. (2002). *Content area reading: Literacy and learning across the curriculum* (7th ed.). Boston: Allyn & Bacon.

Vaughan, J., & Estes, T. (1986). *Reading and reasoning beyond the primary grades*. Boston: Allyn & Bacon.

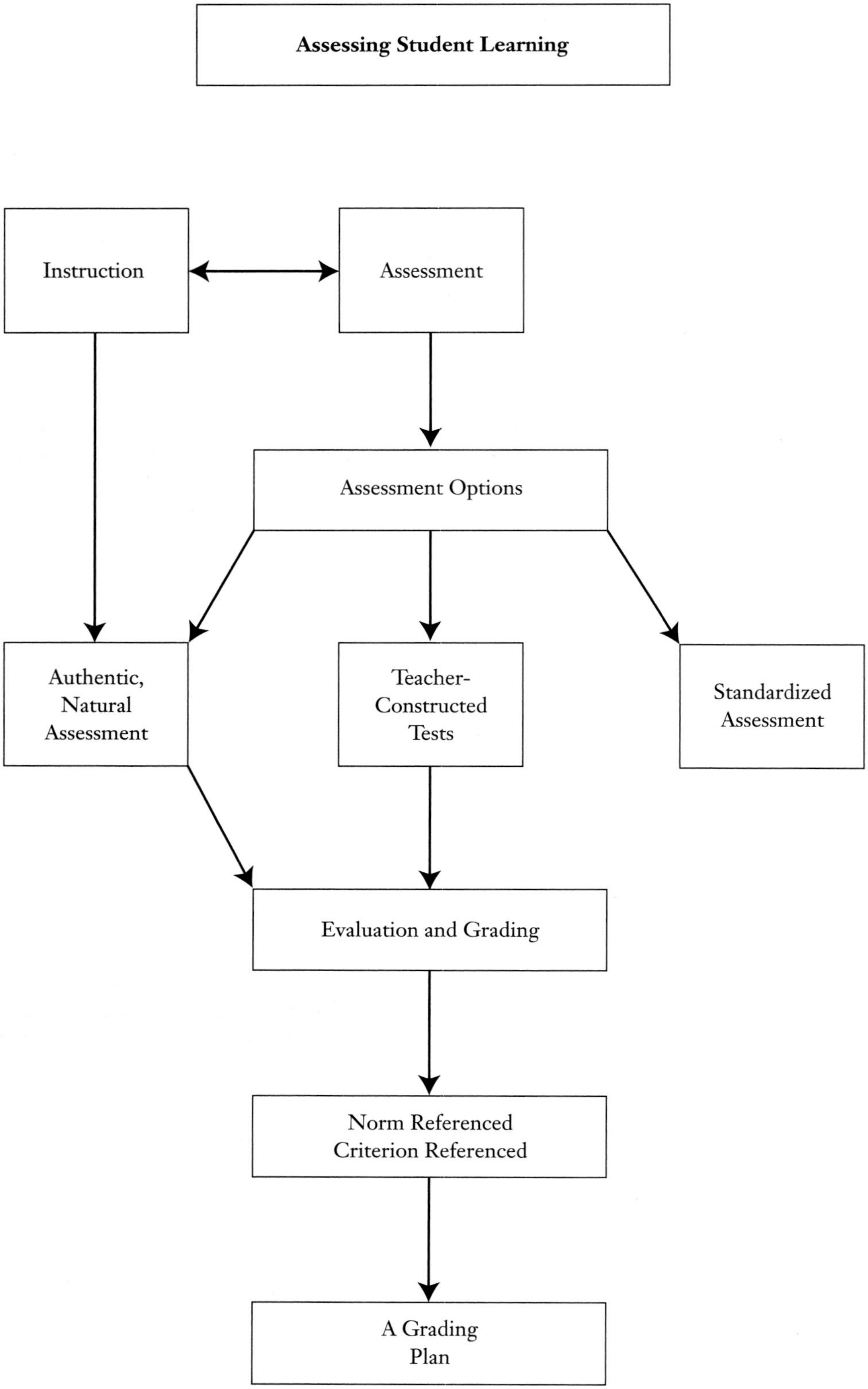

Figure 13.1
Graphic Organizer

CHAPTER 13

Assessing Student Learning

OBJECTIVES

This chapter will help you

- identify the relationship between assessment, evaluation, and grading;
- state basic principles of assessment;
- identify assessment options;
- write test items and construct a test;
- define authentic, natural assessment;
- construct a rubric;
- understand the uses of standardized assessment;
- define norm-referenced and criterion-referenced evaluation and grading; and
- establish a grading plan.

Introduction

Assessment and evaluation are at the heart of much discussion about education, and entire books are devoted to the topic. Our purpose in this chapter is not to try to reduce this complex topic to a single chapter. Rather, our purpose is to provide you with an introduction to some of the basic concepts and issues in order to help you make informed decisions that will help you improve as a teacher and assist your students in learning. We certainly hope that you will pursue this topic in more depth as a part of your professional growth.

The graphic organizer at the beginning of this chapter illustrates that there should be a reciprocal relationship between instruction and assessment. We should assess what we teach, and assessment should inform our teaching. There are several assessment options, including authentic assessment, teacher-constructed assessment, and standardized assessment. Evaluation should be built on the data gathered in the assessment. This in turn relates to grading, which is the process of communicating the evaluation to other interested parties. As a teacher, you need to have a well-thought-out assessment plan as well as a record-keeping and grading plan.

Like many other educational practices, assessment and evaluation have the potential for both good and bad. The issue is not whether there should be assessment and evaluation but, rather, what type of assessment and evaluation should be used and for what purposes.

When properly used, assessment is a natural part of teaching that leads to improved teaching and learning, increased student confidence, better decisions about the allocation of resources, and increased confidence by the public in the performance of teachers and schools. When used improperly, assessment trivializes education, is a hindrance to good teaching and learning, misdirects scarce resources, discourages students and teachers, and leads to a lack of confidence in teachers and schools.

Assessment and Evaluation

At this point, it might be useful to define *assessment* and *evaluation*. Although many people tend to use the terms synonymously, they are not. They are, however, related. *Assessment* refers to the process of gathering information or measuring the presence or absence of something. It is the process of gathering evidence of learning following certain rules of evidence gathering that should be followed. These rules focus attention on the type of evidence gathered, the conditions under which the evidence was gathered, whether there is a sufficient sample of evidence, and the validity of the evidence.

Numerous measurement tools and procedures can be used to gather evidence about student learning, such as a teacher-constructed test. It is important that the measurement tool be appropriate for the task. For example, we would not propose to measure the weight of an item using a yardstick. Other measurement tools that might be used in education include observations of performances, work samples, interviews, and standardized tests.

Evaluation refers to the process of interpreting and making judgments about the evidence gathered in the assessment process. Just gathering evidence is not enough. It must be interpreted and judged. Evaluation can be viewed as a systematic analysis of the evidence. Certain questions must be addressed when making judgments from the evidence. Is there a sufficient sample to warrant a valid judgment? What is the possibility of error? Is the judgment free of bias? What criteria or standards are being used to make the judgment? Is the evaluation actually based on the evidence?

If the evaluation is performed in the absence of data or if evaluation is biased, it is likely to lead to flawed judgments that can have serious consequences. Student motivation can be diminished, learning stifled, and self-concepts diminished, and in some situations, students may not pass or graduate. For example, few of us would be comfortable with a physician who diagnosed an illness or prescribed medication in the absence of some tests or who based a diagnosis on questionable data. Similarly, we would be uncomfortable if we knew certain medications were prescribed based on some extraneous variable such as the attractiveness of the packaging. Unfortunately, similar practices occur in education all too frequently.

Basic Assessment Principles

The key to understanding any subject is the identification of major principles. These principles can assist you in understanding issues and in making good professional judgments. In assessment, several key ideas lead to effective assessment and evaluation regardless of the grade level or subject area. The following are a few of the basic principles that can get you started. There are others that can be added as you develop increased competence and skill.

1. **Assessment Should Focus on the Measurement of Important and Worthwhile Goals and Objectives.** Although this principle might seem obvious, it is frequently violated. The primary reason why it is violated is that many of the important and worthwhile goals of education are difficult to measure. The temptation is to measure those things that are easiest to measure.

2. **Effective Assessment Requires the Use of a Variety of Procedures.** The goals of education are complex. Among the many goals of education are for students to learn how to apply principles and concepts, become creative problem solvers and decision makers, develop lifelong learning habits, become productive citizens, and develop prosocial behaviors. It is unreasonable to think that any one assessment tool or procedure will measure all these goals.
3. **Good Assessment Requires Adequate Sampling.** The more extensive the sample, the more valid the evaluation. This means that assessment should be something that is done on a regular and frequent basis. Making a judgment about a student based on one observation, one project, or responses on one test is likely to be erroneous and invalid.
4. **Good Assessment Requires Multiple Measures.** This principle is related to the previous one. Not only should there be frequent assessment, but the assessment procedures should vary as well. Student learning is best determined using multiple measures. For example, a student might be able to identify the characteristics of a good paragraph on a multiple-choice test. However, this does not mean the student can write a paragraph. A complete picture of what a student knows and is able to do is best constructed using evidence gathered from a variety of sources.
5. **Good Assessment and Evaluation Should Be Ethical and Fair.** The purpose of valid assessment is to distinguish between those who know or have learned and those who have not. Assessment that results in evidence tainted by extraneous variables such as gender, ethnicity, socioeconomic status, disability, linguistic background, learning style, or test-taking ability is unfair, unjust, and a barrier to educational improvement.
6. **Assessment Is an Important Component of Teaching and Learning.** Teachers have a professional obligation to know the impact of their teaching and to use the results of assessment to assist students in achieving success. Good assessment should inform teachers about the strengths and weaknesses of the students they are teaching, the level of instruction that is appropriate for a given group, the activities and assignments that are most useful, and when it is appropriate to move on (Rudner & Schafer, 2002). You need to realize that your assessment techniques will have an important influence on student motivation, study habits, learning, and attitude about the subject. The absence of good valid data is an impediment for both teachers and students.

Keeping these few principle in mind can help you make good professional decisions and can assist you as you move toward competence in the area of assessment and evaluation.

Connecting Instruction and Assessment

Both instruction and assessment should have a common starting point. They should address questions regarding the goals and purposes of education and what an educated person is. We should be teaching students in ways that lead to the accomplishment of important personal and societal goals. We should then assess and evaluate the extent to which these goals are being met. Although there would be widespread agreement on this point, there is one serious difficulty, namely, a lack of consensus on what those broad educational purposes should be.

Reasonable people disagree on the definition of an educated person or the goals of education in a free society. This makes the assessment and evaluation task a difficult one. As a beginning point, you need to arrive at some personal understanding of the important goals for teaching your subject. This provides you with a needed focus for both what you teach and what you assess.

Focusing on Important Outcomes

An important component in both instruction and assessment is to focus on important objectives. Are we teaching and assessing what we value? One of the main charges leveled by opponents of high-stakes assessments is that they do not measure important outcomes. Important outcomes are usually more difficult to measure and usually require multiple assessments. However, this requires considerable time and resources and cannot easily be accomplished using standardized tests. As a result, many of the assessments end up measuring less important or even trivial educational outcomes.

In order to assess important outcomes, first identify clear objectives that focus on what students should know or be able to do. Then plan assessment items for the objectives.

BOX 13.1 Example of Assessment Specifications Table

Unit title: Weather and Climate

Objective	**Assessment Strategy**	**Assessment Activity**
Defines basic terms and vocabulary	Teacher-made test	Multiple-choice and matching Items
Illustrates influence of wind currents	Assessment of student-created map	Develop checklist to use when evaluating accuracy of wind-current map
Discusses importance of air pressure	Teacher-made test	Short-answer items
Interprets symbols on weather maps	Portfolio entry	Weather maps will be provided, and the student will identify symbols and identify fronts, low-pressure zones, high-pressure zones, and precipitation.
Makes weather predictions	Video project	Student will be videotaped making a weather prediction based on a map provided. Each student will be given 20 minutes to prepare the presentation and will be given 3 minutes to make the presentation. Develop a rubric to evaluate the presentation.

A common mistake made by teachers is to wait until the last minute to construct a test. Frequently, tests that are developed under those conditions gather evidence on a limited number of objectives. For this reason, it is useful to begin developing an assessment plan at the same time the course or unit is being planned. When objectives are identified, an assessment procedure for each objective should also be identified. This can be accomplished by developing an assessment table of specifications. This table lists your objectives in one column, the assessment strategy in the second column, and the specific assessment technique in the third column.

The approach allows you to build assessment into your instructional plans, helps you consider multiple types of assessment, and keeps you focused on all the objectives. Box 13.1 is an example of a table of specifications.

Assessment Options

There are a variety of assessment options that can be used in the classroom, including teacher-constructed tests, authentic assessment, performance checklists, rubrics, and standardized tests. One of the most common and useful assessment tools is the teacher-constructed test. However, good test construction requires knowledge and skill. In this section, we will provide information on how to write test items for teacher-constructed tests; define authentic, natural assessment; and discuss the uses of standardized tests.

Constructing a Test

The teacher-constructed test is the most common form of assessment and is used most often for assigning grades. These tests have the potential advantage of increased validity because they usually measure what has been taught. However, this advantage is often lost because of poorly constructed test items. When items are poorly constructed, they are confusing to students and increase the probability of chance and guessing. When this happens, the results may not accurately discriminate between those who know the content and those who do not. In the following sections, we will discuss several guidelines that can help you write tests and test items that increase the quality and the validity of your tests.

The types of items used on teacher tests are of two types: selected response items and constructed response items. Selected response items are those that ask the student to choose the correct answer from those provided. Examples of selected response item examples include multiple choice, true or false, and matching. Constructed response items are those that require the student to construct or develop an answer. Examples of constructed response items are essay, short answer, and completion. Tanner (2001) points out that the difference is in how students respond. Constructed response items require students to produce what they know, while selected response items require that students recognize the best response among alternatives.

Both types of items have advantages and disadvantages. Being aware of the advantages and disadvantages will help you develop better and more valid classroom tests.

Essay Items One of the most common types of test items used in teacher-constructed tests in secondary schools is the essay question. Essay items are powerful because they can be used to assess complex and higher-level objectives. They are best directed to objectives that call on students to apply, analyze, synthesize, or evaluate. The student is asked to produce something. These items can be used to probe learning more deeply than other types of items, and they help eliminate guessing. Thus, well-constructed essay items can be useful in discriminating between those who know and those who do not. Another potential advantage of essay items is that they are relatively easy to construct.

However, there are some potential disadvantages to essay items. The advantage of ease of construction is countered by the difficulty in scoring. First, each response takes considerable time to read. Second, scoring essay items can be difficult, and the subjective bias of the reader can influence the scoring. Yet another disadvantage is that variables such as handwriting and writing style can influence the scoring. This can be especially troublesome when assessing the learning of students whose first language is not English.

Essay items also require more time for students to respond, and therefore only a few items can be included on a test. This means that only a limited number of objectives can be assessed. Thus, student success might be based on their knowledge of a limited range of content. In addition, poorly written items can mislead students and lead to erroneous judgments regarding who has learned and who has not.

Although guessing is reduced on essay items, bluffing is increased. Skilled writers often know how to bluff, often receiving good grades for responses that do not answer the central question.

Although the disadvantages of essay items are serious ones, you can overcome most of them by following a few guidelines. First, use essay items to assess higher-level objectives and main ideas. Tanner (2001) points out that some essay items are little more than elaborate recall items. If the intent is to assess specific bits of information, other types of items would be more appropriate.

Another suggestion is to include several shorter, more specific questions rather than a few general ones (Ward & Murray-Ward, 1999). This allows you to select a broader range of content and helps sort out those students who have learned from those who have not.

Third, take care in structuring essay questions. This means that the directions regarding what is to be included in a response need to be as precise as possible. Notice the difference in the following two sets of instructions:

1. Write an essay in which you discuss the chromosome hypothesis and the gene theory.
2. Write an essay, about five pages in length, in which you compare and contrast the chromosome hypothesis and gene theory. In your answer, provide specific references to (a) essentials of each position, (b) modifications that have been made to each position since it was initially adopted, and (c) strengths and weaknesses that have been attributed to each view by leading experts.

Students receiving instructions similar to those in instruction 1 are not provided many clues as to what is expected. They may be inclined to ramble or to try and bluff. Further, there are no references to the length the response should be. One student may write one paragraph and another several pages. In light of this imprecise item, the problem of scoring is compounded, and confidence in knowing who has accomplished the objective is diminished.

Instruction 2 is much better. Students will have a clear indication of what is expected of them. Its precision also helps eliminate bluffing and provides some clues for what will be included in the scoring.

Finally, try to reduce subjectivity when scoring responses. Begin by establishing a method to score papers anonymously. This helps eliminate a "halo effect" where the scores on a paper are influenced by what the reader knows about the student. You might use student numbers or a code that you later match to students' names.

It is also useful to construct a sample response so that you have a clear understanding of what you expect. Another option is to use a scoring protocol that indicates how many points will be given to different aspects of the response (Tanner, 2001).

Completion Items Another type of constructed response item is the completion item. This type of item requires the student to fill in a blank that correctly completes a sentence. Completion items are attractive to teachers because they are easy to construct. In addition, a wide array of content can be sampled because students can respond to a large number of completion items during the time they might spend responding to just one essay item.

However, completion items have some serious limitations. First, they are much less powerful in the kind of thinking that can be assessed. They generally sample only recall learning. However, some teachers tend to prefer these to true-or-false answers because they eliminate guessing.

There are, however, some potential scoring problems with completion-type items. One problem is that it is difficult to construct a completion item for which a single answer is the only one that is logically correct. It is especially difficult to decide what to do about student answers that are partially correct. To get some perspective on this issue, look at the following completion-type item:

The person who succeeded George Washington as President of the United States was __________.

Probably, the answer the teacher had in mind was "John Adams." Other plausible answers exist, however. For example, students might respond with answers such as "from New England" or "a man." These are technically correct answers, and marking them wrong is certain to cause some serious disagreements with students. The students should not be expected to try to guess what the teacher is thinking.

In order to avoid these problems, completion items need to be written in such a way that students clearly understand the type of response that is required. For example, the previous item could be rewritten to narrow the range of plausible answers. A revised version might be as follows:

The name of the person who succeeded George Washington as President of the United States was __________.

In addition, when constructing completion-type items, it is important to restrict the number of blanks in a given item. Too many blank spaces or poorly placed ones results in confusion and diminishes the validity of the item. Consider this poor example:

__________ affects __________ independently of __________ except on those occasions when __________ and __________ are inversely related.

This item has too many blanks and does not contain enough information to assist a learner in choosing an appropriate response. In addition to restricting the number of blanks, it is useful to put the blanks near the end of the sentence. This helps provide the context for the answer and eliminates the need for the student to reread the item in order to respond.

Another scoring problem relates to misspelled answers or partial answers. Will you give credit for answers that are misspelled? What will you do if the answer is partially correct? For example, on a completion item asking students to fill in the name of the author of *Alice in Wonderland*, one student wrote "Carroll Lewis." How would you score this answer? In order to accommodate this concern, you need to establish some rules that will guide your decisions on giving credit for completion items. For example, you might provide students with a list of items that are to be used when responding to the completion items. This helps eliminate spelling errors and partial answers. However, it makes it a modified matching item and introduces the possibility of guessing. Box 13.2 is an example of a completion test with a provided list of terms.

In general, completion items do not represent a particularly good technique for assessing students' proficiencies. In most cases, other types of items can measure the same learning with fewer problems.

Matching Items Matching items are selected response items. A selection of responses is provided, and the person taking the test must select the correct or the best one. They are generally used to measure less sophisticated levels of student thinking. They are easy to construct, they can be corrected quickly, and there is little subjectivity in the

BOX 13.2 An Example of Completion Items

Directions: In the following paragraph are a number of blanks. Below the paragraph you will find a list of terms. Choose items from this list and print them carefully in the appropriate blanks. Include only terms in the list at the bottom of the page. Terms must be spelled correctly.

In recent years, there has been a trend for people to move away from the core of the city toward surrounding suburbs. Sociologists call this movement __________*. Another urban phenomenon involves the movement of people from one social class to a part of the city occupied by people in another social class. This is termed* __________*. When a new group in society succeeds in taking over a neighborhood, a situation termed* __________ *results. When minority members of a community are removed by majority members, the situation is called* __________*. When this causes married couples to move to a locale where neither set of parents is resident, their new family residence is said to be* __________*. The group an individual interacts with over time on a more or less continuous basis is called a(n)* __________*.*

Terms

recurrent	segregation	invasion	neolocal
allotropic	suburbanization	deviance	patrilocal
expulsion	concession	succession	separation

grading. Therefore, there is no danger that one student's test will be graded using a standard that is different from another student's test.

Difficulties associated with the use of matching items usually have to do with item construction. One construction problem relates to the types of items selected for both of the lists to be matched. Students become confused when they are confronted with matching items containing a mixture of unrelated terms and definitions. In addition, this reduces the item difficulty because it allows the good test taker to eliminate a number of the possible choices. Therefore, all terms in a matching item should focus on a single topic or theme. For example, if you decided to prepare a matching test on the Civil War, you might have one column with the names of Confederate generals and another column with a number of exploits associated with them. It would not be wise to mix in other names and events unrelated to the Confederate generals.

As a rule of thumb, the list on the right side (the one providing the choices to be selected as possible answers) should contain approximately 25% more items than the list on the left-hand side. For example, if you want the students to match 10 items, you should provide them with 12 or 13 alternative choices on the right side.

The entire matching item should be on one page. It is unacceptable for any portion of the item to be on another page. When this happens, students often overlook the part of the item on the second page, resulting in mistakes and confusion.

The preferred format is to place a blank before each item to be matched and to provide a letter identifying each possible choice so that the student fills in the blank with the letter of their choice. Drawing lines between the two columns is not recommended because the result can be a confusing tangle of lines that are hard to follow. This may result in disputes, as when a student claims that you didn't follow the correct line. Box 13.3 is an example of a properly formatted matching test.

Multiple-Choice Items Multiple-choice items are also selected response items. Evaluation experts have long shown a preference for multiple-choice items (Hattie, Jaeger, & Bond, 1999) because they are very flexible. They can measure a variety of subjects and have the capacity of testing not only knowledge but also higher-level thinking abilities. They can be scored easily and quickly, and subjectivity in scoring is very low. Because a person can respond to a number of multiple-choice items in the time it takes to respond to a single essay or short-answer question, content coverage is another advantage of multiple-choice items.

A disadvantage of multiple-choice items is that writing good items can be difficult. It takes a good deal of skill and thought to write items that measure worthwhile outcomes. In fact, the negative reaction that some individuals have to multiple-choice items is related to the hurried and careless construction of items.

Another possible problem with multiple-choice items is that they do allow for a certain measure of guessing. If four choices are provided, a student has a 25% probability of getting the item right simply by guessing. You can overcome these construction problems by following a few basic guidelines.

Do not wait until the night before a test to write the items. Construct an item bank of possible test items as you are teaching the unit. These can be keyed to the content and the particular objective they are intended to measure. Then, when the time comes to construct a test, these items can be reviewed and the test constructed.

Actual item construction poses other challenges that need to be addressed. Poorly constructed items either give away the correct response or confuse students so they do

BOX 13.3 Example of a Properly Formatted Matching Test

Matching Test:

Tennis Terminology

Directions: Find the term in the right-hand column that is defined by the definition in the left-hand column. Place the letter identifying this term in the blank space provided before its definition. Only one term is correct for each definition. Do not draw lines connecting the terms and the definitions.

_____ 1. The point that, if won, wins the match for a player
_____ 2. The area between the net and the service line
_____ 3. Hitting the ball before it bounces
_____ 4. Stroke made after the ball has bounced, either forehand or backhand
_____ 5. The line that is perpendicular to the net and divides the two service courts
_____ 6. The initial part of any swing; the act of bringing the racket back to prepare for the forward swing
_____ 7. A ball hit high enough in the air to pass over the head of the net player
_____ 8. A ball that is served so well that the opponent fails to touch it with his or her racquet.
_____ 9. A shot that bounces near the baseline
_____10. Start of play for a given point

a. Ace
b. Backswing
c. Center, service line
d. Deep shot
e. Forecourt
f. Set point
g. Lob
h. Match point
i. Serve
j. Volley
k. Dink
l. Ground stroke

not know what is being asked. In either case, the evidence gathered through the test becomes suspect, and an evaluation about what a student knows or does not know is invalid.

In terms of format, multiple-choice items consist of two parts: (a) a stem and (b) some alternative choices. Among the choices are the correct answer and some distracters. Good distracters should be plausible choices that would be chosen by individuals who do not know the correct answer. The difficulty of the item depends on the level of thinking that is required to distinguish correct answers from the distracters. For example, good distracters might require working out a problem or engaging in some high-level thinking in order to identify the correct answer.

You will find it challenging to prepare multiple-choice items where the distracters all appear to be plausible answers. Carelessly written distracters tend to give away the correct answer, even to students who do not know the content. Good items take time to develop; hence, high-quality multiple-choice items cannot be prepared in haste.

When you construct multiple-choice items, make sure that the stem is clear and that you write all distracters in a way that ensures grammatical consistency with the stem. Consider this example:

Nils Johansen, in his novel of the Canadian prairies, West from Winnipeg, *called trapping an*

a. science b. art c. duty d. nuisance

A student totally unfamiliar with this novel who read the question carefully would identify "b" as the correct answer simply because it is the only choice grammatically consistent with the article "an" at the end of the stem. To correct this problem, the writer of the item might have concluded the stem in this way: ". . . called trapping a(n)." This revision makes any of the four distracters plausible.

A stem that is too brief fails to cue the students regarding the kind of information they should be looking for in the distracters. Consider this example:

Roger Williams

a. sailed on the Mayflower.

b. established the Thanksgiving tradition.

c. founded the Rhode Island colony.

d. developed the New World's first distillery.

Because the stem is so incomplete, students are really faced with four true-or-false items to ponder rather than with one good multiple-choice item. A better way of writing this question would be as follows:

The founder of the Rhode Island colony was

a. Sir Walter Raleigh.

b. John Winthrop.

c. Roger Williams.

d. William Bradford.

As noted earlier, multiple-choice items can be designed to test quite sophisticated levels of thinking. Consider the example in Box 13.4. It challenges students to make inferences based on their analysis of the prose.

As this example illustrates, it is possible to use multiple-choice questions to assess students' abilities to engage in quite challenging levels of thinking. However, you will find that constructing multiple-choice questions such as the one in this example takes time. You may decide that essay questions better suit your needs when you want to test your students' abilities to apply, analyze, synthesize, and evaluate.

True-or-False Items True-or-false items, though most frequently used to assess knowledge-level thinking, do have some limited applications when you are interested in assessing your students' abilities to engage in more complex levels of thinking. True-or-false items can be prepared relatively quickly. They provide a format that ensures consistency of scoring. Finally, true-or-false items can be corrected quickly.

There are also some disadvantages of true-or-false items. For one thing, they encourage guessing. Because there are only two choices, your students have a 50/50 chance of getting an item correct even when they have no grasp of the content being tested. True-or-false items require you to prepare statements that are absolutely true

BOX 13.4 A Multiple-Choice Item Focusing on Higher-Level Thinking Abilities

Directions: Read the passage and circle the letter of the answer you select.

Ellison has the flair of genius, but he was not a genius. Though pedestrian in his approaches, he was a phenomenon. His was a talent of concentration, not of innovation. No other man of his time rivaled his ability to shunt aside irrelevancies to focus on a problem's essentials. For him, noncritical considerations were a trifling bit of detritus to be swept away in a moment. His resolute attack on the nuggety essence of an unresolved issue obviated even the serious possibility of egregious error. Contemporaries described his reasoning as "glistening." Only an audacious few ventured public challenges to his positions. It is not too much to say that he lived out his days surrounded by a nervously approving silence. Later generations have seen his conclusions as less than revolutionary. But, in his own time, Ellison's ability to "will" an impeccable solution to a complex issue made others seem small figures destined ever to walk lightly in the dark shadows of a giant.

One assumption revealed in the preceding paragraph is that

a. Ellison was truly competent, but he had a flair for impressing people with the logical structure he built to support his solutions.

b. Ellison really was a genius whose "glistening" logic resulted in novel solutions to problems.

c. Today, people tend to be more impressed with Ellison than they were in his own day.

d. Ellison's form probably was more a significant contributor to his reputation than was the substance of his thought.

---

or absolutely false. Much course content tends toward gray areas. For this reason, you may feel constrained by the true-or-false format, which may require you to stay away from the main focus of your instruction to find the odd example that is absolutely true or absolutely false.

One way to eliminate potential scoring disputes is to include the words "True" and "False" before each item and instruct the students to circle the correct response. An example of a properly formatted true-or-false test that asks questions about expected changes in numbers of employed teachers as projected by the National Center for Educational Statistics (Gerald & Hussar, 1999) is provided in Box 13.5.

Authentic, Natural Assessment

A few years ago, some experts pointed out that both teacher-made and standardized tests are contrived and artificial situations generated to provide evidence of student knowledge or ability. They claimed that rather than gathering evidence in artificial situations, it would be better to base evaluations on evidence gained from the actual performance of "authentic" or "real" tasks. For example, rather than giving a paper-and-pencil test relating to an important objective such as problem solving, they advocated assessing the performance of a student when confronted with a real or authentic problem. Advocates point out that assessment should be related to life beyond the classroom. These individuals were critical of the power of conventional testing techniques to

BOX 13.5 Example of a True-or-False Test

Directions: Use the data provided in the chart below to respond to the following true-or-false items. If the statement is true, circle the word "True." If the statement is false, circle the word "False."

Number of Individuals Expected to Be Employed as Teachers (in thousands)

Year	Elementary	Secondary
1998	1,866	1,243
1999	1,885	1,260
2000	1,903	1,276
2001	1,920	1,291
2002	1,935	1,306
2003	1,943	1,325
2004	1,949	1,347

True False 1. There will be an increase in number of both elementary and secondary teachers in each year from 1998 through 2004.

True False 2. The number of additional elementary teachers added each year from 1998 through 2004 will be larger in years at the beginning of this time period than in the years toward the end.

True False 3. From this information, we can infer that numbers of secondary students will increase at a slower rate than numbers of elementary pupils in the years 1998 through 2004.

True False 4. There will be a larger total increase in the number of secondary teachers than the number of elementary teaches over the entire time period from 1998 through 2004.

True False 5. The smallest annual increase in the number of elementary teachers will occur between the same 2 years as the largest annual increase in the number of secondary teachers.

Source: Data are from D. E. Gerald & W. J. Husser (1993). *Projections of education statistics to 2009* (p. 72). Washington, DC: Department of Education, Office of Educational Research and Improvement, National Center for Education Statistics.

do this. Too frequently, students viewed tests as meaningless hurdles to be cleared, and the information to be forgotten as soon as the test was over. Wiggins (1989) argues that "authentic assessments replicate the challenges and standards of performance that typically face writers, business people, scientists, community leaders, designers, or historians" (p. 704).

"Natural assessment" extends the notion of authentic assessment. Natural assessment is a term used to make the point that assessment should be a natural part of the instruction process rather than an add-on (Smith, Smith, & De Lisi, 2001). This view puts learning first and suggests that the purpose of assessment is facilitating learning rather than as just auditing what students have learned.

Proponents of natural assessment emphasize that assessment tasks can be the same as instructional activities. This opens up numerous options for gathering evidence about student learning. Instructional activities such as working on a research paper, working with a group of students on a project, conducting an experiment, or giving a class presentation can all become assessment tasks that are useful in gathering data about student learning.

Authentic, natural assessment is also a response to the increased diversity of students in classrooms (Tanner, 2001). In typical classrooms, there are students from a variety of backgrounds with a variety of academic, cultural, and linguistic abilities. Some of these abilities interfere with the ability of students to read and respond on a typical test. Thus, natural or authentic assessment opens up multiple ways of allowing students to demonstrate what they know and have learned.

One of the first steps in natural assessment is to identify specific tasks or performances that would be the basis for an assessment. These should be complex tasks that have a clearly defined product or performance related to important objectives and should be as similar as possible to real-life tasks.

Once these important tasks have been identified, you need to define the criterion for assessing the performance or the product. This can be done using tools such as checklists, rating scales, or rubrics. Therefore, authentic, natural assessment requires considerable thought and planning. You can justify the time commitment because what students experience during authentic assessment activities is really an extension of your basic instruction. Authentic, natural assessment seeks to teach as well as reveal what students know and can do.

Not everyone agrees that authentic assessment is a good idea. One concern relates to the amount of subjectivity involved in evaluating authentic assessment. Some people worry that few standards presently exist to ensure the quality of authentic assessment procedures. The quality of authentic assessment is related to the quality of the tasks defined by the teacher and the specificity of the criteria used in the evaluation. Thus, the evaluation might differ greatly, depending on the skill and the ability of the teacher.

In addition, it is more difficult to make sure that all students have met the same standards if they are all involved in different tasks or performances. Traditional tests often yield scores that can be averaged together to suggest how well the students in a given class are doing when compared to a national sample. These scores are used by those interested in accountability to compare and contrast schools. It is difficult to make these kinds of comparisons when authentic assessment procedures are used.

Professionals at the Educational Testing Service have identified the issues that need attention when authentic assessment is being considered as an option:

- Authentic assessment tasks can be difficult to develop.
- Teachers need to be involved in developing authentic assessment experiences, and they should have some training in how the approach works.
- Deciding how to score authentic assessment exercises can be problematic.
- Authentic assessment procedures often require more class time than traditional approaches.

- Use of authentic assessment often also implies a commitment to use different kinds of instructional techniques.
- Establishing high levels of reliability when using authentic assessment is a continuing challenge (Educational Testing Service, 1995).

Using Rubrics Engaging students in authentic assessment requires the use of nontraditional evaluation approaches. When your purpose is to make judgments about complex sets of behaviors, you need to establish some guidelines or standards that will provide you with clear indicators of what is expected. Often, those using authentic assessment techniques use *rubrics* to perform the evaluation. A *rubric* consists of a set of guidelines that tell you what to consider as acceptable evidence when you make a judgment about the quality of a performance or product. Rubrics can also be viewed as behaviorally anchored rating scales. Usually, they are a rating scale indicating different levels of performance. However, each point of the rating scale specifies behaviors or characteristics that relate to that rating point. For example, you might judge a student product on a 5-point scale with the "5" being the highest score and the "1" the lowest. In a rubric, each one of the 5 points are to be defined as clearly as possible. The content of the rubric defines what to look for in a student's performance or product to determine its quality. Therefore, it is important that the rubric cover the essential qualities and leave out the trivial (Arter & McTighe, 2001). The purpose of these clear definitions is to provide some assurance that different raters would assign the same numbers to the same performance or product.

Rubrics are usually one of two types. One type is a holistic rubric that gives a single score or rating for an entire performance or product. The other type is an analytical rubric that divides the performance into essential dimensions so that each dimension can be rated separately. Holistic rubrics are generally best when evaluating a relatively simple product that may have only one important dimension. They are useful for giving a general view of the overall quality. However, they do not give a detailed analysis of the strengths and weaknesses of a performance or product and therefore are of limited use to a student in knowing what is required for improvement (Arter & McTighe, 2001).

Analytic rubrics are best for complex performances where there are several important dimensions. They also provide more specific feedback to students and parents and are more useful in helping you pinpoint areas that might need more instruction (Arter & McTighe, 2001).

One of the drawbacks with rubrics is that good ones can be difficult to construct. You need to have a very clear understanding of your objectives and what is expected of students. You then need to be able to identify, in detail, different performance levels.

While there is no one way to construct rubrics, there are some suggestions that can help you. One that we have found useful is to start by trying to define what we would accept as minimally acceptable performance. Avoid defining this as "average" because if you do a good job of defining the rubric and you share it with students, you will probably have many students who do much better than "average." Then identify what you would define as an outstanding performance and what you would see as unacceptable. This provides you with a basic 3-point rubric. Additional levels can be defined as you refine your rubric.

A review of the literature to see how others define this knowledge or skill or a review of rubrics developed by others for this same type of performance is also very useful in defining what should be included. When you have the beginnings of a rubric, share it with others who know the subject and get their thoughts. You may also gather some samples of student work and sort them according to quality into three or more piles. Then describe the elements that make them different. This will help you conceptualize the dimensions of a work that contribute to its quality (Arter and McTighe, 2001).

Once you have a rubric, test it on some student work with some others to see if there is consistency between raters. This final step can be very valuable in adding some fine detail to your rubric that will make it useful when used with your students. Box 13.6 is an example of a holistic rubric that could be used to evaluate an oral presentation. Review it and think about how you might alter it to fit your definition of a good oral performance.

Evaluative Checklists Another approach to evaluating student performance or products is the use of a checklist. Checklists also require a clear understanding of your expectations. A major difference with rubrics is that they allow more flexibility in

BOX 13.6 Example of a Rubric for an Oral Presentation

5 A clear statement of the topic or question is made.
A persuasive argument is presented for the importance of the topic.
Facts and information gathered from research are smoothly integrated.
Eye contact is maintained throughout.
Correct grammar is used.
Students refer to notes but do not read.
Presentation has a smooth and logical flow.

4 A clear statement of the topic or question is made.
Importance of the topic or question is adequately stated.
Knowledge and data drawn from research are incorporated.
There are few grammatical errors.
Speech is clear.
There is a generally smooth flow and logical organization with minimal digressions.
Eye contact is made with some lapses.
Use of notes is prominent.

3 The question or topic is stated.
There are occasional errors in grammar and sentence structure.
Knowledge and data drawn from research are superficially included.
Speech and diction are adequate.
There is evidence of organization.
Considerable reading of the material is done.
Occasional eye contact is made.

2 The question or topic is not clear.
Few facts or information from research are included.
There is a lack of enthusiasm in the presentation.
Little eye contact is made.

Most of the presentation is read.
There are significant grammatical and sentence structure errors.
Logic of the presentation is unclear.
1 The question or topic is not stated.
No attempt is made to justify importance of topic.
The presentation is fragmented with no logical flow.
There are major grammatical and structural errors.
There is little evidence of research.
Presentation is read.
Minimal eye contact is made.

determining the adequacy of a given student's performance. Usually checklists are used when there is a yes/no decision and degrees of performance variability are unimportant. For example, a checklist would be an appropriate tool for evaluating the ability to drive a car. A person either knows how to start the car or does not, or they can shift into gear or cannot. There are few degrees of performance variability. It is useful to arrange items on a checklist in the order they occur. This will save you time when you are scoring the performance.

If there are certain items on the checklist that are more important than others, you can give those items more points than those that are important but relatively minor. For example, in the driving example, while it is important to know how to insert the key and start the car, it is probably not as important as signaling and making a safe lane change. Thus, items such as changing lanes safely or stopping at signals would be given more weight and more points.

Portfolios In recent years, the portfolio has become a popular assessment tool. The portfolio is a collection of artifacts relating to important objectives. The task of the student is to select those items that will best reflect on his or her knowledge and ability. The claimed advantages for portfolios as an assessment tool are that the assessment is more closely related to instruction and to reality, focuses on important educational outcomes, and includes a wider sample of student performances over time and in multiple settings. Additionally, students can include material that relates to a wide variety of goals and objectives so that the assessment becomes a natural part of instruction. Portfolio assessment blends instruction and assessment by including student work samples. A portfolio should not be just a static collection of a student's work. The key to the effectiveness of a portfolio is an ongoing dialogue between the teacher and the student where students are encouraged to engage in self-evaluations on their work and to reflect on their progress.

However, just gathering material together in a portfolio does not automatically mean it is a more valid assessment technique. Care must be taken in selecting the items to be included in the portfolio, and there must be a clear set of criteria used in performing the evaluation. Portfolios do have the disadvantage of taking much more time to gather and evaluate, and there can be a greater degree of subjectivity in evaluation.

Components of portfolios vary depending on the subject being taught and the preferences of teachers and students.

Some examples of the items that might be contained in a portfolio include the following:

- Completed assignments
- Journal entries (reflections by the students about content that has been learned)
- Answers to prompt questions supplied by the teacher
- Photos, sketches, and other visuals
- Special projects
- Summary statements made at different points regarding what has been learned
- Self-assessment statements regarding areas of strength and areas needing additional work

The use of portfolios is consistent with reflective teaching. Comments made on students' portfolios can prompt them to think about what they have done, help them consider alternatives, and speculate about new issues. Writing in the portfolio can encourage an ongoing dialogue and can help personalize the relationship between teacher and student. The portfolio provides a tangible piece of evidence for students that they are learning and making progress. This can be a powerful motivator. Porter and Cleland (1995) suggest that from time to time, students be asked to look over their portfolio and self-validate their learning by citing specific examples of how more recent work represents growth and learning over what was done earlier.

The evidence gathered in a portfolio also provides an opportunity for one-on-one discussions at grading time. With a portfolio to discuss, tangible evidence can be discussed that leads to the grading decision. This helps take some of the mystery out of the grading process. It can help students feel as if they had some input in the grade.

Proponents of portfolios argue that students who prepare them recognize that grading is data based, and hence they tend to accept the grades they receive. Supporters also argue that portfolios help base grading on significant learning and emphasize the importance of effort. They contrast this to the more traditional assessment where grades are based on tests that may be only loosely tied to significant learning and where students view the grade as highly subjective and related more to chance than to effort.

Gathering material for the portfolio is only the first step of the process. To make the process meaningful, the portfolio must be evaluated. Because the content and the complexity of a portfolio can vary widely, the approach to evaluating them can also vary widely. Rubrics are the most common method for evaluating portfolios.

Standardized Assessment

Standardized assessment is an assessment where there are established standards for administration, scoring, and reporting of results. These standardized assessments usually focus on achievement or on aptitude. In simple terms, the purpose of standardized assessment is to assess the performance of large numbers of individuals from a variety of backgrounds on some similar trait or characteristic (Tanner, 2001). One of the common uses of standardized assessment is in the area of student achievement. Its use in schools is usually to compare student performances in content areas such as reading, mathematics, science, social science, and English.

MORE FROM THE WEB

Several Websites provide help to teachers who are concerned about evaluation and assessment. The following are just a few examples that can provide assistance as you consider your needs in your classroom.

Rubistar for Teachers

This site provides assistance to those teachers who want to create rubrics for their students' projects. They provide a variety of formats and allow you to modify them and add your own descriptors if you prefer. Your rubrics can be saved and accessed whenever you need to modify them.

Website: http://rubistar.4teachers.org

National Center for Fair and Open Testing

The mission of this site is to end the misuses and flaws of standardized testing and ensure fair evaluation of teachers, students, and schools. Excellent links provide access to a number of worthwhile books and articles that stimulate thoughtful consideration of this topic.

Website: http://www.fairtest.org

A second type of a standardized test is the aptitude test. The purpose of the aptitude test is to measure potential ability or capacity to learn. For example, most of the entrance examinations required for admission to a university are aptitude tests designed to indicate the potential of the person to be successful in higher education.

For decades, standardized assessments have been used to monitor student progress over time, to serve as a benchmark to understand how a given group of students was doing when compared to a national sample, to predict performance, and to identify students who might be eligible to receive special services (McMillan, 2001). However, in recent years, large-scale standardized assessment has become an important and almost universal feature. Much more time is spent giving standardized tests and preparing students to take them. Standardized achievement tests have become a key element of the movement to hold students, teachers, and schools accountable for their performance. This is usually called "large-scale, high-stakes assessment." This refers to the fact that large numbers of students are usually tested (frequently all the students at a given grade level in the state) and that the results have important consequences. In numerous states, the results of standardized testing are used to promote or retain students, reward and evaluate teaches, and label schools as successful or unsuccessful. Many opponents of this movement claim that this is an inappropriate and dangerous use of standardized achievement tests.

Standardized tests are usually developed by companies for profit (McMillan, 2001). As a result, they often include relatively well-written test items that have been developed by experts and have been tested and revised. Because they are usually developed by companies for profit, they also focus on broad outcomes and content that is taught in schools across the nation. Usually, standardized tests are applied to population samples in order to establish "norms." These norms then allow comparisons of the achievement of students across the country.

The disadvantage of this approach is that there might be a significant mismatch between the objectives and the curriculum of a local school district and what is included on a standardized test developed for a national audience. This is the issue of content validity. Is the content being assessed important content that has been taught? In an attempt to meet this concern, some states have developed standardized tests that focus on state standards. Rather than focusing on a comparison with other students, these tests focus on whether the students achieved state standards.

Another disadvantage of standardized tests is that because they are so general, they do not provide the teacher with much useful information in making instructional decisions. Often the tests are given near the end of the year, and by the time the results are returned, the students have moved on to the next year. This might be helpful in a general way for preparing for the next year. However, since the teacher now has a new group of students with a different set of needs and abilities, the possibility of making significant instructional improvement is diminished.

Bias is yet another issue that needs to be considered when interpreting standardized achievement scores. Some experts argue that the testing practices clearly favor students from the majority culture. Socioeconomic level is clearly related to success on standardized achievement tests. There have been other well-documented cases of ethnic, gender, linguistic, and geographical bias (Tanner, 2001).

The most common type of a standardized test is a comprehensive series of tests called an "achievement test battery" (McMillan, 2001). These test batteries often include subtests in areas such as mathematics, science, social science, and study skills. Students may take one subtest per day for several days. When administering standardized tests, it is important that the administration be consistent and follow the procedures established by the test developers so that all test takers take the test under similar conditions.

Because of the importance now being placed on the use of standardized tests, some ethical issues have been raised. One of the major ethical issues relates to coaching. Students should be told what the test is like and why they are taking it. They should also be coached on appropriate test-taking techniques. However, coaching becomes unethical when students are given specific information about items on the test (Ward & Murray-Ward, 1999). When there are high stakes on a test and a teacher has seen past tests, there is a temptation to teach the students specific information contained on the test.

Another ethical issue relates to the administration of standardized tests. Again, there is a temptation for teachers to provide extra assistance to those who may have limited English ability or those with some problem that makes it difficult for them to respond appropriately. Many tests do establish standards to be followed in making special accommodations for individuals who need them.

In summary, standardized tests are an important feature of the school system, and you should learn as much as you can about them. Because important decisions about students' lives are being made on the basis of standardized tests, it is imperative that you become informed about the tests you will be required to give students, their validity, any possible bias, and how the results are reported and interpreted.

Evaluation and Grading

Assessment is the process of gathering data about student learning. Evaluation is the process of judging the performance. Grading is the process of communicating the judgment to students and other interested parties. The value of a particular grading system should be the degree to which it communicates valuable information to those

Explaining grading criteria to students is an important component of the assessment process.

who have an interest in the evaluation. For example, does the grade provide the student and the parents with valuable information? Does the grade contribute to important decisions, such as promotion or retention? Does the grade communicate information needed by future employers or institutions of higher education? Current grading processes in America have long been a tradition in education. As a result, the traditional grading system has been challenged less and has probably changed less than just about any other aspect of education (Guskey & Bailey, 2001).

Grading is one dimension of teaching that many dislike. This dislike has many dimensions. One reason is that it places teachers in a position that conflicts with what they see as their major responsibility. While many see themselves as advocates for students, grading places them in the role of a judge. This conflict is not as apparent when formative judgments are meant to help students learn. However, when grades or a summative judgment are the product, the situation is quite different.

A second aspect that makes grades difficult is that they require teachers to make difficult choices. It is difficult to be a dispassionate judge when you know the students well. There is always an element of subjectivity that enters the picture. For example, what do you do when you have a student who always scores at the top of the class with little effort or interest? Is giving the student a top grade providing the student with the type of feedback that will help him or her achieve success outside of school? What about the opposite type of student who has put forth considerable effort, has good work habits, and has made excellent growth but still falls short of the prescribed standard? Will he or she be less motivated and turned off if he or she gets a disappointing grade?

For the most part, teachers get their ideas about how to grade from their own experience. Over the years, you have had numerous teachers and have seen various grading systems. You will favor those that you thought were most fair for you. This is also based on your personal philosophy of teaching and learning. Those individuals who see their role as one of identifying and rewarding talent will probably have a different method of awarding grades than those who believe it is their role to foster the personal growth of all students (Guskey & Bailey, 2001). Another source of information about grading systems is school district or department policy regarding grading. One study found that about two thirds of the school districts have grading policies. However, many teachers reported that they were vague and ambiguous (Guskey & Bailey, 2001). Even though there is a high probability that you will teach in a school district with a grading policy, ultimately, you will have to rely on your knowledge and philosophy to determine how to give grades.

Types of Criteria

The beginning point for grading is to make sure it is done in reference to a set of criteria. There are two types of criteria that can be used in evaluating student performance: norm-referenced criteria and criterion-referenced criteria.

Norm-Referenced Evaluation In a norm-referenced system, the performance of an individual is evaluated based on the performance of a reference group. The score of an individual is compared to a frequency distribution, often the normal distribution, or the bell-shaped curve. The distribution is based on the assumption that given traits will be distributed throughout the population on a normal distribution with few cases at each of the extremes and most cases in the middle.

In classrooms, teachers use norm-referenced evaluation when they compare the performance of each class member to the performance of the rest of the class. This is what is generally called "grading on the curve." The grades are plotted on a distribution and cutoff points determined for different grades.

This practice has several limitations. First, the grade of an individual is based on the quality of work of other class members. A student in a class that contained a high percentage of high-performing students might receive a low grade yet outperform students who received high grades in a class that contained a high number of low-performing students. Therefore, the grade doesn't say what a student has learned or is able to do. It only identifies the relative standing of the student in a given group.

Second, this system introduces unhealthy competition between students. It is to an individual's advantage that others do poorly. All of us probably remember being upset when we were assigned to a group of high-performing individuals who "inflated the curve." These practices are counter to the conditions that foster a good learning environment.

Finally, it is important to remember that competition motivates individuals who believe they have a chance to win. Therefore, students who find themselves in a class with several talented individuals are often not motivated because they do not believe they have a chance to obtain a good grade.

For these reasons, some individuals have criticized norm-referenced grading systems. The normal distribution is best applied to chance and random activities, not to purposeful activities that do not include a random sample of the general population (Guskey & Bailey, 2001).

Criterion-Referenced Evaluation In a criterion-referenced system, the performance of an individual is compared to a standard, or specific, criteria. In most classrooms, is it based on the extent to which the students have mastered the objectives established for the class. Teachers who use this system often define at the beginning of the class exactly what must be done in order to receive a particular grade. This has the effect of changing responsibility for the grade from the teacher to the students. They know the expectations and can choose to work or not work toward a particular grade. The role of the teacher is setting the criterion levels for the grades.

Criterion-referenced systems are most compatible with mastery learning environments. This provides students with feedback on their performance and allows them to redo assignments or tests in order to get a higher grade.

Implementing a criterion system is considerably more difficult than implementing a norm-referenced system. Identifying the learning goals for the course and the criterion level for each level of performance and deciding what type of evidence will be used to validate student performance are the most challenging dimensions of establishing a criterion-referenced system. You need to develop a grading rubric for each objective. You want to make sure that the highest performance levels really are indicative of high-quality performance. On the other hand, you don't want the criterion level so high that no one can attain it, thus discouraging your students. Establishing criterion levels that are fair and appropriate for the students you are teaching requires careful attention and experience.

Establishing a Grading Plan

When you begin teaching, the school or the district will generally have a reporting system that you will be required to use. The traditional reporting system has been the use of the 5-point letter grade. Accompanying the letter grade are descriptors of each of the letter grades. For example, the grade of "A" is defined as outstanding, "B" above average, "C" average, "D" below average, and "F" failing. These descriptors are clearly norm-referenced terms. A more criterion-referenced set of descriptors would be "A" for excellent, "B" for good, "C" for satisfactory, "D" for poor, and "F" for unacceptable.

In recent years, some schools have rejected these value-laden labels that stigmatize students in favor of more descriptive categories. In some instances, they have rejected letter grades altogether (Guskey & Bailey, 2001). For example, Nebraska established a four-category reporting system that is clearly more criterion referenced. It includes the categories "beginning," "progressing," "proficient," and "advanced."

Another common system bases grades on percentages. Students who get between 90% to 100% receive an "A," between 80% and 89% a "B," between 70% and 79% a "C," and so forth. This allows for maximum discrimination between students because the difference between a score of 90% and a score of 99% indicates a difference in performance level even though both qualify for a grade of "A."

In all these systems, you will generally have a great deal of responsibility in recording student grades on various assessment activities and pulling all of them together into a single grade. One of the most important responsibilities is to keep good student records. This will assist you greatly in providing the basis for grades when the grading period is over. In addition, records provide you with support should your grades be challenged.

Several sources of evidence can be included in your grading plan: homework assignments, major projects, test scores, laboratory projects, student portfolios, and oral presentations. Some individuals also include a score for classroom participation and attendance. Some suggest that those factors relating to something other than student achievement, such as work habits, classroom behavior, and effort, should be recorded separately, or else the validity of the grade is compromised (Tanner, 2001). In other words, if the grade is to be a good communication tool, it should clearly reflect the basis for the grade so that others can easily interpret what the grade means.

Once you have identified those sources of evidence that you will use in arriving at a grade, you should decide how much weight you are going to give each one. For example, how much weight you will you give homework scores? Will they count as 25% of the grade? How much will the tests and the major projects count? You will want to take into account the importance of each source of data and how it relates to important course objectives.

Although a grading and reporting system can be complicated and elaborate, you can develop systems for deciding how to weight various scores and determining a final grade. We suggest you keep it simple. Begin with something that keeps a focus on important objectives, is objective, is consistent with your philosophy, takes into account school or district policies, and is fair for the students. Develop a good record-keeping system and keep the data that you will include in calculating a final grade to a reasonable amount. Then you will find that the final grading period is not overwhelming, and you will end up with few disputes.

FOR YOUR PORTFOLIO

Given the fact that assessment and evaluation has become such an important part of education, it would be important to include evidence of your understanding of assessment and evaluation in your portfolio. INTASC Standard 8 focuses on evaluation. Keep in mind that you want to present evidence that you have a solid understanding of the issues and processes of assessment and evaluation. Review what you have learned from this chapter and from assignments you may have completed for your class. You may also choose to do some of the learning extension activities. From these, choose up to three items to include in your portfolio. For each of the items included, write a brief statement indicating why you chose this particular entry and what it indicates about your knowledge of assessment and evaluation.

You might also review the material to determine if your entries relate to any of the other standards. Identify which INTASC standards these entries address using the following chart.

Item of Evidence Number	**INTASC Standards**									
	S1	S2	S3	S4	S5	S6	S7	S8	S9	S10
1										
2										
3										

KEY IDEAS IN SUMMARY

- Assessment refers to the process of gathering evidence about student learning. Evaluation is the process of making judgments about the evidence. Grading is communicating the judgment to other interested parties.
- Assessment should gather data about important and worthwhile goals, should include a variety of procedures, should include adequate sampling of student learning, and should be ethical and fair to the students.
- There should be a clear connection between assessment and instruction. If done properly, assessment and instruction are complementary components of good teaching and learning.
- Developing a table of specifications at the same time that unit planning takes places helps ensure that important objectives are measured.

- Teacher-made tests are a common assessment tool. Their value as an assessment tool relates to the quality of the test items that are included. There are two basic types: constructed responses and selected response. Both types have strengths and weaknesses. Constructed response items include essay and completion types. Selected response items include matching, multiple-choice and true-or-false types.
- Authentic, natural assessment refers to the idea that assessment should be a natural part of the teaching process and that evaluation should be based on real or authentic tasks rather than the data gathered through artificial and controlled methods generally associated with traditional tests.
- Individuals interested in authentic assessment often use portfolios. A portfolio is a systematically organized collection of a student's work that covers specific objectives and a specific period of time. They allow for the inclusion of multiple sources of evidence concerning student learning.
- Assessment rubrics are tools that are often used to evaluate the quality of student products or performances that are commonly associated with authentic, natural assessment. They are behaviorally anchored rating scales that have clear indicators for each performance level.
- Evaluative checklists are useful tools when a yes/no decision is appropriate or where degrees of performance are unimportant. The checklist should identify all the important components of a required performance. If the items on the checklist can be arranged in the order they generally appear, scoring will be easier.
- Standardized assessment has become an important component in the educational landscape. It is increasingly used for high-stakes purposes, such as determining student promotion, teacher evaluations, and school accreditation. Standardized assessment is an assessment where there are controlled standards for administrating, scoring, and reporting results. They often include well-written items. However, because they are developed by for-profit corporations that seek to sell them across the nation, they focus on broad outcomes and may not match the objectives of a given school district.
- Grading is one dimension of teaching that many teachers dislike. This is due to several reasons, including the fact that grading is time consuming and places teachers in the role of a judge that is counter to the role of student advocate.
- Norm-referenced evaluation and grading compares the performance of an individual to the performance of a group. Criterion-referenced evaluation and grading compares the performance of an individual to a standard or a set of criteria. In recent years, there has been a movement away from norm-referenced grading in favor of more criterion-referenced grading.
- Letter grading is still the most common form of grading. However, some places have moved away from the definition of grades as norm referenced in favor of a standards approach. Another common form of grading bases grades on percentages.
- The role of the teacher is defining the sources of data for gathering evidence, how to weight the evidence, keeping accurate records, and deciding how to summarize the data into a final grade. It can be a very time-consuming process, so it is important to try to develop a simple yet fair grading system.

LEARNING EXTENSIONS

1. There has been much debate concerning the role of standardized testing in education. Do some additional research and identify a list advantages and disadvantages of standardized assessment.

2. Design an assessment plan for a unit in your subject area. Identify at least five objectives and state the assessment technique you will use and how you will specifically implement it.
3. Construct a sample test that you might use for assessing student learning in your subject area. Construct at least two essay items, several completion items, a matching item, at least five multiple-choice items, and at least five true-or-false items.
4. Develop a sample rubric that you could use to evaluate a student performance for an objective in your content area.
5. Define some authentic, natural assessment tasks that you could use in your classroom.
6. Identify your philosophy of teaching and learning and how it will influence how you grade students. Will you use norm-referenced or criterion-referenced grading? How will your grading system work?

REFERENCES

Arter, J., & McTighe, J. (2001). *Scoring rubrics in the classroom.* Thousand Oaks, CA: Corwin Press.

Educational Testing Service. (1995). *Performance assessment: Different needs, different answers.* Princeton, NJ: Author.

Gerald, D. E., & Hussar, W. J. (1999). *Projections of educational statistics to 2009.* Washington, DC: U.S. Department of Education, Office of Educational Research and Improvement, National Center for Educational Statistics.

Guskey, T. R., & Bailey, J. M. (2001). *Developing grading and reporting systems for student learning.* Thousand Oaks, CA: Corwin Press.

Hatlie, J., Jaeger, R. M., & Bond, L. (1999). Persistent methodological questions in educational testing. In A. Iran-Nejad & P. D. Pearson (Eds.) *Review of Research in Education.* Vol 24. Washington, DC: American Educational Research Association.

McMillan, J. (2001). *Essential assessment concepts for teachers and administrators.* Thousand Oaks, CA: Corwin Press.

Porter, C., & Cleland, J. (1995). *The portfolio as a learning strategy.* Portsmouth, NH: Boynton/Cook.

Rudner, L., & Schafer, W. (2002). *What teachers need to know about assessment.* Washington, DC: National Education Association.

Smith, J., Smith, L., & De Lisi, R. (2001). *Natural classroom assessment.* Thousand Oaks, CA: Corwin Press.

Tanner, D. E. (2001). *Assessing academic achievement.* Needham Heights, MA: Allyn & Bacon.

Ward, A. W., & Murray-Ward, M. (1999). *Assessment in the classroom.* Belmont, CA: Wadsworth.

Wiggins, G. (1989). A true test: Toward more authentic and equitable measurement. *Phi Delta Kappan,* *70*(8), 703–713.

PART 4 *The Professional Context*

14 Legal Issues

15 Career-Long Professional Growth

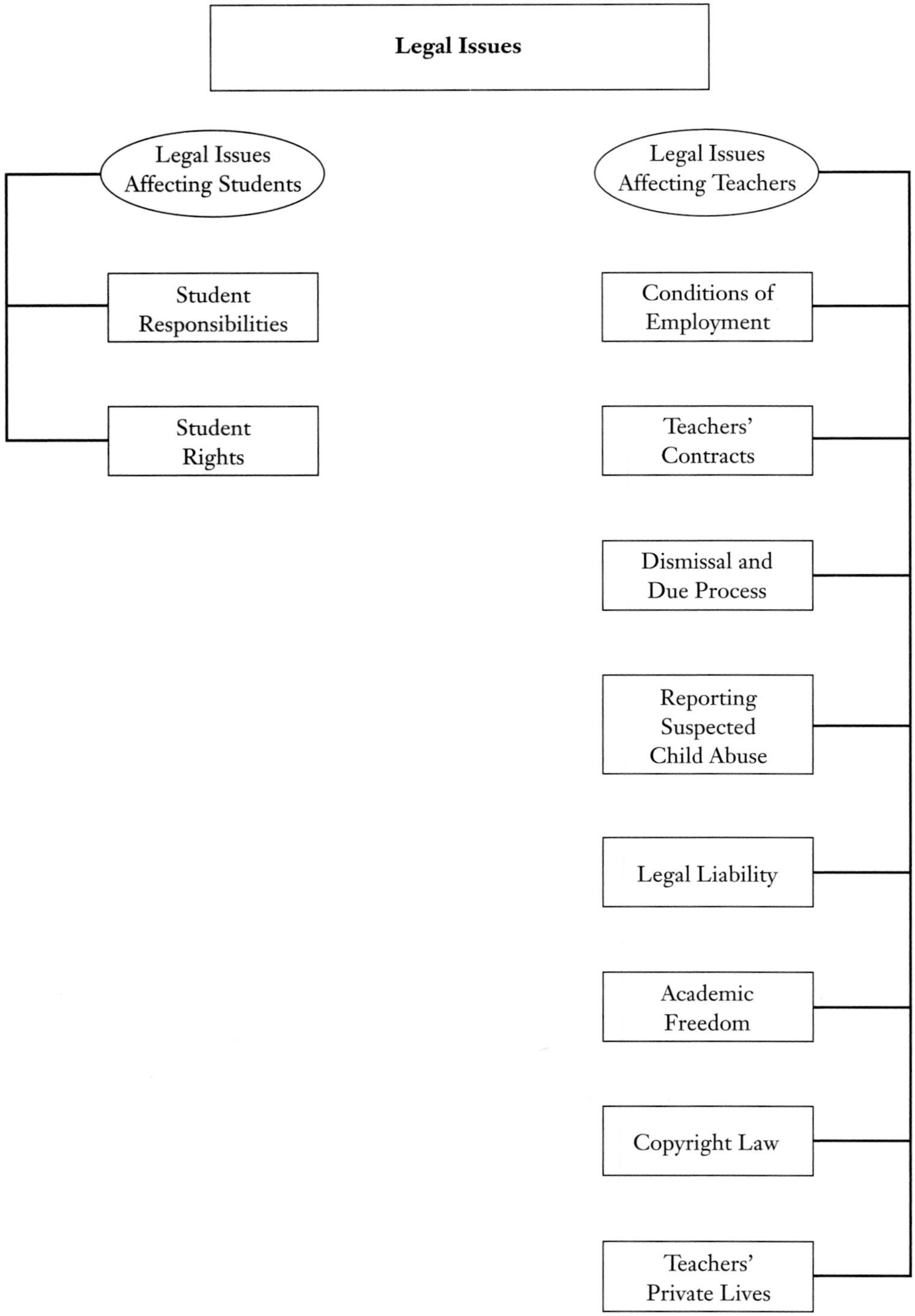
Legal Issues
Legal Issues Affecting Students
Student Responsibilities
Student Rights
Legal Issues Affecting Teachers
Conditions of Employment
Teachers' Contracts
Dismissal and Due Process
Reporting Suspected Child Abuse
Legal Liability
Academic Freedom
Copyright Law
Teachers' Private Lives

Figure 14.1
Graphic Organizer

CHAPTER **14**

Legal Issues

OBJECTIVES

This chapter will help you

- describe some of the rights and responsibilities of students and teachers;
- state conditions under which school officials may limit student rights;
- explain basic principles that guide court decisions regarding student and teacher rights;
- define limitations that can legally be placed on teachers' out-of-school behavior;
- define various forms of teacher negligence;
- explain teachers' responsibilities for reporting suspected cases of child abuse; and
- describe implications of copyright law for teachers.

Introduction

Just a couple of decades ago, few teachers worried about how legal issues and decisions would affect their work. However, times have changed. Legal questions permeate education. For example, in recent years, cases have been brought against schools and teachers focusing on such diverse topics as curriculum content, library books, required reading material, school assemblies, access to the Internet, censorship of student publications, condom distribution, student discipline, and even what material can be duplicated for classroom use.

The graphic organizer illustrates two major areas that this chapter will discuss. One important dimension is legal issues that affect students. Students have both responsibilities as well as rights. Their responsibilities include attendance, following school rules, not interfering with the right of the school to have a safe school environment, and behaving in socially appropriate ways. Their rights include freedom of speech, freedom of conscience, dress and appearance, freedom from unreasonable search and seizure, privacy of records, and the right to due process.

A second dimension of the chapter discusses legal issues impacting teachers. These include conditions of employment, types of contracts, dismissal and due process procedures, requirements regarding required reporting of suspected child abuse, legal liability that includes excessive use of force in discipline and teacher negligence, academic freedom, copyright law, and dimensions of teachers' private lives that can lead to legal problems.

As a teacher, you need to have a basic understanding of the pattern of court decisions regarding these issues. You also should have an understanding of other issues that can affect you personally, such as (a) legal principles associated with teacher contracts, (b) your authority in areas relating to the retention and promotion of students, and (c) constraints on your own personal behavior (both in school and out of school). As is true with legal issues in general, ignorance is no excuse. What you do not know can harm your career and your finances.

Legal issues are complex, and the purpose of this chapter is not to provide you with legal advice or with unequivocal answers to every situation. That is simply not possible. Each court case is decided on its own merits, and each case is unique.

However, legal precedents have been established, and by looking at these cases we can identify some basic principles that will provide you with guidance in this complex area.

Legal Issues Affecting Students

Few issues in secondary schools generate as much discussion as student rights and responsibilities. In recent years, the legal relationship between students and school authorities has been greatly altered. Since the 1980s, students in school have enjoyed legal rights that are basically the same as those extended to all adult citizens.

As a beginning point, you need to understand that legal issues are generally the result of a conflict between different sets of rights. For example, legal issues relating to student rights have arisen because of a conflict between the legal rights of students as citizens and the rights and responsibilities of a school to create a safe and orderly learning environment. At one time, the rights of school officials were given precedent, and students in school had few rights. With the change in the legal rights of students in schools, many school rules and practices were challenged. Those established by school officials must respect the rights of students and must be related to the establishment of a safe and orderly learning environment.

Contrary to what some believe, legal decisions have not just defined student rights. They have also defined student responsibilities. In fact, in recent years, because of incidents such as the violence at Columbine High School, in Littleton, Colorado, more attention has been directed to the area of student responsibilities. A few individuals have suggested that student rights need to be severely limited in order to prevent tragic occurrences such as these.

Student Responsibilities

School Attendance An educated and informed citizenry is essential to the health of a democratic society. Therefore, the state has a compelling interest in the education of all students. Students have a duty to participate in educational experiences. The courts have consistently upheld this principle. However, in recent years, there have been many cases regarding the meaning of the regulations regarding the education of students. These cases have emphasized the rights of the state to require an education for students. However, they have indicated that this does not necessarily mean that the only place this can occur is in a school.

There have been numerous challenges to compulsory attendance laws. In general, court decisions have reflected the view that the interest of the state is in promoting a quality education for each person, not in defining the place or the manner of the education. This has raised some legal questions concerning what constitutes a quality education and what is required in order to satisfy the state interest in an education for all citizens. Much of this discussion relates to an increased interest in home schooling.

Again, this legal issue is the result of a conflict between the compelling interest of the state in an education for all citizens and the rights of parents to direct the upbringing of their children. Because most parents lack the breadth and depth of knowledge required to prepare young people for the complex roles they will face as adults in a rapidly changing society, the courts have generally supported the rights of the state to insist that their students either attend a state-supported school or undertake an acceptable alternative.

What constitutes an acceptable alternative varies from state to state. In a typical situation, an acceptable alternative must be equivalent to what is provided in the public school curriculum. These alternatives might be either private schools or home schools. Some states require that a qualified individual teach students who enroll in acceptable alternatives to the regular public schools. In some places, this means that the person teaching the students must have a teaching credential. In other locations, other evidence of expertise is acceptable. Some school districts require that students not attending the public school be given examinations at regular intervals to make sure they are learning the required content.

A few challenges to compulsory attendance have been made on the grounds that school conditions place the students in physical or emotional danger. Court decisions relating to these challenges have followed a consistent pattern. The judges have usually placed a heavy burden of proof on the parents to prove their contention that the school environment is unsafe (Valente, 1994).

Another challenge to compulsory attendance has been based on the claim that school attendance can have a negative impact on religious beliefs. Most challenges of this sort have not been successful. An interesting exception was a ruling made in response to a challenge brought by Amish parents in Wisconsin (*Wisconsin v. Yoder*, 1972). These parents refused to send their children to school beyond the eighth grade. They contended that the general emphasis in the secondary schools was contrary to the basic tenets of their religion and way of life. The U.S. Supreme Court ruled in their favor, holding that the Amish way of life constituted an acceptable alternative to formal secondary education. However, the court was careful to note that this did not set a precedent for other groups who wished to challenge compulsory attendance laws (Fischer, Schimmel, & Steelman, 2003).

Following Reasonable School Rules Because schools have the right to establish a safe and orderly educational environment, school officials have the right to establish reasonable school rules. Students have the responsibility to obey them and to submit to the authority of the teachers. For example, the California School Code states that every teacher in a public school has an obligation to hold each student accountable for conduct on the way to and from school, on the school grounds, and during breaks from classroom activities. Any certified employee is given the right to exercise reasonable control over a student in order to protect property, ensure the safety of others, or maintain conditions conducive to learning. Willful violation of teacher authority by students is grounds for suspension or expulsion (California Teachers Association, 1992).

The operative word is *reasonable*. Arbitrary rules and regulations that have nothing to do with the establishment of a safe school or a climate conducive to learning are not legally protected. If a school attempts to impose or enforce rules that fail to meet the "reasonableness" test, these rules are unlikely to survive a legal challenge.

Not Interfering with the Maintenance of a Safe School Environment School officials have an obligation to protect the health and safety of those who are present in the school and to maintain a school environment that is conducive to learning. Students have a responsibility to refrain from actions such as bringing weapons or controlled substances that might endanger the safety and health of others. Most states provide for immediate suspension of individuals who violate this responsibility. The increased fear of violence has led many schools to establish a zero-tolerance policy. This means that students do not get a second chance and that any violations result in immediate suspension.

Similarly, threatening violence or harm to another person is grounds for suspension of expulsion. Thus, a student who threatens you or another student with violence can be immediately suspended. In some instances, this has been followed to the letter of the law, and young children pretending to shoot each other with paper guns have been suspended. One of your obligations is to ensure that students understand their responsibilities and realize the serious consequences of such behavior.

Socially Appropriate Behavior When political and social leaders suggest that one of your jobs as a teacher is to inform young people about the boundaries of socially acceptable behavior, they assume there are restrictions that can be placed on student behavior. Further, this perspective implies that behavior that might be appropriate in other settings may not be acceptable in school. Several court cases have endorsed this view.

In one case, a high school student who was nominating a friend for a school office gave a speech that was filled with sexual metaphor and innuendo. Although the student did not use explicit language, he was suspended from school for 3 days. The student sued, claiming that his First Amendment rights of freedom of speech had been violated. The court upheld the school district, ruling that the rights of the student were outweighed by society's interest in educating young people within the bounds of socially appropriate behavior (Zirkel & Richardson, 1988). The finding in this case suggests that students must accept that they have responsibilities to behave in ways that permit schools to maintain a productive learning environment.

To summarize, your students do have certain responsibilities that you can require them to fulfill. However, you and others in your school must recognize that you face certain constraints in establishing expectations related to student behavior. For example, courts will not be sympathetic if your school adopts and attempts to enforce capricious regulations. Rules and expectations must be reasonable and consistent with defensible educational purposes.

Student Rights

Legal issues relating to the rights of students focus on the concept that students are citizens who enjoy the legal status guaranteed to all citizens by the U.S. Constitution. Court cases have focused on two key areas. First, there has been litigation concerned with the limits of the power of school authorities to interfere with student actions. Second, cases have considered the appropriateness or fairness of procedures used by school authorities when making decisions affecting students.

In reviewing information related to students' rights cases, you need to keep in mind that each case is considered by the courts on its own merits as well as in light of laws and decisions in previous, related cases. Laws and precedents change over time. Therefore, you cannot always presume that when courts consider new cases, they will follow the same course of action they have tended to take in the past. For reasons we cannot predict today, future courts may take quite different views of some issues related to students' rights.

Freedom of Speech and Expression One of the fundamental rights guaranteed by the Constitution is *freedom of expression*. This issue has caused school officials considerable concern. In the past, school officials were quite free to limit students' freedom of expression. School officials took the position that these restrictions were necessary in order to preserve an orderly school environment. This situation began to change in the late 1960s and early 1970s. One of the landmark freedom of expression cases was the *Tinker v. Des Moines Independent Community School District* (1969).

This important case, while focusing on the issue of freedom of expression, had a wider impact on schools when the Supreme Court ruling stated that neither students nor teachers give up their constitutional rights at the classroom door. The *Tinker* case evolved out of a situation that developed in Des Moines, Iowa, during the Vietnam War.

Children from several families who opposed the war decided to express their opposition by wearing black armbands to school. When school officials learned of this protest, they quickly adopted a school policy forbidding the wearing of these armbands. According to this policy, students who refused to remove the armbands would be suspended.

Three students refused to remove the armbands and were suspended. Suit was brought on behalf of the students, and the case ultimately worked its way to the Supreme Court. In its decision in the *Tinker* case, the Court viewed the wearing of the armbands as symbolic free speech. The Court, arguing that students do have constitutional rights in classrooms and that the First Amendment of the Constitution protects free speech and expression, ruled that the wearing of the armbands was protected and that the school authorities had erred in passing the regulation and enforcing it. This decision means that if you or the school officials wish to limit student freedom of expression, you have to demonstrate that the exercise of unrestricted freedom of speech would result in material and substantial disruption of the educational environment. For example, if it could be demonstrated that the exercise of this right would result in disruptions such as fights among students, then the courts might be sympathetic to a regulation limiting certain kinds of student expression.

Another freedom-of-expression issue that has prompted much interest over the years concerns the authority of school officials to limit what is printed in official school publications as well as in "underground" or unauthorized student publications. In many places, school officials have censored student publications and forbidden unauthorized publications. Some of these actions have been challenged.

In general, the courts have determined that school administrators' power to regulate a publication depends on whether the publication in question is sponsored by the school in some official way. Courts have tended to support more administrative control over the content of student publications produced as a part of a regular journalism course than publications that are not officially connected with the school. An important precedent in this area was established in the case of *Hazelwood School District v. Kuhlmeier* (1988).

The *Hazelwood* case focused on the actions of a school principal who deleted two articles from the school newspaper. One article referred indirectly to some pregnant students. Though names in the article had been changed to mask the true identities of these students, the principal felt that many readers might be able to identify them. In a second article, a student had written a complaint about her father, but the father had not been given an option to respond. The principal felt the treatment was unbalanced and unfair. In its decision, the court upheld the right of the principal, noting that educators have the authority to exercise considerable control over school-sponsored publications.

The courts have generally supported educators' decisions to reject articles that are poorly written, insufficiently researched, clearly biased, vulgar, or otherwise unacceptable for immature audiences. They may prohibit articles that advocate unacceptable (and often illegal) social practices such as alcohol or drug abuse and irresponsible sexual activities. Control can be exercised when actions by school leaders are undertaken to ensure some consistency in the ongoing instructional responsibilities of the school.

Authority to limit the content of school publications does not extend to the censorship of controversial issues or views that may be unpopular with administrators, teachers, or parents. If you and others in your school want to place limitations on what students can print in school publications, you must be able to demonstrate that your actions are for valid educational reasons, not for capricious, convenient, or punitive ones.

Underground and other publications that are produced without formal school recognition and support generally lie outside the control of school officials. These publications ordinarily cannot be regulated unless their contents can be challenged on grounds that would invite legal actions against any type of a publication. Although you and your colleagues may find some of these articles to be highly irritating, you generally lack legal grounds for barring publications from the school or for punishing the writers. However, school leaders generally have legal authority to place some limits on how and when these publications can be distributed, but the regulations cannot be so restrictive that they prohibit distribution.

In considering freedom-of-expression and freedom-of-speech cases, most court decisions have supported the idea that students enjoy constitutional freedom-of-speech rights. They cannot be limited because they discuss controversial issues or because they criticize school officials. They can be limited only when there is a legitimate educational concern that they disrupt the orderly operation of the school.

Students' Freedom of Conscience Legal questions focusing on the issues of separation of church and state and the place of religious expression in schools have generated much controversy. Two basic First Amendment principles usually clash in these disputes. One principle guarantees the right to free exercise of religion; the other bars government involvement in establishing or supporting religion.

Courts have consistently affirmed the idea that freedom of religion cannot be abridged unless the state and its officials demonstrate an overwhelmingly compelling need to do so. This means that school officials cannot arbitrarily require all students to do something that may interfere with their fundamental religious principles. For example, court cases have upheld the right of individual students to refrain from participating in the daily Pledge of Allegiance on the grounds that their participation conflicts with religious beliefs. In Pledge of Allegiance cases, the courts have taken the position that a refusal to recite the pledge does not threaten any major public interest; hence, the state has no compelling interest in requiring all students to participate.

However, suppose you encountered a situation in which a religious group claimed that teaching students to read was contrary to fundamental religious beliefs. It is doubtful the courts would excuse these students from reading instruction because the state does have a compelling interest in the literacy of all citizens.

Courts have ruled that your students' religious views may excuse them from certain parts of the school program. For example, courts have upheld the rights of some students from activities such as dancing and viewing films. In recent years, there have been numerous challenges from parents to ban the teaching of such literary works as *The Wizard of Oz* and *Macbeth* on the grounds that they promote witchcraft. For the most part, the courts have upheld school officials' contentions that familiarity with literature such as this is essential to the complete educational development of students, something in which the state has a compelling interest.

The issue of prayer and meditation as forms of religious expression continues to draw considerable attention. To understand this complex issue, you must remember that the First Amendment states that Congress shall make no law respecting the establishment of religion or prohibiting the free exercise of religion. Therefore, the schools, as government agencies, cannot promote a particular religious belief or impose a particular religious practice on students. However, neither can the school prohibit a student from exercising his or her own religious freedom.

Trying to sort out the boundaries between these ideas continues to be a challenge. For the most part, individuals have accepted that practices such as a required morning prayer over the loudspeaker or the posting of certain religious documents seem to further a particular religious belief and are therefore not allowed. However, there is still some ambiguity regarding prayers at events such as school graduations.

Student Dress and Appearance The topic of student dress and appearance has resurfaced in recent years as some school districts have considered requiring all students to wear a uniform. Proponents claim that uniforms improve the educational environment and result in a decrease in discipline problems. However, many students and parents have not found this idea appealing and have challenged the authority of the school to place restrictions on what students can wear to school.

While the issue of dress and appearance is still one where there is some ambiguity, the courts have generally recognized that schools do enjoy some rights to govern what students wear to school. In one case, the courts ruled that requiring uniforms is permissible if it meets certain requirements, such as that the dress code furthers a substantial government interest, such as reducing discipline problems, and is unrelated to the suppression of student expression (Fischer et al., 2003). Some court rulings have indicated that the school does have a responsibility to exclude persons who are unsanitary or obscenely or scantily clad (Fischer et al., 2003). As a general rule, dress and appearance standards established by schools must bear a reasonable relationship to the educational process or to the health and safety of students.

Hairstyle and grooming standards have also been the subject of several court cases. Some courts have ruled that hairstyle is a more fundamental right than clothing style. The argument has been that a restriction on hairstyle represents an unacceptably intrusive invasion of individual privacy. Where hairstyle regulations have been upheld, it is usually on the grounds of student health and safety or to prevent a clear and documented interference with the educational process.

Search and Seizure Concerns about drugs and weapons on school campuses have prompted much interest in the issue of the right of school officials to conduct searches and seize property. For example, school officials may have a desire to search school lockers, automobiles parked in the student parking lot, student possessions such as backpacks and purses, and even students themselves. The need to search for weapons, drugs, and other illegal items that can threaten the safety of the general student population has had to be weighed against Fourth Amendment guarantees against unreasonable search and seizure.

In general, the court decisions relating to this issue require school officials to apply four basic tests as they attempt to decide whether a proposed search violates Fourth Amendment rights. The first test relates to the *nature of the material or object* they are seeking. The greater the potential danger posed by the material or the object to the safety of the students, the stronger the justification for the search. For example, a weapon or a bomb poses a tremendous threat to the safety of the students, and an intrusive search would usually be justified. However, a search for a stolen book does not pose a danger, and an intrusive search would probably not be justified.

The second test to be applied in determining the legality of a search relates to the *quality of the information* that has led to the consideration of a search. This means that the reliability and validity of the information must be evaluated. If several reliable people provide similar information, a stronger case can be made for the search than if it is based on an anonymous phone tip. If the nature of a proposed search is to be potentially invasive (i.e., that it involves the search of a person or his or her private possessions), then the search must meet the test of *probable cause*. This requires a very high standard of evidence as a justification for a search and is equivalent to what courts require before issuing a search warrant.

The third test concerns *the nature of the place to be searched*. If the place to be searched (e.g., a school locker, a private possession, or a car) is a place where an individual has a high expectation of privacy, school officials must have very reliable information in order to justify the search. This would apply to searches of a person, a person's clothing, a purse, a wallet, or a private possession. However, there is much less of an expectation of privacy in areas such as a school locker or a school desk, where there is not much expectation of privacy. Therefore, a search of these places could be justified on less supporting evidence.

The case of *New Jersey v. T.L.O.* (1985) established some important search-and-seizure precedents. In this case, a vice principal questioned a girl suspected of smoking, a violation of school rules. At the vice principal's request, the girl opened her purse. It contained not only cigarettes but also drug paraphernalia. This led to a further search of the purse. In court, the girl challenged the search on the grounds that it violated her Fourth Amendment rights of freedom from unreasonable searches. The case ended up in the Supreme Court.

In its decision, the Court stated that the initial suspicion that the girl had been smoking and might have cigarettes in her possession was sufficient reason to ask her to open her purse. Once this was done, the physical evidence of drug paraphernalia provided sufficient justification for the extensive search of her purse.

The ruling in *New Jersey v. T.L.O.* seems to give school officials considerable latitude in search and seizure. However, there are some important limits. For example, if you want to conduct a search, you must have *reasonable suspicion* that the student has violated a specific rule. Reasonable suspicion refers to the presence of evidence that is sufficiently compelling to convince a prudent and cautious individual that a violation has occurred. General "fishing expeditions" are not permitted, and when a search is undertaken in the absence of reasonable suspicion, it is likely to be viewed by the courts as an illegal invasion of students' privacy rights.

To summarize, case law relating to search and seizure does not provide you with absolutely clear guidelines. In general, we advise that you not attempt searches on your own initiative. Responsibility for school searches should be left in the hands of school administrators who are in a better position to check the legality of search-and-seizure procedures.

Due Process Discussion of student rights and responsibilities inevitably leads to the issue of *due process*. Due process is a principle requiring that certain procedures and safeguards be followed when students are denied a right, such as school attendance.

Until after World War II, school attendance was widely regarded as a privilege to be enjoyed by those who were willing to abide by the rules established by the school authorities. Because schooling was not viewed as a fundamental right protected by the Constitution, students had no legal recourse if they were suspended or expelled from school for a rule violation. In this earlier era, absence of schooling or possession of a high school diploma was not viewed as imposing any serious hardships on an individual.

However, after World War II, it became evident that the possession of a high school diploma was important for the future economic well-being of individuals. Thus, to deprive an individual of an education has serious consequences. This view, coupled with the fact that the public schools were tax-supported institutions, soon led to the idea that education was more than a privilege extended to those who were willing to conform to the rules of the school officials. It began to be viewed as a substantial right. This right merited due process protection.

The legal precedent extending due process protection to public schools was established in the *Goss v. Lopez* case (1975). In its decision, the court noted that while the Constitution does not require states to establish public schools, once they are established, the right to attend them is a constitutionally protected property right. Therefore, efforts to deny students access to schooling through suspension or expulsion must be accompanied by due process procedures in conformity with the Fourteenth Amendment to the Constitution.

There are two basic components to due process. The first, or the substantive component, consists of a set of principles on which the process is based. The second, or the procedural component, delineates procedures that must be followed to ensure that due process rights have not been violated.

The following are the substantive components of due process:

- Individuals are not to be disciplined on the basis of unwritten rules.
- Rules must not be unduly vague.
- Individuals charged with rules violations are entitled to a hearing before an impartial body.
- Identities of witnesses are to be revealed.
- Decisions must be supported by substantial evidence.
- A public or a private hearing can be requested by the individual accused of the rule violation.

The following steps are consistent with the guidelines to be followed by schools to ensure compliance with the procedural steps component of due process:

- Rules governing students' behavior are to be distributed in writing to students and their parents/guardians at the beginning of the school year.
- Whenever a student is accused of a serious violation of rules that can lead to the loss of a right, charges must be provided in writing to the student and to his or her parent or guardian.
- Written notice of the hearing to consider the alleged violation must be given, with sufficient time for the student and his or her representatives to prepare a defense. However, the hearing must be scheduled within a timely manner (usually within 2 weeks).
- A fair hearing must include the following: right of the accused to be represented by legal counsel, right of the accused to present a defense and to introduce evidence,

right of the accused to face his or her accusers, and right of the accused to cross-examine witnesses.

- The decision of the hearing board must be based on evidence presented and must be rendered within a reasonable time.
- The accused must be informed of his or her right to appeal the decision.

The need to comply with due process requirements means that you and others in your school need to exercise great care in initiating actions against a student who is suspected of having violated important rules or regulations that might result in suspension or expulsion.

Suspension is defined as a temporary separation from school. A suspension of less than 10 days is considered a short-term suspension. Short-term suspensions require only minimal due process procedures. In these situations, a student must receive (a) at least an oral (preferably a written) notice of the charges that led to the suspension, (b) an explanation of the evidence supporting the action, and (c) the opportunity to provide his or her version of facts relevant to the situation. When short-term suspension is used, it is not required that legal counsel be present to represent the student.

A suspension exceeding 10 days in length is considered long-term suspension. Long-term suspension has the potential to seriously interfere with the education of students, so school officials are obligated to follow all the due process guidelines.

Expulsion is a more serious action. It permanently separates a student from school. In situations where expulsion is likely to be the end result of a disciplinary action against a student, very strict due process procedures must be followed. Usually, you and the administrators at your school do not, by yourselves, have the authority to make an expulsion decision. This tends to be the prerogative of the highest governing officials of the school district. The policy of referring this kind of decision to higher authorities helps ensure that procedures that adequately protect and represent the student's interests are followed. If they are not, the student and his or her legal representatives may initiate potentially expensive legal actions against the school district and the school board.

There are important implications of due process for you as a teacher. First, you need to recognize that your students have been legally defined as citizens whose rights are protected by the Constitution. This means that you must proceed in a fair and appropriate manner in making and enforcing school rules. However, the need to observe due process guidelines by no means diminishes your authority to control students in the classroom. The courts have affirmed your rights, as a teacher, to establish and maintain a safe and orderly educational environment.

Family Rights and Privacy Since the 1960s, concerned citizens have raised questions about potential misuses of school records. Much of the discussion has focused on long-term damage to students that might occur as a result of their being stigmatized by comments made about them in school records.

In response to these, Congress passed what was originally know as the Buckley Amendment in 1975 and what later became known as the Family Rights and Privacy Act (1996). This legislation requires schools to protect students' privacy rights by denying access to their files by anyone except individuals immediately concerned with their education. Files can be opened to others only with the consent of students' parents or, in the case of students who are age 18 or older, the students themselves. The law also gives parents free access to school files and records pertaining to their children. Students age 18 or older have similar rights to see this information. After parents or individuals over age 18 have viewed the records, they may request to amend any records they believe to be (a) inaccurate, (b) misleading, or (c) a violation of privacy rights.

The access to student records by parents and students over age 18 authorized by the Family Rights and Privacy Act means that you need to exercise care when placing information in student files. Your comments should be descriptive rather than judgmental. It is particularly important to avoid malicious or other kinds of general statements that might be considered a negative summary judgment about a student. Such comments may subject you to legal action (Connors, 1991).

You also need to be careful about the kinds of comments you make to others about individual students. A person who knowingly spreads false information that hurts another's reputation (in this case a student) has committed slander, a punishable offense.

Emerging Issues Several current issues are likely to result in legal action in the future. One of the most volatile issues relates to high-stakes testing. High-stakes testing is the practice of using the results of standardized tests to make important decisions, such as promotion and graduation. There is evidence that students from low-socioeconomic communities do less well on these tests. This would seem to set the stage for challenges to the validity of the tests. Challenges would appear likely when there is considerable evidence a given student has performed well on all other indicators of achievement but is denied a diploma based on the outcomes of one test. Other challenges are sure to arise on behalf of students with disabilities and those with limited English proficiency.

Another issue that is generating considerable attention is the issue of computers and free speech. This relates to the issue of censorship. In the past, the courts have ruled that schools cannot remove controversial books or deny students access to ideas and content with which they disagree. However, they have been given the right to remove material that is educationally unsuitable or vulgar (Fischer et al., 2003). Computer use opens up a whole new set of circumstances that result in a conflict between these rulings. Some individuals are concerned that restricting computer use and access in order to protect students from pornographic and commercial material may violate student rights by arbitrarily denying them access to important ideas and material. No doubt that there will some interesting cases relating to computer use and censorship.

MORE FROM THE WEB

Trends and Issues: School Law

This site has excellent articles on a variety of topics relating to school law. It is a good source for keeping current on current issues in education.

Website: http://eric.uoregon.edu/issues/law/index.html

Legal Issues Affecting Teachers

Legal issues concerned with schools and schooling do not pertain only to students. There are also important legal dimensions related to your rights and responsibilities as a teacher. These include such areas as conditions of employment, contracts, freedom of expression, academic freedom, drug and alcohol abuse, copyright, and professional performance of duties.

Conditions of Employment

Generally, a person must possess a valid *teaching certificate* as a condition of employment. Some states prohibit school districts from paying the salaries of teachers who do not hold a valid certificate. Several court cases have declared that people who sign contracts and perform teaching duties without possessing valid certificates are "volunteers" who have donated their services to the district.

Most school districts will require you to register your certificate with the personnel office of the school district prior to the issuance of a paycheck. Some states prohibit payment by a school district until proof of certification is provided. It is important when you apply for a teaching position to accurately represent your certification status. If you suggest that you have a certificate when, in fact, you do not, this misrepresentation may eliminate your future prospects not only in the district where you are seeking employment but elsewhere in the state as well. You need to make sure you have clarity of your certification status before you leave your teacher preparation program.

Certification is a state responsibility. Each state has its own requirements for people who wish to teach in its schools. Because teacher certification requirements vary

CRITICAL INCIDENT

Completing the Employment Application

Rodney Harte started a business after he graduated from college. The business prospered, but his day-to-day routines did not satisfy his need to be involved in service-oriented work. Since Rodney always enjoyed being around young people and he had several friends who were teachers, he decided to pursue a teaching credential.

Rodney proved to be an excellent student and earned high evaluations in his student teaching. As a result of his strong performance, he received excellent recommendations and submitted his application to the state for a teaching credential.

When he was completing the application for the credential, he noted a question asking for information about any previous legal problems. He had been caught shoplifting an item in a shopping center many years earlier when he was an undergraduate. He carefully explained the circumstances on the application form and submitted it to the state department of education. After some additional correspondence with the state, he was granted a teaching credential.

In his job search, he was interviewed for a teaching position that he felt was ideal. It was in a good school district, it was close to where he lived, and it offered him an opportunity to assist in the athletic program. On the district application form was a question asking if he had ever been convicted of a felony. He reflected on the matter and concluded that since he had been cleared by the state for a credential, there was no need to reopen the issue and answered "no."

He was hired in the school district and began teaching. At the end of September, he received a note requesting him to report immediately to the director of human resources. When he arrived, he was informed that his employment was being terminated because the school district had learned of his earlier conviction and that he had entered false information on his application.

■ ■ ■

What do you think Rodney should do? Do you think that since this was cleared by the state and he had been granted a teaching credential, the district had a right to pursue it? Do you think he has any legal recourse? What is the legal principle that should be learned?

from state to state, obtaining a teaching certificate in one state may not mean that you have met the certification requirements in another state. If you are interested in teaching in another state, you should contact the Teacher Certification Office in the State Department of Education in the state where you wish to seek employment. This office will be able to provide you with information about the procedures you will need to follow to qualify for a teaching certificate.

Teacher certificates are not guaranteed for the life of the holder. They may be terminated for a variety of reasons, and states can establish conditions that must be met to renew them or keep them in force. In many states, certificates have fixed expiration dates. For example, you may find regulations that require you to meet renewal conditions, such as taking additional college courses or participating in other professional development opportunities. Certificates may be revoked for conviction of a felony, public displays of immorality, incompetence, or extreme examples of socially unacceptable behavior.

Teachers' Contracts

Teachers' contracts are important documents. They contain information related to such issues as conditions of employment, salary, sick leave provisions, insurance coverage, and grievance procedures. For a contract to be valid, it must include four basic features:

- Language that reflects a meeting of the minds of the signatories
- Signatories who are competent parties
- Obligations from each of the signatories to the others
- Definite and clear terms delineating what is to be done and by whom (Fischer et al., 2003)

The phrase "*meeting of minds*" means that all parties must agree on the contents of the contract. One party must offer the contract, and the other must accept it. In the case of teaching contracts, the formal process of offer and acceptance is not over until the contract is approved by action of the school board.

For a contract to be between competent parties, the individual signatories must be of legal age and be legally and intellectually able to engage in and conclude needed negotiations. As a prospective teacher, you must have a teaching certificate (or be eligible to receive one before you begin work) to be competent to enter into a contract.

Teaching contracts are legal documents. When a contract is breached or broken, the other party is entitled to a legal remedy that will compensate for the injury the breaching party causes. For example, a school district may sue to collect monetary damages if you sign and break a contract. Likewise, you could seek damages from a school district if it failed to honor a legal contract. In general, a teacher is entitled to damages that equal the salary described in the contract minus any money the teacher earned in another teaching position. Individuals may also collect additional damages related to the costs of seeking another teaching position (Fischer et al., 2003). However, a person must look for other teaching positions. If the school board can demonstrate that other teaching jobs are available, the amount of damages can be reduced.

In addition, some states have regulations regarding the breach of contract by teachers. These regulations call for the suspension or revocation of the teaching credential of a teacher who breaches a contract. Therefore, the signing of a contract to teach is a serious issue that should be done only with careful consideration. If you have a compelling reason to be released from a signed contract, the appropriate procedure is to make a formal request to the school district requesting a release from the contract. There is no legal obligation on the part of the school district to grant your request. However, if it is based on a solid reason, such requests are often honored. As a practical matter, school districts do not want people who would really prefer to be somewhere else working for them.

There are several types of teachers' contracts. Typically, new teachers are offered a term contract (a contract that offers employment for a specific period of time) usually for one school year. Near the conclusion of the term of the contract, a decision is made about renewing the contract. The term contract allows either party (the school district or the teacher) to negotiate new terms of employment or to terminate the relationship at the end of the contract period. No reason for terminating the contract needs to be provided. In some places, term contracts are issued to all teachers. In others, regulations require that term contracts be issued only to new teachers. Usually after they have taught for a number of years, teachers must be offered a different type of a contract.

A second type of a contract is the continuing contract. Unlike term contracts, basic provisions of the contract do not have to be renewed after a specified term (ordinarily, there are allowances for adjustments of salaries). This type of contract is renewed automatically at the end of each year. Before a district can make a decision not to renew a continuing contract, it must provide specific and legal reasons for the termination, and it must follow strict procedural guidelines. This means that teachers holding continuing contracts enjoy more employment security than teachers who hold term contracts.

A third type of a contract is the tenure contract. Like a continuing contract, a tenure contract remains in force from year to year. Usually, teachers holding tenure contracts can be dismissed only when they have been found guilty of violating state statues relating to tenure. The school board has the burden of proving that there is legal cause for dismissing a tenured teacher.

Tenure contracts are generally not awarded to teachers until they have worked successfully in a given district for several years. A typical probationary period is 3 years. During their initial years of service, teachers are issued term contracts. Laws that establish tenure contracts were passed, in part, to protect teachers from political interference on the part of parents and others who might try to influence the content of what is taught in the classroom. Tenure laws also represent attempts to provide more stability to the group of teachers working in a particular school by offering them employment security.

Some critics have attacked tenure contracts because they are perceived as guaranteeing lifetime employment for teachers, therefore protecting incompetent teachers from dismissal. This is a misconception. Tenure does not guarantee lifetime employment. What it does guarantee is that due process procedures will be followed in any proceedings that might lead to a dismissal and that dismissal will occur only when certain conditions have been met. Some reasons for the dismissal of tenured teachers include (a) evidence of gross incompetence, (b) physical or mental incapacity, (c) neglect of duty, (d) immorality, (e) unprofessional conduct, and (f) conviction of a crime.

In recent years, contracts often followed a standard form. In many places, what is included in the contract is dictated by the state or agreed on by the school district and the local teacher association. Therefore, you do not need to be too concerned about the type of contract or what is included in the contract. However, you should carefully read the contract to make sure you understand your responsibilities and obligations.

Dismissal and Due Process

There is no general answer to the question of whether you, as a teacher, always have the right to challenge nonrenewal of your contract or actions undertaken to dismiss you from your teaching position. Legal discussions of this matter have focused on two basic rights: liberty rights and property rights. Liberty rights free individuals from having personal restraints imposed on them. These rights give them, among other things, opportunities to engage in the common occupations of life (*Meyer v. Nebraska*, 1923). Some court decisions relating to this issue have established that school districts cannot use unconstitutional reasons to deny teachers employment. As a result, you cannot be dismissed because of such things as age, gender, religious beliefs, or association with groups such as unions or clubs.

Property rights, among other things, give individuals rights to enjoy the benefits associated with employment. Courts have wrestled with the question of whether teaching, as defined in a teacher's contractual agreement with a school district, is a property right. In general, the answer depends on the type of contract a teacher holds and the specific language it contains. Sometimes the issue becomes murky. For example, term contracts ordinarily terminate a teacher's employment on a given date. On the surface, it appears that the teacher has no property rights after the termination date of the contract. However, in places where it has been customary for districts to almost automatically reissue new term contracts to teachers, teachers may enjoy some property rights to employment even beyond the strict terminology in their contracts. The courts tend to weigh questions about such matters in terms of the specifics of the particular case.

In circumstances where there is agreement that the teachers have either liberty rights or property rights that merit legal protection, actions undertaken by school districts to interfere with these rights (typically, actions taken to dismiss teachers) must follow strict due process guidelines. If you were in such a situation, you would have to be given a notice of charges against you, provided with an opportunity to state your position in a hearing, given a chance to respond to charges made against you, and allowed to be represented by legal counsel. Some states with stricter due process procedures would also require the district to provide you with an opportunity to remediate any deficient skills before initiating a formal dismissal proceeding.

Reporting Suspected Child Abuse

There continues to be considerable concern about child abuse. As a result, all 50 states now have legislation requiring people in certain positions to report suspected cases of child abuse. You, as an educator, are included among the group of people with special legal obligations to report suspected abuse.

No state requires a teacher to know beyond a reasonable doubt that a child is being abused before reporting suspicions to authorities. All you need is reasonable suspicion of abuse (Monks & Proulx, 1986).

Each state has a set of specific procedures that are followed when reporting suspected cases of child abuse. Some states have established a 24-hour telephone hot line to make it easier for suspected cases to be reported. In most cases, there is a requirement that an oral report be followed by a written report within a few days (often about 3 days). Many school districts provide teachers with forms they can use in preparing reports of suspected child abuse.

All states provide teachers with some immunity from lawsuits for reporting suspected child abuse. This offers protection to individuals who may otherwise hesitate to file a report for fear of reprisal. Immunity from lawsuits is not unlimited. Immunity is guaranteed only when reports are filed in good faith. For example, if you are found to have filed a report maliciously for the purpose of "getting even" with the parents, you may find yourself facing a lawsuit.

Many states have established penalties to be levied against required reporters of suspected abuse who fail to do so. Penalties range from fines up to about $1,000 to jail terms of up to 1 year. These penalties and the long-term negative consequences of abuse on the development of a student make it imperative for you to learn how to recognize signs of potential abuse and to become familiar with the required reporting process.

Legal Liability

There are a number of grounds for lawsuits against teachers. One major category of liability lawsuits against teachers is tort liability. A tort is a civil wrong against another that results in either personal injury or property damage. There are many categories of torts, including negligence, invasion of privacy, assault, and defamation of character. The areas that draw the largest number of lawsuits against teachers are (a) excessive use of force in disciplining students and (b) negligence.

Excessive Use of Force Many court cases have focused on the issue of using physical punishment as a means of disciplining students. In the landmark case of *Ingraham v. Wright* (1977), the Supreme Court held that teachers could use reasonable but not excessive force in disciplining students. The justices further noted that corporal punishment did not constitute cruel and unusual punishment and therefore was not a violation of a student's constitutionally protected rights.

Some individuals mistakenly conclude that this makes the use of corporal punishment legal. This is not the case. Because of the great national concern for child abuse and the message that is conveyed by hitting students, numerous states and school districts have prohibited corporal punishment as a means of disciplining students. Even in those places where it is still allowed, teachers usually must follow strict guidelines before administering corporal punishment. For example, they may be required to have an administrator or some other designated person act as a witness. Even then, legal action is possible if the punishment worsens a student's preexisting health condition. This is the case even if the person administering the punishment was unaware of a preexisting health condition. In addition, allegations of excessive force by students by their legal representatives may result in criminal assault and battery charges. In such situations, juries often decide cases on the basis of whether the teacher acted as a prudent parent would have acted.

Corporal punishment or the use of force in disciplining students is a very controversial topic. In light of concerns about child abuse and the possibility of legal action against teachers who are judged as having used excessive force, we subscribe to the view that the risks associated with corporal punishment outweigh any potential benefits. It is a practice you should avoid.

Negligence Negligence is a failure to use reasonable care and/or take prudent actions to prevent harm from coming to someone. There are three basic types of negligence:

- Nonfeasance
- Misfeasance
- Malfeasance

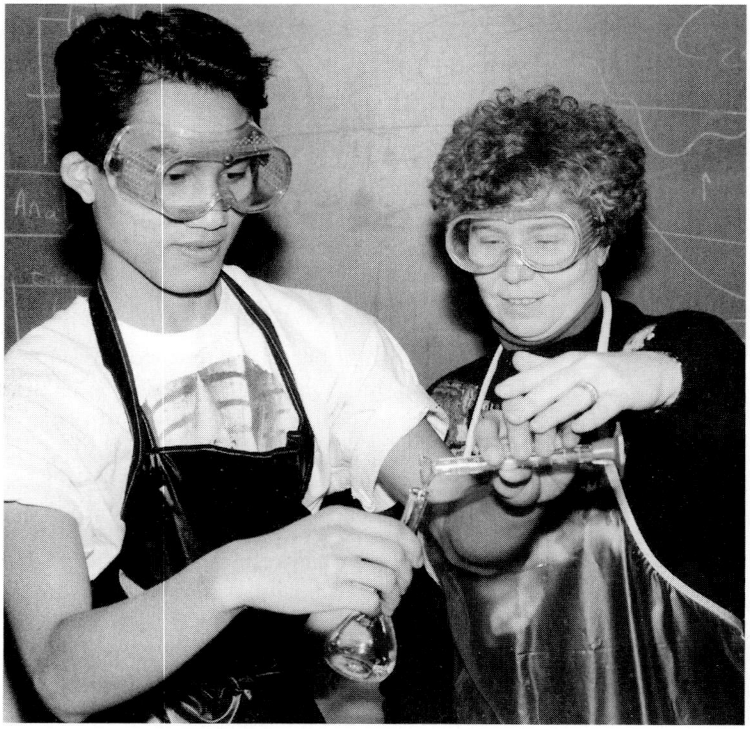

Teachers need to make sure that protective equipment is used in order to avoid charges of negligence.

Nonfeasance occurs when an individual fails to act when there is a responsibility to do so. Many lawsuits filed against teachers fall into this category. Ordinarily, they are the result of a teacher being absent from his or her place of assigned responsibility when an injury occurs to a student. For example, nonfeasance might occur when you are assigned the responsibility of supervising students. However, you are not present, and a student is injured. Another example might be when you slip out of your classroom while students are present and an injury occurs.

By no means does this imply that there are no circumstances that can justify your absence from your designated area of responsibility. There can be compelling reasons for being away from your designated area. For example, if an incident or an event outside the classroom poses potential harm to students, your absence from the room would be justified. However, you should avoid the practice of one secondary teacher we know who regularly leaves his classroom while students are present to visit with other teachers!

Misfeasance occurs when a person fails to act in a proper manner to prevent someone from harm. In misfeasance, a person acts but in an unwise or unprofessional manner. Misfeasance might occur in the classroom if proper precautions and instruction are not given when students work with potentially dangerous material or equipment or when they engage in potentially harmful activities. Thus, misfeasance might occur in a science classroom where students are allowed to handle a dangerous substance without proper instruction, in a shop class where students are using potentially dangerous equipment, or in a physical education class. For example, one teacher was charged with misfeasance when a student was injured during wrestling practice. The assertion was that the teacher had not given proper instruction about a particular wrestling hold. However, misfeasance could also occur in other classrooms where students are using paper cutters, electronic equipment, or tools.

An important step in avoiding many suits based on misfeasance is to make sure that clear and specific instructions are provided to students regarding such issues as the safe use of equipment and the proper uses of tools and chemicals. You must also provide proper supervision when students are working with potentially dangerous material or equipment.

Malfeasance occurs when a person deliberately acts in an improper manner and thereby causes harm to another. One example might be the situation where a teacher becomes angry with a student and gives him or her a shove that results in a fall or an injury.

Academic Freedom and Freedom of Expression

Academic freedom issues for teachers often involve conflicts between (a) teachers' rights to conduct their classes according to their best professional judgment and (b) school authorities' responsibilities to make sure the prescribed curriculum is taught. Court decisions in this area do not reflect a consistent pattern.

One principle that has often been supported by the courts is that school officials have the right to expect that the prescribed curriculum is taught and to require you to teach the subject matter content of the class you have been assigned. For example, if you have been assigned to teach mathematics, you cannot avoid teaching the content prescribed for this particular class and instead spend time promoting your personal political views on the grounds that you are protected by academic freedom. In other words, academic freedom does not give a teacher total freedom to teach and say whatever he or she pleases.

However, the courts usually have ruled that districts cannot require you to avoid dealing with controversial issues or prohibit you from teaching certain topics that are a legitimate component of the subject you teach. An example is the case of an American history teacher who used a simulation activity that evoked strong racial feelings. The school district informed the teacher that she was not to continue using the simulation. However, she continued to do so. The courts upheld the rights of the teacher on the grounds that it was a legitimate part of the curriculum (*Kingsville Independent School District v. Cooper*, 1980). In another case, the courts supported a teacher who challenged an administrative ruling that forbade her from using a particular book. In this decision, the court ruled that the book was appropriate for high school students, that the book contained nothing obscene, and that the ruling to ban its use had violated the teacher's academic freedom rights (*Parducci v. Rutland*, 1979).

In the *Parducci* case, the court noted that the right to teach, evaluate, and experiment with new ideas is fundamental to a democratic society. In other cases, however, courts have upheld the rights of the school boards to prohibit the use of certain books, even literary classics. Decisions in this area have tended to be responsive to specific characteristics of the work in question, the age and sophistication of the students, and the nature of the local community.

Freedom of expression refers to the rights of individuals to state their views on a subject without fear of reprisal. Court cases in this area that involve teachers have often arisen from situations in which school authorities have attempted to punish teachers for out-of-classroom speech.

A landmark freedom-of-expression case is *Pickering v. Board of Education of Township School District 205, Will County* (1968). Pickering, a teacher, wrote a letter to the editor of the local newspaper criticizing the way school funds were being allocated. Members of the school board were outraged. They claimed that Pickering had made untrue statements in the letter and thereby had damaged the reputations of school board members and leading school administrators. The board took action to dismiss Pickering. Pickering protested and challenged the dismissal action in court. The case ultimately made its way to the Supreme Court.

In arriving at its decision in the *Pickering* case, the Court considered two key issues. The first focused on whether a teacher can be dismissed for making critical comments about the school district and district policies in public. On this issue, the Court ruled that teachers have a right to speak out on school issues as a part of a general effort to provide for a more informed public. The second issue the Court considered had to do with whether a teacher could be dismissed for making false statements. In this particular case, the Court found that Pickering had made only one false statement in his letter. In the absence of any information that Pickering knowingly or deliberately made the false statement, the Court ruled in favor of Pickering. In other cases, dismissal actions taken against teachers have been upheld when evidence has been presented that they knowingly made false statements with a clear understanding that they were recklessly disregarding the truth.

However, these rulings by no means suggest that, as a teacher, you have a right to complain about everything. There are some activities of schools and school districts that may not be seen as matters of public concern by the courts. In addition, the style and manner of your complaints are important. Complaints cannot be made at a time or in a manner that interferes with the operation of the school or the responsibility of the administrators to perform their assigned responsibilities.

Copyright Law

Copyright law seeks to protect the works of authors and artists. Federal copyright law covers the use of material copied from books, journals, computer programs, and videotapes.

The doctrine of fair use is an exception to copyright law that has implications for you as a teacher. Fair use seeks to balance the rights of a copyright owner with the public's interest in having easy access to new ideas and information. The fair use doctrine makes it permissible for you to make single copies of book chapters, articles from journals, short stories or poems, or charts and graphs for your own scholarly research or as a part of your preparation for teaching lessons. Multiple copies (not to exceed one for each student in the class) may be made if guidelines related to (a) brevity, (b) spontaneity, and (c) cumulative effect are met (Committee on the Judiciary, 1976).

Brevity (as the term applies to fair use) for different kinds of material is defined as follows:

- A complete poem may be used if it is not more than 250 words and not more than two pages in length.
- An excerpt from a longer poem may be used consisting of no more than 250 words.
- A complete article or story may be used that is less than 2,500 words long.
- From a larger work, an excerpt may be used that is less than 1,000 words in length or that consists of no more than 10% of the length of the total work, whichever is less.
- One chart, diagram, picture, or cartoon per book or periodical may be used.

The spontaneity criterion refers to situations when your need to use the work is so close to the time it must be provided to students in your class that it would be unreasonable or impossible to request and receive permission. If this is the situation, then you would be allowed to use the material one time and then would be expected to seek permission for continued use.

Cumulative effect is defined as the following:

- The material is used for only one course.
- No more than one short poem, article, short story, or essay or two excerpts from works by the same author and no more than three excerpts from the same collective work or periodical volume may be used without permission.
- There are no more than nine instances of such multiple copying for one course during one term.

Unless these fair use guidelines can be met, you are obligated to secure permission from authors, artists, or other copyright holders before making and distributing copies. If you fail to do so, you may face legal action brought by copyright holders or their representatives.

It is also important to note that computer software programs are not covered by fair use doctrine. It is illegal to make copies of commercially produced programs and to use them on different computers in the classroom unless specific permission has been granted. Many software vendors will sell a site license to a school or business authorizing the purchaser to make and distribute a given number of copies of a specific program.

There are special copyright provisions that apply to videotaping for educational purposes. A copyrighted program may be videotaped and used for instructional purposes, provided that you use it within 10 days and keep the videotape for no more than 45 days. The only legal use that can be made of the videotape between the 10th and the 45th day is evaluating its content. If you wish to keep a given program for some time and to repeatedly use it in your classes, you need to secure written permission from the copyright holder.

Failure to abide by copyright regulations can result in significant penalties. There can be an award to the copyright holder equivalent to the loss of profits resulting from the illegal use or an amount of money determined by the court ranging between $500 and $20,000. If the court determines that the violator acted willfully, it can increase monetary damage to an amount as high as $100,000. However, if the violator can prove that the infraction was unintentional, the court can scale back damages to a figure as low as $220.

Teachers' Private Lives

The case of *Board of Trustees v. Stubblefield* (1971) helped establish the principle of higher standards of conduct for people in certain professions, such as teaching. The argument is that because teachers work with impressionable young people, they should be held to especially high personal standards.

There have been many cases involving allegations of immoral teacher behavior. Typically, the courts have dealt quite harshly with teachers who have been found to be "immoral." The difficulty in deriving general principles from a review of these cases is that the terms "moral" and "immoral" tend to take on different meanings from place to place.

A theme that runs through many of these cases has to do with the perceived impact of a given teacher's behavior on his or her classroom performance and his or her standing in the local community. When a teacher has been dismissed for alleged immoral behavior and there is evidence that the behavior violates prevailing community standards, the courts have tended to support the dismissal. However, if the alleged immoral behavior has been shown to have little impact on the teacher's ability to teach effectively and has elicited little negative reaction in the community, the courts have often held for the teacher and against the school officials.

Consequences have been severe for teachers whose immoral behaviors have involved students. Courts have upheld dismissals of a teacher who was found playing strip poker with a student in a car, of another teacher whose offer to "spank" two female students was interpreted as a sexual advance, and of a teacher who tickled and used suggestive language to female students on a class field trip.

In still another case, a teacher was dismissed when a high school girl he had been dating became pregnant. He admitted having an affair with the student but contended that since the girl was not a student at the school where he taught, there was no adverse impact on his teaching. The teacher felt he should be reinstated. The court disagreed, stating that in situations like this no evidence of interference with the classroom performance of the teacher was needed (*Denton v. South Kitsap School District No. 402*, 1973). The court ruled that the relationship between the teacher and any student constituted sexual misconduct that was inherently harmful to the school district.

Other cases in which teacher dismissal action has been upheld have involved situations where teachers have been arrested for public intoxication, had repeated drunk driving convictions, shoplifted, lied about being sick in order to collect sick leave, taken school property, engaged in welfare fraud, and allowed students to consume alcohol in their home. Conviction of any serious crime, such as a felony, ordinarily is grounds for dismissal.

To summarize, because of the sensitive role you play as a nurturer of young people, as a teacher you are expected to reflect standards of personal behavior that are higher than those expected of average citizens. Hence, you have to be a careful monitor of your own behavior. In particular, you have to avoid personal behaviors that interfere with your ability to function as an effective teacher or that clearly conflict with standards of morality prevalent in your community.

KEY IDEAS IN SUMMARY

- Students not only have rights but also have responsibilities. Among those responsibilities are following reasonable rules and regulations, attending school regularly, refraining from the possession of unsafe articles such as weapons and controlled substances, and behaving in socially acceptable ways.
- Students enjoy considerable freedom-of-expression rights. Administrators have limited rights to oversee the contents of student publications that are produced as a part of the regular school program. However, they may not censor material simply on the grounds that they are controversial or on other grounds that clearly violate students' constitutional rights. Administrators have even less authority over student publications that are not produced under the auspices of the school. Students also enjoy constitutional protection of oral speech.
- In general, the courts have allowed students' religious beliefs as grounds for excusing them from school activities that cannot be demonstrated to be essential to their health or welfare or essential to the welfare of the state. In practice, this means that religious reasons have been viewed as grounds for excusing students from activities such as the Pledge of Allegiance but not from such basic school subjects as reading.
- Regulations regarding dress and appearance have been reported most frequently when the courts have found a demonstrable connection between student's dress or appearance and (a) safety or health of the student body or (b) disruption of the instructional process. Recent cases have also supported decisions to ban items of dress associated with gang membership.
- The Fourteenth Amendment to the Constitution guarantees due process rights to citizens. These provide certain procedures or safeguards that must be followed whenever a person is denied a constitutionally protected right.
- Search-and-seizure cases have considered the authority of school officials to search students, their property, and such areas as school lockers. In determining the appropriateness of a search, the courts have generally considered (a) the nature of what is being sought, (b) the quality of the evidence leading to the decision to conduct a search, (c) the degree of the expectation of privacy associated with the place to be searched, and (d) the intrusiveness of the search.
- The federal Family Educational Rights and Privacy Act gives parents and students who are 18 years of age or older the right to look at school records. Further, the law prohibits the records from being shown to anyone not immediately concerned with the students' education. Requests can also be filed to amended records that are identified as (a) inaccurate, (b) misleading, or (c) in violation of privacy rights. Individuals who have entered defamatory comments on student records can be sued.

- Teachers' contracts are legal documents that establish a working relationship between the individual and the school district that employs them. For contracts to be valid, they must be approved by the school board. There are several types of contracts, including term contracts, continuing contracts, and tenure contracts. There are penalties attached whenever either party violates a contract.
- Dismissal procedures must be followed when a school district decides to release a teacher with a continuing or a tenure contract. Dismissal actions against a teacher with a term contract cannot be initiated for reasons that are inconsistent with constitutional rights.
- All states have laws requiring that teachers report suspected child abuse. These laws also protect teachers who make such reports in good faith from reprisals. There are penalties associated with failure to report suspected cases of child abuse.
- Teachers may be held liable for certain types of actions. Many teacher liability suits have resulted from charges of (a) excessive use of force in disciplining students or (b) negligence. Negligence cases often have focused on nonfeasance (a failure to act when there is a duty to do so), misfeasance (a failure to act in a proper manner), or malfeasance (acting to deliberately harm another).
- In considering issues of academic freedom, courts have weighed both teachers' rights to conduct their classrooms according to their own professional judgment and the needs of school officials to make sure that the prescribed curriculum is taught. In general, the courts have supported the actions of administrators to ensure that the mandated curriculum is taught and have supported teachers in cases where administrators have attempted to stifle the study of controversial or embarrassing content that is directly related to the content being taught.
- Copyright regulations are designed to protect the interests of the developers of intellectual property, such as books, music, works of art, radio and television programs, and computer programs. In general, teachers must request and receive written permission for making and distributing multiple copies of copyrighted material. Fair use guidelines allow some limited classroom use of copyrighted material without securing permission.
- Actions teachers take in their private lives sometimes come to the attention of the courts. The courts have declared that, because of their potential influence on young people, teachers can be held to higher moral and behavioral standards than citizens in general. Dismissal actions against teachers have frequently been upheld when courts have found their actions to undermine their credibility in the community and to make them ineffective as instructional leaders.

LEARNING EXTENSIONS

1. Survey recent articles that have appeared in the press for articles on legal issues relating to education. Identify the legal principles that were applied to the situation.
2. Interview a local high school principal on the procedures followed when it becomes necessary to suspend or expel a student. Pay particular attention to how due process guidelines are implemented.
3. Interview a human resources director of a local school district and discuss the various elements of a teaching contract.
4. Obtain information regarding the laws governing reporting suspected child abuse. This information should be filed so that you will have easy access to it when you begin teaching.

FOR YOUR PORTFOLIO

Your understanding of legal issues can be very important for you as you move toward a teaching career. You might want to gather information regarding what is required to obtain a credential in your state, information regarding tenure and due process for teachers, the process and phone numbers for reporting suspected child abuse, contract information, and recent court decisions in your region regarding student rights and responsibilities. In addition, select at least one activity related to the content of the chapter. Reflect on the importance of this information and how it impacts your choices as a teacher and include it in your portfolio.

Material on the legal issues relates most directly to INTASC Standard 9 (evaluating the effect of choices and actions on others). However, some legal issues could relate to Standard 10 (fostering relationships with colleagues, parents, and agencies in the larger community). Decide how the material in your portfolio relates to each of these standards.

REFERENCES

Board of Trustees v. Stubblefield, 94 Cal. Rptr., 318, 321 (1971).

California Teachers Association. (1992). *Guide to school law*. Burlingame, CA: Author.

Committee on the Judiciary, H.R. No. 94-1476, 94th Congress, 201 Sess. 68–70 (1976).

Connors, E. (1991). *Educational tort liability and malpractice*. Bloomington, IN: Phi Delta Kappa.

Denton v. South Kitsap School District No. 402, 516 P2d 1080 (Wash. 1973).

Family Education Rights and Privacy Act. (1996, November 21). FERPA final regulations. *Federal Register*.

Fischer, L., Schimmel, D., & Steelman, L. R. (2003). *Teachers and the law* (6th ed.). Boston: Allyn & Bacon.

Goss v. Lopez, 419 U.S. 565 (1975).

Hazelwood School District v. Kuhlmeier, 484 U.S. 260 (1988).

Ingraham v. Wright, 430 U.S. 651 (1977).

Kingsville Independent School District v. Cooper, 611 F2d 1109 (5th Cir. 1980).

Meyer v. Nebraska, 262 U.S. 390, 399 (1923).

Monks, R., & Proulx, E. (1986) *Legal basics for teachers* (Fastback No. 235). Blomington, IN: Phi Delta Kappa.

New Jersey v. T.L.O. 105 S.Ct. 733 (1985).

Parducci v. Rutland, 316 F. Supp. 352 (m.d. Ala. 1979).

Pickering v. Board of Education of Township School District 205, Will County, 225 N.E. 2d 1 (1967); 391 U.S. 563 (1968).

Tinker v. Des Moines Independent Community School District, 393 U.S. 513 (1969).

Valente, W. (1994). *Law in the schools*. (3rd ed.). Upper Saddle River, NJ: Merrill/Prentice Hall.

Wisconsin v. Yoder, 406 U.S. 205 (1972).

Zirkel, P., & Richardson, S. (1988). *A digest of Supreme Court decisions affecting education*. Bloomington, IN: Phi Delta Kappa.

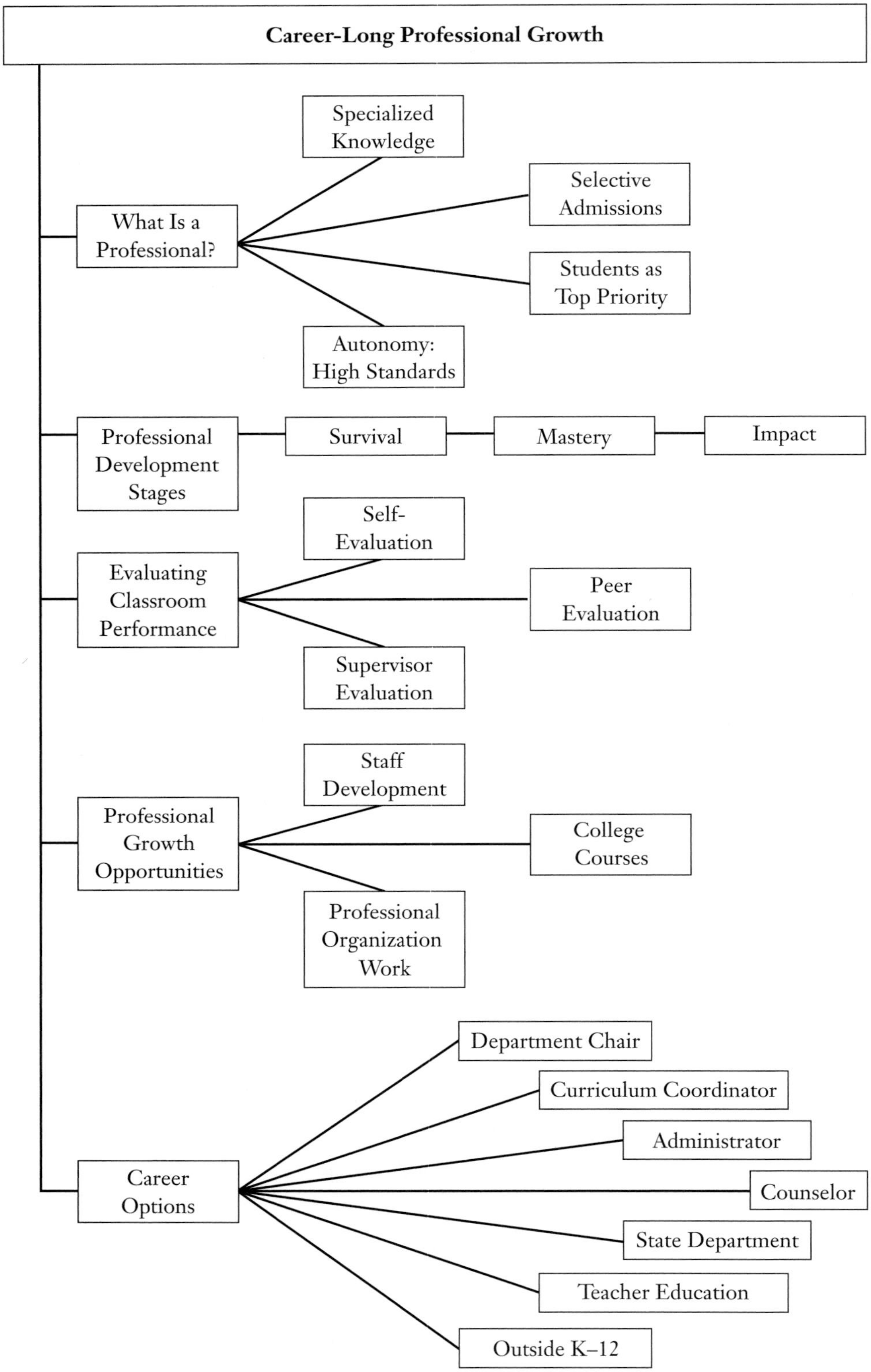

Figure 15.1
Graphic Organizer

CHAPTER **15**

Career-Long Professional Growth

OBJECTIVES

This chapter will help you

- understand your need for career-long preparation and development;
- define characteristics of professionalism as they apply to teaching;
- identify teachers' professional growth stages;
- state the purposes of teacher evaluation;
- define different types of teacher evaluation;
- point out some alternative approaches you can use to seek additional expertise you will need as you work throughout your career to be a more effective teacher;
- distinguish between general organizations and specialty organizations for teachers;
- describe advantages for beginning teachers of affiliating with a professional group; and
- identify career options that may be open to you as someone who has a background in classroom teaching.

Introduction

Although you are almost at the end of this text, most of you are just in the beginning phases of your professional preparation program. When you complete your studies, we hope you will be a highly talented beginning teacher. However, to reach a high level of professionalism and obtain the rich personal satisfaction that goes along with this kind of competence, you will need to engage in career-long professional growth.

When you survey the contemporary world of education, you may be struck by the complexity of changes taking place. You should take some comfort in knowing that these kinds of unsettled conditions have always characterized our profession. The likelihood is high that throughout your career, you will confront proposals for change related to issues including the following:

- The nature of the curriculum
- The degree of available school choice
- Basic processes of teaching and learning
- The use of technology to support instruction
- A proper balance of required student testing and instruction
- Preparation and performance standards for teachers
- Approaches to assessing teacher performance

If you are the type of individual who desires predictability and a career that will change little during the next 10 to 20 years, you should consider a field other than teaching. Successful educators understand that change is a constant professional companion. The expertise you leave with at the conclusion of your preparation program is something you should see simply as the end of the beginning phase of your professional preparation.

Throughout this text, we have emphasized the importance of reflective practice. This approach to teaching can provide you with the basis for establishing a career-long professional growth agenda. Reflective teaching encourages you to accept responsibility and open-minded attitudes that are essential if professional improvement is to occur.

You need to embrace the idea that what you do as a teacher makes a difference and that your actions have consequences. This means accepting responsibility for your actions and avoiding any temptation to blame difficulties on external factors, such as parental indifference, negative student attitudes, or administrative decisions that conflict with your beliefs. While certainly not all conditions you face will please you, it is important to avoid falling into the trap of assuming that these circumstances can overwhelm your ability to adjust and respond in ways that provide sound educational experiences for your students. You need to remain open, flexible, and committed to responding proactively to the special situations you will face. That is what professionals do.

What Is a Professional?

As you consider a career in teaching, you may find it useful to reflect on the definition of the term professional. Education specialists John Jarolimek and Clifford Foster (1996) characterize professional teachers as follows:

- Individuals who possess specialized knowledge and skill
- Individuals who have been admitted to a professional development program after having met specified criteria
- Individuals who place students as their number one priority
- Individuals who exercise a certain amount of autonomy and set high standards for their own professional practice

Specialized Knowledge and Skill

The value of professional knowledge in education is often brought into question. There are several reasons for this. Some see teaching as an art, not as a science. If it is an art, then some people have the skill, and some do not. If it is an art, then they see little specialized knowledge relating to teaching and learning.

Others do not view teaching as an especially difficult skill. They see it as based on common sense and thus requiring little specialized knowledge beyond what an average person would know. They focus on the personal characteristics and academic qualifications of a person seeking to be a teacher.

How can you tell if a given occupation demands professional preparation? The basic measure is to look for answers to this question: Can a person be successful without specialized knowledge and formal preparation?

A growing body of research attests to the fact that a solid preparation in professional education is important. As you will recognize, when you begin to work in the classroom, you will need a depth of knowledge in the subjects you teach, an understanding of the developmental dimensions of those you teach, and sound professional knowledge related to instructional design and delivery issues. Experts suggest that specialized expertise acquired in areas related to transmitting what you know (as opposed to simply acquiring this kind of knowledge yourself) correlates highly to the quality of instruction you are likely to provide your students (Darling-Hammond, 2000). Yet another factor lending support to the idea that specialized knowledge is important is the high attrition rate of individuals who enter the teaching profession without adequate professional preparation.

However, we need to be clear that good teaching, like most other professions, requires more than just specialized knowledge. In other words, successfully completing a teacher preparation program will not guarantee success. There is something of an art in knowing when and how to apply the specialized knowledge that you have. In essence, there is a scientific basis to the art of teaching.

Acquisition of specialized knowledge will not end when you meet qualifications for a degree or a teaching license or credential. Remember, you are dealing with one of the most complex and sophisticated organisms: the human brain. How the brain develops and how learning occurs is still largely a mystery. To make things even more complicated, you are dealing with a whole room full of these complex organisms, and they are all programmed differently! In addition, the students you teach are influenced by their culture and their background. As the world changes, culture will change, as will students. Thus, as society changes and we learn more about how individuals learn, professional knowledge will change. Therefore, you and your professional teaching colleagues will need to be involved in a career-long process of professional development. If you reach the point where you feel you have nothing more to learn, then it is probably time to consider another profession.

Selective Admission to Preparation Programs

Teacher preparation programs are "professional," in part, because candidates selected meet specified criteria. These criteria seek to identify people with the knowledge and attitudes that are necessary for successful professional practice. Not everyone meets these requirements; not everyone should be a teacher.

It should also be clear to anyone who has been a student that more than subject matter and pedagogical knowledge is required for a person to be a successful teacher. Good teachers also need to have personality characteristics and emotional dispositions that allow them to achieve success in the school environment. As a teacher, you will find yourself interacting with a wide array of people. You need to be able to establish good working relationships with students, other teachers, administrators, parents, and members of the general community. Some individuals simply do not have the values and the interpersonal skills needed to facilitate the establishment of these important personal relationships. Thus, good teacher preparation programs consider characteristics beyond just academic success in selecting individuals who complete the teacher preparation program.

Students as a Top Priority

Professionals in all fields accord a high priority to providing service to clients. As a teacher, your "clients" are your students. When you become a teacher, you accept responsibility for one of our society's most important obligations: educating young people. The importance of this role has been recognized for centuries. For example, the great Roman orator Cicero remarked that there is no nobler profession than teaching the youth of the Republic (Clark & Starr, 1996).

In practice, "putting students first" means that professional teachers place service to students higher than competing interests and obligations. There will be occasions when you spend time with individuals far beyond the end of the regular school day, and there will be times when you willingly listen to students' concerns even when you have stacks of paperwork to attend to. You will devote extra time outside of class to ensure that the lessons you provide are responsive to your students' needs. In summary, everything you do is framed by a commitment to helping the young people under your charge grow into secure, informed, and contributing members of society.

An additional dimension of this priority requires you to express informed judgments about policies and practices that involve students. In the contemporary world, people often feel free to make proclamations and decisions regarding what should be done to educate our youth. Unfortunately, some of these proposals have the potential for harming the educational development of some students. Your role as a professional educator obligates you to speak out against policies and practices that are potentially detrimental to students.

Autonomy and High Standards

As a professional, you will exercise a certain amount of autonomy and accept responsibility for setting high standards of professional practice. Although adopted curriculum requirements and other rules and regulations give some external direction to what you can do, you still have a certain amount of authority as a teacher to decide exactly what you will do each day. As a professional, you will not be subject to minute-by-minute scrutiny, and your teaching methods are not likely to be prescribed by some external body.

Along with this autonomy comes responsibility. You need to be a thoughtful decision maker who constantly seeks to improve your professional expertise. Teachers who resist change are insensitive to the unique needs of a given class of students, and repeating units or lessons from year to year is simply unprofessional. This kind of behavior has the potential to diminish the profession and to invite intervention by dissatisfied external authorities.

Professional Development Stages

As you enter the field of teaching, you need to realize that there will be different stages you will experience as you continue to grow professionally. You need to understand the dimensions of each of these stages in order to cope with them. The sad fact is that many new teachers do not cope well. Current trends indicate that approximately 50% of new teachers leave within the first 5 years. Typically, about 15% leave after the first year and another 15% after the second year (Kronowitz, 1999).

Much of this high attrition rate can be ascribed to what is called "reality shock." Reality shock is what happens when an individual experiences unexpected events during the early years at a job. Everyone experiences some unease on undertaking a new responsibility. However, there is evidence that this problem is especially acute among new teachers. People who have studied this problem note that part of the difficulty is the disconnection between what new teachers remember about their own school days and what they encounter when they begin teaching (Ryan et al., 1980). Consider your own situation. You spent many years sitting in school classrooms. You may have had contact with 50 to 100 teachers by the time you graduated from high school. Some were good, some were not so good, and some probably fell somewhere in between. You have clear memories of the sights, the smells, and the pace of daily life in secondary schools.

You may well begin your work in the profession feeling confident that you really understand what your life as a teacher will be like. However, your confidence may be shaken once you have your own classroom and begin teaching. For the first time, you will be viewing education exclusively from the perspective of the teacher. In your former student days, you may have been largely unaware of those students who were not enthusiastic about school. You may have had only the vaguest understanding of the "behind the scenes" issues and problems your teachers were confronting.

Even the experiences you will have had as a student teacher may not prepare you for the fact that some (often quite a large number) of your students, initially at least, may be indifferent to the subjects you are teaching. You may also find that large numbers of students do not have as much background information as you imagined they would have had. You may also be surprised at how much work is required to motivate students and to maintain good order in the classroom. Finally, you may not initially be prepared for the huge time investment required to handle out-of-school responsibilities, including lesson planning, correcting papers, attending meetings, and supervising student activities.

Do not be surprised if some of these realities surprise and concern you when you accept your first teaching position. The good news is that thousands of teachers have successfully made the adjustment to their new professional roles and take great personal and professional satisfaction in their ability to promote the educational development of young people.

For years, researchers have been interested in how new teachers adjust to the profession. Experts who have studied this issue have identified three important teacher growth and development stages (Fuller, 1969):

- The survival stage
- The mastery stage
- The impact stage

Survival Stage

Given the above discussion, it should come as no surprise to you that the initial stage of development is called the survival stage. When you first begin teaching, you are likely to be worried about your adequacy as a teacher. You may well be concerned that problems will arise for which you are not prepared. It would not be unusual for you to worry about whether your students and professional colleagues will like and respect you. Initially, you are likely to focus on surviving each period, getting through the day, and making it to the next break in the school calendar.

The survival stage may vary in length. Some people quickly solve their survival problems and begin to develop confidence in their ability to handle the multiple dimensions of their teaching. You may be one of these individuals who develops a strong sense of teaching efficacy within a few months and completes your first year of teaching eagerly anticipating the next group of students. However, others who start at the same time as you do may struggle. They may have a difficult time adjusting and experience frustration and failure. By the end of the first year, some of these individuals may well decide to leave the teaching profession. Others will persist and return for a second year with the hope that things will surely improve. For many, the second year will prove to be more satisfying. Others, however, will continue to find it difficult to deal with all the problems and frustrations involved in teaching and will remain in the survival stage. Many of them will leave at the end of the second or third year. A few people remain in the survival stage for a large portion of their careers and go on to become unhappy, even bitter, teachers.

CRITICAL INCIDENT

I Wasn't Prepared for This

Arlene Newby has been struggling through her first year of teaching mathematics to eighth graders at King Middle School. She teaches a pre-algebra course to some of her students and a regular algebra class to the others. After a particularly difficult day, she made her way into the faculty lounge. Her friend, Veronica Linn, was sitting on one of the battered couches.

"So, another day in the bag, Arlene. Get some coffee and sit down. What's new with you?" asked Veronica.

"My day . . . my week . . . they've just been the pits," Arlene replied. "Even my best algebra kids have been on a tear. As for the rest of them, well, I just feel I'm barely keeping the lid on."

"Well, eighth graders will be eighth graders. Remember you've got all those surging hormones and the football game with Madison coming up tomorrow night. I mean the Pied Piper and Mother Theresa combined would have a hard time convincing these kids that quiet attention to mathematics should be their top priority."

"That's fine for you to say. You've been here for years. The principal thinks you're great. Parents support what you're doing. But what about me? I'm the new kid on the block. I feel like I'm really under the microscope. I've had several parents make a big point of telling me that they expect their kids to become engineers or scientists and that they want them to 'really be prepared' for their high school math classes. If the kids thought math was half as important as their parents, my job would be a breeze."

"Anything else on your mind?" asked Veronica.

"Well, since you asked yes. These pre-algebra classes are driving me nuts. The students just don't have the basics. I mean, some of them don't even know their multiplication tables. What did those elementary school teachers teach these kids? Not much. Sometimes I wonder why I struggled through all of those calculus classes only to be given a bunch of students who hate math and who can't even manage basic arithmetic. I just wasn't prepared for this."

"All right, so some of your kids don't think the sun rises and sets on math. And you think this wasn't true when you were in school? Give me a break." Veronica continued, "Do you think all my kids love English? Do you think Mr. Harmon's students turn hand-flips at the prospects of studying science? Are Ms. Knight's kids just lusting to study history? No way. That's not how the world is. Part of our job is seeing to it that kids tolerate our instruction. Beyond that, we try to motivate them to like it. Enthusiasm doesn't come from any inherent interest in the subject itself; it comes from what we do. You've got to get beyond this idea that these kids are just going to sit there and let you build on enthusiasm and interest that are already there. Won't happen."

"Well, thanks a lot, Veronica," sputtered Arlene, "you've just made my day. Now even you don't think I'm being professional. I'm so frustrated right now I can't believe it. I feel like a real square peg in a round hole. I'm working hard, getting by on less sleep than I need, and for what? I can't seem to please anybody . . . least of all myself. I just don't know what I'm going to do."

■ ■ ■

What do we learn about some things that are important to Arlene? What aspects of her teaching responsibilities seem to challenge some of her values? What are her assumptions about how students and schools ought to be? What discrepancies are there between these assumptions and what she encounters?

How do you explain differences in perspectives revealed in Arlene's comments and in Veronica's comments? What do these reveal about differences in values and in other priorities? What might account for these differences?

What kinds of personal responsibilities does Arlene have in trying to respond to the problems she feels she is facing? Has she assumed that professional development ceased before she began her first teaching job? Does she have an obligation to take specific actions that might lead to different patterns of behavior and to different expectations of students? Does she have a place in education, or should she pursue a different career option? What should her next steps be?

Your focus during the survival stage should be on mastering the basics of teaching. Develop routines for predictable and recurring events. Make sure that you have completely thought through your daily lessons. Have rules and clear expectations for your students. Make sure you have all your material ready to go before the school day begins. Working on these basics will allow you to focus your energy on those unpredictable events that are bound to occur. You need to seek out "older hands" who can give you advice. You will find most of your colleagues to be highly sympathetic to the stresses and challenges you will be experiencing. Remember that even the most confident teachers in your building at one time were newcomers to the profession.

When you begin teaching and are at the survival stage, there are several things you can do to make your life more manageable. First, have realistic expectations. Developing excellence in teaching takes time. Don't feel bad if every lesson does not work out well. Avoid negative self-judgments. You need to understand that even highly experienced teachers have forgettable days.

Second, if your school does not assign newcomers an official mentor, seek out experienced people on the faculty. They will likely remember the adjustments they had to make as newcomers to the profession. Many of these people will reach out and befriend a beginner. Their support can be invaluable as you work to retain and extend your self-confidence.

You also need to think about how people-intense the activity of teaching is. Prolonged interactions with others on a daily basis can produce stress. To counteract this situation, consider developing outside activities that you particularly enjoy. Many teachers find that exercise programs and other activities that free the mind from job-related concerns add a much-needed dose of psychological serenity.

Finally, remember that the first year of teaching is a unique time. Even if you were fortunate enough to have experienced an exemplary preparation program, you still have much to learn. You will find that much professional development occurs during your first year on the job. In fact, the benefits of this early, on-the-job learning are so great that we often counsel frustrated beginners who want to leave the profession to wait at least 2 years before making a decision.

Mastery Stage

After you solve survival-stage issues, you will move on to the mastery stage. Once you have arrived at this stage, you will have developed confidence in your ability to deal with your students and in delivering the curriculum. You will understand how to plan and use time wisely. You will have confidence that you can handle those unpredictable events. Your concerns now will turn away from worrying about getting through the day or the week and become more focused on your skill as a teacher.

You will pay more attention to mastering the fundamentals of teaching and are likely to develop interest in approaches that promise to enhance your instructional effectiveness. You are also likely to look more carefully at the contents of the curriculum and to consider ways to augment basic information you have been sharing with your students. Basically, you are seeking to become a "master" teacher. You want to use the latest and the best approaches and stay up with new approaches.

If you are typical of teachers at this stage, you will be eager to seek out professional development opportunities. You will want to learn more about your subject area and about new approaches to teaching and learning. This phase of your professional development can last a long time. Learning new ideas and developing increased confidence in your teaching can generate great personal satisfaction. During this time of your professional life, you may well become interested in serving as a mentor for new teachers.

Impact Stage

The third stage that you are likely to enter as your career progresses is the impact stage. Once you have developed a strong repertoire of teaching skills and have developed confidence in your teaching abilities, your concerns are likely to turn from how to master more teaching approaches to a focus on the impact you are having on students. To be sure, you will have some concern about your impact even during the survival and mastery stages. However, during earlier stages, it is a secondary concern. During the impact stage, this concern assumes a position of primacy.

This priority will be reflected in several ways. For example, when a new teaching approach is promoted, you will not be inclined to adopt it simply to expand your repertoire of techniques. Rather, your first question will be, "What do we know about how this approach affects students and their learning?" Your acceptance or rejection of approaches will depend on your relative confidence that new ways of doing things have excellent potential to help students learn.

Your life as a teacher can be highly satisfying when you arrive at the impact stage. Seeing students grow and change and being able to adapt your instruction to meet the needs of individuals can be highly rewarding. At the same time, your concern for "impact" can produce some personal frustration as you witness adoption and implementation of policies that, in your view, may interfere with your ability to have a positive and lasting influence on students.

Teacher Development Stages: Summary

You need to understand that teachers do not necessarily move through these stages in lockstep fashion. At various times during your career, you may find yourself moving back and forth through the categories. In general, these changes occur when you face significant and expected personal and professional circumstances. For example, if you change schools at some point in your career and find conditions drastically different from where you previously were employed, you may shift back (initially at least) to the survival stage. There can also be unexpected stresses in personal life that affect your abilities to cope with challenges at school, and these events can cause a backward developmental-stage shift.

Thinking about these stages can assist you in several ways. First, they can help you understand that these are stages that all teachers experience. At one time or another, every teacher in your building will have gone through the survival stage. Knowledge about these stages will help you appreciate that feelings of being overwhelmed during your first year are not signs of personality flaws or professional failings. You are merely experiencing a normal stage of professional development. Further, you should understand that the survival phase will pass and that, in time, you will move on to professional stages you are likely to find more satisfying.

Second, you can use these stages to evaluate your own growth. If you are struggling to get through the day, you will know that you are in the survival stage. You may then turn your attention to the kinds of professional growth opportunities that will allow you to master tasks that are challenging you and that will help you to move on to the next stage.

Finally, an understanding of the development stages can help you better understand your colleagues. Without understanding these stages, you might find yourself intimidated when you see some of your fellow teachers getting excited about a new program or growth opportunity that you see as a threat because you are still struggling just to get through the day. But knowing what you now know about patterns of teachers' development, you should feel secure in understanding that these teachers have moved beyond the survival stage and have arrived at the point in their careers where they are concerned with expanding their instructional capacities and increasing their impact on students' lives.

Evaluating Classroom Performance

Productive growth as a teacher requires useful data on which to base your reflections and your professional growth plans. Good teacher evaluation can supply data that can serve this function.

There are basically two purposes for teacher evaluation. One of those is what might be called "quality assurance." The public demands that each classroom is taught by a quality teacher. This has received more emphasis in recent years as the concept of teacher quality has been given more importance in educational policy. Today, almost everyone recognizes that the quality of an individual teacher matters (Danielson, 2001).

A second purpose of teacher evaluation is to provide the basis for making decisions about professional growth. This purpose has also been recognized in recent years. However, many point out that teacher evaluation for the purposes of growth and for quality assurance may be incompatible. For example, evaluation for growth requires trust between the individuals involved in the process and requires that the person being evaluated be open and honest in discussing one's strengths, weaknesses and concerns. However, evaluation that carries the possibility of serious consequences can lead to a lack of trust between those involved in the evaluation process, and those being evaluated may be reluctant to share their concerns for fear that they will be held against them on the evaluation. As a result, three different types of evaluations have emerged: self-evaluation, peer evaluation, and supervisor evaluation.

Self-Evaluation

Self-evaluation requires more than merely guessing about your instructional skills and your teaching effectiveness. During self-evaluation, you need to consider how you can gather information about your teaching and reflect on the meaning of that information. You can use your own creativity in identifying ways of gathering information that will inform your teaching. If meaningful professional growth is to occur, you need to be open to the possibility that you will find areas where growth is needed.

Several arguments support self-evaluation as an important professional growth tool. First, it is something that you can do to generate information about your teaching more frequently than supervisor or peer observations. This means that you can use the approach to fill any information gap that results from infrequent peer or supervisor observations.

A second reason for self-evaluation is that you will be more inclined to change your behavior when you personally identify something you do not think is satisfactory (Airasian & Gullickson, 1997). When you make changes based on self-evaluation, you gain a sense of personal control over your needs and how they should be accommodated (Rodriguez & Johnstone, 1986).

Third, self-evaluation is a nonintrusive way of gathering information and making judgments. When it is used, you don't have to do anything that interferes with your normal classroom procedures. Because self-evaluation preserves a normal teaching environment, the information you gather may be a better reflection of how you teach under typical classroom conditions than information gathered by others who visit your classroom and thereby alter the normal classroom environment.

Finally, self-evaluation can build your confidence. Over time, modifications in your teaching behavior adopted as a result of your own personal reflections will be changes you believe in. If your self-evaluation information is compelling enough to commit you to make changes, it is typically a rationale you can use to explain your teaching to others.

You will discover a few negatives associated with self-evaluation. If you don't implement self-evaluation carefully, you may be gathering information in a haphazard, unsystematic manner so that it is of little value. To be effective, self-evaluation should be based on the systematic gathering of data about those teaching dimensions that are of interest or concern to you.

Researchers have discovered that teachers who are unable to describe and defend the procedures they used in gathering information about their teaching often draw conclusions about their teaching that correlate poorly with the observations of others (Brown, 1983). This suggests that poorly conceived self-evaluation is not very helpful in providing the basis for instructional improvement.

Another difficulty with self-evaluation is that it is difficult to make accurate records of what goes on in the classroom. Classrooms are fast-paced environments. So much happens that you will find it impossible to reconstruct the lesson from memory. In addition, you may be so focused on your concerns that you miss significant events that occur during the lesson. One method that is useful in overcoming this problem is the use of video- and audiotape to capture your teaching. Although this can be threatening, making a tape and viewing it in the privacy of your own classroom can be very beneficial.

When using tapes of lessons, it is useful to develop a checklist or a rating scale of things you want to observe in the lesson. This will help you focus on the specifics and help you pinpoint behaviors. It is not necessary for you to tape an entire lesson every time. You might find it useful to focus on small pieces of your lesson. For example, you might just tape the beginnings of lessons to see how you capture attention and get lessons started. Or you might just focus on the directions you give to make sure they are clear and concise. These "samples" are often easier to tape and do not require large amounts of time to analyze.

Your portfolio can be another source of information that can be used for evaluation. It can serve as a repository for ideas about teaching as well as a basis for both self- and supervisor evaluation.

When you use a portfolio either as part of a self-evaluation process or as a data source for others who will be evaluating you, you need to pay particular attention to how you organize materials. If others are going to review your portfolio, you need to have a clear understanding of their assessment standards. Portfolio evaluators often use clear sets of standards, or "rubrics," to enhance their ability to make consistent judgments. Often these rubrics are based on descriptions of good teaching. They address questions such as "What should a good teacher know and be able to do?" "Does the teacher have a clear understanding of the content?" "Does the teacher know how to communicate clearly?" and "How does the teacher assess student learning?" You will want to make sure that you understand the rubrics and the types of evidence that would be useful in demonstrating your knowledge and skill. You should then make sure that the items in your portfolio address these rubrics and standards and that you can use the rubrics as a basis for your self-evaluation. Where would you place yourself on the scale of descriptors provided on the rubric?

Consider the advantages to your being evaluated based on information contained in a portfolio you have assembled. More traditional evaluation schemes depend on data gathered during one or two classroom observations. Information in a portfolio, on the other hand, includes items you have gathered over a considerable period of time from a variety of sources. The portfolio can provide a more comprehensive picture of what you know and are able to do than information gathered during a couple of classroom observations.

In addition, since you assemble the portfolio, you are in a position to play an active role in the evaluation process by selecting items to be included. This gives you some "ownership" of the evaluation process (Painter, 2001).

Another useful tool for self-evaluation is the reflective journal where you keep a record of classroom events and your reactions and thoughts. One of the serious problems in promoting teacher growth is that teachers get so busy that they rush from day to day and seldom have the time to pause and reflect. Choosing a regular pattern of writing in a reflective journal can provide you with some useful benefits that help overcome the disadvantages of the hectic life of a teacher.

When using a reflective journal, you will want to look for recurring patterns or themes. It might be helpful to generate questions that you might want address when you read through your reflective journal. Are there recurring patterns or themes? What does the journal indicate about your decision making? Does the journal reflect growth or change over time? What might account for the change or the lack thereof? These questions will help you move beyond superficial reading and analysis.

You may also include student achievement data in your self-evaluation. Rather than looking at student scores on daily work and tests as just a measure of assigning grades, look at them as indicators of your teaching effectiveness. Are students growing in understanding as the year unfolds? Where are they having difficulty? Why might they be having difficulty? These are often difficult questions for us to ask about our students because sometimes we find that we are a part of the problem.

Peer Evaluation

Collaboration with a respected peer can help you gain insight into your behaviors and can give you a glimpse of your teaching performance through a different set of eyes. When a colleague observes your work, there is an opportunity for a rich discussion that allows both individuals to gain insights and to grow. Basically, data gathered from multiple perspectives is more comprehensive than data gathered from one source (Dyer, 2001). This provides a good rationale for having others observe your teaching and work with you.

In recent years, a major emphasis has been on peer coaching, a situation in which two or more individuals voluntarily work together to help each other solve problems and grow professionally. In peer coaching, no person is regarded as superior to another. The purpose here is not quality assurance but professional growth and change. This requires that the two people who work together have a high degree of mutual respect and trust.

It is best to begin the peer coaching relationship by discussing perspectives about teaching and sharing ideas. In time, peer coaching teams begin observing lessons and sharing insights and ideas. The approach should be a positive one that helps individuals build confidence and enhances a sense of professional self-worth.

The normal cycle of activity during a peer coaching observation is a preconference, the observation, and a postconference. During the preconference, the purpose is to share information about the lesson that will be taught. Together the team members then plan the observation and make decisions about the primary focus.

During the observation, the observing peer coach gathers information on the areas discussed in the preconference. The peer coach may take some notes on some things that he or she feels should be shared or discussed.

The postconference is the time when the information is shared in a nonjudgmental fashion. A good peer coach will present the data and then ask the observed individual to look for patterns and draw conclusions. This is also a time to affirm those things that were done well and to suggest some things to try in the future. Ideally, the postconference is a two-way discussion between equals.

Another form of peer evaluation involves what is called mentoring. Mentoring is different from peer coaching because it is more of a superior–subordinate relationship.

It is a more experienced or skilled person helping a less experienced or skilled person. The mentor serves as a guide, adviser, role model, or consultant.

In many places, mentors have become a regular part of the induction process for a new teacher. When you are hired, a person might be appointed as your mentor. This person has the responsibility of serving as your guide and adviser through the difficult beginning stage of teaching.

If you take a position in a school district with a formal mentoring program, the benefit you derive from the program will depend on the mutual trust and respect between you and your mentor. One of the problems associated with formal mentoring is that because it is forced, the two individuals may not be philosophically or interpersonally compatible. This then leads to a lack of openness that hinders professional growth.

If your school does not have a formal mentoring program, we recommend that you try to identify a more senior member of the faculty with whom you feel comfortable. Then try to develop an informal mentoring relationship with that person. Many experienced teachers are willing to serve as informal mentors to new teachers. However, be cognizant of the fact that they also have responsibilities and demands on their time, so carefully choose the times to discuss questions with your mentor.

Supervisor Evaluation

Supervisor evaluation occurs when someone in a position of authority is given the responsibility of evaluating your performance. Although professional growth has long been a major thrust of supervisor evaluation, the basic purpose of supervisor evaluation is quality assurance. School leaders are increasingly being held accountable for how well teachers in their schools perform. Many school districts require a supervisor evaluation process, and results of supervisor evaluations can have serious consequences relating to personnel decisions, such as retention or tenure.

Because supervisory evaluations have important consequences, they are often accompanied by high levels of anxiety. Thomas Sergiovanni (1994), a scholar who has studied these relationships, argues that the traditional supervisor–subordinate relationship often results in negative outcomes because new teachers are unwilling to share concerns and problems out of a fear that these will be used against them when personnel decisions are made. Sergiovanni advocates replacing traditional supervisor evaluation with a conception of schools as communities where the status relationships among people are minimized and interpersonal communication is enhanced. While this is a worthwhile concept, it is unlikely that the role of supervisors in quality assurance and accountability will disappear anytime soon.

Even though you might have concerns about supervisor evaluations, researchers have found that, in general, teachers want and value this type of assessment (McLaughlin & Pfeifer, 1988). This is especially true if the supervisor is perceived as knowledgeable, credible, and trustworthy. One teacher who reflected on this finding indicated general agreement but also noted an important condition: "We need people to come in and check on us just like anybody else. As long as it is done in a positive and constructive manner, all it can do is benefit education" (McLaughlin & Pfeifer, 1988, p. 63). When supervisors provide constructive and positive feedback, they can help you overcome any fears you have about the evaluation process.

Supervisor evaluation tends to be done in more systematic ways than peer evaluation. For example, supervisors often use formal evaluation instruments that have been developed by specialists and are used across all teachers in the district. When

Teacher workshops are an important component of teacher growth.

preparing for supervisor visits to your classroom, you will find it useful to review the observation instruments. This will provide you with an understanding of the behaviors that will be assessed and the expectations of the supervisor. If possible, it is useful to follow the sequence of a preconference, an observation, and a postconference.

Whether supervisors see a truly representative sample of teachers' work is a matter of debate. When a supervisor comes into your room, the classroom environment is altered. The changes can be positive and negative. On the one hand, sometimes your students will behave better and be more responsive than usual. On the other hand, the presence of the supervisor can make you nervous, and this may significantly alter your normal teaching style.

In summary, evaluation is likely to be an important component of your teaching career. Currently, there is considerable attention to making sure that teacher evaluation is directed toward significant dimensions of teaching. You need to learn that teacher evaluation can be productive and is an important component in helping you improve and make choices for your professional growth.

Professional Growth Opportunities

Regardless of the excellence of your teacher preparation and regardless of where you begin teaching, you are likely to recognize early in your first year of teaching that there are some gaps in what you need to know to become an effective teacher. This situation is inevitable, given the tremendous differences among students, physical facilities, materials availability, levels of parental involvement, and administrative support that vary from one school to another. You will have a number of options available to you as you seek to extend your levels of understanding. For example, you may wish to pursue some of these options:

- Staff development activities (including meetings sponsored by the school or school district)
- College and university courses
- Professional organization work (including special programs sponsored by professional education associations)

Staff Development Activities

Many school districts provide development activities for their teachers. These are part of a larger effort to improve the overall quality of the educational program. Sometimes staff development activities for teachers are referred to as in-service education. In many districts, the school calendar is developed in such a way that students are dismissed from school on several days throughout the year to enable teachers to participate in professional development opportunities.

Attendance at district-sponsored staff development is often required for new teachers. When you begin to teach, you should inquire regarding the professional growth opportunities available in the school district. In some places, teachers receive staff development credits for their participation. When teachers accumulate enough of these, they qualify for salary increases.

Staff development takes a variety of forms. Sessions sponsored by school districts often feature speakers, workshops led by teachers with special expertise, and sharing sessions that allow teachers of common subjects to exchange ideas. As a newcomer to the profession, you may find these staff development sessions an excellent source of information as you work to improve your instruction and your approaches to classroom management.

College and University Courses

You also may want to take some college and university courses while you are teaching. To serve this market, many institutions offer courses at night so that local teachers can attend. In some places, Saturday classes are available. You may find yourself working in a school district that places limits on the numbers of courses teachers can take during the school year. This requirement has been adopted in some places out of a concern that teachers may not leave themselves enough time to plan adequately for their teaching responsibilities.

College and university courses, in addition to adding to your knowledge, may help you move to a higher level on the salary schedule. In many places, salaries go up as (a) the number of years a teacher has taught increases and (b) the total number of academic credits the teacher has earned past the time of initial certification goes up. This scheme is built on the idea that your expertise will increase in tandem with years of experience and additional college-level study.

In addition to helping you become a more effective teacher, college courses you take may be applied toward an advanced degree. Teachers often qualify for a master's degree after taking courses for several years in the evening and attending several summer sessions. We caution against using applicability toward a degree as a reason for selecting any college courses you might take during your first year or two in the classroom. Advanced degree programs often prescribe specific programs of study. These courses may not meet the kinds of needs you face every day in your classroom. We think it makes much more sense for you to select courses that will be of immediate help in your day-to-day work. After these initial knowledge gaps have been filled, there will be plenty of time for you to enroll in a more formal program of study leading to an advanced degree.

Professional Organization Work

Professional organizations regularly sponsor events that include sessions designed to improve teachers' levels of expertise. They provide opportunities for teachers to interact with others who share similar interests. This is important in a profession where individual practitioners do not come into much direct contact with other professionals during the major part of the day when they are working with students in the classroom. An affiliation with professional groups can help you appreciate the bonds that join all who teach.

This kind of involvement can give you access to information through several channels. Professional organizations sponsor meetings that almost always feature presentations and workshops that allow participants to gain up-to-date information about content and instructional methodologies. Many of them also publish journals and newsletters with helpful information. Simply coming into contact with others who share your professional concerns can be a confidence builder as you come to recognize that many others share an interest in issues that are important to you.

There are two broad types of professional organizations that serve educators: general organizations and specialty organizations. The two largest general organizations, the National Education Association (NEA) and the American Federation of Teachers (AFT), seek their members from the total national population of teachers. Members include teachers working at all grade levels and in all subject areas. Specialty organizations seek members from among teachers who are interested in specific subject areas or certain categories of learners. Both of these types of organizations provide professional growth opportunities for teachers.

General Organizations The NEA and AFT are particularly interested in issues associated with teachers' working conditions. In many parts of the country, local affiliates of these groups represent teachers in negotiating salary and working conditions with representatives of the school board and administration. At the state and national levels, representatives of these organizations work to support passage of legislation of interest to teachers.

Representatives also serve as members of accrediting agencies that are responsible for examining and certifying the adequacy of practice within individual school districts. They sometimes also serve as members of bodies considering curriculum changes. In general, representatives of the major general professional organizations are involved in almost all situations when issues of great concern to teachers are considered.

Teachers who belong to these groups are in a position to keep informed about issues affecting the profession. For more information about these groups and their programs, write or go to their Websites:

National Education Association
1201 16th Street NW
Washington, DC 20036-3207
http://www.nea.org

American Federation of Teachers
555 New Jersey Avenue NW
Washington, DC 20001-2029
http://www.aft.org

Specialty Organizations There are dozens of specialty organizations in the field of education. Affiliation with one will give you opportunities to exchange ideas and share perspectives with others who share your interests and who work with similar kinds of students. Thousands of teachers belong to these groups.

Specialty organizations provide numerous services to their members. Most of the large ones have annual meetings. These bring together educators from throughout the country to share ideas and discuss issues. Many national organizations also have state and local affiliates that also sponsor meetings. Typically, these meetings include presentations that inform teachers of promising approaches to instruction and issues of special interest in that particular state.

Most of the national specialty groups publish professional journals for their members. Articles often focus on up-to-date research findings, descriptions of innovative teaching practices, and discussions of other relevant issues. Many new teachers find these journals to be an excellent place to discover new teaching ideas.

Many specialty groups encourage people who are preparing to become teachers to join. We think this is a good idea. If you join and become active in one of these organizations, you will have opportunities to become acquainted with employed teachers and gain insights on some aspects of their professional lives that may not have received much attention in your education courses.

Box 15.1 introduces a number of specialty groups. This listing is by no means comprehensive. We have selected these organizations to illustrate the broad range of those that invite secondary school teachers to join. We encourage you to visit those sites that are of particular interest to you, particularly the one affiliated with your content field.

Organizations profiled in Box 15.1 typify those that draw much of their membership from teachers. These groups help members build communities of shared concern. Many of the groups also have state and local affiliates that provide easy access for local teachers.

Finally, they function as catalysts for political action. Many federal and state laws that influence schools began as lobbying efforts of educational specialty groups. For example, present laws about serving students with disabilities can be traced to pressures first brought to bear on legislatures by organizations committed to better serving the needs of these young people.

You may wish to visit Websites of some additional specialty organizations. The home page titled "Educational Associations and Organizations" is a good place to start. You will find links here to many public and private groups with interests in education. For example, you will find sites for groups such as Achieve (an organization that draws together governors, business leaders, and others interested in improving students' achievement levels), the American Educational Research Association (a group

BOX 15.1 Specialty Groups

American Alliance for Health, Physical Education, Recreation, and Dance (AAHPERD)
http://www.aahperd.org

Association for Career and Technical Education (ACTE)
http://www.avaonline.org

Council on Exceptional Children (CEC)
http://www.cec.sped.org

International Reading Association (IRA)
http://www.reading.org

International Society for Technology in Education (ISTE)
http://www.iste.org

Music Teachers National Association (MTNA)
http://www.mtna.org

National Art Education Association (NAEA)
http://www.naea-reston.org

National Association for Gifted Children (NAGC)
http://www.nagc.org

National Business Education Association (NBEA)
http://www.nbea.org

National Council for the Social Studies (NCSS)
http://www.ncss.org

National Middle School Association (NMSA)
http://www.nmsa.org

National Council of Teachers of English (NCTE)
http://www.ncte.org

National Council of Teachers of Mathematics (NCTM)
http://www.nctm.org

National Science Teachers Association (NSTA)
http://www.nsta.org/

dedicated to promoting research on topics related to education), the Council of Great City Schools (a group dedicated to improving the education of inner-city youth), and the National Rural Education Association (a group interested in improving education in rural areas). Here is the URL that will take you to the Web page with links to these and other education-related associations and organizations: http://www.ed.gov!EdRes/EdAssoc.html.

Meetings of national organizations provide opportunities for teacher growth and professional involvement.

Career Options

As you have been working to complete your preparation program, you may not have thought much about the wide range of career options in education. Many of these will be open to you only after you have spent some time actually working as a classroom teacher. A few of these roles would require you to leave classroom teaching entirely.

Department Chair

The department chair in a secondary school is the person designated to exercise leadership in a specific subject area (English, social studies, mathematics, science, and so forth). Duties vary but often include responsibilities in areas such as evaluating new faculty members, coordinating staff development opportunities, disseminating information about school policies, and ordering supplies for department members. In general, the department chair functions as a liaison between school administrators and faculty members in the department.

Typically, department chairs are selected from among the most experienced teachers in their respective departments. They tend to be individuals who have credibility both with their teaching colleagues and with school administrators. Often, department chairs teach a reduced load to allow them time to perform other assigned duties. They sometimes receive extra salary and often must work more days each year than regular classroom teachers.

Opportunities for people to become department chairs are limited. Only one chair is appointed for each department. In some schools, many years go by before a new chair needs to be appointed. One potential advantage of the department chair's role is that it allows an individual to assume some administrative and supervisory responsibilities while continuing to teach. Elevation to the position of department chair is one of the few promotions in education that does not remove a teacher completely from the classroom.

Curriculum Coordinator

This position often goes by one of a number of titles other than curriculum coordinator. Among them are curriculum director, curriculum supervisor, and curriculum leader. By whatever title it is known, this position requires the designated individual to assume leadership in such areas as curriculum planning, in-service planning, and instructional support planning. In small school districts, the curriculum coordinator may have responsibilities for several subject areas and may even continue to teach part time. In larger districts, curriculum coordinators do not teach. Typically, curriculum coordinators have their offices in the district's central administrative headquarters.

Curriculum coordinators are individuals with a great deal of knowledge about up-to-date trends in the subject area (or areas) for which they are responsible. They are in a position to influence the nature of the instructional program throughout the district in their areas of responsibility. Many curriculum coordinators hold advanced degrees. Curriculum coordinators often work a longer school year than teachers and are paid more. Their primary audience is teachers in the district. Especially in medium- and large-size districts, curriculum coordinators only infrequently work with students in the classroom.

School Administrator

Nearly all school administrators begin their work in education as classroom teachers. By taking advanced courses, often including completion of at least a master's degree and relevant administrative certification requirements, they qualify for administrative positions. These positions exist both at the school level and at the central district administrative level. Some typical administrative positions at the school level are assistant principal and principal. Positions often found in central school administrative headquarters are director of personnel, assistant superintendent, and superintendent.

Administrators have responsibilities that require some skills that are different from those required of classroom teachers. Much of their work involves preparing budgets, planning, scheduling, supervision of noncertified personnel, paperwork related to state and federal guidelines, and evaluation reports on teachers.

Administrators function as official representatives of the schools to the community; hence, they must have good public relations skills. School administrators almost always work a longer school year than classroom teachers and are paid higher salaries than teachers. Because demands of administration are quite different from those of teaching, some individuals who are outstanding teachers may not much care for administrative positions.

School Counselor

Many school counselors begin their careers as classroom teachers. In most parts of the country, school counselors must take additional graduate training to qualify for a counseling certificate, usually by completing master's degrees with a school counseling emphasis. Counselors typically work a longer school year than teachers and are paid more.

In addition to personal and academic counseling, many school counselors also are expected to perform a number of administrative tasks. Sometimes counselors are responsible for establishing the master teaching schedule for a school. Often they are in charge of all standardized testing. They must spend a great deal of time attending special meetings. Time available for working with individual students often is surprisingly limited.

State Education Agency Employee

All states have education departments or agencies that are staffed primarily by professionals with backgrounds in education. State education agencies hire people with a variety of backgrounds and for diverse purposes. There often are subject-area specialists who are charged with coordinating curriculum guidelines and in-service training throughout the state for teachers in specific subjects. There often also are assessment specialists who coordinate statewide testing programs. Teacher education specialists work with colleges and universities to ensure that teacher preparation programs are providing new teachers with appropriate backgrounds.

Employees of state education agencies often have had considerable prior experience working in the schools. Most of these positions require people to have at least a master's degree, and some of them require a doctoral degree. Considerable travel often is required. Employees of state education agencies work all year long. Levels of remuneration typically are considerably higher than those of classroom teachers.

Teacher Educator

Individuals who have taught successfully sometimes seek opportunities to share their expertise with future teachers. One way for them to do this is to become a teacher educator. Most teacher educators are faculty members of colleges and universities. A few are employed by large school districts.

Almost always, teacher educator positions require a doctoral degree. Because most teacher educators are members of college and university faculties, this degree is essential for the teacher educator to meet employment and tenure standards at most institutions of higher learning.

The role of the teacher educator is more varied and complex than is sometimes imagined by those viewing it from the outside. Although exemplary teaching certainly contributes to success as a faculty member in teacher education, still more is necessary. Faculty members must also demonstrate initiative in improving preparation programs, keep up to date on findings of researchers, conduct research, write for publication, seek opportunities to make presentations at regional and national meetings, maintain good working relations with other departments and with the schools, serve on large numbers of committees, maintain good links with state education agencies, and counsel students. All these obligations require the processing of massive quantities of paperwork.

A person who enters a doctoral program must devote considerable time to intensive study. About 3 years of full-time study after the award of the master's degree is typical. Many institutions require that prospective doctoral students spend at least 1 full year as resident, full-time students on the campus. This means that a teacher interested in doing this must leave his or her teaching position for at least 1 year. Many who do decide to pursue a doctorate resign their positions to devote their full attention to their studies. Most universities have graduate assistantships and fellowships that provide modest financial support to individuals doing advanced doctoral work.

Teacher educators typically are employed for 9 months out of the year. Many of them also have opportunities to work during the summer months as well. Salaries are not particularly high. In fact, some beginning teacher educators are paid less than some experienced public school classroom teachers. However, although beginning salaries of teacher educators tend to be modest, top salaries for experienced teacher educators tend to be higher than those paid to classroom teachers.

Individuals considering pursuing a doctoral program and becoming a teacher educator should seek information from reputable and accredited universities that offer doctorates. Some universities that offer doctorates are not widely respected, and an individual holding such a degree is going to have difficulty finding employment as a teacher educator. Discussions with practicing teacher educators can provide useful information. Once several possible universities have been identified, it makes sense to write to them for information about the specific features of their doctoral programs in education. There are important differences among institutions, and someone considering advanced study should look for one that is compatible with his or her own objectives. For example, one university may have an outstanding program in mathematics education, and another may have special strengths in social studies education.

Opportunities Outside of Education

For a variety of reasons, some teachers decide to leave the classroom after teaching for just a few years. If you decide to do this, does it mean that your time spent preparing to teach was wasted? Not at all. There are employment options outside the K–12 classroom for individuals with backgrounds in teaching.

Many large firms employ people with good teaching and curriculum development skills to work in their employee training programs. Education in industry is becoming big business. Many large corporations have special training divisions. The term human resource development, often abbreviated HRD, is frequently used to describe the corporate training function. There is a large national professional organization, the American Society for Training and Development (ASTD), devoted exclusively to promoting the interests of its members who are educators in industry. The group produces a fine journal titled *Training and Development*. People interested in the possibility of working as an educator in industry should look through several issues to get a feel for the kinds of things corporate trainers do.

In addition, individuals with skills developed in education find work in what is called the *human services sector*. Positions in this sector involve working in places such as museums or in youth organizations such as the Boy or Girl Scouts or the YMCA or YWCA.

Some individuals with educational backgrounds have also found employment working as educational material salespersons. The types of communication and interpersonal relations skills typically developed in education can also be transferred to success in other occupations that demand face-to-face contact with the general public.

Final Comments

The teaching profession is complex. Changing student populations, federal and state education regulations, public expectations, and knowledge about what works in the classroom require a commitment to career-long professional development. It is a process that may take unexpected twists and turns but that, despite these surprises, promises to go resolutely onward. If you embrace the idea that change is going to be a regular feature of the life of a teacher, you probably will be satisfied with your career choice. If you expect to enter an ordered and predictable world that will be in the future much as it was in the past, you will be disappointed.

When you teach, you will find yourself making dozens of decisions each day. Our intent in this book has been to provide you with some principles that have been followed by successful teachers. We know that a good part of teaching is unpredictable. However, if you have a set of guiding principles and have learned how to routinely handle most tasks, the unpredictable nature of teaching will not overwhelm you. We hope that some of the material we have presented will be of help to you.

We also recognize that teaching is not for everyone. Our intent has not been to try to convince all readers that they should be a teacher. Rather, we have attempted to provide you with information that will assist you in making an intelligent decision.

For those who do decide to teach, we hope you will enjoy some of the same exciting moments and rewards we have experienced as teachers. We are proud of what we do, and we look forward to welcoming you to one of civilization's proudest callings: teaching.

FOR YOUR PORTFOLIO

INTASC Standards 9 and 10 both relate to the content of this chapter. Standard 9 indicates that a professional educator is one who continually evaluates the effects of his or her actions and constantly seeks to grow professionally. Standard 10 indicates that professional educators participate in the professional community and foster relationships with colleagues, agencies, and parents. With that in mind, identify two or three entries for your portfolio.

1. Reflect on the items you chose for the portfolio. Why did you choose them? Write a reflection cover for each entry that describes the entry and what it indicates about you and your teaching.
2. How do these entries communicate how you profit from evaluation?
3. How do these entries communicate your involvement in the professional community of educators?

KEY IDEAS IN SUMMARY

- You will be involved in professional development throughout your career. Conditions change over time, as will your professional interests and needs. You cannot expect to have mastered all you need to know during your teacher preparation program.
- Teaching is a profession. This means you need to be prepared to accept special responsibilities. Professionals are individuals with specialized knowledge who have met selection criteria for entry, who place service to their clients as a priority, and who have a high degree of autonomy and responsibility.
- At least three distinct growth stages have been observed in the professional development of teachers. The first stage is that of survival, where the concerns are focused on self and being able to get through the day or the week. The second stage is mastery, where the concerns are still on self but are focused on becoming an expert or "master" teacher. The third stage is impact, where the concerns now shift from self to that of the impact on students.
- There are two basic purposes of teacher evaluation. One purpose is for accountability and quality assurance. There is much public interest in making sure that there are quality teachers in every classroom. The second purpose is to provide a database for professional growth and development.
- There are three types of evaluation that can be performed. Perhaps the most powerful type of evaluation is self-evaluation. However, it needs to be done systematically and with care.
- Peer evaluation has become an emphasis in recent years as a way of bringing about growth and development. One type of peer evaluation is peer coaching. This is where individuals are considered to be equals and they share ideas together. The second type is mentoring, where a more experienced and skilled individual helps a beginning teacher.
- Supervisor evaluation is focused on accountability and quality assurance. The results of this type of evaluation are usually used for retention and tenure. Although this type of evaluation can be threatening, it can be useful if the supervisor is knowledgeable, credible, and trustworthy.
- Many kinds of staff development activities are available to classroom teachers. These include school-based development activities, college courses, and participation in professional organizations.
- There are two types of professional organizations. General organizations represent interests of the entire teaching profession. Specialty organizations serve interests of teachers working with a given subject area or type of student.
- Although many individuals who choose teaching as a career do so because they want to work in classrooms with students, there are career opportunities beyond the classroom. These include department chair, curriculum coordinator, state agency employee, and teacher education. These roles often require additional preparation.
- Some individuals with backgrounds in education do not work in K–12 schools. Some work in training departments in industry or in human services organizations. The skills acquired in teacher education program are transferable to other occupations that need individuals with good organization and human relations skills.

REFLECTIONS

1. This chapter emphasized that a person in education must be prepared to accept and adapt to change. How do you react to change and unpredictable events?

2. There has been debate about whether teaching is a profession. Using the standards discussed in this chapter, do you think teaching is a profession? Why or why not?
3. One of your obligations as a professional is to speak out against actions and policy decisions that might not be in the best interest of students. Are there some actions now that you see as detrimental to students? What could you do about them?
4. How do you react to supervision and evaluation? What would be your reaction to a mentor relationship and supervisor evaluation?
5. Where do you see yourself 5 years after entering teaching? Ten years after entering teaching? What will it take for you to accomplish that status?

LEARNING EXTENSIONS

1. Interview some first- and second-year teachers. Ask them to describe their first year. What surprised them? Did they experience reality shock? How did they cope with the survival stage? What contributed to their growth to the next stage?
2. Begin the process of self-evaluation by taking the time to honestly evaluate your growth toward successful teaching. What have you learned? What do you need to learn? What actions and responsibility can you take to make sure you arrive at the place you need to be to assume responsibility for a classroom?
3. Visit some local school districts or go on the Internet to see what types of professional growth opportunities are provided by different school districts.
4. Conduct some research on career opportunities outside of education for people who have completed teacher education programs. What do these positions entail? How do salaries compare to those in schools? What do you think would be the professional and personal satisfactions and frustrations of these positions?

REFERENCES

Airasian, P., & Gullickson, A. (1997). Teacher self-evaluation. In J. Strong (Ed.), *Evaluating teaching: A guide to current thinking and best practice* (pp. 215–241). Thousand Oaks, CA: Corwin Press.

Brown, R. (1983). Helpful and humane teacher evaluations. In W. Duckett (Ed.), *Teacher evaluation: Gathering and using data* (pp. 9–26). Bloomington, IN: Phi Delta Kappa.

Clark L., & Starr, I. (1996). *Secondary and middle school teaching methods* (7th ed.). Upper Saddle River, NJ: Merrill.

Danielson, C. (2001). New trends in teacher evaluation. *Educational Leadership, 58*(5), 12–15.

Darling-Hammond, L. (2000). Teacher quality and student achievement: A review of state policy evidence. *Educational Policy Archives, 8*(1). Available at http://epaa.asu.edu/epaa/v8n1

Dyer, K. (2001). The power of 360-degree feedback. *Educational Leadership, 58*(5), 35–38.

Fuller, F. (1969). Concerns of teachers: A developmental conceptualization. *American Educational Research Journal, 6*, 207–226.

Jarolimek, J., & Foster, C. (1996). *Teaching and learning in the elementary school* (6th ed.). Upper Saddle River, NJ: Merrill.

Kronowitz, E. (1999). *Your first year of teaching and beyond* (3rd ed.). New York: Longman.

McLaughlin, M., & Pfeifer, R. (1988). *Teacher evaluation: Improvement, accountability, and effective learning*. New York: Teachers College Press.

Painter, B. (2001). Using teacher portfolios. *Educational Leadership, 58*(5), 31–34.

Rodriguez, S., & Johnstone, K. (1986). Staff development through collegial support groups. In K. Zumwalt (Ed.), *Improving teaching: 1986 ASCD yearbook* (pp. 87–99). Alexandria, VA: Association for Supervision and Curriculum Development.

Ryan, K., Newman, K., Mager, G., Applegate, J., Lasley, T., Flora, R., et al. (1980). *Biting the apple: Accounts of first year teachers*. New York: Longman.

Sergiovanni, T. (1994). Organizations of communities? Changing the metaphor changes the theory. *Educational Administration Quarterly, 30*(2), 214–226.

Name Index

Subject Index